Lecture Notes in Computer Science 7587

Commenced Publication in 1973
Founding and Former Series Editors:
Gerhard Goos, Juris Hartmanis, and Jan van Leeuwen

T0172205

Mirco Tribastone   Stephen Gilmore (Eds.)

Computer Performance Engineering

9th European Workshop, EPEW 2012
Munich, Germany, July 30, 2012, and
28th UK Workshop, UKPEW 2012
Edinburgh, UK, July 2, 2012
Revised Selected Papers

 Springer

Volume Editors

Mirco Tribastone
Ludwig-Maximilians University
Department for Informatics
Oettingenstrasse 67, 80538 Munich, Germany
E-mail: tribastone@pst.ifi.lmu.de

Stephen Gilmore
The University of Edinburgh
School of Informatics
Informatics Forum
10 Crichton Street, Edinburgh EH8 9AB, UK
E-mail: stephen.gilmore@ed.ac.uk

ISSN 0302-9743   e-ISSN 1611-3349
ISBN 978-3-642-36780-9   e-ISBN 978-3-642-36781-6
DOI 10.1007/978-3-642-36781-6
Springer Heidelberg Dordrecht London New York

Library of Congress Control Number: 2013931752

CR Subject Classification (1998): C.4, D.2.7-9, C.2.1-2, C.2.4, I.6.3-6, J.2

LNCS Sublibrary: SL 2 – Programming and Software Engineering

Typesetting: Camera-ready by author, data conversion by Scientific Publishing Services, Chennai, India

Printed on acid-free paper

Springer is part of Springer Science+Business Media (www.springer.com)

Preface

This volume of LNCS contains papers from the 9th European Performance Engineering Workshop held at the Ludwig Maximilians University of Munich, Germany, on July 30, 2012, and papers from the 28th UK Performance Engineering Workshop held at the University of Edinburgh on July 2, 2012.

The accepted papers reflect the breadth of interest across Europe in performance engineering of software and hardware in computer systems. A healthy range of types of papers are in evidence: papers from classical performance modelling areas such as wireless network protocols and parallel execution of scientific codes to hot topics such as energy-aware computing to unexpected ventures into ranking professional tennis players. In addition to new case studies, the accepted papers also present new techniques for dealing with the modelling challenges brought about by the increasing complexity and scale of systems today.

We extend our thanks to all members of the Program Committees for the two workshops and all of the additional reviewers for their helpful and constructive comments and reviews. The workshops were enriched by keynote talks given by Isi Mitrani (EPEW) and Katinka Wolter and Nigel Thomas (UKPEW). We were delighted to have their contributions.

We would like to express our gratitude to everyone involved in making EPEW 2012 and UKPEW 2012 a success, in particular the staff of both the Ludwig Maximilians University and the University of Edinburgh, who helped with many organizational and logistical challenges. We are grateful to the EasyChair site for their excellent conference system and to Springer for their continued support of this workshop series. The UK Performance Engineering Workshop received financial support from the Scottish Informatics and Computer Science Alliance (SICSA) for which we are very grateful. Finally, we thank the authors of all the papers in this volume for their contribution and for meeting all of the deadlines for the workshops.

July 2012

Mirco Tribastone
Stephen Gilmore

Organization

Chairs

EPEW Chair

Mirco Tribastone   Ludwig Maximilians University of Munich, Germany

UKPEW Chair

Stephen Gilmore   University of Edinburgh, UK

Proceedings Chair

Robert Holton   University of Bradford, UK

Publicity Chair

Steven Wright   University of Warwick, UK

Program Committee

Steffen Becker	University of Paderborn, Germany
Marco Bernardo	University of Urbino, Italy
Luca Bortolussi	University of Trieste, Italy
Jeremy Bradley	Imperial College London, UK
Allan Clark	University of Edinburgh, UK
Antinisca Di Marco	University of L'Aquila, Italy
Nick Dingle	University of Manchester, UK
Paulo Fernandes	PUCRS, Brazil
Jean-Michel Forneau	University of Versailles-Saint-Quentin, France
Vashti Galpin	University of Edinburgh, UK
Nicholas Gast	EPFL, Switzerland
Stephen Gilmore	University of Edinburgh, UK
Richard Hayden	Imperial College London, UK
Andras Horvath	University of Turin, Italy
Samuel Kounev	Karlsruhe Institute of Technology, Germany
Catalina M. Lladó	University of the Balearic Islands, Spain
Dorina Petriu	Carleton University, Canada
Marco Scarpa	University of Messina, Italy
Markus Siegle	University of the Federal Armed Forces, Munich, Germany
Miklos Telek	Budapest University of Technology and Economics, Hungary

Nigel Thomas   Newcastle University, UK
Mirco Tribastone   Ludwig Maximilians University Munich,
                          Germany
Petr Tuma   Charles University Prague, Czech Republic
Antonio Vallecillo   University of Malaga, Spain
Katinka Wolter   Free University of Berlin, Germany

Sponsoring Institutions

The Scottish Informatics and Computer Science Alliance (SICSA)

Table of Contents

UKPEW Poster

Trading Power Consumption against Performance by Reserving Blocks of Servers

Isi Mitrani

School of Computing Science, Newcastle University, NE1 7RU, UK
isi.mitrani@ncl.ac.uk

Abstract. We consider the problem of managing a service center where it is desirable to keep power consumption low. Customers may be patient or they may defect (i.e. leave the system) if waiting times are too long. Several blocks of servers are designated as 'reserves'. They are powered up and down when the queue size increases above or falls below certain thresholds. Objective functions to be minimized take into account the number of servers that are powered up, the number of occasions when blocks are powered up and a performance measure involving either waiting time or number of jobs lost through defections. The question of how to choose the blocks of reserves is answered by analyzing a suitable queueing model. Heuristic policies are proposed and numerical results are presented.

Keywords: Cloud Computing, Power saving, Performance, Dynamic server allocation, Reneging, Queueing models.

1 Introduction

Service centers are supporting the operations of major organizations. They also form the basis of a business model, sometimes referred to as *Cloud Computing*, whereby a company makes money by selling computing services to paying customers. A typical service center may contain thousands of computers, which require large amounts of power to run and to keep cool (not to mention the hidden costs associated with greenhouse gas emissions). Consequently, it is important to devise strategies for reducing the power consumption while maintaining acceptable levels of performance.

Despite much research on the design of servers whose power consumption is proportional to their utilization, progress in that direction has been limited. Even with the best current designs, the power consumed by an idle server is about 65% of its peak consumption [6]. Hence, the only realistic way to reduce significantly the power consumption of a service center is to power down blocks of servers whenever that can be justified by the demand conditions. That is the policy that this paper proposes to investigate.

Note the emphasis on 'blocks': the servers in a large-scale service center are usually grouped into logical or physical units of equal or unequal sizes.

M. Tribastone and S. Gilmore (Eds.): EPEW/UKPEW 2012, LNCS 7587, pp. 1–15, 2013.

The problem of managing these blocks efficiently is to ensure that they are switched on readily enough to respond to increased demand, yet not leave them powered up unnecessarily when they are under-utilized.

The behaviour of users depends on the way the service center is run. In some cases, submitted jobs are obliged to remain in the system until their service is completed (e.g., users pay for services in advance). Then the objective to be optimized would include some measure of performance such as the average response time. If, on the other hand, long waits can cause jobs to depart before receiving service, then a major part of the objective would be to minimize the number of these 'defections'. In both cases, a trade-off arises: the user experience is improved by increasing the number of powered-up servers, while power consumption is lowered by increasing the number of powered-down servers.

We propose a dynamic operating policy where a subset of the available servers are left powered on all the time, while the remainder is divided into k 'reserve' blocks. The latter are powered up and down depending on the number of jobs in the system. The problem is to decide how many and how big should the reserve blocks be. Answers are provided by analyzing two queueing models of the system: with and without defections. Closed-form solutions are obtained in both cases. These also lead to easily implementable and very efficient heuristic policies.

There is a large volume of literature on improving the power consumption of computer systems. For an overview and many references, see Berl et al [3]. A system for monitoring demand and adaptive allocation of servers was proposed by Chase et al [4]. However, the set of studies where a specific dynamic policy is quantitatively modeled with a view to predicting its behaviour, is much smaller. It is to that set that the present paper belongs.

Perhaps the closest models to ours were examined by Artalejo et al. [2], Gandhi et al. [5], Mitrani [8,9], Schwartz et al [10] and Mazzucco et al [7]. In [2] and in [5], servers are powered up and down one at a time. Exact results are obtained when at most one server can be in the set-up mode (i.e., in the process of being powered up), or when the number of servers is infinite. In [8], there is a single reserve block with set-up times; no defections are allowed. The same model without set-up times was subsequently examined in [10]. A similar system, again with a single reserve block but allowing defections, was studied in [9]. Reneging was also considered in [7], in the context of a static policy which employs a fixed number of servers. The objective was to examine what that number should be. For some further aspects of queues with defections, see for example Ancker and Gafarian [1], and Ward and Glynn [11].

At the time when [8] and [9] appeared, the question was asked "Why a single block of reserves?" Could one not reduce costs further by allowing several blocks of servers to be designated as reserves and be turned on and off dynamically in response to different loading conditions? We now aim to answer that question by evaluating to what extent the increased flexibility would lead to lower costs. It should be pointed out that such a generalization comes at a price: in order to maintain tractability, it is assumed that both the power-on and the power-off operations are instantaneous. However, those operations are still assumed to incur costs and the latter are included in the cost functions to be minimized.

Our numerical experiments will show that using more than one reserve block makes in fact only a small difference to the achievable costs. So the result of this paper is in a sense negative: a complex operating policy is not much better than a simple one. However, that conclusion was not a priori obvious; to arrive at it, it was necessary to go through the process of modelling, analysis and evaluation.

The queueing model without defections, and its solution, are described in sections 2 and 3, respectively. The model with defections, and its solution, are presented in sections 4 and 5. Both solutions are essentially in closed form, in the sense that they do not involve simultaneous sets of equations. Numerical experiments examining different aspects of the control policies, together with comparisons between the optimal policy and some simple heuristics, are shown in section 6.

2   The Model without Defections

The service center contains N servers, of which n_0 are permanently operative (they are referred to as the 'main' block). The remaining $N - n_0$ servers are divided into k reserve blocks, of sizes m_1, m_2, ..., m_k, respectively. (Note that even if the real or logical blocks are all the same size, one can easily construct blocks of different sizes by appropriate groupings.)

Requests, or 'jobs', arrive in a Poisson stream with rate λ. Operative servers accept one job at a time, service times being distributed exponentially with mean $1/\mu$. There is an unbounded FIFO queue for those jobs that have to wait for a server.

There are two increasing sequences of 'up' and 'down' thresholds, U_i and D_i, which control the availability of the reserve blocks $i = 1, 2, \ldots, k$. If the ith reserve block is inoperative and the number of jobs in the system increases from $U_i - 1$ to U_i, then that block is powered up. All of its servers become operative instantaneously. If the ith reserve block is operative and the number of jobs in the system drops from $D_i + 1$ to D_i, then that block is powered down instantaneously. Any job whose service is interrupted because its server is powered down, is immediately and instantaneously transferred to another server if one is available. If not, the job goes to the head of the queue and its service is eventually resumed from the point of interruption.

Let n_i be the number of servers that would be operative if only blocks $0, 1, \ldots, i$ are powered up. That is, $n_1 = n_0 + m_1$, $n_2 = n_0 + m_1 + m_2 = n_1 + m_2$, ..., $n_k = n_{k-1} + m_k = N$. It is sensible to power up reserve block i when all of its servers can come into use, i.e. when the number of jobs in the system reaches n_i: we thus choose $U_i = n_i$. Similarly, it is sensible to power down reserve block i when its servers are not needed, i.e. when the number of jobs in the system drops to n_{i-1}: hence, choose $D_i = n_{i-1}$. This choice of thresholds is not essential for the analysis, but is made in order to reduce the number of control parameters.

server blocks

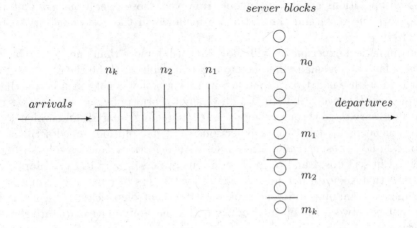

Fig. 1. A service center with reserve blocks

The system is illustrated in figure 1. The system state at time t is described by a pair of integers $[I(t), J(t)]$, where $I(t)$ specifies the current state of the reserve blocks: $I(t) = 0$ if only the main block is operative; $I(t) = 1$ if only the main block and reserve block 1 are operative; $I(t) = 2$ if only the main block and reserve blocks 1 and 2 are operative; $\ldots$; $I(t) = k$ if all the reserve blocks are powered up.

The second integer, $J(t)$, represents the number of jobs present. The admissible values for $J(t)$ depend on the value of $I(t)$. Thus, if $I(t) = 0$, then $0 \leq J(t) < n_1$; if $I(t) = 1$, then $n_0 < J(t) < n_2$; $\ldots$; if $I(t) = k$, then $n_{k-1} < J(t) < \infty$. In general, if $J(t) > n_{I(t)}$ the queue is non-empty.

The above assumptions imply that $[I(t), J(t)]$ is a Markov process. That process is ergodic when the offered load, $\rho = \lambda/\mu$, is smaller than the total number of servers: $\rho < N$. Assuming that that condition holds, denote the steady-state distribution of the process by

$$p_{i,j} = \lim_{t \to \infty} P[I(t) = i, J(t) = j], \tag{1}$$

for $i = 0, 1, \ldots, k$ and the corresponding admissible values for j. A portion of the transition diagram of the Markov process $[I(t), J(t)]$, for $i = 0, 1, 2$, is illustrated in figure 2. The 'instantaneous departure rates' that appear in figure 2, $\mu_{i,j}$, depend on the number of operative servers and on the number of jobs present. When there are no defections, those rates are given by

$$\mu_{i,j} = \min(j, n_i)\mu . \tag{2}$$

Let $p_{i,\cdot}$ be the steady state marginal probability that $I = i$, i.e. that only blocks $0, 1, \ldots, i$ are powered up. For $i = 0$ this is given by

$$p_{0,\cdot} = \sum_{j=0}^{n_1-1} p_{0,j} . \tag{3}$$

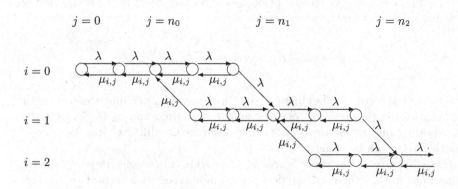

Fig. 2. Transition diagram

For $i = 1, 2, \ldots, k - 1$, we have

$$p_{i,\cdot} = \sum_{j=n_{i-1}+1}^{n_{i+1}-1} p_{i,j} . \tag{4}$$

The corresponding expression for $i = k$ is

$$p_{k,\cdot} = \sum_{j=n_{k-1}+1}^{\infty} p_{k,j} . \tag{5}$$

The steady state average number of operative servers, S, is equal to

$$S = \sum_{i=0}^{k} n_i p_{i,\cdot} . \tag{6}$$

The average number of instances, per unit time, when block i is powered up, is denoted by Q_i; it is given by

$$Q_i = \lambda p_{i-1,n_i-1} ; \quad i = 1, 2, \ldots, k . \tag{7}$$

In the steady state, that is also the average number of instances, per unit time, when block i is powered down.

Performance is measured by the average number of jobs in the system, L (one could just as easily have taken the average response time per job):

$$L = \sum_{i=0}^{k} \sum_{j} j p_{i,j} , \tag{8}$$

where the sum with respect to j extends over the admissible numbers of jobs in the system when the reserve blocks are in state i.

In assessing the cost incurred by the system per unit time, we wish to include job holding costs, power consumption costs and unit costs for powering servers up. Thus, the cost function has the form

$$C = c_1 L + c_2 S + c_3 \sum_{i=1}^{k} Q_i m_i \, , \tag{9}$$

where c_1 is the cost for holding one job in the system per unit time, c_2 is the power consumption cost for one server per unit time and c_3 is the unit cost of powering one server up (if powering down incurs different, non-zero costs, another term can be added).

The objective of the analysis will be to provide expressions for computing L, S and Q_i, so that the cost function can be minimized with respect to the sizes of the main and reserve blocks.

3   Solution of Model without Defections

The first step to computing the cost function (9) is to determine the steady state probabilities (1), which in turn necessitates the solution of the corresponding set of balance and normalizing equations.

The main task will be to express all probabilities in terms of one of them. For numerical reasons, it is convenient to select the latter as p_{0,n_0}. The computational procedure would start by setting $p_{0,n_0} = 1$. The recurrences provided below enable all remaining probabilities to be computed sequentially, at the same time accumulating their sum and their contribution to the quantities of interest L, S and Q_i. Having computed all these values, they are re-normalized by dividing them by the sum of all probabilities.

When $i = 0$ and $j \leq n_0$, the process behaves in a simple birth-and-death manner. The corresponding probabilities are expressed recurrently in terms of p_{0,n_0} as follows:

$$p_{0,j-1} = \frac{j\mu}{\lambda} p_{0,j} \; ; \; j = n_0, n_0 - 1, \ldots, 1 \, . \tag{10}$$

If the probability p_{i,n_i} has already been expressed, the probabilities $p_{i,j}$, for $j = n_i + 1, n_i + 2, \ldots, n_{i+1} - 1$, can be obtained as follows. Making cuts in the steady state diagram around sets of states $\{(i, n_{i+1} - 1), (i, n_{i+1} - 2), \ldots, (i, j)\}$, for $j = n_{i+1} - 1, n_{i+1} - 2, \ldots, n_i + 1$, we write a set of balance equations:

$$(\lambda + n_i \mu) p_{i,n_{i+1}-1} = \lambda p_{i,n_{i+1}-2}$$
$$\lambda p_{i,n_{i+1}-1} + n_i \mu p_{i,n_{i+1}-2} = \lambda p_{i,n_{i+1}-3} \tag{11}$$
$$\cdots$$
$$\lambda p_{i,n_{i+1}-1} + n_i \mu p_{i,n_i+1} = \lambda p_{i,n_i} \, .$$

These yield expressions for the desired probabilities, first in terms of $p_{i,n_{i+1}-1}$:

$$p_{i,j} = p_{i,n_{i+1}-1} \sum_{s=0}^{n_{i+1}-1-j} r_i^s , \qquad (12)$$

where $r_i = n_i \mu / \lambda$; $j = n_i, n_i + 1, \ldots, n_{i+1} - 2$.

Then it is not difficult to express the same probabilities in terms of p_{i,n_i}:

$$p_{i,j} = \frac{1 - r_i^{n_{i+1}-j}}{1 - r_i^{m_i}} p_{i,n_i} ; \quad j = n_i + 1, \ldots, n_{i+1} - 1 . \qquad (13)$$

The next step is to express the probabilities $p_{i+1,j}$, for $j = n_i + 1, \ldots, n_{i+1}$, in terms of $p_{i,n_{i+1}-1}$. First, since the average number of power-up events for block $i + 1$ per unit time is equal to the average number of power-down events for block $i + 1$, we have

$$\lambda p_{i,n_{i+1}-1} = (n_i + 1)\mu p_{i+1,n_i+1} . \qquad (14)$$

The remaining probabilities $p_{i+1,j}$, for $j = n_i + 2, \ldots, n_{i+1}$, satisfy the balance equations

$$\lambda p_{i,n_{i+1}-1} + \lambda p_{i+1,j-1} = j\mu p_{i+1,j} . \qquad (15)$$

These recurrences allow the probabilities $p_{i+1,j}$, for $j = n_i + 1, \ldots, n_{i+1}$, to be expressed in terms of $p_{i,n_{i+1}-1}$ and hence in terms of p_{i,n_i}.

Repeating the above procedure for $i = 0, 1, \ldots, k - 1$, all the probabilities $p_{i,j}$ where $j \leq N$, up to and including $p_{k,N}$, are expressed in terms of p_{0,n_0}. This enables the computation of $p_{i,\cdot}$ for $i = 0, 1, \ldots, k - 1$, using equations (3) and (4). At the same time, Q_i is obtained for $i = 1, 2, \ldots, k$ via equation (7), and the appropriate contributions to L are accumulated.

The remaining infinite tail, $p_{k,j}$, for $j = N + 1, N + 2, \ldots$, is determined by remarking that in that region the process behaves like an $M/M/1$ queue with parameters λ and $N\mu$. The relevant probabilities are geometric, satisfying the recurrences

$$p_{k,j+1} = \rho_k p_{k,j} ; \quad j \geq N , \qquad (16)$$

where $\rho_k = \lambda / (N\mu)$. The sum of the tail probabilities (needed for computing $p_{k,\cdot}$ and for the subsequent re-normalization) is equal to

$$\sum_{j=N+1}^{\infty} p_{k,j} = \frac{\rho_k}{1 - \rho_k} p_{k,N} . \qquad (17)$$

The contribution of the tail to the mean, L, is given by

$$\sum_{j=N+1}^{\infty} j p_{k,j} = \frac{\rho_k}{1 - \rho_k} \left[N + \frac{1}{1 - \rho_k} \right] p_{k,N} . \qquad (18)$$

We are thus able to compute the cost function for a given set of parameters.

4   The Model with Defections

Again the system consists of N servers, with a main block of size n_0 and k reserve blocks of sizes $m_1, m_2, \ldots, m_k$, respectively. Block i is powered up (instantaneously) when the number of jobs in the system reaches n_i and is powered down when that number drops to n_{i-1}. The job arrival and service assumptions are the same as before.

The important difference in this model is that customers are impatient. Upon arrival, each job starts a personal independent timer which is an exponentially distributed random variable with mean $1/\gamma$. If that timer expires before the job is admitted into service, that job leaves the system ('defects', or 'reneges'). Similarly, if the job is returned to the queue as a result of a power-down operation, it starts a new impatience timer with parameter γ.

Thus, if there are j jobs in the queue (excluding the ones in service), then the instantaneous total defection rate is $j\gamma$.

Using the notation of section 2, the system state at time t is described by a pair of integers $[I(t), J(t)]$, where $I(t)$ specifies the current state of the reserve blocks and $J(t)$ is the number of jobs present. Because the rate of defections is proportional to the size of the queue, the Markov process $[I(t), J(t)]$ is always ergodic. The corresponding steady state probabilities, $p_{i,j}$, determine the average number of operative servers, S (as in equation (6)), and the average number of instances per unit time when block i is powered up, Q_i (equation (7)).

Denote by R the average number of defections per unit time. This quantity is given by

$$R = \sum_{i=0}^{k} \sum_{j>n_i} (j - n_i)\gamma p_{i,j} \,, \tag{19}$$

where the second summation extends over the values of j that are admissible for the corresponding value of i and exceed n_i.

The cost function to be minimized in this model has the form

$$C = c_1 R + c_2 S + c_3 \sum_{i=1}^{k} Q_i m_i \,, \tag{20}$$

where c_1 is the revenue lost due to one defection, c_2 is the power consumption cost for one server per unit time and c_3 is the unit cost of powering one server up.

5   Solution of Model with Defections

The balance diagram for this model is similar to the one in figure 2. The instantaneous departure rates are now state-dependent for all i and j. They are given by

$$\mu_{i,j} = \min(j, n_i)\mu + \max(j - n_i, 0)\gamma \,. \tag{21}$$

These differences cause small changes to the analysis of the finite part of the process, i.e. the states (i,j) for which $j \leq N$. However, the infinite tail will require a radically different treatment.

Equations (10) continue to hold. Equations (11) now take the form

$$(\lambda + n_i\mu + (m_i - 1)\gamma)p_{i,n_{i+1}-1} = \lambda p_{i,n_{i+1}-2}$$
$$\lambda p_{i,n_{i+1}-1} + (n_i\mu + (m_i - 2)\gamma)p_{i,n_{i+1}-2} = \lambda p_{i,n_{i+1}-3}$$
$$\cdots$$
$$\lambda p_{i,n_{i+1}-1} + (n_i\mu + \gamma)p_{i,n_i+1} = \lambda p_{i,n_i} .$$

Again, these equations allow us to express the probabilities $p_{i,j}$, for $n_i < j < n_{i+1}$, first in terms of $p_{i,n_{i+1}-1}$, and then in terms of p_{i,n_i}.

Equations (14) and (15) hold without change. In those states, the queue is empty and hence there are no defections.

This covers the finite part of the process. It remains to determine the tail probabilities $p_{k,j}$, for $j = N+1, N+2, \ldots$. In this region the model behaves like an an $M/M/1$ queue with arrival rate λ, service rate $N\mu$ and defection rate γ per job in the queue. The corresponding set of balance equations is

$$\lambda p_{k,j} = [N\mu + (j+1-N)\gamma]p_{k,j+1} \; ; \quad j = N, N+1, \ldots . \tag{22}$$

A simple way to solve that set of equations (other solutions exist, e.g. see [7,11]) is by introducing the generating function

$$g(z) = \sum_{j=N}^{\infty} p_{k,j} z^{j-N} . \tag{23}$$

Multiplying the jth equation in (22) by z^{j-N} and adding them together yields, after some manipulations, a first order ordinary differential equation for $g(z)$:

$$g'(z) = \left[\frac{\lambda}{\gamma} - \frac{N\mu}{\gamma z}\right] g(z) + \frac{N\mu}{\gamma z} p_{k,N} . \tag{24}$$

The solution of this equation is available in closed form:

$$g(z) = \frac{N\mu}{\gamma} p_{k,N} e^{\frac{\lambda}{\gamma}z} z^{-\frac{N\mu}{\gamma}} \int_0^z e^{-\frac{\lambda}{\gamma}x} x^{\frac{N\mu}{\gamma}-1} dx . \tag{25}$$

After a change of variable $x \to \lambda x/\gamma$, this becomes

$$g(z) = \frac{N\mu}{\gamma} p_{k,N} e^{\frac{\lambda}{\gamma}z} z^{-\frac{N\mu}{\gamma}} \left(\frac{\gamma}{\lambda}\right)^{\frac{N\mu}{\gamma}-1} \Gamma(\frac{\lambda}{\gamma}z, \frac{N\mu}{\gamma}) , \tag{26}$$

where $\Gamma(z,y)$ is the incomplete gamma function:

$$\Gamma(z,y) = \int_0^z e^{-x} x^{y-1} dx .$$

The sum of all tail probabilities is equal to the value of $g(1)$:

$$g(1) = \frac{N\mu}{\gamma} p_{k,N} e^{\frac{\lambda}{\gamma}} \left(\frac{\gamma}{\lambda}\right)^{\frac{N\mu}{\gamma}-1} \Gamma\left(\frac{\lambda}{\gamma}, \frac{N\mu}{\gamma}\right). \tag{27}$$

The contribution of the infinite tail to the rate of defections, R, is provided by $\gamma g'(1)$. According to (24), this is equal to

$$\gamma g'(1) = (\lambda - N\mu)g(1) + N\mu p_{k,N}. \tag{28}$$

Routines for computing the incomplete gamma function are readily available.

6   Numerical Results

A number of numerical experiments were carried out, where the models with and without defections were solved in a variety of settings. The aims were (a) to illustrate the effect of reserving different numbers and sizes of blocks on the cost function, and (b) to devise efficient heuristic policies that would avoid having to carry out expensive searches for the optimum. In all cases, the number of servers was $N = 20$ and the average service time was chosen as the time unit, so that $\mu = 1$. In the model with defections, it was assumed that customers are willing to wait for about one service time before departing, i.e. $\gamma = 1$.

The plots in figure 3 show the average cost per unit time as a function of k, the number of reserve blocks ($k = 0, 1, \ldots, 9$), in a system without defections. The main and reserve blocks were chosen to be of approximately the same size, as far as possible. Thus, when $k = 2$, the 20 servers were divided into 3 blocks of sizes 7, 7 and 6, respectively; when $k = 5$, the division was 4,4,3,3,3,3; when $k = 8$ it was 3,3,2,2,2,2,2,2,2. Three arrival rates were used: $\lambda = 6$, $\lambda = 10$ and $\lambda = 14$, representing average system utilizations of 30%, 50% and 70%, respectively. The holding, power consumption and power-on unit costs were $c_1 = 2$, $c_2 = 1$ and $c_3 = 1$, respectively. In other words, reducing waiting times was considered to be twice as important as saving power or avoiding server state changes. The figure shows that, with one slight exception, the most expensive system is the one where all servers are in the main block ($k = 0$). Significant cost savings can be achieved by introducing one or two reserve blocks, particularly when the offered load is medium or low. However, further increasing the number of reserve blocks (and hence reducing the block sizes), tends to make little difference or even increase costs.

One might suspect that equal size blocks are not necessarily best. This is indeed the case, as figure 4 illustrates. The servers are now divided into three blocks, with the main block having three sizes: $n_0 = 6$, $n_0 = 10$ and $n_0 = 14$. In each of these cases, the system cost is plotted against the size of the first reserve block, m_1 (the size of the second reserve block is of course $20 - n_0 - m_1$). The arrival rate is $\lambda = 10$, i.e. the system is 50% utilized.

We see that for each main block size, there is an optimal value for m_1. When $n_0 = 6$, that value is $m_1 = 7$, resulting in three almost equal blocks of sizes 6,

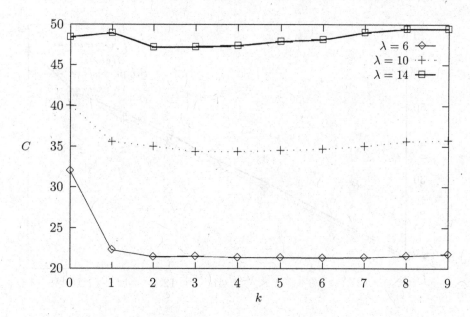

Fig. 3. Cost as a function of the number of blocks, for different arrival rates
$N = 20$; $\mu = 1$; $c_1 = 2$; $c_2 = 1$; $c_3 = 1$

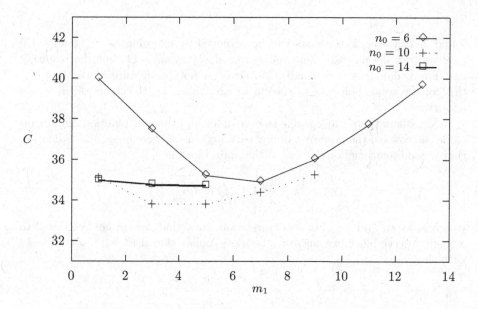

Fig. 4. Cost as a function of m_1, for different main blocks n_0
$N = 20$; $\lambda = 10$; $\mu = 1$; $c_1 = 2$; $c_2 = 1$; $c_3 = 1$

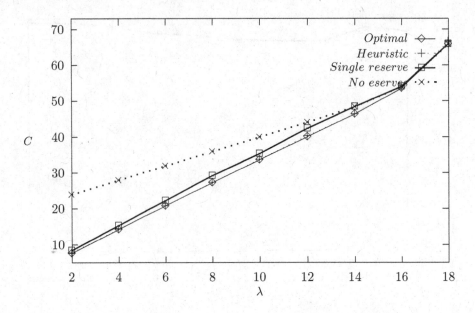

Fig. 5. Comparison between reserve policies for different arrival rates
$$N = 20 \; ; \; \mu = 1 \; ; \; c_1 = 2 \; ; \; c_2 = 1 \; ; \; c_3 = 1$$

7 and 7. However, lower costs can be achieved by choosing $n_0 = 14$ and still lower ones when $n_0 = 10$ (an even better choice is $n_0 = 11$, but the resulting cost improvement is very small). Moreover, a notable feature of the figure is that for the good choices of n_0 the curves are flatter, i.e. the choice of m_1 is less important.

In [8], where there was a single reserve block and the cost function did not include the costs of the power-on operations, arguments were presented indicating that a good heuristic for the size of the main block is

$$n_0 = \left\lfloor \rho + \frac{1}{2} \left[1 + \sqrt{1 + 4\rho \frac{c_1}{c_2}} \right] \right\rfloor , \tag{29}$$

where $\rho = \lambda/\mu$ and $\lfloor \cdot \rfloor$ indicates truncation. Now that we are not restricted to a single reserve block, we suggest a heuristic policy that uses two reserve blocks such that

$$n_0 = \lfloor \rho \rfloor + 1 , \tag{30}$$

and

$$m_1 = \left\lfloor 0.5 + \sqrt{\rho \frac{c_1 + c_3}{c_2}} \right\rfloor . \tag{31}$$

That is, make the main block just large enough to be able to cope with the offered load. Let the first reserve block be roughly of the size indicated by the second term in (29), bearing in mind that the unit cost c_3 discourages frequent powering on and hence argues for larger blocks. Leave the remaining servers, if any, for the second reserve block.

This heuristic agrees with the results in figure 3 (which suggested a small number of reserve blocks) and with those in figure 4: it provides the partition $n_0 = 11$, $m_1 = 5$ and $m_2 = 4$, which is almost optimal.

A more extensive comparison between the above heuristic and the optimal policy (obtained by searching through all possible numbers and sizes of reserve blocks) is presented in figure 5. The offered load is varied by increasing the value of λ. Also plotted are the costs of the policy that uses no reserves at all, and the one using a single reserve block, with n_0 given by a similar expression to (29)

$$ n_0 = \left\lfloor 0.5 + \rho + \sqrt{\rho \frac{c_1 + c_3}{c_2}} \right\rfloor . $$

A rather striking feature of the figure is that the heuristic policy is practically indistinguishable from the optimal policy. There are some differences but most of the time they are too small to show up in the figure. Using a single reserve block is, on the whole, a little worse. However, the advantages of using two reserve blocks rather than one are not great. The costs of having all servers powered on all the time are, in general, considerably higher.

It is worth mentioning that the great majority of the configurations that achieve the optimal costs consist of a main block and two reserve blocks. A few partitions contain three reserve blocks and none use more than three.

The gains in costs that can be achieved by using a dynamic policy, compared to not powering servers down, are of course largest when the system is lightly loaded; they are smallest, or non-existent, when the system is heavily loaded.

We now turn our attention to the system with defections. Remember that the question of stability does not arise here, since the servers can always cope with the load. In [9], it was suggested that if only one reserve block is used, a good heuristic for the size of the main block is $n_0 = \lfloor \rho \rfloor + 1$ (rather that the value given by (29)).

For the present model, where more than one reserve block is allowed, we suggest the same heuristic policy as in the case without defections: use two reserve blocks, with n_0 and m_1 given by (30) and (31), and $m_2 = N - n_0 - m_1$.

Figure 6 shows a similar comparison between different policies to the one in figure 5. Since losing jobs due to defections is a serious matter resulting in lost revenue, the cost of losing a job was assumed to be four times greater than the running cost of a server: $c_1 = 4$, $c_2 = 1$. The unit cost of powering a server on is again $c_3 = 1$.

This time the differences between the optimal and heuristic policies are a little more noticeable. However, even here those differences are less than 10%. The relative advantage of using two reserve blocks, rather than one, is again quite small; it is of about the same order of magnitude as in the case without defections.

Note that the cost of the system without reserves is now mostly flat, whereas it increased roughly linearly in figure 5. This is because of the different first term

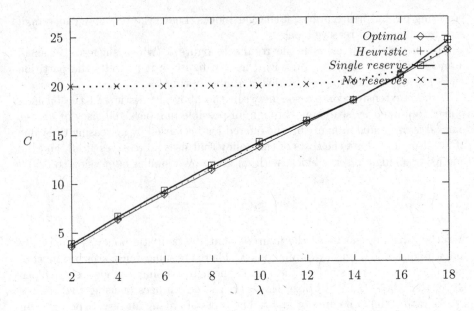

Fig. 6. Comparison between reserve policies: job defections
$$N = 20 \; ; \; \mu = 1 \; ; \; \gamma = 1 \; ; \; c_1 = 4 \; ; \; c_2 = 1 \; ; \; c_3 = 1$$

in the cost function: defections only affect the cost of the static system when it becomes heavily loaded.

7   Conclusion

This paper provides an analysis and evaluation of an energy-saving mechanism whereby several blocks of servers are kept in reserve and are powered up and down dynamically, according to the number of jobs present. This is an extension of previously studied policies based on a single reserve block.

Two queueing models of the system are examined, one disallowing and one allowing customer defections. In both cases, efficient closed form solutions for evaluating the cost function are obtained. Heuristic policies which are very close to optimal are presented.

The experiments carried out appear to indicate that the advantages derived by using multiple reserve blocks instead of a single reserve block, are quite small. In a large scale enterprise, small savings can mount up, but even if they do not, a negative result of this nature is valuable. It tells us that a simple policy can do really well, and therefore there is no need to go through an expensive search for an optimal policy which may be quite complex.

References

1. Ancker, C.J., Gafarian, A.: Queueing with Impatient Customers Who Leave at Random. Journal of Industrial Engineering 13, 84 (1962)
2. Artalejo, J.R., Economou, A., Lopez-Herrero, M.J.: Analysis of a multiserver queue with setup times. Queueing Syst. Theory Appl. 51(1-2), 53–76 (2005)
3. Berl, A., Gelenbe, E., di Girolamo, M., Giuliani, G., de Meer, H., Dang, M.Q., Pentikousis, K.: Energy-Efficient Cloud Computing. The Computer Journal 53(7), 1045–1051 (2010)
4. Chase, J.S., Anderson, D.C., Thakar, P.N., Vahdat, A.M., Doyle, R.P.: Managing energy and server resources in hosting centers. In: Procs. 18th ACM Symposium on Operating Systems Principles, NY (2001)
5. Gandhi, A., Harchol-Balter, M., Adan, I.: Server farms with setup costs. Performance Evaluation 67(11), 1–22 (2010)
6. Greenberg, A., Hamilton, J., Maltz, D.A., Patel, P.: The Cost of a Cloud: Research Problems in Data Center Networks. SIGCOMM Comp. & Comm. Rev. 39(1), 68–73 (2009)
7. Mazzucco, M., Dyachuk, D., Dikaiakos, M.: Profit-Aware Server Allocation for Green Internet Services. In: MASCOTS 2010, Miamy Beach (2010)
8. Mitrani, I.: Managing Performance and Power Consumption in a Server Farm. Annals of Operations Research (2011), doi:10.1007/s10479-011-0932-1
9. Mitrani, I.: Service Center Trade-Offs Between Customer Impatience and Power Consumption. Performance Evaluation 68(11), 1222–1231 (2011)
10. Schwartz, C., Pries, R., Tran-Gia, P.: A queuing analysis of an energy-saving mechanism in data centers. In: Procs. Information Networking Conf. (ICOIN), pp. 70–75 (2012)
11. Ward, A.R., Glynn, P.W.: A diffusion approximation for a Markovian queue with reneging. Queueing Systems 43, 103–128 (2003)

Operational Semantics
for Product-Form Solution

Maria Grazia Vigliotti

Department of Computing, Imperial College London,
180 Queen's Gate, London SW7 2BZ, UK
maria.vigliotti@imperial.ac.uk

Abstract. In this paper we present product-form solutions from the
point of view of stochastic process algebra. In previous work [16] we have
shown how to derive product-form solutions for a formalism called Labelled Markov Automata (LMA). LMA are very useful as their relation
with the Continuous Time Markov Chains is very direct. The disadvantage of using LMA is that the proofs of properties are cumbersome. In
fact, in LMA it is not possible to use the inductive structure of the language in a proof. In this paper we consider a simple stochastic process
algebra that has the great advantage of simplifying the proofs. This simple language has been inspired by PEPA [10], however, detailed analysis
of the semantics of cooperation will show the differences between the
two formalisms. It will also be shown that semantics of the cooperation in process algebra influences the correctness of the derivation of the
product-form solutions.

1 Introduction

In this paper we present product-form solutions from the point of view of stochastic process algebra. The main motivation for this work is twofold: on one side, our
formalisation clarifies the basic mechanisms that govern product-form solutions
in Continuous Time Markov Chains (CTMCs), on the other side, we can generalise the notion of product-form solutions beyond queuing theory. Product-form
solutions are efficient solutions for stationary distributions in CTMCs in general,
while so far product-form solutions have been studied mostly in the area of performance evaluation/ queuing theory. The work presented here is an extension
of previous work [16] where we have shown how to derive product-form solutions
for a formalism called Labelled Markov Automata (LMA). In very simple terms,
LMA describe the state space of CTMCs as labelled graph decorated with transition rates. LMA are equipped with a basic mechanism to build complex CTMCs.
LMA have proved very useful in helping to understand basic mechanisms that
govern product-form solutions, and in providing a very elegant proof of the theorem GRCAT [16]. However, the disadvantage in using LMA is that the proofs,
even for simple properties, are cumbersome. In LMA it is not possible to use the
inductive structure of the language in a proof.

M. Tribastone and S. Gilmore (Eds.): EPEW/UKPEW 2012, LNCS 7587, pp. 16–31, 2013.

In this paper we improve on previous work [16] by considering a simple stochastic process algebra (SSPA), which preserves the semantics of cooperation of LMA. This simple language has been inspired by PEPA [10], however detailed analysis of the semantics of cooperation will show the differences between the two formalisms.

In this paper we investigate the general principle that determines product-form solutions in CTMCs, and we show that the semantics of cooperation is crucial for the correct derivation of product-form solutions. We will introduce a simple language equipped with a rather unique, and possibly counterintuitive semantics, which guarantees the existence of product-form solutions. We will argue that the semantics presented here, is precisely what is needed to model rigorously product-form solutions for CTMCs. We shall also consider a biological example to show an interesting application of product-form solutions to a context different from queuing theory.

2   Related Work

There is vast literature on the topic of product-form solutions and process algebra, and on the formalisation of the intrinsic mechanisms that determine product-form solution [19,12,8,2,9,7,2,3]. On the relationship between process algebra and product-form solutions, Hillston, Thomas and Clark, played a major role [13,12,8,11,6,19]. The common denominator in these papers is the use of PEPA to model processes that are known to enjoy product-solution, and to extract, via PEPA, the modular properties of such processes. This body of work has demonstrated to the community the modelling power of PEPA. It was shown in [8] that quasi-reversible structures can be modelled in PEPA, together with a large variety of product-from solutions. We differ from the work carried out in PEPA, as our goal is not to define 'yet another stochastic process algebra' to model product-form solutions, but to design a language and a semantics to describe only the CTMCs that enjoy product-form solutions. With our formalism it is relatively easy to find new product-form solutions for CTMCs. This was not achieved in previous work.

Another formalism that has been extensively used is the Generalised Stochastic Petri Nets (GSPN) [2,7,2,3]- to cite a few articles. The emphasis is to understand which GSPN enjoy product-form solutions, and what conditions on GSPN are necessary to yield product-form solution [7]. We differ from the work on the GSPN as we use process algebra, and also because of the generality of our results. In this paper, and in previous work, the effort has been directed in defining a set of sufficient conditions that guarantee product-form solutions for time-homogenous CTMCs. Finally, it must be mentioned that similar efforts have been carried out by the community in performance [14,5,18].

The class of product-form solutions considered by [18] is rather limited, while a true advancement was made by [14,5] with the notions of *quasi-reversibility*. Quasi-reversibility was introduced by Kelly [14], and used only on the context of queuing networks. In [5], great efforts were successfully made to show generality and robustness of quasi-reversibility. Nearly all product-form solutions known in queueing networks are derived using quasi-reversibility. It was proved in [5] that quasi-reversibility is a sufficient condition for product-form solutions. The conditions of Theorem 1 can be seen as formalisation of quasi-reversibility. The main difference between Theorem 1 and quasi-reversibility lies in the formalisation of the 'connection' of CTMCs. The way in which queues are connected together is expressed in natural language [5]. This is the main weakness of the work. Since it is not clear how to 'connect' CTMCs together, only networks of queues are considered. Understanding of how to connect queues together is clear in the community of performance evaluation. Our work goes further as it specifies, in a rigorous way, the 'connection' or, better, the cooperation among CTMCs. Note that we have *only* sufficient conditions for product-form solutions, not necessary conditions. As consequence, there are product-form solutions that we cannot characterise, for example [4]. We leave for future work formal development to deal with such product-form solutions.

3   A Simple Language

In this section we introduce a simple stochastic process algebra, SSPA. The main motivation to introduce such a formalism is to verify that the conditions for product-form solutions can be modelled in a language. SSPA is defined in a rather unusual way, but follows in the spirit ideas that were discussed in [13,12]. We initially define simple processes. These are composed essentially by choice and by recursion.Similarly to PEPA, simple processes may or may not characterise a CTMC. Some simple process are *incomplete*, according to PEPA terminology, in the sense that some transitions lack the information about the rate. Such information can be inserted via a new operator: the *closure*. A second layer of processes is defined, as cooperation of simple processes. The operator for cooperation has been inspired by PEPA, but differently form PEPA is an n-nary -operator, like choice. Such operator, differently form PEPA-bow, cannot be expressed as multiple composition of the binary association.

To formally define the language we assume the existence of a set of variables Var, and a set of actions *Act* on which the letter $a, b, c \ldots$ range over it.

Definition 1 (Simple processes). *The set of* simple process, $\mathcal{P}$, *is is given by the following syntax:*

$$\mathsf{E} ::= 0 \mid \mathsf{D}$$
$$\mathsf{M} ::= \sum_{i \in I} (a_i, r_i).\mathsf{E}_i \mid \mathsf{M}_{[a \leftarrow \lambda]}$$

where I is a finite set of indexes.

For clarity in the notation we use the greek letters $\lambda, \mu, \ldots$ range over the set of positive real numbers $\mathbb{R}^+$, the letters $x, y, x, \ldots$ range over Var and the letter r ranges over $\mathbb{R}^+ \cup$ Var. When writing a variable in processes, we use a subscript that refers to the label. For example we would write $(a, y_a).\mathsf{E}$ but not $(a, y_b).\mathsf{E}$. A simple processes stand for the building blocks which are ultimately used to compose complex CTMCs. Nil, written 0, is the empty process; D is the symbol for the identifier. Identifiers are equipped with *identifier equations* such as D $\stackrel{df}{=}$ M. The *choice*, $\sum_{i \in I}(a,r).E_i$, represents the standard selection of one of the possible transitions, and finally there is a new operator *closure* M$_{[a \leftarrow \lambda]}$. This operator transforms all transitions labelled with the pair a and a variable into transitions labelled with the pair a and the real number λ. The role of closure will become clear in the later development of the paper. The grammar of simple process aims to define the transition graph of a labelled CTMC, but not all transition graphs derived from this grammar are CTMCs due to the presence of variables. Examples of this kind can be seen in Fig. 1.

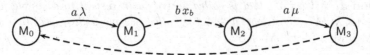

Fig. 1. Transition diagram of the process M$_0$

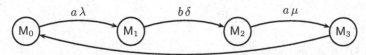

Fig. 2. Transition diagram of the process M$_{0[b \leftarrow \delta]}$

Informally, we can say that the closure operator would transform a transition graph of the simple process M$_0$ $\stackrel{df}{=}$ $(a,\lambda).(b,x_b).(a,\mu).(b,x_b).M_0$ as in Fig. 1 as one in Fig.2 for the simple process M$_{0[b \leftarrow \delta]}$.

If all transitions of a process are decorated with a real number, as in in Fig. 2, then the underlying model description is a time-homogenous CTMC, similar to PEPA. To formally define how to derive the CTMC of a given simple process, we need to give a formal semantics to SSPA via *labelled transition system*.

Definition 2. *A labelled transition system for simple processes written* →: $\mathcal{P} \times$ ($Act \times \mathbb{R}^+ \cup$ Var) $\times \mathcal{P}$ *is the smallest multi-relation that satisfies the rules in Table 1.*

We write M $\xrightarrow{a,r}$ M′ *if* (M, (a,r), M′) $\in$→, *and* →* *for the transitive closure of* →.

In what follows, we consider a relation that is generally defined in π-calculus [17] *structural congruence*. Structural congruence is a relation preserved by all operators of the calculus, i.e a congruence, that identifies terms that should not be distinguished for semantical reasons. Hillston [10] defined a similar relation in a operational way as *isomorphism*.

Definition 3. *Structural congruence, written* ≡ *over the set of simple processes* $\mathcal{P}$ *is the smallest congruence that allows the reorder of terms in the choice.*

We use structural congruence as a relation to talk about individual terms in the summation, and to to avoid to be bothered by the order of terms in the summation. For example $(a, \lambda).E_1 + (b, \mu).E_2 \equiv (b, \mu).E_2 + (a, \lambda).E_1$. We use S to indicate a set of terms of the summation that we do not wish to identfy i.e. $(a, \lambda).E_1 + (b, \mu).E_2 + (c, \gamma).E_3 \equiv (a, \lambda).E_1 + S$.

Differently from CTMC, not all transitions in SSPA have a real number attached. These are called *passive transitions*. Passive transitions are transitions whose delay has not yet been specified. The difference between passive and active transitions, is crucial in this work, so we proceed now to define such entities via analysis of the labels in a process.

Definition 4. *A label $a \in Act$ is called* active *with respect to a simple process* M *if* $M \equiv (a, \lambda).M' + S$. *A label $a \in Act$ is called* passive *with respect to a simple process* M *if* $M \equiv (a, x_a).M' + S$.

We now define a the set of labels that are active or passive in any possible evolution of the simple process.

Definition 5. *The sets of* active labels, *written $\mathcal{A}(M)$, is recursively defined as follows:*

(Nil) $\mathcal{A}(0) = \emptyset$;

(Def) $\mathcal{A}(D) = \mathcal{A}(M)$ *if* $D \overset{df}{=} M$;

(Choice) $\mathcal{A}(\sum_{i \in I}(a_i, r_i).E_i) = \cup_{i \in I}\{a_i : (a_i, r_i).E_i, r_i \in \mathbb{R}^+\} \cup \mathcal{A}(E_i)$;

(Closure) $\mathcal{A}(M_{[a \leftarrow \lambda]}) = \mathcal{A}(M) \cup \{a\}$.

Definition 6. *The set of* passive labels, *written $\mathcal{P}(M)$, is recursively defined as follows:*

(Nil) $\mathcal{P}(0) = \emptyset$;

(Def) $\mathcal{P}(D) = \mathcal{P}(M)$ *if* $D \overset{df}{=} M$;

(Choice) $\mathcal{P}(\sum_{i \in I}(a_i, r_i).E_i) = \cup_{i \in I}\{a_i : (a_i, r_i).E_i, r_i \in Var\} \cup \mathcal{P}(E_i)$;

(Closure) $\mathcal{P}(M_{[a \leftarrow \lambda]}) = \mathcal{P}(M) \backslash \{a\}$.

We simply write $\mathcal{P}$ and $\mathcal{A}$ for the set of passive and active labels when it is clear from the context which simple process we are referring to.

Definition 7. *A simple process* M *is* closed *if $\mathcal{A}(M) = \emptyset$, it is open otherwise.*

The closure operator transforms each open automata into a closed one. We now present a few properties of the closure operator, with respect to the semantics equivalence of *strong bisimilarity*.

Definition 8. *We define* strong bisimilarity *as the largest symmetrical relation $\cong$ such that if $M_1 \cong M_2$, then if for all M_1' it holds that $M_1 \overset{a,r}{\longrightarrow} M_1'$ then there exists M_2' such that $M_2 \overset{a,r}{\longrightarrow} M_2'$ and $M_1' \cong M_2'$.*

Proposition 1. *1.* $M_{[a \leftarrow \lambda]} \cong M$ *if* M *is closed.*

2. $M_{[a \leftarrow \lambda][b \leftarrow \mu]} \cong M_{b \leftarrow \mu][a \leftarrow \lambda]}$.

3. *Let* $\mathcal{P}(\mathsf{M}) \cong \{a_1, a_2, \ldots a_N\}$ *be the set of passive actions of* M. $\mathsf{M}_{[a_1 \leftarrow \lambda_1]} \ldots [a_N \leftarrow \lambda_N]$ *is closed.*

Proof. By induction on grammar of simple processes.

Sometimes, in the presence of multiple applications of the closure operator, we write $\mathsf{M}_{\mathcal{P} \leftarrow R}$, where R is a set of rates $R = \{r_1, r_2, \ldots, r_N\}$ and $\mathcal{P} = \{a_1, a_2, \ldots, a_N\}$ is the set of passive labels in M. Clearly, by generalisation of Proposition 1 this abbreviation is well defined, as it does not matter the order in which the closure is performed. Now we define the interaction among simple processes.

Table 1. Transition semantics of simple processes

$$
\frac{}{\sum_{i \in I}(a_i, r_i).\mathsf{E}_i \xrightarrow{a_i, r_i} \mathsf{E}_i} \qquad \frac{\mathsf{E} \xrightarrow{a, r} \mathsf{E}'}{D \xrightarrow{a, r} \mathsf{E}'} \quad \text{if } D \stackrel{df}{=} \mathsf{E}
$$

$$
\frac{}{(a, x).\mathsf{E} \xrightarrow{a, x} \mathsf{E}} \qquad \frac{}{(a, \mu).\mathsf{E} \xrightarrow{a, \lambda} \mathsf{E}}
$$

$$
\frac{}{(a, \lambda).\mathsf{E}_{[a \leftarrow \lambda]} \xrightarrow{a, \lambda} \mathsf{E}_{[a \leftarrow \lambda]}} \qquad \frac{}{(a, \mu).\mathsf{E}_{[a \leftarrow \lambda]} \xrightarrow{a, \mu} \mathsf{E}_{[a \leftarrow \lambda]}}
$$

Table 2. Transition semantics of interacting processes

$$
\frac{\mathsf{M}_i \xrightarrow{a, r} \mathsf{M}_i'}{\bigotimes_L(\mathsf{M}_1, .., \mathsf{M}_i, ..\mathsf{M}_n) \xrightarrow{a, r} \bigotimes_L(\mathsf{M}_1, .., \mathsf{M}_i', ..\mathsf{M}_n)} \qquad (a \notin L)
$$

$$
\frac{\mathsf{M}_i \xrightarrow{a, \lambda} \mathsf{M}_i' \qquad \mathsf{M}_k \xrightarrow{a, x_q} \mathsf{M}_k'}{\bigotimes_L(\mathsf{M}_1, .., \mathsf{M}_i, ..\mathsf{M}_k, ..\mathsf{M}_n) \xrightarrow{a, \lambda} \bigotimes_L(\mathsf{M}_1, .., \mathsf{M}_i', .., \mathsf{M}_k', ..\mathsf{M}_n)} \qquad (a \in L, k \neq i)
$$

Definition 9. *The set of* interacting processes, $\mathcal{L}$, *is defined by the following syntax:*

$$
\mathsf{C} ::= \mathsf{M} \mid \bigotimes_L (\mathsf{M}_1, \ldots, \mathsf{M}_N)
$$

where $L \subseteq Act$, M *was defined in Definition 1, and for all* $i, j \leq N$ *if* $i \neq j$ *it holds that* $\mathcal{A}(\mathsf{M}_i) \cap \mathcal{A}(\mathsf{M}_j) \cap L = \mathcal{P}(\mathsf{M}_i) \cap \mathcal{P}(\mathsf{M}_j) \cap L = \emptyset$.

Definition 10. *The labelled transition system for the interacting processes written* $\rightarrow: \mathcal{L} \times (Act \times \mathbb{R}^+ \cup Var) \times \mathcal{L}$ *is the smallest multi-relation that satisfies the rules in Table 1.*

We write $\mathsf{C} \xrightarrow{a, r} \mathsf{C}'$ *if* $(\mathsf{C}, (a, r), \mathsf{C}') \in \rightarrow$, *and* $\rightarrow^*$ *for the transitive closure of* $\rightarrow$.

Crucial to this definition is that the interaction happens pairwise. For example, in queueing networks such as the Jackson network [5], this captures the idea that customers hop from one node to one other.

Comparison with PEPA. The semantics of the interaction in SSPA has been inspired by PEPA [10], but it is not identical. PEPA's interaction operation works on *broadcasting* while in SSPA the interaction/cooperation is strictly pairwise.

In PEPA, cooperating processes over the same set of actions L is commutative and associative with the respect to a notion of strong bisimulation. Strong bisimilarity ($\cong$) identifies processes that can carry out the same transitions with respect to the transition relation defined in Definition 10. Therefore, we assume that Definition 8 is adapted to the interacting processes.

In SSPA, the cooperating operator is commutative, but *not* associative with respect to strong bisimilarity, even under the same set of cooperating actions. Commutativity says that the order in which processes cooperate does not matter. If fact, two processes that differ only for the order of simple processes in the cooperation are strongly bisimilar, and, we will see, they have the same product-form solution. However, as far associativity goes, the reader can verify that $(\mathsf{M}_1 \oplus_L \mathsf{M}_2) \oplus_L \mathsf{M}_3$ and $\mathsf{M}_1 \oplus_L (\mathsf{M}_2 \oplus_L \mathsf{M}_3)$ have different transitions i.e they are not strongly bisimilar. To see this it suffices to take the following processes ($\mathsf{M}_1 = (a, \lambda).0$ and $\mathsf{M}_2 = \mathsf{M}_3 = (a, x_a).0$ with $L = \{a\}$ and verify that $(\mathsf{M}_2 \oplus_L \mathsf{M}_3)$ has no transition according to the semantics of SSPA. Therefore $\mathsf{M}_1 \oplus_L (\mathsf{M}_2 \oplus_L \mathsf{M}_3) \cong 0$ while $(\mathsf{M}_1 \oplus_L \mathsf{M}_2) \oplus_L \mathsf{M}_3 \not\cong 0$, which implies, differently from PEPA semantics, that $(\mathsf{M}_1 \oplus_L \mathsf{M}_2) \oplus_L \mathsf{M}_3 \not\cong \mathsf{M}_1 \oplus_L (\mathsf{M}_2 \oplus_L \mathsf{M}_3)$. If we had used PEPA transition system we would have been able to prove that the two processes are strongly bisimilar.

3.1   CTMC

In this paper, we deal only with product-form solutions for *time-homogenous* CTMCs. For a time-homogenous CTMC, the generator matrix $\mathbf{Q}$ contains all the information to compute the *transient* and *steady-state* probability distribution. From the matrix $\mathbf{Q}$ it is possible to describe the state space of the CTMC and vice versa. Generally, in process algebra such as PEPA, the language is a means to describe in a modular way the state space of the underlying CTMC. The generator matrix is then appropriately recovered for computation purposes. If the interacting process C does not contain passive transitions, we can recover the CTMC by taking the set of all derivatives of C as the state space of the CTMC, and by generating the entries of the generator matrix $\mathbf{Q}_C$ as the sum of all the real numbers of the transitions between two derivatives. Rates of self-loops should be ignored, and the diagonal of the generator matrix $\mathbf{Q}_C$ is constructed as usual to ensure that the sum of the entries of the rows equals 0. Even in the presence of passive transitions in a process, the generator matrix can be recovered. However, the matrix may not be used for computation purposes, as it may contain the variables from the passive transitions. For this reason, in what follows, we describe how to build the generator matrix, and we will leave it to the reader, or to the context in which it is used, to establish if the generator can be used straightforwardly for computation purposes, or instantiation of variables is necessary.

Given a process, we define the *set of derivatives* as the set of processes derived via the transitive closure of the labelled transition system.

The set of derivatives of an interactive process C is defined as $\mathcal{S}_C = \{C' : C \xrightarrow{a,r}^* C'\}$. The transition rate from the state of the chain C to C' is given by the sum of the rates of all the labelled transitions of the process i.e.:

$$q(C \to C') = \sum_{\substack{(a,r):C \xrightarrow{a,r} C' \\ C \neq C'}} r.$$

If all transition rates $q(C \to C') \in \mathbb{R}^+$ then $\mathbf{Q}_C$ is the generator matrix of the underlying CTMC of the interactive process. If for some rates it holds that $q(C \to C') \notin \mathbb{R}^+$ then we must specify that the variables in the prefix $(a, x).E$ are considered the same if they occur with the same label. This observation has a huge impact in correct derivation of the generator matrix. For all intents and purposes, variables are considered the same if they are associated with the same label. For example we could write $M = (a, x).(b, \mu).M + (a, y).(c, z).M$, however, in the construction of the generator matrix, either x or y will appear in the definition of the rate. This concept has no meaning from the point of view of the process algebra, but it has huge impact in the building of the generator matrix, and in the computation of probabilities. The generator matrix of M, written $\mathbf{Q}_M$, will be

$$\mathbf{Q}_M = \begin{pmatrix} -2x & x & x \\ \mu & -\mu & 0 \\ 0 & z & -z \end{pmatrix}$$

while the matrix

$$\mathbf{Q}_M = \begin{pmatrix} -(x+y) & x & y \\ \mu & -\mu & 0 \\ 0 & z & -z \end{pmatrix}$$

is not what we intended. We impose that $x = y$, since they appear with the label a and therefore we can treat x as a variable, and apply standard numerical operations. The semantics for the variables is such that $x, y \neq z$ as z occurs with the label c, not a. For this reason the subscript of the label of the action in variables is used in this paper.

For convenience we write $q(C \xrightarrow{a} C') = \sum_{r:C \xrightarrow{a,r} C'} r$ for the transition rate with respect to a label a. We note that for the latter definition we also consider rates from a state to itself i.e. $q(C \xrightarrow{a} C)$. This will be useful later in Theorem 1. We observe that $q(C \to C') = \sum_{\substack{a \in Act \\ C \neq C'}} q(C \xrightarrow{a} C')$.

Given an interacting process C, we can generate the state space of the CTMC as $\mathcal{S}_C$ and the generator matrix $\mathbf{Q}_C$, then with an abuse of notation we refer to the properties of the process meaning the properties of the CTMC. Therefore, we can talk about a stationary or steady-state distribution of the process, π_C, meaning that its CTMC has a stationary or steady-state distribution π. If $\mathbf{Q_C}$ is the generator matrix of the underlying CTMC of C, then we write $\pi(C)$ for *invariant measure* meaning the $\pi\mathbf{Q_C} = \mathbf{0}$. In other words, we use in the notation $\pi(C)$ instead of $\pi\mathbf{Q_C}$. For $C' \in \mathcal{S_C}$ we write $\boldsymbol{\pi_M}(C')$ meaning the value of the vector $\boldsymbol{\pi_M}$ for the element C'. If $\sum_{C' \in \mathcal{S_C}} \pi(C') = 1$ then the CTMC is ergodic and π is the state-state distribution of C [5].

4   Product-Form Solution

We now present the main theorem of the paper regarding product-form solution for SSPA. The theorem asserts that for a given class of processes, that satisfies certain conditions on the rates and on the structure of state space, the product-form solution exists. We start with the definition of structure of the processes.

Definition 11. *In a simple process* $M = \sum_{i \in I}(a_i, r_i).E_i$ *the label a is the* unique passive label *if and only if* $M \equiv (a, x_a).E + S$ *and* $M \equiv (a, x_a).E' + S'$ *then* $S' = S$ *and* $E = E'$.

We now define a set of unique passive labels for a process. Such a set is not empty if in all possible evolution of the process, one passive transition with a given label is possible.

Definition 12. *The set of* unique passive labels *in a simple process* M, *written* $\mathcal{U}(M)$, *is recursively defined as follows:*

(Nil) $\mathcal{U}(0) = Act;$

(Def) $\mathcal{U}(D) = \mathcal{U}(M)$ *if* $D \stackrel{df}{=} M$

$$\mathcal{U}(\sum_{i \in I}(a_i, r_i).E_i) = \begin{cases} \emptyset & \text{if there exist a passive label in } \sum_{i \in I}(a_i, r_i).E_i \text{ which is not unique} \\ (\cup_{i \in I}\{a_i\}) \cap_{i \in I} \mathcal{U}(E_i) & \text{if } a_i \text{ is a unique passive label in } \sum_{i \in I}(a_i, r_i).E_i \end{cases}$$

(Choice)

(Closure) $\mathcal{U}(M_{[a \leftarrow \lambda]}) = \mathcal{U}(M) \backslash \{a\}$

Such a definition is necessary as we need to use process that have one passive transition. This restriction could be relaxed, but it would involve a more complicated statement of Theorem 1.

We now provide the definition of well-formed simple processes, which are the building blocks for the correct definition of product form solutions. Well-formed processes are processes that will generate no confusion in the construction of product form solutions. Informally, we can think product-form as a way of decomposing the invariant measure of a CTMC. Now, if the CTMC has been built using simple processes and an empty cooperation set, then each simple process is independent of the other, and trivially the invariant measure can be written as the product of the invariant measures of each simple process. However, if a complex CTMC has been built using simple processes and a *non-empty* cooperation, then the behaviour of each simple process can be influenced by the others in the cooperation. If, however, in each simple process, the reversed rates of the cooperating transitions are constant in each state, then the invariant measure of a complex CTMC can be written as the product of the invariant measures of each simple process, in a similar fashion as if they were independent. To perform all these calculations correctly, we need to make sure that no confusion arises when writing the processes in SSPA, and therefore we need the notion of *well-formed processes*.

Definition 13 (Well-formed processes). *A simple process* M *is well-formed if:*

1. $\mathcal{A}(M) \cap \mathcal{P}(M) = \emptyset$ *and*
2. *if* $\mathcal{P}(M) \neq \emptyset$ *then* $\mathcal{P}(M) = \mathcal{U}(M)$.

From a syntactic point of view, we have done the work for the following result for the product-form solution. The theorem considers only complex CTMCs composed by well-formed processes. A further condition is added on the outgoing rates of the simple processes to guarantee that on average, we can quantify the dependency among the various processes.

Theorem 1. *Given an interacting process* $C = \bigoplus_L(M_1, M_2, \ldots, M_N)$ *composed by be well-formed simple processes* $M_1, M_2, \ldots, M_N$ *that cooperate on a finite set of actions* $L = \{a_1, a_2, \ldots a_M\}$.
Assume that the state space of $\mathcal{S}_C = \mathcal{S}_{M_1} \times \mathcal{S}_{M_2} \times \cdots \times \mathcal{S}_{M_N}$ *is irreducible. If for all labels in the cooperation set* L *there exists a set of positive real numbers* $K = \{\kappa_1, \ldots, \kappa_M\}$ *such that, for any simple process* M_i, *the following equations are satisfied*

$$\frac{\sum_{M' \in \mathcal{S}_{M_i}} q(M' \xrightarrow{a_r} M)\pi_i(M')}{\pi_i(M)} = \kappa_r \qquad M \in \mathcal{S}_{M_i}, \ a_r \in L \cap \mathcal{A}(M_i) \quad (1)$$

where π_i *is the invariant measure of the closed process* $M_i^c = M_{i[\mathcal{P} \cap L \leftarrow K]}$. *Then the following statements hold:*

1. *The invariant measure of the process* $\bigoplus_L(M_1, M_2, \ldots, M_N)$ *has the product-form:*

$$\pi(\bigoplus_L(M_1, M_2, \ldots, M_N)) = \pi_1(M_1^c) \otimes \pi_2(M_2^c) \otimes \ldots \otimes \pi_2(M_N^c) \quad (2)$$

   where $\otimes$ *is the Kronecker product[1].*
2. *If* $\sum_{M \in \mathcal{S}_{M_i}} \pi_i(M) = 1$ $(i \in [1, \ldots, N])$ *then* π *is the steady-state probability distribution of* $\bigoplus_L(M_1, M_2, \ldots, M_N)$.

---

[1] If π_1, π_2 are two vectors, $\pi_1 \in \mathbb{R}^{1 \times n}$ and $\pi_2 \in \mathbb{R}^{1 \times m}$ then he Kronecker product is $\pi_1 \otimes \pi_2 = (p_1\pi_2, p_2\pi_2, \ldots p_n\pi_2) \in \mathbb{R}^{1 \times nm}$.

Proof. For (1) we first show that for all states $(M_1, M_2, \ldots, M_N) \in \mathcal{S}_{M_1} \times \mathcal{S}_{M_2} \times \cdots \times \mathcal{S}_{M_N}$ we can derive $\pi(M_1, M_2, \ldots, M_N) = \prod_{i=1}^{N} \pi_i(M_i)$ for $M_i \in \mathcal{S}_{M_i^c}$. Since we are considering the whole state space, the result $\pi(\bigoplus_L(M_1, M_2, \ldots, M_N)) = \pi_1(M_1^c) \otimes \pi_2(M_2^c) \otimes \ldots \otimes \pi_2(M_N^c)$ follows. We show now, for $N = 2$ that $\pi(M_1, M_2) = \pi_1(M_1)\pi_2(M_2)$ when $M_1 \oplus_{\{a,c\}} M_2$. Generalisation to N is straightforward. We observe, that with an abuse of notation we write M_1 to indicate the simple process in the cooperation, but also the process that forms the state space of $\mathcal{S}_{M_1}$. The context distinguishes between these two mathematical objects.

The global balance equations for the process M_1 or M_1^c are the following, assuming that $\mathcal{A}(M_1) \cap L = \{a\}$ and $\mathcal{A}(M_2) \cap L = \{c\}$

$$\pi_{M_1^c}(M_1)\Big(\sum_{M_1' \in \mathcal{S}_{M_1^c}} q_{M_1^c}(M_1, a, M_1') + \underbrace{q_{M_1^c}(M_1, c, M_1')}_{x_c} + \sum_{\substack{M_1' \in \mathcal{S}_{M_1^c} \\ b \neq a,c}} q_{M_1^c}(M_1, b, M_1'))\Big) =$$

$$\sum_{M_1' \in \mathcal{S}_{M_1^c}} q_{M_1^c}(M_1', a, M_1)\pi_{M_1^c}(M_1') + \sum_{M_1' \in \mathcal{S}_{M_1^c}} \underbrace{q_{M_1^c}(M_1', c, M_1)}_{x_c} \pi_{M_1^c}(M_1') +$$

$$\sum_{\substack{M_1' \in \mathcal{S}_{M_1^c} \\ b \neq a,c}} q_{M_1^c}(M_1', b, M_1)\pi_{M_1^c}(M_1'). \quad (3)$$

We have underlined the transition rates what would have a variable in M_1 but a real number in M_1^c. By definition of well-formed simple process, we know that there is only one instance of $q_{M_1^c}(M_1, c, M_1')$.

For M_2 or M_2^c the global balance equations would be similar by reverting the role of the rates of the actions a and c.

We write now the global balance equations for the global state (M_1, M_2) as follows:

$$\pi\big((M_1, M_2)\big)\Big(\sum_{\substack{M_1' \in \mathcal{S}_{M_1} \\ b \neq a,c}} q((M_1, M_2), b, (M_1', M_2)) + \sum_{\substack{M_2' \in \mathcal{S}_{M_2} \\ b \neq a,c}} q((M_1, M_2), b, (M_1, M_2')) +$$

$$\sum_{(M_1', M_2') \in \mathcal{S}_{M_1} \times \mathcal{S}_{M_2}} q((M_1, M_2), c, (M_1', M_2')) + \sum_{(M_1', M_2') \in \mathcal{S}_{M_1} \times \mathcal{S}_{M_2}} q((M_1, M_2), a, (M_1', M_2'))\Big)$$

$$= \sum_{\substack{M_1' \in \mathcal{S}_{M_1} \\ b \neq a,c}} q((M_1', M_2), b, (M_1, M_2))\pi\big((M_1', M_2)\big) +$$

$$\sum_{\substack{M_2' \in \mathcal{S}_{M_2} \\ b \neq a,c}} q((M_1, M_2'), b, (M_1, M_2))\pi\big((M_1; M_2')\big) +$$

$$\sum_{(M_1', M_2') \in \mathcal{S}_{M_1} \times \mathcal{S}_{M_2}} q((M_1', M_2'), a, (M_1, M_2))\pi\big((M_1', M_2') +$$

$$\sum_{(M_1', M_2') \in \mathcal{S}_{M_1} \times \mathcal{S}_{M_2}} q((M_1', M_2'), c, (M_1, M_2))\pi\big((M_1', M_2')\big).$$

We assume that we can write the joint invariant measure in product-form, dividing by $\pi_{M_1}(M_1), \pi_{M_2}(M_2)$ and writing down the contribution of the rates of each simple process for the labels $b \notin L$ we have:

$$\sum_{\substack{M_1' \in S_{M_1} \\ b \neq a,c}} q(M_1, b, M_1') + \sum_{(M_1', M_2') \in S_{M_1} \times S_{M_2}} q((M_1, M_2), c, (M_1', M_2')) +$$

$$\sum_{\substack{M_2' \in S_{M_2} \\ b \neq a,c}} q(M_2, b, M_2') + \sum_{(M_1', M_2') \in S_{M_1} \times S_{M_2}} q((M_1, M_2), a, (M_1', M_2'))$$

$$= \sum_{\substack{M_1' \in S_{M_1} \\ b \neq a}} q(M_1', b, M_1) \frac{\pi_{M_1}(M_1')}{\pi_{M_1}(M_1)} + \sum_{\substack{M_2' \in S_{M_2} \\ b \neq a,c}} q(M_2', b, M_2) \frac{\pi_{M_2}(M_2')}{\pi_{M_2}(M_2)} +$$

$$\sum_{(M_1', M_2') \in S_{M_1} \times S_{M_2}} q((M_1', M_2'), a, (M_1, M_2)) \frac{\pi_{M_1}(M_1')\pi_{M_2}(M_2')}{\pi_{M_1}(M_1)\pi_{M_2}(M_2)} +$$

$$\sum_{(M_1', M_2') \in S_{M_1} \times S_{M_2}} q((M_1', M_2'), c, (M_1, M_2)) \frac{\pi_{M_1}(M_1')\pi_{M_2}(M_2')}{\pi_{M_1}(M_1)\pi_{M_2}(M_2)}.$$

We consider the rates in the terms with joint states. We observe that since we impose that the simple processes are well formed, this means that there is only one passive action in each process: in M_1 the passive action will be labelled c while in M_2 will be labelled a. The number of transitions in the joint state space $S_{M_1} \times S_{M_2}$ will the same number as the active transitions. Therefore we can rewrite the global balance equation as follows:

$$\sum_{\substack{M_1' \in S_{M_1} \\ b \neq a,c}} q(M_1, b, M_1') + \sum_{\substack{M_2' \in S_{M_2} \\ b \neq a,c}} q(M_2, b, M_2') + \sum_{M_2' \in S_{M_2}} q(M_2, c, M_2') +$$

$$\sum_{M_1' \in S_{M_1}} q(M_1, a, M_1') = \sum_{\substack{M_1' \in S_{M_1} \\ b \neq a}} q(M_1', b, M_1) \frac{\pi_{M_1}(M_1')}{\pi_{M_1}(M_1)} +$$

$$\sum_{\substack{M_2' \in S_{M_2} \\ b \neq a,c}} q(M_2', b, M_2) \frac{\pi_{M_2}(M_2')}{\pi_{M_2}(M_2)} + \sum_{M_2' \in S_{M_2}} \sum_{M_1' \in S_{M_1}} q(M_1', a, M_1) \frac{\pi_{M_1}(M_1')\pi_{M_2}(M_2')}{\pi_{M_1}(M_1)\pi_{M_2}(M_2)}$$

$$+ \sum_{M_1' \in S_{M_1}} \sum_{M_2' \in S_{M_2}} q(M_2', c, M_2) \frac{\pi_{M_1}(M_1')\pi_{M_2}(M_2')}{\pi_{M_1}(M_1)\pi_{M_2}(M_2)}.$$

We can now rewrite the global balance equations in Equation 3 in the following convenient way:

$$\sum_{M_1' \in S_{M_1^c}} \mathbf{q}_{M_1^c}(M_1, a, M_1') + \kappa_c + \sum_{\substack{M_1' \in S_{M_1^c} \\ b \neq a, c}} \mathbf{q}_{M_1^c}(M_1, b, M_1') =$$

$$\kappa_a + \sum_{M_1' \in S_{M_1^c}} \kappa_c \frac{\pi_{M_1^c}(M_1')}{\pi_{M_1^c}(M_1)} + \sum_{\substack{M_1' \in S_{M_1^c} \\ b \neq a, c}} \mathbf{q}_{M_1^c}(M_1', b, M_1) \frac{\pi_{M_1^c}(M_1')}{\pi_{M_1^c}(M_1)})$$

By subtracting each term side of the last two equation we obtain:

$$\sum_{\substack{M_2' \in S_{M_2} \\ b \neq a, c}} \mathbf{q}(M_2, b, M_2') + \sum_{M_2' \in S_{M_2}} \mathbf{q}(M_2, c, M_2') - \kappa_c =$$

$$\sum_{\substack{M_2' \in S_{M_2} \\ b \neq a, c}} \mathbf{q}(M_2', b, M_2) \frac{\pi_{M_2}(M_2')}{\pi_{M_2}(M_2)} + \sum_{M_2' \in S_{M_2}} \kappa_a \frac{\pi_{M_2}(M_2')}{\pi_{M_2}(M_2)} - \kappa_a$$

The latter equation can be rewritten to see that the global balance equation of M_2 by expanding the Definition of κ_a, κ_c as in Condition 1 of Theorem 1.

The proof is very elegant, not because it uses global balance equations, but because it solidly relies on the semantics of the cooperation. Such semantics establishes the contribution of each component to transform the global balance equations of the joint processes into the global balance equations of each simple process. Further considerations on the cooperation operator will lead to conclude that the semantics given in this work is the right one, as it allows the correct substitution of the rates in condition 1 of Theorem 1 in the passive transitions. As Hillston pointed out in [10], passive transitions lack of information about the speed of the transition. Such information is given by the cooperation with the active partner. In this work we embrace this view fully, but we also find out the right rates (the ones given by condition 1 of Theorem 1) for the passive transitions to proceed in isolation. We could have chosen an arbitrary rate to be substituted into the passive transition. This would have made no sense at all. The product form solution relates the rates of the joint process with the rates of the single components. We can see why it is important that cooperation is not associative, and the broadcasting semantics of PEPA would not work here. Consider three well-formed simple processes M_1, M_2, M_3 specified as follows $M_1 = (a, \lambda).M_1', M_2 = (a, x_a).M_2', M_3 = (a, x_a).M_3'$ such that condition 1 of Theorem 1 is satisfied for M_1. Assume that we have PEPA semantics and $M_2 \oplus \{a\}M_3 \xrightarrow{a, x_a} M_2' \oplus \{a\}M_3'$ and $M_1 \oplus \{a\}(M_2 \oplus \{a\}M_3) \xrightarrow{a, \lambda} M_1 \oplus \{a\}(M_2' \oplus \{a\}M_3')$. Now, to identify the product-form solution we would need to substitute in both processes the rate κ_a $M_{2[a \leftarrow \kappa_a]}, M_{3[a \leftarrow \kappa_a]}$. The product from would not work at all. The reader can verify this by inspecting the proof of theorem 1. Now consider the equivalent process $(M_1 \oplus \{a\}M_2) \oplus a M_3 \xrightarrow{a, \lambda} (M_1' \oplus \{a\}M_2') \oplus \{a\}M_3'$ such that $(M_1 \oplus \{a\}M_2) \xrightarrow{a, \lambda} (M_1' \oplus \{a\}M_2')$. We would obtain a series of substitutions

$M_{2[a \leftarrow \kappa_a]}$ and, if $(M_1 \oplus \{a\}M_2)$ satisfy the conditions in theorem 1 for a, then we would have $M_{3[a \leftarrow \kappa_a^*]}$, where $\kappa_a^* = \sum_{(M_1^*, M_2^*)} \lambda \frac{\pi(M_1^*, M_2^*)}{\pi(M_1', M_2')}$ Clearly this would lead to different product-form solution from $M_1 \oplus \{a\}(M_2 \oplus \{a\}M_3)$. In conclusion, differently from PEPA semantics, we do not wish to have associativity as the rates used for the closure of each simple process matters. Such rates depend on how we group simple processes together. The semantics of the cooperation is the exactly was is needed to correctly interpret product-form solutions. In this work we are not concerned about numerical or analytical methods for solution equations in the form of 1. Such methods can be found in [5].

5   Product-Form Solutions for Biological Systems

As stated in the introduction, product-form solutions have been mostly used in queueing theory. There has been a recent interest in product-form solution for biological system [15,1]. In particular in [15,1] consider only chemical reactions, while we show here a variation of the product-form solutions for more complex systems.

Assume we have a cancerous cell, that grows, in a limited way provided that there is enough energy. In absence of energy the cell could die, with a certain probability p. We model the cell as follows:

$$C_0 = (a, x_a).C_1$$
$$C_1 = (a, x_a).C_2 + (c, \gamma_1).C_0 + (c, \kappa_c).C_1$$
$$\vdots \quad \vdots$$
$$C_N = (a, x_a).C_N + (c, \gamma_N).C_0 + (c, \kappa_c).C_N.$$

The transitions labelled a stand for the energy that will allow the cell to grow. As energy is provided by the environment, we model it as a passive transition. We note that the cell has a finite growth: even in the presence of an infinite amount of energy, the cell will stop growing. The transitions labelled c stands for cancerous events: they could inhibit growth and kill the cell.

We model the energy as a switch, either there is energy for the cell to grow, or there is no energy:

$$E_0 = (a, \lambda).E_1 + (a, \delta).E_0$$
$$E_1 = (d, \delta).E_0.$$

The rate δ represents the speed at which the environment supplies energy. Similarly, we model the trigger for cancer which reduces the size of the cell as a switch:

$$T_0 = (c, x_c).T_1 + (c, x_c).T_0$$
$$T_1 = (e, \nu).T_0.$$

f The system is the following: $\oplus_{\{a,c\}}(E_0, C_0, T_0)$, and the steady state probabilities are $\pi(\oplus_{a,c}(E_0, C_0, T_0)) = \pi_1(E_0) \otimes \pi_2(C_{0[a \leftarrow \delta]}) \otimes \pi_3(T_{0[c \leftarrow \kappa_c]})$ where $\kappa_c = \frac{\gamma_3 \pi_1(C_3) + \gamma_2 \pi_1(C_2) + \gamma_1 \pi_1(C_1)}{\pi_1(C_0)}$. We observe that E_0, C_0, T_0 are well formed process and that the conditions of Theorem 1 are satisfied.

The transition graphs of the state-space processes can be found in Figure 5.

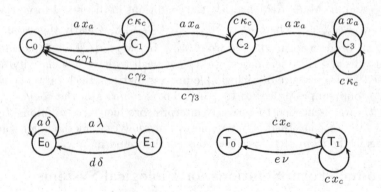

Fig. 3. Transition graphs of the state-space of the processes E_0, C_0, T_0

6   Conclusion

The main interest for product-form solutions arises when a CTMC contains a rather large state space, and the analytical computation of the steady state probability/invariant measure can be computationally prohibitive. In this paper, we have analysed the cooperation operator for a simple process algebra and its relationship with product-form solution. We have clarified the semantics of such operator, and we have shown that such semantics is necessary to derive correctly product-form solutions.

Acknowledgments. I gratefully acknowledge Jane Hillston for useful discussions on product-form solutions and operational semantics. Jane pointed out some mistakes and typos in earlier version of the proof of theorem 1. A lot of generous support and encouragement was given by Gianfranco Balbo. I had very interesting discussions with Andrea Marin, who also pointed out to the work done by Mairesse on biological systems. My interest in product-form solution has arisen during research work I conducted with Peter Harrison. His unique way of working has been great inspiration for me.

References

1. Anderson, D., Craciun, G., Kurtz, T.: Product-form stationary distributions for deficiency zero chemical reaction networks. Bulletin of Mathematical Biology 72, 1947–1970 (2010)
2. Balbo, G., Bruell, S.C., Sereno, M.: Product form solution for Generalized Stochastic Petri Nets. IEEE Trans. on Software Eng. 28, 915–932 (2002)
3. Balbo, G., Bruell, S.C., Sereno, M.: On the relations between BCMP Queueing Networks and Product Form Solution Stochastic Petri Nets. In: Proc. of 10th Int. Workshop on Petri Nets and Performance Models, pp. 103–112 (2003)

4. Boucherie, R.J.: A characterisation of independence for competing Markov chains with applications to stochastic Petri nets. IEEE Tran. on Software Eng. 20(7), 536–544 (1994)
5. Chao, X., Miyazawa, M., Pinedo, M.: Queueing Networks. John Wiley & Sons Ltd. (1999)
6. Clark, G., Hillston, J.: Product form solution for an insensitive stochastic process algebra structure. Performance Evaluation 50, 129–151 (2002)
7. Coleman, J.L., Henderson, W., Taylor, P.G.: Product form equilibrium distributions and a convolution algorithm for Stochastic Petri nets. Perform. Eval. 26, 159–180 (1996)
8. Harrison, P., Hillston, J.: Exploiting quasi-reversible structures in Markovian process algebra models. The Computer Journal 38(7), 510–520 (1995)
9. Harrison, P.G.: Turning back time in Markovian process algebra. Theoretical Computer Science 290(3), 1947–1986 (2003)
10. Hillston, J.: A Compositional Approach to Perfomance Modelling. PhD thesis, Department of Computer Science, Edinburgh (1994)
11. Hillston, J., Thomas, N.: Product Form Solution for a class of PEPA Models. In: Proceedings of IEEE International Computer Performance and Dependability Symposium, Durham, NC (September 1998); An extended version appeared in Performance Evaluation 35(3-4) (1999)
12. Hillston, J., Thomas, N.: Product form solution for a class of PEPA models. Perform. Eval. 35(3-4), 171–192 (1999)
13. Hillston, J.: A class of PEPA models exhibiting product form solution over submodels. Technical Report ECS-LFCS-98-382, University of Edingburgh (February 1998)
14. Kelly, F.P.: Reversibility and Stochastic Networks. Wiley (1979)
15. Mairesse, J., Nguyen, H.-T.: Deficiency Zero Petri Nets and Product Form. In: Franceschinis, G., Wolf, K. (eds.) PETRI NETS 2009. LNCS, vol. 5606, pp. 103–122. Springer, Heidelberg (2009)
16. Marin, A., Vigliotti, M.G.: A general result for deriving product-form solutions in Markovian models. In: Proceedings of First Joint WOSP/SIPEW International Conference on Performance Engineering (January 2010)
17. Milner, R.: Communicating and Mobile Systems: the π-calculus. Cambridge University Press (1999)
18. Thomas, G.: Robertazzi. In: Computer Networks and Systems. Springer (1994)
19. Sereno, M.: Towards a product form solution for stochastic process algebras. The Computer Journal 38(7), 622–632 (1995)

Moment Closures for Performance Models with Highly Non-linear Rates

Marcel C. Guenther, Anton Stefanek, and Jeremy T. Bradley

Imperial College London, 180 Queen's Gate,
London SW7 2AZ, United Kingdom
{mcg05,as1005,jb}@doc.ic.ac.uk

Abstract. Fluid analysis of Population CTMCs with non-linear evolution rates requires moment closures to transform a linear system with
infinitely many ordinary differential equations (ODEs) into a non-linear
one with a finite number of ODEs. Due to the ubiquity of kinetics with
quadratic rates in physical processes, various closure techniques have
been discussed in the context of systems biology and performance analysis. However, little research effort has been put into moment closures for
higher-order moments of models with piecewise linear and higher-order
polynomial evolution rates.

In this paper, we investigate moment closure techniques applied to
such models. In particular we look at moment closures based on normal
and log-normal distributions. We compare the accuracy of the moment
approximating ODEs with the exact results obtained from simulations.
We confirm that by incorporating higher-order moment ODEs, the moment closure techniques give accurate approximations to the standard
deviation of populations. Moreover, they often improve the accuracy of
mean approximations over the traditional mean-field techniques.

Keywords: Fluid analysis, Normal closure, Log-normal closure.

1 Introduction

Population models assume that a large number of identical individuals belonging to a particular population interact with individuals from other populations
and thereby alter population levels. This abstraction from individuals to populations vastly reduces the complexity and the state-space of the underlying
model. Common examples of population models are: chemical reaction models [1] where populations represent molecule concentrations; ecology models [2]
describing the behaviour of groups of animals or plants; and software performance models [3] capturing the interactions between components in massively
parallel systems. The analysis of such models focuses on the evolution of different populations over time and modellers often assume exponentially distributed
rates depending on the prevailing population levels. Under those assumptions
a population model can be represented as a lumped Continuous Time Markov
Chain (CTMC), which we will refer to as a Population CTMC (PCTMC). The

M. Tribastone and S. Gilmore (Eds.): EPEW/UKPEW 2012, LNCS 7587, pp. 32–47, 2013.

class of PCTMC models is popular among modellers since the statistical moments of the underlying stochastic process can be approximated using ordinary differential equations (ODEs) [4]. As populations become larger, these so-called "fluid approximations" become more accurate, while at the same time the evaluation cost remains unaffected. As the cost of stochastic simulation increases with the population size, fluid analysis is often the only computationally feasible method for evaluating models with large populations.

1.1 Moment Closures and Non-linear Rates

The evolution of moments over time in a PCTMC with finitely many populations can always be described exactly by a system of linearly coupled ODEs. This system of ODEs is only finite if all the evolution rates of the PCTMC are linear combinations of population levels. In case of non-linear evolution rates, the right-hand sides of the moment ODEs contain terms that require higher-order moments, which have to be captured by ODEs requiring even higher-order moments, thus resulting in an infinite system of ODEs. For example the evolution of the mean approximating ODEs may depend on population covariances, covariance ODEs on skewness and so on. To allow numerical evaluation of such unclosed systems of ODEs, moment closure functions can be applied, which transform an infinite system of linearly coupled ODEs into a finite system of non-linear ODEs. Since there are infinitely many possible closure functions, a common approach is to assume that the population levels at each point in time are distributed according to a particular multivariate distribution, e.g. the multivariate normal or the log-normal distribution.

PCTMCs with quadratic evolution kinetics have been extensively covered in the theoretical ecology and systems biology literature [5,6]. Many performance analysis models, however, exhibit other non-linear evolutions rates such as the piecewise linear min and max functions in stochastic process algebras [7], stochastic Petri nets [8] or multi-server queueing networks, or higher-order polynomial rates. While piecewise linear functions allow modellers to restrict the speed of evolutions and the size of population levels, higher-order polynomial rates are useful when modelling non-linear feedback. Moreover, when evolution rates contain fractions, logarithmic or exponential rates, Taylor expansions of these functions also yield higher-order polynomials.

1.2 Overview of the Paper

While the first order moments of piecewise linear and higher-order polynomial rates can often be accurately approximated using the mean-field closure [9], the evolution of second and higher-order moments using ODEs is more sensitive to the choice of the closure. In this paper we will investigate the effect of different normal and log-normal moment closures on the accuracy of first and second order moment approximating ODEs for different types of models with piecewise linear and cubic polynomial evolution rates. The paper is organised as follows. In Section 2 we formally introduce PCTMCs and moment closure techniques.

Section 3 introduces three benchmark models and describes the test framework used to conduct the error comparison experiments. The resulting data is presented and analysed in Section 4. Finally we conclude and highlight further work in Section 5.

2   PCTMCs

A Population continuous time Markov chain (PCTMC) consists of a finite set of species $S = \{s_1, \ldots, s_n\}$, and a set E of transition classes. Each state in a PCTMC is expressed as an integer vector $\boldsymbol{P} = (P_1, \ldots, P_n) \in \mathbb{Z}^n$, with the ith component representing the current population level of a species i. A transition class $e = (r_e(\cdot), \boldsymbol{c}_e) \in E$ describes stochastic events with exponentially distributed duration d at rate $r_e : \mathbb{Z}^n \to \mathbb{R}$ and change the current population vector according to the change vector $\boldsymbol{c}_e$, that is sets

$$\boldsymbol{P}(t + d) = \boldsymbol{P}(t) + \boldsymbol{c}_s$$

The analogue to PCTMCs are Chemical Reaction Systems, where $\boldsymbol{P}$ describes a molecule count vector and transition classes represent chemical reactions between the molecules with r being the reaction rate function and $\boldsymbol{c}$ the stoichiometric vector. For clarity, we will adapt a notation similar to that of chemical reactions and denote by

$$s_{i_1} + \cdots + s_{i_k} \to t_{j_1} + \cdots + t_{j_l} \qquad \text{at } r(\boldsymbol{P})$$

the transition class with change vector $(\#_1(I) - \#_1(J), \ldots, \#_n(I) - \#_n(J)) \in \mathbb{Z}^n$ where $I = i_1, \ldots, i_k$, $J = j_1, \ldots, j_l$ and $\#_h(L)$ gives the count of h in the list L, and rate

$$\begin{cases} r(\boldsymbol{P}) & \text{if } P_i \geq \#_i(I) \text{ for all } i = 1, \ldots, n \\ 0 & \text{otherwise} \end{cases}$$

An important aspect of PCTMC models is that the approximations to the evolution of moments of the underlying stochastic process of the population levels can be represented by a system of ODEs [10,11]

$$\frac{\mathrm{d}}{\mathrm{dt}} \mathbb{E}[M(\boldsymbol{P}(t))] = \sum_{e \in E} \mathbb{E}[(M(\boldsymbol{P}(t) + \boldsymbol{c}_e) - M(\boldsymbol{P}(t)))r_e(\boldsymbol{P}(t))] \qquad (1)$$

where $M(\boldsymbol{P})$ defines the moment to be calculated. To obtain the ODE describing the evolution of the mean of a population s_i for instance, all we need to do is to substitute $M(\boldsymbol{P}) = P_i$ in the above equation. Similarly, for higher moments we use a suitable moment function $M(\boldsymbol{P})$, for example $M(\boldsymbol{P}) = P_1 P_2$ for the evolution of the mean product of the populations of s_1 and s_2.

2.1 Moment Closures

In many PCTMC models, Equation (1) results in a linear but infinite system of moment approximating ODEs. This happens if there are evolution rates $r_e(\boldsymbol{P})$ with non-linear polynomials in the population counts, such as $r_e(\boldsymbol{P}) = P_i P_j$. When expanding Equation (1) for such systems, moment ODEs will depend on higher-order moment ODEs. In a simple example with a transition class

$$s_1 + s_2 \to s_3 \qquad\qquad \text{at } r(\boldsymbol{P}) = P_1 P_2$$

the ODE describing the mean of s_1, $\mathbb{E}[P_1(t)]$, depends on a second order moment $\mathbb{E}[P_1(t)P_2(t)]$, the ODE for this moment depends on third order moments such as $\mathbb{E}[P_1(t)^2 P_2(t)]$ and so on. To numerically solve such infinite systems of coupled ODEs, one option is to close these equations at some order, e.g. approximating any higher-order moments using moments with order no larger than the order of the highest moment we wish to obtain. Generally this involves changing the linear but infinite system of moment ODEs into a finite non-linear system of ODEs. In the literature this transformation is referred to as a moment closure.

To express a higher-order moment in terms of lower-order moments, moment closure techniques often assume that the populations at each point of time are (approximately) realisations from a particular family of probability distributions. Many closure methods such as the *normal* [5], *log-normal* [6] or *beta-binomial* [12] are named after such an assumption.

We briefly describe four types of moment closures, the *mean-field* [9], *normal*, *min-normal* and *log-normal* closure methods respectively. In the following we will write $\mathbb{E}[\boldsymbol{P}^{(\boldsymbol{m})}]$ for the raw joint moment $\mathbb{E}[P_1^{m_1} \cdots P_n^{m_n}]$ for a random population vector $\boldsymbol{P}$, where $\boldsymbol{m} = (m_1, \ldots, m_n) \in \mathbb{Z}^n$. We say $o(\boldsymbol{m}) = m_1 + \ldots + m_n$ is the order of the joint moment.

Mean-Field. *Mean-field* analysis [9] methods investigate the evolution of the mean of population vectors. The mean-field closure approximates higher-order moments such as $\mathbb{E}[P_i(t)P_j(t) \cdots P_k(t)]$ by the product of the individual expectations $\mathbb{E}[P_i(t)]\mathbb{E}[P_j(t)] \cdots \mathbb{E}[P_k(t)]$. In other words, the mean-field approach ignores the covariance between any two populations. This produces good approximations for population means, especially when the populations are high. However in some model, for instance in the circadian clock model the mean-field closure does not perform well [11,13].

Normal Closure. The *normal moment closure* [5] can be applied to any system of ODEs originating from a PCTMC for which we want to find 2nd or higher-order moments. It assumes that the populations at each point in time are approximately multivariate normal and therefore all third- and higher-order moments can be expressed in terms of means and covariances. This relationship is captured by the Isserlis' theorem [14]: For $\boldsymbol{P}(t)$ multivariate normal with mean $\boldsymbol{\mu}$ and covariance matrix (σ_{ij}) we have

$$\begin{aligned}
\mathbb{E}[(\boldsymbol{P} - \boldsymbol{\mu})^{(\boldsymbol{m})}] &= \mathbb{E}[(P_1 - \mu_1)^{m_1} \cdots (P_n - \mu_n)^{m_n}] = 0, &&\text{if } o(\boldsymbol{m}) \text{ is odd} \\
\mathbb{E}[(\boldsymbol{P} - \boldsymbol{\mu})^{(\boldsymbol{m})}] &= \sum \prod \mathbb{E}[(P_i - \mu_i)(P_j - \mu_j)], &&\text{if } o(\boldsymbol{m}) \text{ is even}
\end{aligned} \qquad (2)$$

where $\sum \prod$ sums through all the distinct partitions of $1, \ldots, n$ into disjoint sets of pairs i, j. If some elements in $\boldsymbol{m}$ are greater than one, then certain pairs i, j will appear multiple times in the resulting sum. To obtain the raw moment, we need to expand the central moment in Equation (2) first and subsequently rearrange the equation. For example, instead of including an ODE for the third order joint raw moment $\mathbb{E}[P_1(t)P_2(t)^2]$ we can close the expansion at second order by using the approximation

$$
\begin{aligned}
\mathbb{E}[P_1(t)P_2(t)^2] \approx{} & 2\mathbb{E}[P_2(t)]\mathbb{E}[P_2(t)X_1(t)] + \mathbb{E}[P_1(t)]\mathbb{E}[P_2(t)^2] \\
& - 2\mathbb{E}[P_1(t)]\mathbb{E}[P_2(t)]^2
\end{aligned}
\tag{3}
$$

which yields $\mathbb{E}[(P_1(t) - \mu_1(t))(P_2(t) - \mu_2(t))^2] = 0$ as required, since the multivariate normal distribution is not skewed.

Min-Normal Closure. The *min-normal moment closure* has been previously applied in the analysis of feedback reward models where the min function guarantees a feedback rate to stay non-negative [15]. It aims to improve the mean-field approximation of expectations such as $\mathbb{E}[\min(P_i(t), P_j(t))]$, often arising in PCTMC models coming from the PEPA process algebra or stochastic Petri nets. The mean-field closure with the approximation $\min(\mathbb{E}[P_i(t)], \mathbb{E}[P_j(t)])$ on the right hand side of the ODEs is accurate in the absence of switch points [16], that is the time intervals when the two means $\mathbb{E}[P_i(t)]$ and $\mathbb{E}[P_j(t)]$ are sufficiently distant. This depends on the variance of the two random variables and large errors occur whenever $\mathbb{E}[P_i(t)] \approx \mathbb{E}[P_j(t)]$. Moreover, if switch points only appear during the transient phase of the model then the steady-state mean-field approximation is usually accurate.

However, we can produce a better estimate for the min expression under the assumption that populations are approximately multivariate normal. Using a result for the moments of a minimum of two bivariate normal random variables [17], we can use the following identity for P_1, P_2 bivariate normal (where Φ and ϕ are the CDF and PDF of a standard normal random variable):

$$
\begin{aligned}
\mathbb{E}[\min(P_i, P_j)] = {} & \mathbb{E}[P_i]\Phi\left(\frac{\mathbb{E}[P_j] - \mathbb{E}[P_i]}{\theta}\right) + \mathbb{E}[P_j]\Phi\left(\frac{\mathbb{E}[P_i] - \mathbb{E}[P_j]}{\theta}\right) \\
& - \theta\phi\left(\frac{\mathbb{E}[P_j] - \mathbb{E}[P_i]}{\theta}\right)
\end{aligned}
\tag{4}
$$

where $\theta = (\mathrm{Var}[P_i] - 2\mathrm{Cov}[P_i, P_j] + \mathrm{Var}[P_j])^{1/2}$. The right hand side of higher-order moment ODEs contains terms such as $\mathbb{E}[P_k \min(P_i, P_j)]$. In that case, experiments suggest that a good heuristic is to insert P_k into the above equation, capturing some covariance:

$$
\begin{aligned}
\mathbb{E}[P_k \min(P_i, P_j)] \approx {} & \mathbb{E}[P_k P_i]\Phi\left(\frac{\mathbb{E}[P_j] - \mathbb{E}[P_i]}{\theta}\right) + \mathbb{E}[P_k P_j]\Phi\left(\frac{\mathbb{E}[P_i] - \mathbb{E}[P_j]}{\theta}\right) \\
& - E[P_k]\theta\phi\left(\frac{\mathbb{E}[P_j] - \mathbb{E}[P_i]}{\theta}\right)
\end{aligned}
\tag{5}
$$

All other terms are closed using the normal moment closure described above.

Log-Normal Closure. Instead of assuming a multivariate normal distribution it is also possible to use the *log-normal moment closure* which provides a purely multiplicative way of closing higher-order moments. In [6], Singh *et al.* explain how this closure can be applied to chemical reaction systems. Assume we want to approximate the uncentered joint moment $\mathbb{E}[\boldsymbol{P}^{(\boldsymbol{m})}]$ where $o(\boldsymbol{m}) = m + x$, $m, x \in \mathbb{Z}^+$ using only joint moments of order up to m. Let $\mathcal{M} = \{\boldsymbol{m}_1, \ldots, \boldsymbol{m}_k\}$ be the ordered set containing all these moments up to the order m then the *log-normal closure* is defined by

$$\mathbb{E}[\boldsymbol{P}^{(\boldsymbol{m})}] \approx \prod_{p=1}^{k} \left(\mathbb{E}[\boldsymbol{P}^{(\boldsymbol{m}_p)}]\right)^{\gamma_p} \tag{6}$$

where the exponents γ_p form the unique solution to the following system of linear equations

$$C_{\boldsymbol{m}_s}^{\boldsymbol{m}} = \sum_{p=1}^{k} \gamma_p C_{\boldsymbol{m}_s}^{\boldsymbol{m}_p}, \ \forall s = \{1, \ldots, k\} \quad \text{where} \quad C_{\boldsymbol{l}}^{\boldsymbol{h}} = \binom{h_1}{l_1} \cdots \binom{h_n}{l_n} \tag{7}$$

Further details regarding the derivation of Equation (7) can be found in [6]. If we were to close the third order joint moment $\mathbb{E}[P_1(t)P_2(t)^2]$ at second order using the log-normal closure technique, we obtain

$$\mathbb{E}[P_1(t)P_2(t)^2] \approx \frac{\mathbb{E}[P_2(t)^2]\mathbb{E}[P_1(t)P_2(t)]^2}{\mathbb{E}[P_1(t)]\mathbb{E}[P_2(t)]^2} \tag{8}$$

Apart from the mean-field analysis, all the above closures can calculate second and higher-order moments. As we will show in Section 4, higher-order moments usually improve the accuracy of the mean approximations. In case of PCTMCs with evolution rates using the min function such as in the GPEPA process algebra, it is also possible to obtain higher-order moments without affecting the means. For simplicity, we will refer to this closure as mean-field whenever comparing closures, such as in Figure 4 and Table 2.

3   Evaluation Framework

In this section we describe the techniques and benchmark models we use to compare the different moment closures in the following section. Table 1 gives an overview.

3.1   Hybrid Peer-to-Peer Model

A simple and commonly used non-linear evolution rate in PCTMCs is the quadratic *mass-action* kinetics. As an example, we look at a simple abstract model of a hybrid peer-to-peer system. The system consists of users who already own a copy of some data to be distributed. Other users are trying to obtain the data. Additionally, to increase the speed of data distribution, the system includes dedicated servers that can perform faster seeding. Users with data can leave the system and potentially come back.

Table 1. An overview of the models used to compare the different closures. The second column shows the number n of different species (populations) in the model. The last column shows the number $\#P$ of different parameter configurations we evaluated the models on.

Model	Rates	Closures	n	$\#P$
Peer-to-peer	linear, quadratic	Mean-field Normal order 2, 3	5	30
Client/server	linear, min of linear	Min, min-normal	6	30
Pheromone routing	linear, quadratic, cubic, min of quadratic	Mean-field Normal order 2, 3 Log-normal order 2	15	12

There are 5 populations $(U_l, U_s, U_f, S_{on}, S_{off}) \in \mathbb{Z}^5$ corresponding to users without the data, with the data, those who left the system and servers in on/off states respectively. Initially, there is a fixed number of users and servers in the off state – the initial populations are $(N_l, N_s, 0, 0, N_S)$.

We assume that the users and servers are uniformly distributed across the network and equally likely to initiate communication with each other. This is often captured by the mass action kinetics – for example, the rate of the event where a user seeds the data to a user without the data is proportional to the product of the two populations, i.e. to $U_l(t) \cdot U_s(t)$. The system behaviour can be captured by 6 transition classes

$$
\begin{aligned}
S_{off} &\to S_{on} & &\text{at } S_{off}(t) \cdot r_{on} \\
S_{on} &\to S_{off} & &\text{at } S_{on}(t) \cdot r_{off} \\
U_l + U_s &\to U_s + U_s & &\text{at } U_l(t) \cdot U_s(t) \cdot r_{seed} \\
U_l + S_{on} &\to U_s + S_{on} & &\text{at } U_l(t) \cdot S_{on}(t) r_{seed,s} \\
U_s &\to U_f & &\text{at } U_s(t) \cdot r_{leave} \\
U_f &\to U_l & &\text{at } U_s(t) \cdot r_{return}
\end{aligned}
$$

In the evaluation, we varied the initial count N_S and the rate r_{leave}.

3.2   GPEPA Client/Server Model

The second model we look at demonstrates the use of the *bounded capacity kinetics*. We use the GPEPA process algebra [7] to define a simple client/server model. The modelled system consists of a number of clients and servers. Clients can request data from servers, receive data from one of the servers and then perform some independent action with it. Servers, in addition to providing the data, are susceptible to failure in which case they have to be reset. To cope with the failures, clients repeat the requests after a timeout.

$$Client \stackrel{def}{=} (request, r_{req}).Client\_wait \qquad Server \stackrel{def}{=} (request, r_{req}).Server\_get$$
$$+ (fail, r_{fail}).Server\_fail$$
$$Client\_wait \stackrel{def}{=} (data, r_{data}).Client\_think \qquad Server\_get \stackrel{def}{=} (data, r_{data}).Server$$
$$+ (timeout, r_{timeout}).Client \qquad\qquad + (fail, r_{fail}).Server\_fail$$
$$Client\_think \stackrel{def}{=} (think, r_{think}).Client \qquad Server\_fail \stackrel{def}{=} (reset, r_{reset}).Server$$

$$\mathbf{Clients}\{Client[N_C]\} \underset{\{request, data\}}{\bowtie} \mathbf{Servers}\{Server[N_S]\}$$

Using the operational semantics of GPEPA, we can obtain a PCTMC. There are 6 populations $(C, C_w, C_t, S, S_g, S_b) \in \mathbb{Z}^6$, each corresponding to a state of the client/server components. The initial state given by the system equation is $(N_C, 0, 0, N_S, 0, 0)$. The GPEPA process algebra assumes bounded capacity co-operation – that is, the rate of cooperation between two components is no faster than the individual rates. This introduces the min function into the transition rates. In total, there are 7 transition classes:

$$C + S \rightarrow C_w + S_g \qquad\qquad \text{at } r_{req} \cdot \min(C(t), S(t))$$
$$C_w + S_g \rightarrow C_t + S \qquad\qquad \text{at } r_{data} \cdot \min(C_w(t), S_g(t))$$
$$C_t \rightarrow C \qquad\qquad \text{at } r_{think} \cdot C_t(t)$$
$$C_w \rightarrow C \qquad\qquad \text{at } r_{timeout} \cdot C_w(t)$$
$$S \rightarrow S_b \qquad\qquad \text{at } r_{fail} \cdot S(t)$$
$$S_g \rightarrow S_b \qquad\qquad \text{at } r_{fail} \cdot S_g(t)$$
$$S_b \rightarrow S \qquad\qquad \text{at } r_{reset} \cdot S_b(t)$$

During the evaluation we varied the initial number of clients N_C and the rate $r_{timeout}$.

3.3   Spatial Pheromone Routing Model

The last model we discuss is a spatial model that represents the spread of phero-mone in a multi-hop Wireless Sensor Network (WSN). In nature, pheromone is a hormone laid down by colony-based insects, to indicate popular routes to food sources or new nest sites. In a similar manner pheromone gradients have been adapted in the WSN literature as an abstract means of studying the evolution of routes from source to sink nodes [18]. Figure 1 visualises the topology of our WSN model [19], where 1 is the sink node and node 15 is the sensor furthest from it. The pheromone is at the highest level in the node 1 and the lowest level in the node 15. We assume that the nodes exchange pheromone information us-ing a Manhattan style communication pattern. The resulting fluid pheromone level ph is assumed to decrease exponentially at a cubic rate proportional to $ph@(loc)^3/c_1^3$, where c_1 is a constant. On the other hand the pheromone level in-creases exponentially at a rate governed by the amount of excess pheromone that neighbouring nodes have over the receiving node. For instance the pheromone level at location 3 grows at rate

$$(\max(0, ph@(2) - ph@(3)) + max(0, ph@(6) - ph@(3)))/c_2; \qquad (9)$$

The model can be extended to analyse transient and steady-state routing probabilities as well as packet flows in the network [20], but here we only model the pheromone spread. For the comparison test we varied the constant parameters c_1, c_2.

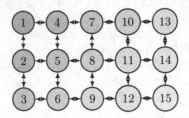

Fig. 1. Node 1 is the sink and has the highest pheromone level. The level decreases with increasing hop distance from the sink [19].

3.4 Accurate Simulation

In order to allow a fair error comparison between simulations and ODEs, we implemented a Gillespie simulator, which creates replications until a certain confidence interval is reached for all the population moments that we are estimating. The confidence interval for the sample statistics is computed using a Student's t-distribution with the degrees of freedom depending on the sample size. In order to compute the confidence interval of distance squared samples, we also keep track of the third and fourth order central sample moments. As an example, in the pheromone model we say that the simulation sample averages of mean and distance squared have converged if the relative half-width of the 95% confidence interval is $< 1\%$ at any point in time. To achieve this, the simulation of this model requires about $125k$ sample traces. The other two models require even more replications. We also noticed that small parameter changes in some models can heavily impact the convergence behaviour of the accurate simulation.

3.5 Computation of Error

To evaluate accuracy of the different closures we compute population moments in each of the 3 models above, trying a large number of parameter configurations. For a particular model and a set of parameters, the simulation provides a confidence interval estimate $[\mathbb{E}[M(t)]^L, \mathbb{E}[M(t)]^U]$ of each moment M at each time point t until a specified time T. At the same time, each closure provides an approximation $\widetilde{\mathbb{E}}[M(t)]$. The absolute error of the closure for the moment M at time t then is

$$
e_{\text{abs}}(M(t)) = \begin{cases} 0 & \text{if } \widetilde{\mathbb{E}}[M(t)] \in [\mathbb{E}[M(t)]^L, \mathbb{E}[M(t)]^U]] \\ \widetilde{\mathbb{E}}[M(t)] - \mathbb{E}[M(t)]^U & \text{if } \widetilde{\mathbb{E}}[M(t)] > \mathbb{E}[M(t)]^U \\ \mathbb{E}[M(t)]^L - \widetilde{\mathbb{E}}[M(t)] & \text{if } \widetilde{\mathbb{E}}[M(t)] < \mathbb{E}[M(t)]^L \end{cases}
$$

To get the relative error, we divide the absolute error by the point estimate, i.e.

$$
e_{\text{rel}}(M(t)) = e_{\text{abs}}(M(t)) \cdot \frac{2}{|\mathbb{E}[M(t)]^L + \mathbb{E}[M(t)]^U|}
$$

For each model, we look at means and standard deviations of all the populations when available. We aggregate the respective errors at each order: For each time t, we will define the average/maximum first order error as the average/maximum relative error across all the means, that is

$$
e_{\text{avg}}^1(t) = 1/n \sum_i^n e_{\text{rel}}(P_i(t)) \qquad e_{\text{max}}^1(t) = \max_{i=1,\dots,n} e_{\text{rel}}(P_i(t))
$$

Similarly, we define the second order aggregate errors $e_{\text{avg}}^2(t)$ and $e_{\text{max}}^2(t)$ by replacing $\mathbb{E}[P_i(t)]$ with $\sqrt{\text{Var}[P_i(t)]}$ above. For each closure, we further aggregate the above errors by taking the average/maximum of each error across a large number of parameter combinations. We define $\bar{e}_{\text{avg}}^i(t)$ and $\bar{e}_{\text{max}}^i(t)$ as the average of $e_{\text{avg}}^i(t)$ and maximum of $e_{\text{max}}^i(t)$ over all parameter combinations respectively. Additionally, we also look at the effects of scaling the initial populations on the error of the moment closure approximations. We pick a single parameter configuration and calculate the aggregate average and maximum errors $e_{\text{max}}^i(t)$ and $e_{\text{avg}}^i(t)$. We repeat this when the initial populations in the model are multiplied by a constant.

4 Closure Comparison

In this section we will evaluate the accuracy of different moment closures with respect to results from the accurate simulation. For each of the above three models, we plot $\bar{e}_{\text{avg}}^i(t)$ and $\bar{e}_{\text{max}}^i(t)$ for $i = 1, 2$ (the relative errors in mean and standard deviation). Additionally, we plot $e_{\text{avg}}^i(t)$ and $e_{\text{max}}^i(t)$ for a single parameter combination at 3 different scales of the system, illustrating the improved accuracy as the model size increases. Table 2 compares the numerical values of the errors.

4.1 Hybrid Peer-to-Peer Model

Figure 2 shows the plots of the average and maximum relative errors $\bar{e}_{\text{avg}}^i(t)$ and $\bar{e}_{\text{max}}^i(t)$ in the sample peer-to-peer model.

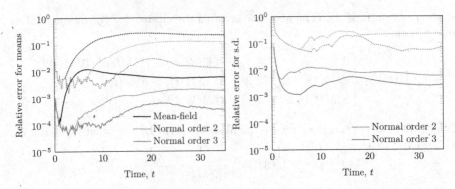

Fig. 2. Comparison of closures for the peer-to-peer model. The dotted lines are maximum relative errors $\bar{e}_{\max}^i(t)$ over all the experiments, the solid lines the average relative errors across a number of different model parameters $\bar{e}_{\text{avg}}^i(t)$.

In case of approximations of the means, the mean-field analysis already gives quite accurate results, with the average error over all populations in the order of 1% and the maximum of 26% occurring only in certain populations and limited time intervals for each parameter configuration. As we use higher-order moments, we can see the error decrease. The second-order normal closure improves these to 0.2% average and 12% maximum error respectively and the third order further to 0.03% and 3%. The normal closures give quite accurate approximations to standard deviations. For a short initial time period, the relative error is higher due to the very small values of the standard deviation. However, for most of the considered time, the second-order normal closure gives a maximum error of around 27% and average error 7% and the third-order closure reduces these to 19% and 0.7% respectively. Figure 3 shows the relative errors for a single parameter combination at 3 different scales of the system – when initial populations are scaled by 1, 10 and 100 respectively.

We can see that the error in all the 3 closures decreases with higher scales, both in case of means and standard deviations. The y axis labels not shown for the plots at scales 10 and 100 are the same as for scale 1. At the scale 100, the normal closures give a zero error with respect to the 2% interval estimate from the simulation for most of the time.

4.2   Client/Server Model

Figure 4 shows the average and maximum relative errors for the client/server model. Similar to the peer-to-peer model, the mean-field mean approximations are quite accurate, with maximum error 29% and average error no more than 4%. The min-normal closures is particularly effective here and brings down the errors to 2% and 0.02% respectively. As mentioned above, in case of bounded capacity rates we can also obtain standard deviation estimates using the mean-field method. Although in many cases this can be at least quantitatively accurate, the maximum error is quite large at 77%, with average at 4%. The min-normal

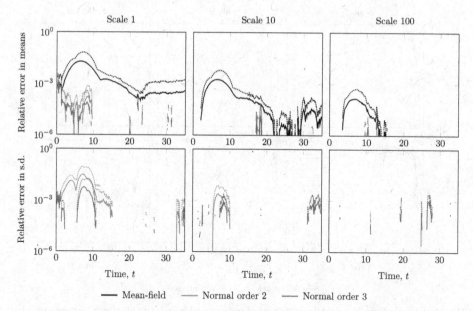

Fig. 3. Effect of scaling on the accuracy of moment closures in the peer-to-peer model. All the plots are shown with the same (logarithmic) scale. The gaps on the plots represent zero error values.

closure results in an improvement to 15% and 0.8% respectively. Figure 5 shows the effect of scaling in the client/server model.

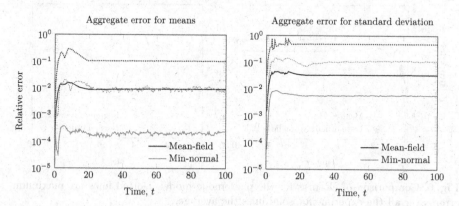

Fig. 4. Comparison of mean-field and min-normal closures for the client/server model

We can see a decrease in both errors as the model size increases, similar to the case of the peer-to-peer model. There are more regions where the errors stay non-zero even at the highest scale. This is possibly caused by the presence of switch points where the used min approximations are particularly inaccurate.

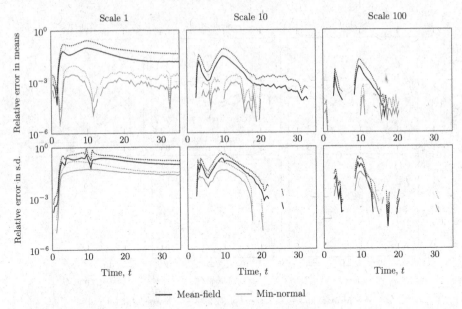

Fig. 5. Effect of scaling on the accuracy of moment closures in the client/server model. The gaps on the plots represent zero values of the error.

4.3 Spatial Pheromone Routing Model

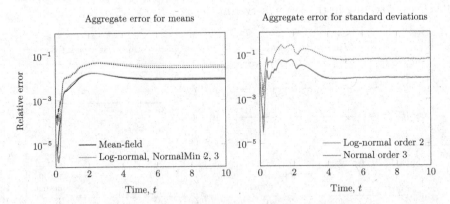

Fig. 6. Comparison of closures for the pheromone model. Dotted lines are maximum errors over all the experiments, solid lines the average.

The comparison results are shown in Figure 6. As can be seen both mean and standard deviation of the pheromone levels are approximated well by the ODEs. It is surprising though, that the aggregated maximum relative error in the means estimated by the mean-field closure is lower than the one of higher-order esti-mates. Further analysis revealed that the mean estimate for larger pheromone

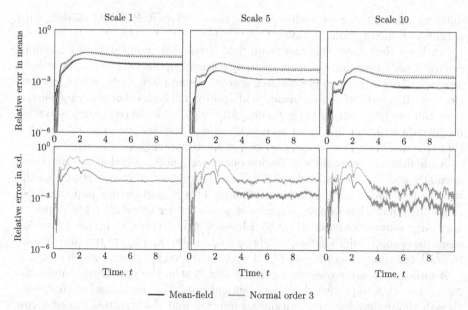

Fig. 7. Effect of scaling on the accuracy of moment closures in the pheromone model. The gaps on the plots represent zero values of the error.

Table 2. Summary of the aggregate relative (%) error in the benchmark models. The numbers on the left of each column are the maximum of $\bar{e}_{\max}^i(t)$ over all t and the numbers on the right the maximum of $\bar{e}_{\mathrm{avg}}^i(t)$ respectively.

	Mean-field				(Min-)normal 2				Normal 3			
	mean		s.d.		mean		s.d.		mean		s.d.	
	max	avg	max	avg	max	avg	max	avg	max	avg	max	avg
Peer-to-peer	26	1	—		12	.2	27	7	3	.03	19	.7
Client/server	29	4	77	4	2	.02	15	.8	—			
Pheromone	4	1	—		4	1	26	5	←			

populations $ph@(1)$, $ph@(4)$ and $ph@(5)$ is actually much better when using a normal closure with ODEs up to and including the third moment. For smaller populations $ph@(12)$, $ph@(14)$ and $ph@(15)$, the mean-field estimate is better in this model, but Figure 7 indicates that this difference becomes smaller as we increase the pheromone population size. Moreover, we found that the normal closure at second order as well as the log-normal closure at second order gave equally good estimates for mean and standard deviation of populations as the third order normal closure.

5   Conclusions and Future Work

We have presented a moment closure comparison framework for ODEs originating from PCTMCs with highly non-linear evolution rates. We evaluated four different moment closure techniques on three different PCTMC models with various parameter configurations.

We have confirmed that the mean-field first-order moment approximations generally produce good approximations of average population traces. However, in presence of quadratic and piece-wise linear minimum rates, higher-order moment closures often outperform the mean-field approximation as shown in the peer-to-peer and the client server experiments. Although the more complex pheromone model indicates that this is not necessarily always the case, we were able to show that this was likely due to the presence of small populations.

Aside from the mean approximation our experiments show that the generated normally and log-normally closed ODEs produce good approximations for the standard deviation of population moments. This is particularly important because the simulation sample averages of second order moments often require a very large number of replications to achieve a tight interval estimate. In certain cases the second order ODEs could be solved in less than 1% of the time it took to finish the simulation with a 95% CI with maximum relative CI width of $< 2\%$.

Another interesting observation is the fact that in the pheromone model the log-normal closure produced almost identical results as the normal closure, even though the underlying distribution assumption and the resulting closed terms are different. Generally, however, we prefer the normal closure over the log-normal one as the latter becomes numerically unstable in models where some populations tend to 0.

Further research is required to make a more informed choice of which moment closure to use for which class of models. To do so, we plan to analyse the actual distributions of the simulated populations in the future and subsequently see if the moment closure corresponding to the distribution family closest to the exact distribution of the stochastic process will indeed produce the most accurate ODE approximations for the underlying moments.

Acknowledgment. Anton Stefanek and Jeremy T. Bradley are funded by EPSRC on the Analysis of Massively Parallel Stochastic Systems (AMPS) project (reference EP/G011737/1).

References

1. Gillespie, D.T.: Exact stochastic simulation of coupled chemical reactions. Journal of Physical Chemistry 81(25), 2340–2361 (1977)
2. Wangersky, P.J.: Lotka-Volterra population models. Annual Review of Ecology and Systematics 9(1), 189–218 (1978)
3. Stefanek, A., Hayden, R.A., Bradley, J.T.: Fluid computation of the performance-energy trade-off in large scale Markov models. SIGMETRICS Perform. Eval. Rev. 39(3) (2011)
4. Van Kampen, N.G.: Stochastic Processes in Physics and Chemistry. North-Holland personal library, vol. 11. North-Holland (1992)
5. Whittle, P.: On the use of the normal approximation in the treatment of stochastic processes. Journal of the Royal Statistical Society Series B Methodological 19(2), 268–281 (1957)

6. Singh, A., Hespanha, J.: Lognormal moment closures for biochemical reactions. In: 2006 45th IEEE Conference on Decision and Control, vol. (2), pp. 2063–2068. IEEE (2006)
7. Hayden, R.A., Bradley, J.T.: A fluid analysis framework for a Markovian process algebra. Theoretical Computer Science 411(22-24), 2260–2297 (2010)
8. Silva, M., Júlvez, J., Mahulea, C., Vázquez, C.R.: On fluidization of discrete event models: observation and control of continuous Petri nets. Discrete Event Dynamic Systems 21, 427–497 (2011)
9. Opper, M., Saad, D.: Advanced Mean Field Methods: Theory and Practice. The MIT Press (2001)
10. Hayden, R.A.: Mean-field approximations for performance models with generally-timed transitions. SIGMETRICS Perform. Eval. Rev. 39(3), 119–121 (2011)
11. Engblom, S.: Computing the moments of high dimensional solutions of the master equation. Applied Mathematics and Computation 180(2), 498–515 (2006)
12. Krishnarajah, I., Cook, A., Marion, G., Gibson, G.: Novel moment closure approximations in stochastic epidemics. Bulletin of Mathematical Biology 67(4), 855–873 (2005)
13. Stefanek, A., Guenther, M.C., Bradley, J.T.: Normal and inhomogeneous moment closures for stochastic process algebras. In: 10th Workshop on Process Algebra and Stochastically Timed Activities (PASTA 2011), Ragusa (2011)
14. Isserlis, L.: On a Formula for the Product-Moment Coefficient of any Order of a Normal Frequency Distribution in any Number of Variables. Biometrika 12(1/2), 134–139 (1918)
15. Stefanek, A., Hayden, R.A., Gonagle, M.M., Bradley, J.T.: Mean-Field Analysis of Markov Models with Reward Feedback. In: Al-Begain, K., Fiems, D., Vincent, J.-M. (eds.) ASMTA 2012. LNCS, vol. 7314, pp. 193–211. Springer, Heidelberg (2012)
16. Stefanek, A., Hayden, R.A., Bradley, J.T.: A new tool for the performance analysis of massively parallel computer systems. In: Eighth Workshop on Quantitative Aspects of Programming Languages (QAPL 2010), Paphos, Cyprus, March 27-28. Electronic Proceedings in Theoretical Computer Science (2010)
17. Cain, M.: The moment-generating function of the minimum of bivariate normal random variables. American Statistician 48(2), 124–125 (1994)
18. Bruneo, D., Scarpa, M., Bobbio, A., Cerotti, D., Gribaudo, M.: Markovian agent modeling swarm intelligence algorithms in wireless sensor networks. Performance Evaluation 69(3-4), 135–149 (2011),
http://www.sciencedirect.com/science/article/pii/S0166531611000137,
doi:10.1016/j.peva.2010.11.007, ISSN 0166-5316
19. Guenther, M.C., Bradley, J.T.: PCTMC Models of Wireless Sensor Network Protocols. In: Tribastone, M., Gilmore, S. (eds.) EPEW/UKPEW 2012. LNCS, vol. 7587, Springer, Heidelberg (2013)
20. Guenther, M.C., Bradley, J.T.: Mean-field analysis of data flows in Wireless Sensor Networks. Submitted to VALUETOOLS 2012 (2012),
http://www.doc.ic.ac.uk/~mcg05/wsnrouting

Scale-Freeness of SPA Models with Weighted Immediate Actions

Johann Schuster and Markus Siegle

University of the Federal Armed Forces Munich, Germany
{johann.schuster,markus.siegle}@unibw.de

Abstract. Whenever a process algebra uses weights for specifying probabilities, it is desirable that the rescaling of a submodel's weights by a constant factor does not affect the resulting overall model. A classical weighted approach, which is independent of rescaling weights in submodels, is the WSCCS approach by Tofts. The stochastic process algebra CASPA also uses weights, but the results are in general not independent of rescaling the submodels' weights. This paper develops necessary and sufficient criteria for CASPA models to be independent of rescalings. In addition to the general notion of scale-freeness, weaker notions that do not regard vanishing states or target on certain measures are also considered.

Keywords: stochastic process algebra, scale-free, CASPA, nondeterminism.

1 Introduction

Stochastic Process Algebra (SPA) is a popular formalism used for performance and dependability modelling and evaluation. In most classical SPAs, all actions are associated with an exponentially distributed delay. However, similar to the area of GSPNs [1], immediate actions which do not consume any time can be a very useful feature, for instance for synchronising processes or for modelling probabilistic decisions.

This paper focuses on SPAs that offer both Markovian and immediate actions. Markovian actions are specified by their name and their rate, while immediate actions are specified by their name and weight. Weights are eventually transformed into probabilities in the following way: When the overall model has been constructed (in a compositional way) from subprocesses, no further synchronisation is necessary. At that point we say that the model is *closed*. On the closed model, weights are then normalised to probabilities.

In order to motivate the problem statement we use an example from [2], written in CASPA SPA (cf. [14,17]). Suppose there are two processes:

$$A:=(*s,1*);A1+(*t,1*);A2$$
$$B:=(*s,2*);B1+(*s,3*);B2$$

M. Tribastone and S. Gilmore (Eds.): EPEW/UKPEW 2012, LNCS 7587, pp. 48–62, 2013.
© Springer-Verlag Berlin Heidelberg 2013

(for details of the syntax and semantics cf. Sec. 2). Synchronising A and B over action s results in a closed model whose behaviour is shown in Fig. 1. The normalised transition probabilities in this case are (from left to right) $\frac{1}{3}$, $\frac{1}{2}$, $\frac{1}{6}$. Rescaling the weights of submodel B by factor 2 to B:=(*s,4*);B1+(*s,6*);B2 would lead to transition probabilities $\frac{4}{11}$, $\frac{6}{11}$, $\frac{1}{11}$, which is clearly a different distribution. Such an effect is undesirable, since the local rescaling of a submodel's weights should not produce any effect on the overall model! In particular, this would be problematic when different modellers work on different parts of the same overall model.

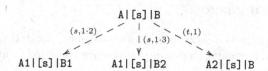

Fig. 1. An example that does not allow rescaling of submodel B's weights

The problem of normalising weights to probabilities in SPA is not new, as the following glance at related work shows: A classical approach, which is independent of rescaling weights in submodels is the WSCCS approach by Tofts [21], where time is discrete and processes proceed in lock-step. However, the present paper is concerned with the continuous-time scenario, where processes evolve in parallel, with the possibility of synchronising on certain events. [7] described such an approach in the context of semi-Markov PEPA, where weights are employed to determine the likelihood of occurrence of certain general distributions. The paper [11] introduces iPEPA, which is PEPA extended by weighted immediate actions. Weights are transformed into probabilities before any parallel composition takes place, and those probabilities are then recomputed at each level of composition. Both approaches just mentioned, however, are not scale-free. EMPA [5] and some versions of TIPP [16] were actually the first Markovian process algebras to offer (weighted) immediate actions, but there the scaling problem did not occur since only local normalisation was required. As investigated in [8], the problem of normalisation is also present in PTPA and some probabilistic variants of LOTOS. In these SPAs there may be competing synchronous and asynchronous transitions, and the possibly nondeterministic choices between them are converted by the semantics to a probabilistic execution fragment in the sense of [19].

Everything is fine as long as the modeller is aware of situations where potential nondeterminism could arise. However, if the modeller misses a potentially nondeterministic situation, the analysis results could be misleading, as they depend on the scaling of certain weights, i.e. their ratios, as the example in Fig. 1 has shown. Therefore it is very important to develop precise criteria for automatically deciding whether a given model is scale-free or not, and this is exactly the topic of this paper. The paper will give a necessary and sufficient criterion for CASPA models to be scale-free, and in addition a sufficient criterion which is considerably easier to prove. The results in this paper are for the stochastic process algebra CASPA [14,17], but the same ideas apply to other SPAs that

1. have both Markovian and immediate actions,
2. use weights to specify probabilities of immediate actions, and
3. use the product of weights for the weight of a synchronised immediate action.

The remainder of the paper is organised as follows: Sec. 2 sketches the CASPA syntax by means of a small example and provides the semantic rules. Sec. 3 defines different notions of scale-freeness and establishes the relationships between them. Sec. 4 proves the main lemmata to characterise scale-freeness in the strong and weak sense, and Sec. 5 concludes the paper.

2   CASPA Language

The CASPA language is a stochastic process algebra, notated in the form of a guarded command language, that is used to specify Weighted Stochastic Labelled Transition Systems:

Definition 1. *A Weighted Stochastic Labelled Transition System (WSLTS) is a tuple $(S, L_M, L_I, \rightarrow, \dashrightarrow, s_0)$ where S is a finite set of states, $s_0 \in S$ is the initial state. Two sets of action labels are present: L_M (Markovian labels) and L_I (immediate labels), $L_M \cap L_I = \emptyset$. Let $Act = L_M \cup L_I$. A special label $\tau \in L_I$ will be used for the internal tau transition. The transition relations are given as $\rightarrow \subseteq S \times L_M \times \mathbb{R}^{>0} \times S$ and $\dashrightarrow \subseteq S \times L_I \times \mathbb{R}^{>0} \times S$. An element $(s_1, a, \lambda, s_2) \in \rightarrow$ is called a* Markovian *transition from s_1 to s_2 with the action label a and the rate λ (describing a negative exponentially distributed random variable). Alternatively we write $s_1 \xrightarrow{a,\lambda} s_2$. An element $(s_1, b, w, s_2) \in \dashrightarrow$ is called an* immediate *transition from s_1 to s_2 with the action label b and the weight w. Alternatively we write $s_1 \xdashrightarrow{b,w} s_2$. A state with at least one outgoing immediate transition is called* vanishing, *otherwise it is called* tangible.

Remark 1. In some modelling frameworks, immediate transitions are given without any weight or probability. This leads to nondeterministic behaviour, as e.g. in the case of Interactive Markov Chains (IMCs) [12]. In our setup we use weights to generate transition probabilities. Both for immediate and for exponentially distributed transitions it is assumed that no "parallel" transitions with the same action label exist. They are grouped together by summing up the parallel weights/rates, i.e. $s_1 \xdashrightarrow{b,w_1} s_2$ and $s_1 \xdashrightarrow{b,w_2} s_2$ will be grouped to $s_1 \xdashrightarrow{b,w_1+w_2} s_2$.

The basic building blocks of the CASPA language are Markovian actions (a, λ) (here action a with rate λ) and immediate actions $(*b, w*)$ (here action b with weight w). Sequential processes are defined by means of the prefix operator ; and the choice operator +. The synchronised parallel composition operator is written as $|[S]|$ for a synchronisation set $S \subseteq L_I$[1]. Finally, the hiding operator

---

[1] Other versions of CASPA also allow the synchronisation over Markovian labels, but since this is irrelevant for the considerations of this paper we decided to omit this feature.

`hide` turns a set of immediate labels into the internal label τ. The complete syntax can be found in [18].

The CASPA semantics in condensed form is given in Tab. 1 (notated in the style of [15]). In the table, P, P', Q and Q' are valid expressions in the language, and λ, μ, ω, σ are positive real numbers. By applying these semantic rules, for every CASPA model C a multi-transition system, and from this by standard flattening [13] a unique WSLTS W is generated. We denote by $\mathcal{C}_{cl}$ the set of *closed* CASPA models, i.e. models which will not be used in further parallel composition. In a closed model

- all immediate action labels can safely be ignored
- time can only evolve in tangible states, (maximal progress assumption [12])
- weights can be normalised to probabilities
- a tangible initial state is required

A CASPA state measure characterises a subset of states. It can be used in connection with transient or steady-state analysis. For a more detailed explanation cf. [2].

Table 1. CASPA language semantics

$$\frac{}{(a,\lambda); P \xrightarrow{(a,\lambda)} P} a \in L_M \qquad\qquad \frac{}{(*b,\omega*); P \overset{(b,\omega)}{\dashrightarrow} P} b \in L_I$$

$$\frac{P \xrightarrow{(a,\lambda)} P'}{P+Q \xrightarrow{(a,\lambda)} P'} a \in L_M \qquad\qquad \frac{Q \xrightarrow{(a,\lambda)} Q'}{P+Q \xrightarrow{(a,\lambda)} Q'} a \in L_M$$

$$\frac{P \overset{(b,\omega)}{\dashrightarrow} P'}{P+Q \overset{(b,\omega)}{\dashrightarrow} P'} b \in L_I \qquad\qquad \frac{Q \overset{(b,\omega)}{\dashrightarrow} Q'}{P+Q \overset{(b,\omega)}{\dashrightarrow} Q'} b \in L_I$$

$$\frac{P \xrightarrow{(a,\lambda)} P'}{P|[S]|Q \xrightarrow{(a,\lambda)} P'|[S]|Q} a \in L_M \qquad\qquad \frac{Q \xrightarrow{(a,\lambda)} Q'}{P|[S]|Q \xrightarrow{(a,\lambda)} P|[S]|Q'} a \in L_M$$

$$\frac{P \overset{(b,\omega)}{\dashrightarrow} P'}{P|[S]|Q \overset{(b,\omega)}{\dashrightarrow} P'|[S]|Q} b \notin S \qquad\qquad \frac{Q \overset{(b,\omega)}{\dashrightarrow} Q'}{P|[S]|Q \overset{(b,\omega)}{\dashrightarrow} P|[S]|Q'} b \notin S$$

$$\frac{P \overset{(s_b,\omega)}{\dashrightarrow} P' \quad Q \overset{(s_b,\sigma)}{\dashrightarrow} Q'}{P|[S]|Q \overset{(s_b,\omega\cdot\sigma)}{\dashrightarrow} P'|[S]|Q'} s_b \in S \subseteq L_I$$

$$\frac{P \overset{(s_b,\omega)}{\dashrightarrow} P'}{\text{hide } S \text{ in } P \overset{(\tau,\omega)}{\dashrightarrow} \text{hide } S \text{ in } P'} s_b \in S \qquad\qquad \frac{P \overset{(s_b,\omega)}{\dashrightarrow} P'}{\text{hide } S \text{ in } P \overset{(s_b,\omega)}{\dashrightarrow} \text{hide } S \text{ in } P'} s_b \notin S$$

$$\frac{P \xrightarrow{(a,\lambda)} P'}{\text{hide } S \text{ in } P \xrightarrow{(a,\lambda)} \text{hide } S \text{ in } P'} a \in L_M$$

2.1 A Small Running Example

Consider a production system with two machines – represented by their input buffers – that are loaded by a shared robot (an extremely simplified version of the model in [20]). The CASPA model of the system is given in Fig. 2. Lines 1-4 describe one input buffer (X is to be substituted by 1 or 2), the robot that loads the buffers is described in lines 5-7 and the system definition is given in lines 8-10 (synchronisations over `start_enqueue`, `stop_enqueue`). The state measures of interest are defined in lines 11-13.

The possibly nondeterministic choice which buffer should be loaded next is resolved by CASPA semantics to a probabilistic execution fragment (cf. [19]) according to the ratios of weights. Suppose that all weights of immediate actions in Buffer2 are changed by the same constant factor α_2. From a subprocess-perspective, this should lead to the *same* resulting probabilities. But this is not the case in this example, as we shall see later.

```
(1)   BufferX(state [2]) :=
(2)        [state = IDLE] -> (*start_enqueue,1*); BufferX(WORKING)
(3)        [state = WORKING] -> (enqueue,5); BufferX(FINISHED)
(4)        [state = FINISHED] -> (*stop_enqueue,1*); BufferX(IDLE)

(5)   Robot(state [1]) :=
(6)        [state = IDLE] -> (*start_enqueue,1*); Robot(BUSY)
(7)        [state = BUSY] -> (*stop_enqueue,1*); Robot(IDLE)

(8)   Sys := ( Buffer1(WORKING)|[]|Buffer2(IDLE) )
(9)             |[start_enqueue, stop_enqueue]|
(10)        Robot(BUSY)

(11) statemeasure buf1working Buffer1(state=WORKING)
(12) statemeasure buf2working Buffer2(state=WORKING)
(13) statemeasure any_working Buffer1(state=WORKING) | Buffer2(state=WORKING)
```

Fig. 2. CASPA model and measure definitions

3   Scale-Freeness

The example from the previous section shows that it is natural to ask for CASPA models that lead to the same results for certain measures, even if weights of immediate transitions are rescaled for any submodel. To make this statement more precise, we will generalise CASPA models to accept also variables (in addition to constants) for their weights. Before doing this, we introduce a powerful tool from algebra, the quotient field.

Definition 2. *For a CASPA model C with N sequential submodels we define*

1. *a generalised weight as an element of the polynomial ring $\mathbb{R}[\alpha_1, \ldots, \alpha_N]$ (note that this is a unique factorisation domain (UFD) [10]),*
2. *the quotient field $\mathbb{R}(\alpha_1, \ldots, \alpha_N) := Quot(\mathbb{R}[\alpha_1, \ldots, \alpha_N])$ is called the field of rational functions in N variables,*
3. *two quotients $\frac{p}{q}$, $\frac{r}{s}$ are equivalent in $\mathbb{R}(\alpha_1, \ldots, \alpha_N)$, i.e. $\frac{p}{q} = \frac{r}{s}$, if and only if $ps = rq$. We say that a fraction $\frac{p}{q}$ "is in $\mathbb{R}$" or "constant" if $\frac{p}{q} = \frac{r}{1}$ for some $r \in \mathbb{R}$.*

For generalised weights w_i, $i \in \{1, \dots, m\}$ we have $\frac{w_i}{\sum_{j=1}^{m} w_j} \in \mathbb{R}(\alpha_1, \dots, \alpha_n)$. So we see that normalising a WSLTS (including generalised weights) leads in general to probabilities in the field of rational functions. In some lucky cases the probabilities are constant. We define:

Definition 3. *For a CASPA model C consisting of sequential submodels S_i, $i \in \{1, \dots, N\}$ we define its* relaxation $\widetilde{C}$ *as the model where every weight in a submodel S_i is multiplied by variable $\alpha_i > 0$ ($i \in \{1, \dots, N\}$). A CASPA model is called* scale-free *if after applying the maximal progress assumption all probabilities in the reachable part of the normalised WSLTS corresponding to $\widetilde{C}$ do not change regardless which actual values for α_i are chosen, i.e. the corresponding probabilities are constant in $\mathbb{R}(\alpha_1, \dots, \alpha_N)$.*

The next definition introduces balancedness that – while on first glance a very different approach – will prove to be equivalent to the scale-free property.

Definition 4. *A CASPA model consisting of sequential submodels S_i, $i \in \{1, \dots, N\}$, is called* balanced *if, after applying the maximal progress assumption, for every reachable state s there is a set $syn(s) \subseteq \{S_1, \dots, S_N\}$ such that for every transition emanating from s the set of participating submodels is equal to $syn(s)$.*

Lemma 1. *For a CASPA model C it holds that: C scale-free $\Leftrightarrow$ C balanced .*

Proof. Let S_i, $i \in \{1, \dots, N\}$ be the sequential submodels of C. Assume without loss of generality that the maximal progress assumption has been applied and the set of transitions has been restricted to the reachable subset. A general transition in the WSLTS of $\widetilde{C}$ emanating from s has the form $s \xrightarrow{a_I, c_I \cdot \alpha_I} s'$ where I is to be understood as the multi-index $(i_1, \dots, i_M)$, $\forall k \in \{1, \dots, M\} : i_k \in \{1, \dots, N\}$ (M denotes the number of synchronising submodels). Furthermore, we have $a_I \in Act$, $c_I = \prod_{k=1}^{M} c_{i_k} \in \mathbb{R}$ and $\alpha_I := \alpha_{i_1} \cdot \ldots \cdot \alpha_{i_M}$. Now the normalisation leads to the following fraction for the corresponding probability: $\frac{c_I \cdot \alpha_I}{c_I \cdot \alpha_I + \dots + c_K \cdot \alpha_K}$. We see that the α product can only be cancelled out if and only if the multi-indices are the *same* for every summand in the denominator.

Remark 2. The idea of balanced models is quite classic. Without calling it this way, [21] uses a semantics that implies balancedness of all weighted decisions for the resulting models. There, only discrete time steps are considered.

For an even stronger formulation we use

Definition 5. *A transition is called* synchronised *if more than one submodel participate in it, otherwise it is called* unsynchronised*. A CASPA model is called* simple *if after maximal progress and reachability for every state s it holds that*

1. *there is at most one synchronised transition emanating from s and no un-synchronised transition, or*
2. *the transitions emanating from s are all are unsynchronised and belong to the same submodel.*

Lemma 2. *For a CASPA model C it holds that: C simple $\Rightarrow$ C balanced .*

Proof. Clear by definition.

Sometimes this definition of scale-freeness is too restrictive. Note that – similar to the elimination of vanishing states in Generalised Stochastic Petri Nets (GSPNs) – all vanishing states in a CASPA model may be eliminated in the case that no timeless trap is present[2] (cf. [18,4]). We denote this process by $el(.)$ (note that this is well-defined up to bisimilarity [18]).

Definition 6. *A CASPA model C is called* quasi scale-free, *if in $el(\widetilde{C})$ all probabilities and rates are constant.*

Example 1. Let C be the example presented in Fig. 2. We see in Fig. 3a the corresponding WLSTS of the relaxation. It can immediately be seen that it is not balanced ($syn((\texttt{IDLE},\texttt{IDLE},\texttt{IDLE}))$, or equivalently multi-index α_I, is not constant) and therefore, by Lemma 1 not scale-free. The same can be seen in Fig. 3b as in the fractions emanating from $(\texttt{IDLE},\texttt{IDLE},\texttt{IDLE})$ only α_3 cancelled out, but nothing more. Fig. 3c shows the that the model is not even quasi scale-free, as the rates of the CTMC depend on α_1 and α_2.

Sometimes even not quasi scale-free models can be useful – if the measure that is to be computed does not depend on the weights chosen.

Definition 7. *Let $\mathcal{M}$ be a set of CASPA state measures. A CASPA model C without timeless traps is called* scale-free with respect to $\mathcal{M}$, *if the analysis results of $el(\widetilde{C})$ for every measure in $\mathcal{M}$ are constant in $\mathbb{R}(\alpha_1,\ldots,\alpha_N)$ (i.e. they do not depend on the scaling parameters α_i, $i \in \{1,\ldots,N\}$).*

Example 2. Let C be the model given in Fig. 2. Doing CTMC analysis on $el(\widetilde{C})$ we see that the results are $\texttt{buf1working} = \frac{\alpha_1}{\alpha_1+\alpha_2}$, $\texttt{buf2working} = \frac{\alpha_2}{\alpha_1+\alpha_2}$ and $\texttt{any\_working} = \frac{\alpha_1+\alpha_2}{\alpha_1+\alpha_2} = 1$. So the model is only scale-free with respect to the trivial measure $\texttt{any\_working}$.

Lemma 3. *The following implications hold*

1. *"scale-free" $\Rightarrow$ "quasi scale-free"*
2. *"quasi scale-free" without timeless trap $\Rightarrow$ "scale-free with respect to all state measures"*

---

[2] In the case that timeless traps are present, we leave vanishing states with timeless self-loops with loop-probability 1 unchanged.

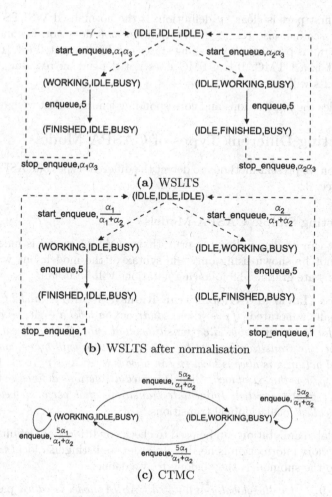

(a) WSLTS

(b) WSLTS after normalisation

(c) CTMC

Fig. 3. State graphs for the example

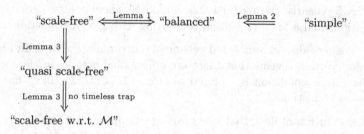

Fig. 4. Different notions of scale-freeness and their relations

Proof. The first part is clear by definition: If the normalised WSLTS does not depend on rescaling, also the result after elimination does not. Second part: If no timeless trap is present, all vanishing states can be eliminated (cf. [18,4]) and so the result is a CTMC. If a CTMC does not depend on rescaling, also the analysis results will not.

Fig. 4 includes the implications and corresponding lemmata that we have shown.

4   Detecting Different Types of CASPA Models

In this section we present methods to detect the different types of CASPA models defined in Sec. 3.

4.1   Detecting Simple CASPA Models

In general it can be demanding to verify that a CASPA model is indeed scale-free. It cannot be shown using only the syntax of the model, but we have to examine the state graph. The following notations will be useful:

Definition 8 (Local and Global Transitions). *A CASPA model C is called* locally/globally annotated, *if every immediate action label $a \in Act \setminus \{\tau\}$ has the suffix* _loc *for local transitions, i.e. transitions that only affect the local submodel or* _glob, *i.e. the transition is used for synchronisation with other components. The internal action τ is always local (τ can always be read as τ_loc). We define Act_{loc} (Act_{glob}) as the set of local (global) immediate actions defined in C — with suffix* _loc *(*_glob*) omitted. Immediate transitions that perform local (global) actions are called* local *(global) transitions.*

The local/global annotation can be used to check condition 1 of Definition 5. For condition 2 more information is needed. In order to distinguish local transitions according to the submodels they belong to, we define:

Definition 9. *A locally/globally annotated CASPA model is called* partitioned, *if every local action has an additional suffix that determines the submodel a local action acts in.*

Example 3. The partitioned transition system from the example in Fig. 1 is shown in Fig. 5. Clearly the model is not simple as there are two concurring global transitions and a local transition concurring with global transitions.

Example 4. We give also an annotated version of our running example in Fig. 6. The annotated version reveals that there are only global actions in the model. But now the simple condition is violated as state (IDLE,IDLE,IDLE) has two outgoing global transitions.

We already saw in Example 1 that our running example is not scale-free. But there – even if it was easy to see – we used the fact that one start_enqueue transition has participants Robot and Buffer1, while the other has participants Robot and Buffer2, which is hard to detect automatically. We will formalise the detection in the next section.

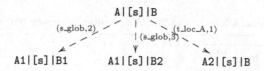

Fig. 5. Partitioned version of example from the introduction

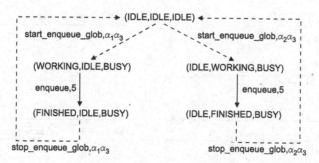

Fig. 6. annotated WSLTS

4.2 Dectecting Balanced CASPA Models

For detecting balanced CASPA models, we introduce an additional signature parameter for every transition that can be derived directly from the syntax of a CASPA model. We need the following notation.

Definition 10. *Let N be fixed and $\mathfrak{B}(N) := \cup_{i=1}^{N} \mathbb{B}^i$ the set of boolean strings of length up to N. There is a canonical outer product $\mathbb{B}^i \times \mathbb{B}^j \to \mathbb{B}^{i+j}$,*

$$((a_1, \ldots, a_i), (b_1, \ldots, b_j)) \mapsto (a_1, \ldots, a_i).(b_1, \ldots, b_j) := (a_1, \ldots, a_i, b_1, \ldots, b_j).$$

The set $\mathfrak{B}(N)$ will be called the set of patterns *for CASPA models with N submodels. For any CASPA process Q we define $|Q|$ as the number of sequential submodels contained in Q.*

The transition relation for a CASPA model with N submodels will be altered to $\dashrightarrow \subseteq S \times L_I \times \mathbb{R}^{>0} \times \mathfrak{B}(N) \times S$, where $\mathfrak{B}(N)$ describes the submodels that participate at a transition. Every participating submodel will be denoted by 1, while every non-participating submodel is set to 0. We will use 0^n to denote the boolean string $\underbrace{(0, \ldots, 0)}_{n \text{ times}}$.

We change the semantics according to Tab. 2 (only the modified semantic rules are depicted, $\mathcal{P}_1$, $\mathcal{P}_2$ and $\mathcal{P}$ denote patterns). With this semantics at hand, it remains to check the closed model (after maximal progress and reachability) whether every vanishing state has its unique pattern of outgoing transitions.

Example 5. In our running example from Fig. 2 after maximal progress assumption there are two patterns for the reachable state (IDLE, IDLE, IDLE), namely $(1, 0, 1)$ and $(0, 1, 1)$, so it is clear that it is not balanced.

Table 2. Changes to CASPA semantics for using patterns

$$\frac{}{(*b,\omega*); P \xrightarrow{(b,\omega,(1))} P} b \in L_I$$

$$\frac{P \xrightarrow{(b,\omega,\mathcal{P})} P'}{P + Q \xrightarrow{(b,\omega,\mathcal{P})} P'} b \in L_I \qquad\qquad \frac{Q \xrightarrow{(b,\omega,\mathcal{P})} Q'}{P + Q \xrightarrow{(b,\omega,\mathcal{P})} Q'} b \in L_I$$

$$\frac{P \xrightarrow{(b,\omega,\mathcal{P})} P'}{P|[S]|Q \xrightarrow{(b,\omega,\mathcal{P}.0^{|Q|})} P'|[S]|Q} b \notin S \qquad\qquad \frac{Q \xrightarrow{(b,\omega,\mathcal{P})} Q'}{P|[S]|Q \xrightarrow{(b,\omega,0^{|P|}.\mathcal{P})} P|[S]|Q'} b \notin S$$

$$\frac{P \xrightarrow{(s_b,\omega,\mathcal{P}_1)} P' \quad Q \xrightarrow{(s_b,\sigma,\mathcal{P}_2)} Q'}{P|[S]|Q \xrightarrow{(s_b,\omega\cdot\sigma,\mathcal{P}_1.\mathcal{P}_2)} P'|[S]|Q'} s_b \in S$$

$$\frac{P \xrightarrow{(s_b,\omega,\mathcal{P})} P'}{\text{hide } S \text{ in } P \xrightarrow{(\tau,\omega,\mathcal{P})} \text{hide } S \text{ in } P'} s_b \in S \qquad\qquad \frac{P \xrightarrow{(b,\omega,\mathcal{P})} P'}{\text{hide } S \text{ in } P \xrightarrow{(b,\omega,\mathcal{P})} \text{hide } S \text{ in } P'} b \notin S$$

Remark 3. In the pattern-based setting we can also characterise simple models quite easily if we define $| \ | : \mathfrak{B}(N) \to \{1,\dots,N\}$, $(a_1,\dots,a_j) \mapsto \sum_{i=1}^{j} a_i$ ($1 \le j \le N$). We consider the reachable part of the state graph after maximal progress assumption (S being the set of reachable states). A model is simple if

- there exists a mapping $\mathcal{P} : S \to \mathfrak{B}(N)$ (i.e. for every state s there is a unique pattern $\mathcal{P}(s)$ such that all transitions emanating from s have this pattern), and
- for every state s with $|\mathcal{P}(s)| > 1$ there is only one transition emanating from s.

4.3   The Quasi Scale-Free Case

So far we have concentrated on the strong form of scale-freeness. For the quasi scale-free case we present two approaches: The first one, which is straight-forward, is to carry out the elimination process with generalised probabilities calculated from generalised weights in $\mathbb{R}(\alpha_1,\dots,\alpha_n)$ (again after maximal progress and reachability analysis). If after the elimination process all remaining rates and probabilities are constant, the model is quasi scale-free by definition.

The second approach uses the patterns introduced in Sec. 4.2. The idea is to find equivalent models under some appropriate equivalence relation that only have emanating transitions with one single pattern per state. We will now construct Markov Automata (MA, cf. [9]) that reflect the problem of un-balancedness by introducing nondeterminism. Informally, an MA is a 5-tuple $(S, Act, \longrightarrow, \dashrightarrow\!\!\!\rightarrow, s_0)$ with state space S, action set Act and inital state s_0. MAs can express both, nondeterminism between action (immediate) transitions ($\longrightarrow$), and races between Markovian (delay) transitions ($\dashrightarrow\!\!\!\rightarrow$).

Remember from Sec. 2 that for closed CASPA models all immediate action labels can safely be ignored. So we would like to stress that the assumption in the following definition poses no restriction for closed CASPA models. For the rest of this section we assume that whenever $C \in \mathcal{C}_{cl}$ then

1. all immediate action labels are equal to τ
2. the maximal progress assumption has been applied.

Definition 11. *Let $C \in \mathcal{C}_{cl}$ be a CASPA model (with N submodels) and S be its set of reachable states, $s_0 \in S$ the initial state, $\rightarrow$ the set of Markovian transitions and $\dashrightarrow$ the set of immediate transitions (annotated by patterns). Let $\mathfrak{P}(s) \subseteq \mathfrak{B}(N)$ be the set of patterns emanating from s (remember that for balanced models $|\mathfrak{P}(s)| = 1$ for every s). Then a corresponding MA can be generated in the following way:*

1. *For every $\mathcal{P} \in \mathfrak{P}(s)$ we calculate $P(s, \mathcal{P}, s') := \dfrac{\sum_{(s,\tau,\omega,\mathcal{P},s') \in \dashrightarrow} \omega}{\sum_{\exists t: (s,\tau,\omega,\mathcal{P},t) \in \dashrightarrow} \omega}$*
2. *$\twoheadrightarrow := \{(s, \tau, \mu) | s \in S, \mathcal{P} \in \mathfrak{P}(s), \mu = P(s, \mathcal{P}, .)\}$*
3. *$\rightarrowtail := \{(s, \lambda, s') | \exists a \in Act : (s, a, \lambda, s') \in \rightarrow\}$*

The corresponding MA $MA(C)$ is then defined as $(S, \{\tau\}, \twoheadrightarrow, \rightarrowtail, s_0)$.

Note that the sum in the numerator of item 1 has either one or zero elements. The combined effect of item 1 and item 2 is a pattern-wise normalisation of weights. This construction has interesting properties, as the following lemmata show.

Lemma 4. *For a CASPA model C the MA $MA(C)$ is always scale-free in the sense that it does not change when submodels are rescaled.*

Proof. This is clear by definition: Only transitions with the *same* pattern are merged into a distribution.

Lemma 5. *When Markovian action labels are ignored, the standard semantics of a CASPA model $C \in \mathcal{C}_{cl}$ describes a probabilistic execution fragment of $MA(C)$ in the sense of [19].*

Proof. We construct a probabilistic scheduler that yields the desired behaviour. We have to show that for every state s every distribution on successor states of s can be realised by some convex combination of the transitions in $\twoheadrightarrow$ emanating from s. Suppose s has the outgoing transitions $s \overset{(\tau, \omega_i, \mathcal{P}_i)}{\dashrightarrow} s_i$, $i \in \{1, \ldots, I(s)\}$, then the probability distribution on the successor states s_i is given as $P(s_i) := \frac{\omega_i}{\sum_{j=1}^{I(s)} \omega_j}$ by standard semantics. Assume without loss of generality (otherwise reorder) that $|\mathfrak{P}(s)| = K$ and that transitions with index in $\{k_m, \ldots, k_{m+1} - 1\}$ belong to pattern $\mathcal{P}_m$, $k_1 = 1$, $k_{K+1} = I(s) + 1$, $k_h < k_j$ for $h < j$. Now the probabilities – in $MA(C)$ – when using the m-th pattern are $P(s, \mathcal{P}_m, s_i) = \frac{\omega_i}{\sum_{j=k_m}^{k_{m+1}-1} \omega_j}$, so it is easy to see that the coefficients c_m for the convex combination have to be chosen as $\frac{\sum_{j=k_m}^{k_{m+1}-1} \omega_j}{\sum_{j=1}^{I(s)} \omega_j}$ to get the distribution that is determined by standard CASPA semantics.

One could now reduce $MA(C)$ modulo weak bisimulation (a relation on distributions) and check whether there is a *deterministic* representative in the equivalence class modulo weak MA bisimilarity, because this would mean that in a nondeterministic choice it does not matter which action is taken. The problem is that this is not the whole story. Looking at our running example, a possible result would be an MA with just one state with a Markovian loop with rate 5, which is clearly deterministic. But we saw earlier that our example is not scale-free!

The solution is that for getting results on the state measures (which only can be specified for stable states) we are not allowed to lump together different stable states (which would be done to get the Markovian loop above). This can be realised by a sort of AP (atomic proposition) bisimulation in the spirit of F-bisimulation [3] or Markov-AP bisimulation [6]: If all stable states have different APs, they can never be grouped together! We recall from [9] that weak MA bisimulation $\approx$ induces an equivalence relation $\approx_\Delta$ on states by defining $x \approx_\Delta y :\Leftrightarrow \Delta_x \approx \Delta_y$ (where Δ_x denotes the Dirac distribution at state x). Therefore, with an appropriate extension of $\approx_\Delta$ to an AP bisimulation $\approx_\Delta^{AP}$ we can conclude that if our MA is weakly AP bisimilar to a deterministic MA, the corresponding CASPA model is quasi scale-free, i.e. this is a sufficient criterion. Note that weak AP bisimulation also generalises the elimination of vanishing states (cf. Sec. V in [9]). The drawback of this approach is that no weak MA bisimulation algorithm has been published so far, but at least we can state:

Lemma 6. *If for a CASPA model $C \in \mathcal{C}_{cl}$ the resulting MA $MA(C) = (S, \{\tau\},$ $\longrightarrow, \twoheadrightarrow, s_0)$ is weakly AP bisimilar to a deterministic MA $M' = (S, \{\tau\}, \longrightarrow'$ $, \twoheadrightarrow, s_0)$, where $\longrightarrow' \subseteq \longrightarrow$, then C is quasi scale-free.*

Proof. Assume that all stable states in S are equipped with different atomic propositions. Weak MA AP bisimilarity ensures that every nondeterministic choice in $MA(C)$ is equivalent to a deterministic one in M'. So each decision "does not matter" with respect to our equivalence relation. Especially it is not important which probabilistic execution fragment of $MA(C)$ is chosen by the probabilistic scheduler induced by CASPA semantics according to Lemma 5. As by Lemma 4 the distributions in $MA(C)$ do not depend on rescaling, also the distributions in M' cannot depend on rescaling of weights of submodels.

We use the diagram in Fig. 7 to prove the claim. Firstly we show that commutativity of the diagram implies our claim. Secondly we prove the commutativity. The diagram is explained as follows: $el(.)$ denotes the elimination of vanishing states (this is also defined for deterministic MA, cf. Sec. V in [9]), $det(.)$ denotes the mapping to a weakly AP bisimilar deterministic representative M'. The canonical mapping from CASPA models to MA by transforming the reachable state graph to MA (disregarding labels of Markovian actions) is denoted by $canon(.)$. Now we observe that quasi scale-freeness can be identified as $canon \circ el(C)$ having constant rates and probabilities – no matter, which rescaling factors for submodels are chosen. But the mapping $el \circ det \circ MA(C)$ surely produces constant rates and probabilities. Commutativity of the diagram follows from the above observation that the actual probabilistic execution fragment of $MA(C)$ does not play any role and by Theorem 7 in [9].

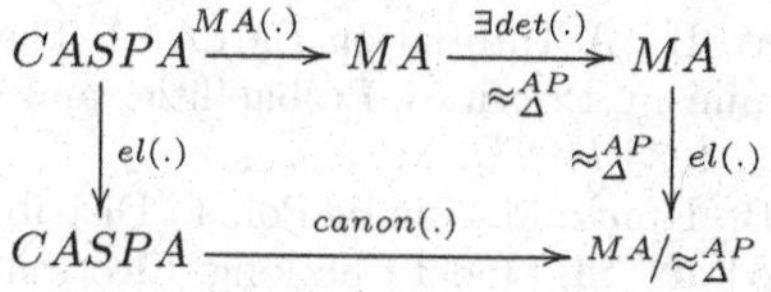

$$
\begin{array}{ccc}
CASPA & \xrightarrow{MA(.)} MA \xrightarrow[\approx_\Delta^{AP}]{\exists det(.)} MA \\
\downarrow{\scriptstyle el(.)} & \approx_\Delta^{AP} \downarrow{\scriptstyle el(.)} \\
CASPA & \xrightarrow{canon(.)} MA/\approx_\Delta^{AP}
\end{array}
$$

Fig. 7. Elimination and weak AP bisimulation

4.4 Scale-Freeness with Respect to Some Measure

The MA-based approach sketched in Sec. 4.3 can also be adapted to the "with respect to some measure" case. Using different state labels (characterising some given measures) for the AP bisimulation, one can use this machinery to check for the weaker case of scale-freeness with respect to some measure $\mathcal{M}$. The basic difference between the two settings is that in the quasi scale-free case *all* stable states get different labels, while in the weaker setting some stable states might share the same label.

5 Conclusion

We have shown necessary and sufficient criteria for scale-free CASPA models and related different kinds of scale-freeness. Patterns have been introduced to easily recognise participating submodels. From the state graph annotated with patterns one can check scale-freeness. Patterns have also been used to transform the problem to the domain of Markov Automata in order to check the quasi scale-free case.

Acknowledgements. We would like to thank the anonymous reviewers for their valuable comments, and DFG who supported this work under grant SI 710/7-1 and for partial support by DFG/NWO Bilateral Research Programme ROCKS.

References

1. Ajmone Marsan, M., Balbo, G., Conte, G., Donatelli, S., Franceschinis, G.: Modelling with Generalized Stochastic Petri Nets. Wiley Series in Parallel Computing (1995)
2. Bachmann, J., Riedl, M., Schuster, J., Siegle, M.: An Efficient Symbolic Elimination Algorithm for the Stochastic Process Algebra Tool CASPA. In: Nielsen, M., Kučera, A., Miltersen, P.B., Palamidessi, C., Tůma, P., Valencia, F. (eds.) SOFSEM 2009. LNCS, vol. 5404, pp. 485–496. Springer, Heidelberg (2009)

3. Baier, C., Haverkort, B., Hermanns, H., Katoen, J.-P.: Model-checking algorithms for continuous-time Markov chains. IEEE Transactions on Software Engineering 29(7) (2003)
4. Bause, F.: No Way Out ∞ The Timeless Trap. Petri Net Newsletters 37, 4–8 (1990)
5. Bernardo, M., Gorrieri, R.: A Tutorial on EMPA: A Theory of Concurrent Processes with Nondeterminism, Priorities, Probabilities and Time. Theoretical Computer Science 202(1-2), 1–54 (1998)
6. Blom, S., Haverkort, B., Kuntz, M., van de Pol, J.: Distributed Markovian Bisimulation Reduction aimed at CSL Model Checking. Electron. Notes Theor. Comput. Sci. 220, 35–50 (2008)
7. Bradley, J.: Semi-Markov PEPA: Modelling with Generally Distributed Actions. International Journal of Simulation 6(3-4), 43–51 (2005)
8. D'Argenio, P., Hermanns, H., Katoen, J.-P.: On generative parallel composition. Electr. Notes Theor. Comput. Sci. 22, 30–54 (1999)
9. Eisentraut, C., Hermanns, H., Zhang, L.: On probabilistic automata in continuous time. In: Proceedings of the 2010 25th Annual IEEE Symposium on Logic in Computer Science, LICS 2010, pp. 342–351. IEEE Computer Society (2010)
10. Fulton, W.: Algebraic Curves. Benjamin (1969)
11. Hayden, R., Bradley, J., Clark, A.: Performance specification and evaluation with Unified Stochastic Probes and fluid analysis. IEEE Transactions on Software Engineering 39(1), 97–118 (2013)
12. Hermanns, H. (ed.): Interactive Markov Chains. LNCS, vol. 2428. Springer, Heidelberg (2002)
13. Hillston, J.: A Compositional Approach to Performance Modelling. Cambridge University Press (1996)
14. Kuntz, M., Siegle, M., Werner, E.: Symbolic Performance and Dependability Evaluation with the Tool CASPA. In: Núñez, M., Maamar, Z., Pelayo, F.L., Pousttchi, K., Rubio, F. (eds.) FORTE 2004. LNCS, vol. 3236, pp. 293–307. Springer, Heidelberg (2004)
15. Plotkin, G.: A structural approach to operational semantics. Journal of Logic and Algebraic Programming 60-61, 17–139 (2004)
16. Rettelbach, M.: Probabilistic Branching in Markovian Process Algebras. The Computer Journal 38(7), 590–599 (1995)
17. Riedl, M., Schuster, J., Siegle, M.: Recent extensions to the stochastic process algebra tool CASPA. In: 5th International Conference on the Quantitative Evaluation of SysTems (QEST 2008), pp. 113–114. IEEE Computer Society (2008)
18. Schuster, J.: Towards faster numerical solution of Continuous Time Markov Chains stored by symbolic data structures. PhD thesis, Universität der Bundeswehr München (2011)
19. Segala, R.: Modeling and Verification of Randomized Distributed Real-Time Systems. PhD thesis, Department of Electrical Engineering and Computer Science, Massachusetts Institute of Technology (1995)
20. Teruel, E., Franceschinis, G., De Pierro, M.: Clarifying the priority specification of GSPN: Detached priorities. In: Proceedings of the 8th International Workshop on Petri Nets and Performance Models (PNPM 1999), pp. 114 –123. IEEE Computer Society (1999)
21. Tofts, C.: Processes with probabilities, priority and time. Formal Aspects of Computing 6, 536–564 (1994), doi:10.1007/BF01211867

Experimental Evaluation
of the Performance-Influencing Factors
of Virtualized Storage Systems

Qais Noorshams, Samuel Kounev, and Ralf Reussner

Chair for Software Design and Quality
Karlsruhe Institute of Technology (KIT)
Am Fasanengarten 5, 76131 Karlsruhe, Germany
{noorshams,kounev,reussner}@kit.edu

Abstract. Virtualized cloud environments introduce an additional abstraction layer on top of physical resources enabling their collective use by multiple systems to increase resource efficiency. In I/O-intensive applications, however, the virtualized storage of such shared environments can quickly become a bottleneck and lead to performance and scalability issues. In software performance engineering, application performance is analyzed to assess the non-functional properties taking into account the many performance-influencing factors. In current practice, however, virtualized storage is either modeled as a black-box or tackled with full-blown and fine-granular simulations. This paper presents a systematic performance analysis approach of I/O-intensive applications in virtualized environments. First, we systematically identify storage-performance-influencing factors in a representative storage environment. Second, we quantify them using a systematic experimental analysis. Finally, we extract simple performance analysis models based on regression techniques. Our approach is applied in a real world environment using the state-of-the-art virtualization technology of the IBM System z and IBM DS8700.

Keywords: I/O, Storage, Performance, Virtualization.

1 Introduction

Today's growth in resource requirements demand for a powerful yet versatile and cost-efficient data center landscape. Virtualization is used as the key technology to cost-optimally increase resource efficiency, resource demand flexibility, and centralized administration. Furthermore, cloud environments enable new pay-per-use cost models to provide resources on-demand.

Modern cloud applications have increasingly an I/O-intensive workload profile (cf. [1]), e.g., mail or file server applications are often deployed in virtualized environments. With the rise in I/O-intensive applications, however, the virtualized storage of shared environments can quickly become a bottleneck and lead to unforeseen performance and scalability issues.

M. Tribastone and S. Gilmore (Eds.): EPEW/UKPEW 2012, LNCS 7587, pp. 63–79, 2013.
© Springer-Verlag Berlin Heidelberg 2013

In current software performance engineering approaches, however, virtualized storage and its performance-influencing factors are often neglected. The virtualized storage is either treated as a black-box due to its complexity or modeled with full-blown and fine-granular simulations. In rare cases, elaborate analysis is applied, e.g., [2,3], however without explicitly considering storage configuration aspects and their influences on the storage performance.

This paper presents a systematic performance analysis approach for I/O-intensive applications in virtualized environments. First, we systematically identify storage-performance-influencing factors by considering a representative virtualized storage environment. These influencing factors are modeled hierarchically and organized categorically by workload, operating system, and hardware. The studied influencing factors and their classification are of general nature and not specific to the considered environment. Second, we propose a general workload and benchmarking methodology in order to reason about the performance of I/O-intensive applications in virtualized environments. By applying our methodology, we quantify the influence of the identified factors by means of a systematic experimental analysis. Finally, we derive simple performance analysis models based on linear regression that can be used in software performance engineering. The approach is applied in a real world environment using the state-of-the-art virtualization technology of the *IBM System z* and *IBM DS8700* with full control of the system environment and the system workload.

In summary, the contributions of this paper are: i) We provide a study of virtualized storage performance in a real world environment using the state-of-the-art virtualization technology of the IBM System z. ii) We systematically identify storage-performance-influencing factors and abstract them by means of a hierarchical feature tree model. iii) We provide an in-depth quantitative evaluation and comparison of the storage-performance-influencing factors. iv) We create simple regression-based performance models for performance prediction of a variety of storage workloads.

The remainder of this paper is organized as follows. Section 2 presents our system environment. Section 3 identifies storage-performance-influencing factors. Section 4 presents our experimental methodology and evaluation. In Section 5, we extract simple performance models based on linear regression. Finally, Section 6 presents related work, while Section 7 summarizes.

2   System Environment

A typical virtualized environment in a data center consists of servers connected to storage systems. The mainframe *System z* and the storage system *DS8700* of IBM comprise our virtualized environment of focus. They are state-of-the-art high-performance virtualized systems with redundant and/or hot swappable resources for high availability. The System z combined with the DS8700 represent a typical cloud environment. The System z enables on-demand elasticity of pooled resources with an inherent pay-per-use accounting system (cf. [4]). The System z provides processors and memory, whereas the DS8700 provides storage space. The structure of this environment is illustrated in Figure 1.

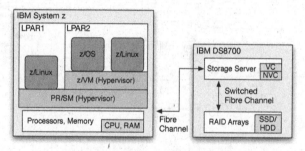

Fig. 1. IBM System z and IBM DS8700

The *Processor Resource/System Manager (PR/SM)* is a hypervisor managing logical partitions (*LPARs*) of the machine (therefore also called *LPAR hypervisor*) and enabling CPU and storage virtualization. For memory virtualization and administration purposes, IBM introduces another hypervisor, *z/VM*. The System z supports the classical mainframe operating system *z/OS* and special Linux ports for System z commonly denoted as *z/Linux*. The System z is connected to the DS8700 via fibre channel. Storage requests are handled by a storage server having a volatile cache (VC) and a non-volatile cache (NVC). Write-requests are written to the volatile as well as the non-volatile cache, but they are destaged to disk asynchronously. The storage server is connected via switched fibre channel with SSD and/or HDD RAID arrays.

In such multi-tiered virtualized environments with several layers between the hosted applications and the physical storage, many questions arise concerning the impact of the workload profile and the storage configuration on the system performance. How do certain workload characteristics, e.g., read/write request ratio, affect the performance? How does the locality of requests affect performance in tiered environments? Further, do current standard system configurations, e.g., the default I/O scheduler, still show to be suitable in such an environment? Our experiments in Section 4 will examine these and more questions.

3   Storage Performance Influencing Factors

For the identification of storage-performance-influencing factors, we created a hierarchical feature tree model aligned along logical borders, i.e., between workload mix and system configurations, and system borders, i.e., between System z and DS8700. The models capturing the performance-influencing factors are shown in Figure 2, however, complex interactions between factors are not depicted for the sake of simplicity. Still, workload-specific effects on system configurations are discussed in our experiment scenarios in Section 4.

3.1   Workload Mix

The top model in Figure 2 shows basic characteristics of a workload mix. The characterization is based on a general, storage-level view on the workload.

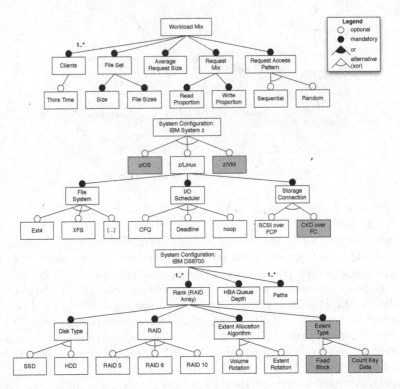

Fig. 2. Storage Performance Influencing Factors (in gray: system-specific factors)

- *Clients*: The requests of the workload are created by a certain number of clients representing e.g., threads or processes. After completion of a request, clients may have a certain waiting time (or *think time*), e.g., to process the data requested, before issuing another request. The number of clients affects performance defining the number of concurrent requests that require scheduling and introduce resource contention.
- *File Set*: Applications read from and write into a set of files. The size of this *file set* influences the locality of requests and the effectiveness of caching algorithms and data placement strategies. Depending on the physical allocation of the files, the *file sizes* affect, i.e., limit, sequential requests.
- *Average Request Size*: Most I/O optimization strategies in the various layers of the storage system aim at maximizing throughput by merging subsequent sequential requests. Serving many small requests results in a lower throughput than serving fewer large requests.
- *Request Mix*: While *read* requests are synchronous, *write* requests can be served asynchronously without blocking the application. This leads to complex optimization strategies when having mixed requests.
- *Request Access Pattern*: The access pattern affects performance due to the physical access of data as well as the optimization strategies in the various layers of

the storage system. Typical request access pattern are random or sequential requests.

3.2 System Configuration

The system configuration space is separated into two systems, System z and DS8700. While the former represents the computing environment including operating system configurations, the latter represents the storage environment including hardware configurations, cf. the middle and bottom models in Figure 2, respectively.

IBM System z – Computing Environment

- *IBM System z*: As mentioned before, the System z runs different operating systems, *z/OS* and *z/Linux*, which both can run on another virtualization layer *z/VM* to ease administration and increase resource sharing.
- *z/Linux*: As previously described, *z/Linux* is a special Linux port for System z and can be regarded as a regular Linux system.
- *File System*: Modern *file systems*, e.g., *EXT4* as the de facto standard for Linux or *XFS*, exhibit significant performance differences under the same workload as they are implemented and optimized differently.
- *I/O Scheduler*[1]: The current Linux standard *completely fair queueing (CFQ)* scheduler performs several optimizations (e.g., splitting/merging and request reordering) to minimize disk seek times, which account for a major part of I/O service times in disk-based storage systems. The *deadline* scheduler imposes a deadline on requests to prevent request starvation with read requests having a significantly shorter deadline than write requests. The *no operation (noop)* scheduler only merges and splits disk requests.
- *Storage Connection*: The System z provides two different protocols embedded in a protocol for fibre channel, classical mainframe protocol (*CKD*) over fibre channel (i.e., FICON protocol) or widespread *SCSI* over fibre channel protocol (*FCP*). The required protocol depends on the storage volume format (cf. *Extent Type*).

IBM DS8700 – Storage Environment

- *IBM DS8700*: The storage system has several configuration parameters, which - although not all directly - can be mapped to configurations of different systems.
- *Rank (RAID Array)*: A RAID array formatted with a type (*extent type*) and sub-divided into equally sized partitions (*extents*) is a *rank*. The extents are used to define volumes that can be used by applications.

---

[1] Note: i) The *antecepatory* scheduler was removed from the latest Linux kernel and is highly discouraged in virtualized environments. ii) The recently announced *FIOPS* scheduler is designed for flash-based storage devices and is still under development.

- *Disk Type*: An array can be created with disks of a specific *disk type* advantageous for different usages: Fast, but more expensive *SSDs* for higher performance requirements or regular *HDDs* (with either 7.2k r/min or 15k r/min) for lower cost per storage space.
- *RAID*: The different RAID types offer a trade-off between performance, reliability and resource efficiency.
- *Extent Type*: The format type of an array can be classical mainframe format, i.e., *Count Key Data (CKD)*, optimized for availability or regular format, i.e., *Fixed Block (FB)*. Each type requires a different protocol (cf. *Storage Connection*).
- *Extent Allocation Algorithm*: Ranks (possibly a SSD/HDD mix) can be pooled. Using multiple ranks to create volumes, the extents of a volume can be allocated on one rank after the other or be striped across ranks to optimize performance by exploiting parallelism.
- *HBA Queue Depth*: The host bus adapter (HBA) receives and queues all requests to the storage system. Having multiple servers accessing the storage system, the HBA queue depth controls fairness among servers, e.g., if one server sends much more storage requests than another.
- *Number of Paths*: To improve availability, multiple logical or physical paths can be defined from an operating system to the storage system. However, this induces routing overhead to determine which path to use for the next request.

4   Experimental Storage Performance Analysis

In this section, we analyze the storage-performance-influencing factors presented in Section 3. We start by introducing our experimental methodology.

4.1   Experimental Methodology

The experimental environment consists of the System z connected to the DS8700 storage system as introduced in Section 2 and illustrated in Figure 1.

As load driver, we used the open source Flexible File System Benchmark (FFSB)[2] because of its fine-grained configuration possibilities needed for our in-depth analysis. The detailed parameters of the workload and the system considered in our experiments are shown in Table 1. The *fixed* parameters are not varied in the experiments. The *variable* parameters are chosen depending on the specific analysis scenario. The workload parameters marked as *full explore* are measured in all combinations in every considered scenario. In our experiments, hardware variations are out of scope due to constraints in the available hardware configuration.

As an example of a benchmark run, assuming 4KB requests and a read/write ratio of 80%/20%, 100 threads repeatedly issue a series of 4096 requests[3] for

---

[2] http://sourceforge.net/projects/ffsb/. Note: There is a known bug in FFSB that miscalculates the throughput, however, it was fixed in the version we used.

[3] This is limited by the smallest file size and the largest request size (128MB/32KB = 4096) and is kept constant in all runs to ensure comparability.

Table 1. Experiment Setup and Parameters

(a) Workload Configurations

Fixed	
Runtime	300sec
Threads	100 (no think time)
O_DIRECT[4]	on
Variable	
File set size	{10x 128MB, 10x 1GB, 150x 1GB}
Full explore	
Read/Write Ratio	{100%/0%, 80%/20%, 50%/50%, 20%/80%, 0%/100%}
Request size	{4KB, 32KB}
Access pattern	{random, sequential}

(b) System Configurations

Fixed	
OS	z/Linux (Debian 2.6.32-5-s390x)
CPU	2 IFLs (cores) with approx. 2760 MIPS
RAM	4GB
Storage Cache	50GB (volatile), 2GB (non-volatile)
Storage Array	One RAID5 array with 7 HDDs (15k r/min)
Connection	SCSI over FCP
Variable	
Hypervisor	{LPAR, z/VM (on top of LPAR)}
File system	{EXT4, XFS}
Scheduler	{CFQ, deadline, noop}

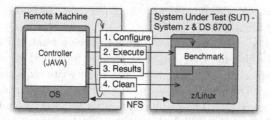

Fig. 3. Experimental Controller Setup

5 minutes. Each thread issues a request as soon as the previous request is completed. For each request series, a thread issues with 80% probability a read request series and with 20% probability a write request series. Thus, during this benchmark run, the system will be exposed to a stochastically mixed read and write workload while the benchmark gathers performance data for both types of requests. If the requests are sequential, the logical addresses of subsequent requests of one thread are ascending and 4KB apart. Further, since having, e.g., 100% read requests implies that there are no write requests during one run, such benchmark runs cannot induce any write performance data (cf. fewer bars in the figures in Section 4.2 depicting 100% read and 100% write requests respectively).

The experiments are fully automated and run by a controller software written in JAVA. Illustrated in Figure 3, the controller software is located on a remote machine that is connected to the System z via NFS. After configuring the controller, the configuration space of the experiments is explored. For every (benchmark) configuration, the controller i) configures the benchmark, ii) executes the benchmark, iii) collects the results during and after the run to the remote machine to not further introduce load on the system under test (SUT), and finally iv) cleans the system by removing the files written by the benchmark.

---

[4] POSIX flag that minimizes caching effects of the host.

For the analysis, we focus on the average system performance, thus, we compared the mean response time and mean throughput for each workload and configuration scenario. We repeated each benchmark run 15 times. As the response times are very small, the means calculated by the benchmark are prone to large outliers. In order to obtain stable and meaningful results, we ordered the response time means, and calculated the mean of the middle 5 values such that the results can be reproduced.

4.2   Experimental Results

In our evaluation, we first provide an analysis of the performance influences of the workload profile under a representative system setting. We then analyze performance characteristics of the system environment, specifically storage level caching effects and z/VM hypervisor overhead. Finally, we analyze operating system influences by varying the file system and the I/O scheduler.

Workload – *Variable Parameters:* LPAR hypervisor, EXT4 file system, noop scheduler, 1280MB file set.

We evaluate the system performance under varying read/write ratio, as well as performance of different sized and of sequential and random access requests.

Figures 4a, 4b show the performance of read and write requests depending on the read/write ratio. The metrics are normalized w.r.t the 100% read and the 100% write workload respectively. The results show that sequential read-requests have higher response times under a higher write-request fraction. This is because the read-requests are retained (i.e., queued) longer under a higher write-request fraction if the system recognizes the sequential access pattern. The goal is to serve multiple read-requests at once to improve throughput. In this scenario, the throughput of sequential and random access read-requests are approximately equal, however, the benefit of this behavior becomes evident later when examining the caching effects. In contrast to the read-requests, the response times of sequential write-requests are lower than the response time of random access write-requests under higher read-request proportion. Again, throughput of sequential and random access write-requests are approximately equal.

To elaborate, Figures 4c, 4d illustrate the relative differences in the measured response time and throughput between sequential and random access requests where the metric values for sequential requests are used as a reference, i.e., a negative value corresponds to a lower value of the respective metric for random requests. Except for the case of 100% read-requests, the sequential requests are always slower than random access requests, for read-requests between 50% and 70% and for write-requests between 20% and 50%, depending on the read/write ratio. However, comparing the throughput metric of the configuration confirms that the differences in throughput are negligible, i.e., less than 4% in most cases and up to 7% in one case.

The previous measurements show no noticeable difference between 4KB and 32KB requests. Figures 4e, 4f illustrate the relative differences of response time and throughput between 4KB (used as reference) and 32KB requests.

As expected, response time and throughput of 32KB requests are consistently higher than of 4KB requests with write- (read-) requests having higher (lower) response times in write-intensive workloads. However, this behavior is specific to this scenario and, as we will show later, it is different for the XFS file system.

Caching Effects – *Variable Parameters:* LPAR hypervisor, EXT4 file system, noop scheduler, {1280MB, 10GB, 150GB} file set.

As described before, this system environment consists of two storage tiers comprising storage server cache and RAID array. These tiers have significantly different performance characteristics. The experimental results in this scenario demonstrate the need for intelligent read-ahead and de-staging algorithms in heterogeneous or multi-tier storage environments. They are illustrated in Figure 5 comparing 1280MB and 10GB as well as 1280MB and 150GB file sets. As explained in [5], the storage system combines the algorithms Sequential Adaptive Replacement Cache (SARC), Adaptive Multi-stream Prefetching (AMP), and Intelligent Write Caching (IWC). This combination was shown to be very effective for workloads exhibiting a certain predictable access pattern, e.g., sequential requests. In case of a 10GB file set, the data exceeds the non-volatile cache leading to frequent de-staging of data from the non-volatile cache to the disk array. In case of a 150GB file set, the file set also exceeds the volatile cache leading to frequent cache misses especially for random access read-requests.

z/VM Layer – *Variable Parameters:* {LPAR, z/VM} hypervisor, EXT4 file system, noop scheduler, 1280MB file set.

Figure 6 illustrates the relative differences in terms of observed response time and throughput when adding another hypervisor layer (using z/VM). This setup benefits larger requests and impairs smaller requests in mixed workloads in terms of the relative response times, however, given that the absolute values are less than 2ms, the respective absolute performance differences are rather low. Furthermore, the throughput differences are not significant given that a SCSI connection is used and the additional hypervisor layer only performs address mapping/translation tasks.

File System – *Variable Parameters:* LPAR hypervisor, {EXT4, XFS} file system, noop scheduler, 1280MB file set.

Figure 7 illustrates the relative differences in terms of observed response time and throughput between EXT4 (used as reference) and XFS. This comparison requires a more fine-grained analysis as it exhibits a number of patterns. While for pure read-workloads the read performance is constant, XFS is able to perform better than EXT4 for sequential reads in mixed workloads. For random reads, XFS exhibits higher response times for smaller read-requests. Large read-requests in a write-intensive workload (read/write = 20%/80%) is the only case where XFS performs better than EXT4 for random reads. For write-requests, XFS shows to have higher response times than EXT4 in mixed workloads. Furthermore, even for pure write workloads, XFS has about 50% higher response times for small random

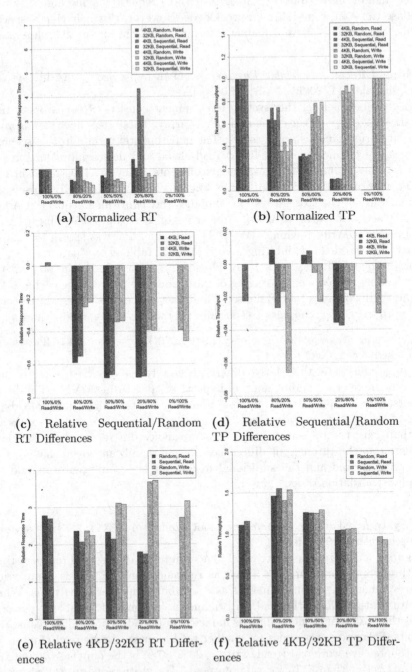

Fig. 4. Workload Performance: Response Time (RT) and Throughput (TP)

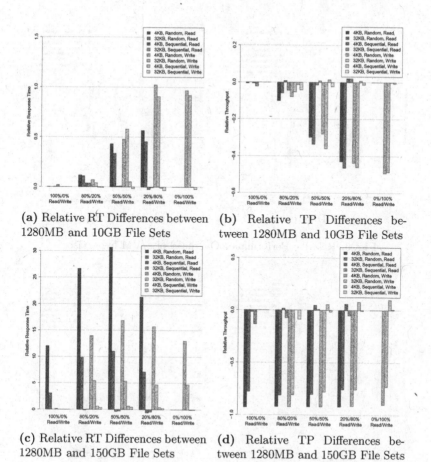

(a) Relative RT Differences between 1280MB and 10GB File Sets

(b) Relative TP Differences between 1280MB and 10GB File Sets

(c) Relative RT Differences between 1280MB and 150GB File Sets

(d) Relative TP Differences between 1280MB and 150GB File Sets

Fig. 5. Caching Effects when Varying File Set Sizes

writes-requests. However, XFS is able to improve throughput for most workloads, most noticeably for small random requests in write-intensive workloads.

I/O Scheduler – *Variable Parameters:* LPAR hypervisor, EXT4 file system, {CFQ, deadline, noop} scheduler, 1280MB & 150GB file set.

As the standard scheduler in Linux distributions, CFQ incorporates a so-called elevator mechanism reordering I/O-requests to minimize disk seek times. Figure 8 illustrates the relative differences in terms of observed response time and throughput between the noop (used as reference) and CFQ I/O schedulers, the top two charts for a file set size of 1280MB, the bottom ones for 150GB. The scheduler queues (especially small) read-requests longer if less write-requests are in the queue, trying to reorder requests and to merge small requests into larger ones. However, while this optimization is important for regular disks and disk arrays, in this tiered environment, this scheduling shows drastic performance degradation. Even if the cache is fully utilized and the response time of random

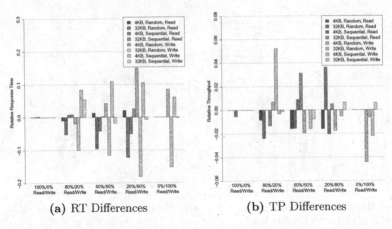

(a) RT Differences   (b) TP Differences

Fig. 6. Relative Performance Overhead of z/VM hypervisor

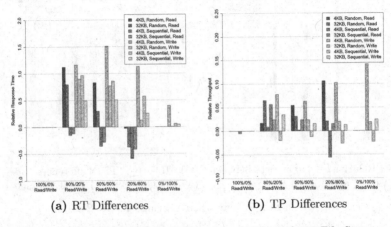

(a) RT Differences   (b) TP Differences

Fig. 7. Relative Performance Differences of EXT4 and XFS File System

read-requests in write-intensive workloads is slightly decreased, the throughput is significantly reduced with this scheduler.

The deadline scheduler assigns deadlines to requests in order to avoid request starvation. Interestingly, in our environment, it exhibited almost no performance differences (less than 5%, mostly less than 1%) to the noop scheduler, therefore, the results are omitted for brevity.

4.3   Discussion

Summarizing the measurement results, the conclusions from our analysis are manifold. In our tiered storage environment, the workload is subject to optimization and queueing in the storage system. The applied read ahead mechanisms (i.e., publicly available caching algorithms) improve performance significantly for requests with

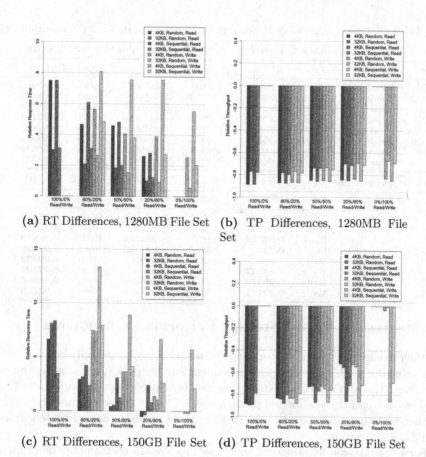

(a) RT Differences, 1280MB File Set   **(b)** TP Differences, 1280MB File Set

(c) RT Differences, 150GB File Set   **(d)** TP Differences, 150GB File Set

Fig. 8. Relative Performance Differences of **noop** and **CFQ** Schedulers

certain access pattern (e.g., sequential). However, the increased queueing of sequential read-requests impairs the response time on fully cached data considerably while still achieving equal throughput of sequential and random requests. More specifically, the response time is highly dependent on the read/write ratio. For fully cached data, sequential read-requests have considerably higher response times under a higher write-request fraction. However, the performance of sequential requests is approximately stable and independent of the file set size. Considering the hypervisor, z/VM introduces very low virtualization overhead. More generally, while the **EXT4** file system is very widespread being the de facto standard for Linux systems, the **XFS** file system showed to be beneficial for sequential reads in terms of response time. In terms of throughput, **XFS** is beneficial for big requests in read-intensive workloads and for random read- and write-requests for balanced and write-intensive workloads. Furthermore, while the **noop** and the **deadline** I/O scheduler showed to perform equally well in our environment, the **CFQ** scheduler impaired performance drastically.

Table 2. Linear Regression Depending on Type (Read or Write) Proportion

(a) Response Time (file set: 1280MB)

Size	Access	Type	R^2
4KB	Random	Read	0.29346
32KB	Random	Read	0.03769
4KB	Sequential	Read	**0.92605**
32KB	Sequential	Read	**0.93349**
4KB	Random	Write	0.69652
32KB	Random	Write	**0.9537**
4KB	Sequential	Write	0.81183
32KB	Sequential	Write	**0.94942**

(b) Throughput (file set: 1280MB)

Size	Access	Type	R^2
4KB	Random	Read	**0.96063**
32KB	Random	Read	**0.98413**
4KB	Sequential	Read	**0.95726**
32KB	Sequential	Read	**0.98101**
4KB	Random	Write	**0.9785**
32KB	Random	Write	**0.93358**
4KB	Sequential	Write	**0.98546**
32KB	Sequential	Write	**0.93377**

(c) Response Time (file set: 150GB)

Size	Access	Type	R^2
4KB	Random	Read	**0.98003**
32KB	Random	Read	**0.96287**
4KB	Sequential	Read	**0.99828**
32KB	Sequential	Read	**0.925**
4KB	Random	Write	0.89803
32KB	Random	Write	**0.94982**
4KB	Sequential	Write	**0.99879**
32KB	Sequential	Write	**0.99711**

(d) Throughput (file set: 150GB)

Size	Access	Type	R^2
4KB	Random	Read	**0.97489**
32KB	Random	Read	**0.95248**
4KB	Sequential	Read	**0.96628**
32KB	Sequential	Read	**0.99029**
4KB	Random	Write	**0.99323**
32KB	Random	Write	**0.98821**
4KB	Sequential	Write	**0.98905**
32KB	Sequential	Write	**0.93505**

5   Regression-Based Storage Performance Modeling

In order to effectively extract storage performance models, we apply linear regression using the read/write ratio as independent and the performance as dependent variables. The aim is to approximate the performance of mixed workloads. This analysis is applied once for a 1280MB and a 150GB file set respectively. The further system configurations are set to LPAR hypervisor, noop I/O scheduler, and EXT4 file system.

For a 1280MB file set, Table 2a and Table 2b show the coefficient of determination R^2 for linear regression models of the system performance when varying the proportion of the operation type. For the response time, sequential read-requests and 32KB write-requests exhibit a strong linear fit. For the throughput, all workloads exhibit a strong fit. In these cases, the linear performance model show to be effective approximations of the real performance. For random read requests and small write requests, we reason that the request queueing and scheduling in the storage system predominate the response time if the file set is fully cached. Therefore, the linear regression models fit nicely unless considering the pure workload for these scenarios, cf. Figure 4a.

For a 150GB file set, the result in Table 2c and Table 2d show to effectively approximate response time and throughput of workloads for varying read/write ratios. Even though there is one lower R^2 value, the approximation is still acceptable.

6   Related Work

Many general modeling techniques for storage systems exist, e.g., [6,7,8], but they are only shortly mentioned here as our work is focused on virtualized environments. The work closely related to the approach presented in this paper can be classified into two groups. The first group is focused on modeling storage performance in virtualized environments. Here, Kraft et al. [2] present two approaches based on queueing theory to predict the I/O performance of consolidated virtual machines. Their first, trace-based approach simulates the consolidation of homogeneous workloads. The environment is modeled as a single queue with multiple servers having service times fitted to a Markovian Arrival Process (MAP). In their second approach, they predict storage performance in consolidation of heterogeneous workloads. They create linear estimators based on mean value analysis (MVA). Furthermore, they create a closed queueing network model, also with service times fitted to a MAP. In [9], Ahmad et al. analyze the I/O performance in VMware's ESX Server virtualization. They compare virtual to native performance using benchmarks. They further create mathematical models for I/O throughput predictions. To analyze performance interference in a virtualized environment, Koh et al. [10] manually run CPU bound and I/O bound benchmarks. While they develop mathematical models for prediction, they explicitly focus on the consolidation of different types of workloads, i.e., CPU and I/O bound. By applying an iterative machine learning technique, Kundu et al. [11] use artificial neural networks to predict application performance in virtualized environments. Further, Gulati et al. [3] present a study on storage workload characterization in virtualized environments, but perform no performance analysis.

The second group of related work deals with benchmarking and performance analysis of virtualized environments not specifically targeted at storage systems. Hauck et al. [12] propose a goal-oriented measurement approach to determine performance-relevant infrastructure properties. They examine OS scheduler properties and CPU virtualization overhead. Huber et al. [13] examine performance overhead in VMware ESX and Citrix XenServer virtualized environments. They create regression-based models for virtualized CPU and memory performance. In [14], Barham et al. introduce the Xen hypervisor comparing it to a native system as well as other virtualization plattforms. They use a variety of benchmarks for their analysis to quantify the overall Xen hypervisor overhead. Iyer et al. [15] analyze resource contention when sharing resources in virtualized environments. They focus on measuring and modeling cache and core effects.

7   Conclusions

We presented a detailed analysis of the performance-influencing factors of I/O-intensive applications in virtualized environments. Our analysis and evaluation is based on a real world deployment of the state-of-the-art virtualization technology of the IBM System z and the storage system IBM DS8700 used in a controlled testing environment. Our multi-tiered storage environment consists of storage caches and RAID arrays and is representative for any virtualized storage environment.

By analyzing our environment, we first systematically identified the relevant storage-performance-influencing factors of I/O-intensive applications in virtualized environments. We modeled the factors using hierarchical feature trees and organized them by workload, operating system, and hardware. The models were of general nature and not specific to the considered environment. Second, we proposed a generic workload and benchmarking methodology and applied it to our environment in order to quantify the impact of the relevant storage-performance-influencing factors. We showed especially high performance influence of the read/write ratio in the workload and the CFQ I/O scheduler in the system configuration. Finally, we effectively extracted performance models based on linear regression for predicting the performance of varying read/write requests. Throughput of requests was approximated very well. Regarding response time, sequential reads and big writes were approximated well for a cached file set and almost all requests were approximated well when the file set size was larger than the cache size.

Acknowledgments. This work was funded by the German Research Foundation (DFG) under grant No. RE 1674/5-1 and grant No. KO 3445/6-1. We especially thank the Informatics Innovation Center (IIC)[5] for providing the system environment of the IBM System z and the IBM DS8700.

References

1. Armbrust, M., Fox, A., Griffith, R., Joseph, A.D., Katz, R., Konwinski, A., Lee, G., Patterson, D., Rabkin, A., Stoica, I., Zaharia, M.: A view of cloud computing. Commun. ACM 53(4), 50–58 (2010)
2. Kraft, S., Casale, G., Krishnamurthy, D., Greer, D., Kilpatrick, P.: Performance Models of Storage Contention in Cloud Environments. Springer Journal of Software and Systems Modeling (2012)
3. Gulati, A., Kumar, C., Ahmad, I.: Storage workload characterization and consolidation in virtualized environments. In: VPACT 2009 (2009)
4. Mell, P., Grance, T.: The nist definition of cloud computing. National Institute of Standards and Technology 53(6), 50 (2009)
5. Dufrasne, B., Bauer, W., Careaga, B., Myyrrylainen, J., Rainero, A., Usong, P.: Ibm system storage ds8700 architecture and implementation (2010), http://www.redbooks.ibm.com/abstracts/sg248786.html
6. Wang, M., Au, K., Ailamaki, A., Brockwell, A., Faloutsos, C., Ganger, G.R.: Storage device performance prediction with CART models. In: MASCOTS 2004, pp. 588–595 (2004)
7. Bucy, J.S., Schindler, J., Schlosser, S.W., Ganger, G.R., Contributors: The DiskSim Simulation Environment - Version 4.0 Reference Manual. Carnegie Mellon University, Pittsburgh (2008)
8. Lebrecht, A.S., Dingle, N.J., Knottenbelt, W.J.: Analytical and simulation modelling of zoned raid systems. The Computer Journal 54, 691–707 (2011)
9. Ahmad, I., Anderson, J., Holler, A., Kambo, R., Makhija, V.: An analysis of disk performance in vmware esx server virtual machines. In: WWC-6, pp. 65–76 (2003)
10. Koh, Y., Knauerhase, R., Brett, P., Bowman, M., Wen, Z., Pu, C.: An analysis of performance interference effects in virtual environments. In: ISPASS 2007, pp. 200–209 (2007)

---

[5] http://www.iic.kit.edu/

11. Kundu, S., Rangaswami, R., Dutta, K., Zhao, M.: Application performance modeling in a virtualized environment. In: HPCA 2010, pp. 1–10 (2010)
12. Hauck, M., Kuperberg, M., Huber, N., Reussner, R.: Ginpex: deriving performance-relevant infrastructure properties through goal-oriented experiments. In: QoSA-ISARCS 2011, pp. 53–62. ACM, New York (2011)
13. Huber, N., von Quast, M., Hauck, M., Kounev, S.: Evaluating and modeling virtualization performance overhead for cloud environments. In: CLOSER 2011 (2011)
14. Barham, P., Dragovic, B., Fraser, K., Hand, S., Harris, T., Ho, A., Neugebauer, R., Pratt, I., Warfield, A.: Xen and the art of virtualization. SIGOPS Oper. Syst. Rev. 37, 164–177 (2003)
15. Iyer, R., Illikkal, R., Tickoo, O., Zhao, L., Apparao, P., Newell, D.: Vm3: Measuring, modeling and managing vm shared resources. Computer Networks 53, 2873–2887 (2009)

Tradeoff between Accuracy
and Efficiency in the Time-Parallel Simulation
of Monotone Systems

J.M. Fourneau and F. Quessette

PRiSM, Université de Versailles-Saint-Quentin, CNRS UMR 8144, France

Abstract. We present a new version of the time-parallel simulation with fix-up computations for monotone systems. We use the concept of monotony of a model related to the initial state of the simulation to derive upper and lower bounds of the sample-paths. For a finite state space with some structural constraints, we prove that the algorithm provides bounds at the first step. These bounds are improved at every fix-up computation steps leading to a natural trade-off between accuracy of the simulation results and efficiency of the parallel computations. We also show that many queueing networks models satisfy these constraints and show the links with the monotone version of the Coupling From The Past technique.

1 Introduction

In a Time Parallel Simulation (TPS in the following), we consider a decomposition of the time axis and we perform the simulations on time intervals in parallel (see [13] chap. 6 and references therein). Afterwards the resulting parts of the path are combined to build the overall sample-path. It is known for a long time that TPS has a potential to massive parallelism [18]. Indeed as the number of logical processes is only limited by the number of times intervals which is a direct consequence of the time granularity and the simulation length, one can expect to efficiently use a large number of processors. This is much easier than the space decomposition approach, in which a grouping of state variables into subsets is assigned to parallel processors. These processors exchange messages about the scheduling of the future events to avoid temporal faults (conservative approach) or to correct them (opportunistic technique). Unfortunately the spatial decomposition approach has a limited parallelism and has in general an important overhead due to this synchronization of future events. Similarly, TPS may exhibit space faults: the final and initial states of adjacent time intervals do not necessarily coincide at interval boundaries, possibly resulting in incorrect state changes.

While both techniques may exhibit faults we need to correct, we advocate that TPS is easier to fix. Indeed, many properties of stochastic models help to handle efficiently these space faults exhibited by TPS. For instance, the parallel prefix computation technique [15] shows how to organize the computation on parallel processors when the simulation is based on the iterative application of

M. Tribastone and S. Gilmore (Eds.): EPEW/UKPEW 2012, LNCS 7587, pp. 80–95, 2013.

an associative operator. Otherwise, the regeneration theory [17], the forecasting of some points of the sample path [13], or the fast mixing property [18] to correct a guessed initial state during some some fix-up computations steps allow to have correct initial states at the beginning of the time-intervals, after some computations. When the parallel prefix technique does not apply the efficiency of TPS depends on our ability to guess the state of the system to initialize the simulation or to efficiently correct the initially guessed states when they are wrong to finally obtain a consistent sample-path after a small number of trials. We have previously introduced two properties of the model both related to monotony (inseq-monotony in [7] and hv-monotony in [6,9]), to increase this ability. In our approaches, the simulation model is seen as a deterministic black box with an initial state and one input sequence which computes one output sequence. All the randomness of the model is stored in the input sequence.

We define some orderings on the sequences and the states. A model is monotone when it preserves the ordering. If this property holds, we have proposed in [6,7] new approaches to improve the efficiency of TPS to compute an upper or a lower bound of the true output sequence. In performance evaluation or reliability studies, we must typically prove that the systems satisfy some quality of service requirements. Thus, it is sufficient to prove that the upper bound (or lower bound, depending on the measure of interest) of the output sequence satisfies the constraint. A bound is a much better information than an approximation which can be computed in a TPS approach when one does not fix the spatial faults [16].

Here we further develop the ideas presented in [6,9] and present some new algorithms for speculative computations and some numerical results. We show how we can build a sample-path for a bound of the exact simulation using some simulated parts and ordering relations without some of the fix-up phases proposed in [18]. The hv-monotony concept is related to the stochastic monotony to compare stochastic processes [10], to the non crossing property [1], and the event monotony which is the main assumption for the monotone Coupling From The Past algorithm for perfect simulation [19].

The technical part of the paper is organized as follows. The next two sections are used to introduce the basic knowledge about monotony of simulation models and the fix-up approach for TPS. In section 2, we define the comparison of sequences, the event monotony and the hv-monotony defined in [6,9]). Then, in Section 3, we give an algorithmic presentation of Nicol's approach of TPS with fix-up computation phases and the computation of bounds we have previously introduced for hv-monotone systems in [12]. Here we propose to compute upper and lower bounds at the same time. We also show that when these two bounds couple, we obtain an exact result. Thus our new algorithm is much more accurate than the other approaches we have previously published. In Section 4, we first present the new algorithm based on coupling and we explain why it allows more speed-up than the other techniques. Finally we present in Section 5 a simple example to illustrate the approach and show it is efficient to compute the sample-path in parallel.

2   A Brief Introduction for Monotone Models in Simulation

We define a simulation model as an operator on a sequence of parameters (typically the initial state) and an input sequence (typically inter arrival times and service times) which produces an output sequence (typically the state of the system or a reward) [7]. Let $\mathcal{M}$ be a simulation model. It is initialised with a state vector a and it receives an input sequence I to compute an output sequence O. This is written as $O = \mathcal{M}(a, I)$. As usual, an operator is monotone iff its application on two comparable inputs provides two output sequences which are also comparable. We have used the following point ordering (denoted as $\preceq_p$ in [7], but various orders are possible. This particular order is interesting, because it implies an easy comparison on the rewards computed on the output sequences as mentioned by Property 1.

Definition 1. *Let I_1 and I_2 be two sequences with length n. $I(m)$ is the m-th element of sequence I. $I_1 \preceq_p I_2$ if and only if $I_1(t) \leq I_2(t)$ for all index $t \leq n$.*

Property 1. *Assume that the rewards are computed with function r applied on state $O(t)$ at time t. If the rewards are non negative, then:*

$$O_1 \preceq_p O_2 \implies R(O_1) = \sum_t r(t, O_1(t)) \leq R(O_2) = \sum_t r(t, O_2(t)).$$

Many rewards such as moments and tails of distribution are non negative.

We have defined two properties which allows to compare the outputs of a simulation model when the change the input sequence (inseq-montone) or the initial state of the simulation (hv-monotone). In the context of queueing networks for instance, this will describe how evolve the sample-path of the population when we change the arrivals (inseq-monotony) or the initial population in the queue (hv monotony). We consider two arbitrary orderings $\preceq_\alpha$ and $\preceq_\beta$.

Definition 2 (inseq-monotone Model). *Let $\mathcal{M}$ be a simulation model, $\mathcal{M}$ is input sequence monotone (or inseq-monotone in the following) with respect to orderings $\preceq_\alpha$ and $\preceq_\beta$ if and only if for all parameter sequence a and input sequences I and J such that $I \preceq_\alpha J$, then $\mathcal{M}(a, I) \preceq_\beta \mathcal{M}(a, J)$.*

Definition 3 (hv-monotone Model). *Let $\mathcal{M}$ be a simulation model, $\mathcal{M}$ is monotone according to the input state or hidden variable (hv-monotone in the following), with respect to orderings $\preceq_\alpha$ and $\preceq_\beta$, if and only if for all parameter sets a and b such that $a \preceq_\alpha b$, then $\mathcal{M}(a, I) \preceq_\beta \mathcal{M}(b, I)$ for all input sequences I.*

We use in the following an event representation of the simulation model. Events are associated with transitions. Let ev be an event in this model and let x be a state, we denote by $ev(x)$ the state obtained by application of event ev on state x. It is more convenient that some events do not have any effect (for instance the end of service event on an empty queue will be a loop). The monotony property has already been defined for events and it is the key idea to design the monotone version of the Coupling From The Past algorithm [19].

Definition 4 (event -monotone). *An event ev is monotone if its probability does not depend on the state and for all states x and y, $x \preceq y$ implies that $ev(x) \preceq ev(y)$.*

We have proved in [12] that stochastic monotony of Discrete Time Markov Chains and event monotonyv implies hv-monotonicty of the simulation model when the state space is fully ordered. Note that hv-monotony or inseq-monotony do not imply strong stochastic monotony in general. It is worthy to remark that increasing the initial state does not in general result in an upper bounding sample-path as shown in Example 2. We first begin to recall the theorem proved in [12] and we illustrate the results with some examples.

Theorem 1. *We consider a state space endowed with a partial ordering. If the simulation model is event-monotone and if the output of the simulation at time t consists in the state at that time, then the simulation model is hv-monotone.*

Example 1 (DTMC). *Consider stochastic matrix M1 defined by:*

$$M1 = \begin{bmatrix} 0.1 & 0.1 & 0.7 & 0.1 \\ 0.1 & 0.1 & 0.2 & 0.6 \\ 0.0 & 0.1 & 0.3 & 0.6 \\ 0.0 & 0.0 & 0.1 & 0.9 \end{bmatrix}.$$

We find an event representation of this DTMC as shown in [8]:

$$M1 = \begin{bmatrix} e5 & e4 & e2+e3 & e1 \\ e5 & e4 & e3 & e1+e2 \\ 0.0 & e5 & e3+e4 & e1+e2 \\ 0.0 & 0.0 & e5 & e1+e2+e3+e4 \end{bmatrix},$$

with $Pr(e1) = 0.1$, $Pr(e2) = 0.5$, $Pr(e3) = 0.2$, $Pr(e4) = 0.1$ and $Pr(e5) = 0.1$, Assume the natural ordering on the integers. Clearly this representation is event monotone. Assume that the output of the model is the state of the Markov chain at each step and that the hidden variable is the initial state of the chain. Further assume a point ordering on the output sequence. Therefore the theorem state that for any input sequence: $\mathcal{M}_1(1, I) \preceq_p \mathcal{M}_1(2, 1)$. Consider the following input sequence of probability $(0.15, 0.65, 0.3, 0.02, 0.98)$ which gives the following sequence of events by an inverse transform method $I = (e2, e3, e2, e1, e5)$. We easily obtain $\mathcal{M}_1(1, I) = (3, 3, 4, 4, 3)$ and $\mathcal{M}_1(2, I) = (4, 4, 4, 4, 3)$ Note also that both simulations have coupled at time 3 on state 4.

Example 2 (DTMC 2). *Consider matrix $M2 = \begin{bmatrix} 0.1 & 0.2 & 0.6 & 0.1 \\ 0.2 & 0.1 & 0.1 & 0.6 \\ 0.0 & 0.1 & 0.3 & 0.6 \\ 0.2 & 0.0 & 0.0 & 0.8 \end{bmatrix}$. It is not st-monotone as row 2 is not stochastically smaller than row 1. Assuming an* *input sequence equal to $I = (0.15, 0.5, 0.15)$, we obtain that $\mathcal{M}_2(1, I) = (2, 4, 1)$ and $\mathcal{M}_2(2, I) = (1, 3, 3)$. Clearly the two vectors cannot be compared with the $\preceq_p$ ordering as the sample-paths cross each other.*

3   Fast Parallel Computation of Bounds of an Hv-Monotone System with TPS

We now present the approach proved in [12] to obtain bounds for the simulation of an hv-monotone system. As usual with many TPS techniques, we first divide the time interval $[0, T)$ into K equal sub-intervals $[t_i, t_{i+1}]$ with $t_1 = 0$ and $t_{K+1} = T$. K is the number of processors and each processor is assigned to the computation of the sample-path for one of these sub-intervals. Without loss of generality, we assume that for all i between 1 and K, logical process LP_i simulates sub- interval $[t_i, t_{i+1}]$. Let $X(t)$ be the state at time t during the exact simulation obtained in a centralised manner. The aim is to build a bound of $X(t)$ for t in $[0, T)$ through an iterative distributed algorithm. For a more detailed presentation of the difference with the classical approach where one compute exact results instead of bounds [18], see [12].

We now assume till the end of the paper that the system is hv-monotone.

The initial state of the simulation a is known and is used to initialise LP_1. In the other logical processes, the initial state is chosen at random or using some heuristics mentioned in [12]. Then the simulations are ran in parallel and the parts of the sample-path are obtained.

To be more precise, we need some notation. Let $Y_j^i(t)$ be the state of the system at time t obtained during the j-th iteration of logical process LP_i. When the simulation of the time intervals are completed, the ending states of each simulation (i.e. $Y_1^i(t_{i+1})$) are obtained. We can now check if the results obtained at the and of LP_i are consistent with the previous initialisation of LP_{i+1} (i.e. we compare $Y_j^i(t_{i+1})$ and $Y_{j-1}^{i+1}(t_{i+1})$). In the original approach [18], both states must be equal and part i must be consistent to prove that part LP_{i+1} is consistent. In our approach when we compute a lower bound, we just have to check that the final point of LP_i is larger than the initial point of LP_{i+1}. Due to the hv-monotone property, this proves that the part computed by LP_{i+1} will be a lower bound of the exact sample-path if LP_i is exact or is a lower bound of the exact sample-path. The consistency test is therefore much easier and we need less iterations until we obtain a complete sequence of consistent parts. Remember that we need such a complete sequence of consistent parts to build a consistent sample-path.

Suppose that the parts are not consistent, we must run a new set of parallel simulations for the inconsistent parts using $Y_j^i(t_{i+1})$ as starting point (i.e. $Y_{j+1}^{i+1}(t_{i+1}) \leftarrow Y_j^i(t_{i+1})$) of the next run on logical process LP_{i+1}. These new runs are performed with the same sequence of random inputs. Indeed, using the same input sequence may speed up the simulation due to coupling. Suppose now that for some t, we find that the new point $Y_k^i(t)$ is equal to a formerly computed point $Y_m^i(t)$. As the input sequence is the same for both runs, both sample-paths have now merged. Thus it is not necessary to build the new sample-path. Such a phenomenon is defined as the coupling of sample-paths. It is important to remark that the coupling of the sample-paths is not necessary for the proof of the TPS but it reduces the number of rounds before the whole simulation becomes coherent.

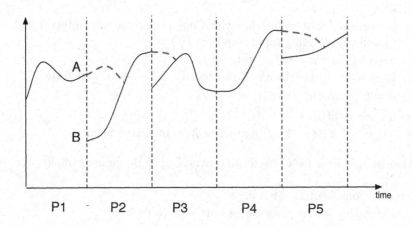

Fig. 1. TPS and bounds of the sample-path for an hv-monotone model

Note that the simulations are ran until all the parts are consistent. After each step, the number of consistent sample-paths will increase and the efficiency of the approach is related to the number of consistent parts at each step. It is clear that at the end of the first run, the simulation performed by LP_1 is consistent. Similarly by induction on i, at the end of round i, LP_i is consistent. It is the worst case we may obtain, and in that case the time to perform the simulation in parallel is equivalent to the time in sequential. Thus, the number of rounds before the whole simulation is consistent is smaller than the number of LP. Clearly computing a bound instead of the exact path leads to an increased number of consistent parts at each step of the simulation. The main result is stated in Theorem 2 and its proof (see [12]) is merely based on the transitivity of the order In Fig. 1, we have depicted two runs in a traditional TPS. The first run is in black lines, while the second is drawn in red doted lines. After the first run, we have obtained a lower bound of the exact sample path. The coupling is obtained during the second run to get an exact result.

Let us now give an algorithmic description of the approach. The computation efforts is distributed among the logical processes LP_i $(i = 1..K)$ which perform simulations and a Master process which must check the consistency of the partial sample-paths. The first logical process in charge of the simulation of the first time interval slightly differs for this general pseudo-code: $Y_1^1(t_1)$ is equal to a the initial state of the whole simulation (see [11] and [12] for a more detailed presentation of these algorithms).

——————————————— Algorithm LP_i ———————————————

1. $k \leftarrow 0$. Read in shared memory input sequence $I(t)$ for all t in $[t_i, t_{i+1}[$.
2. $Y_1^i(t_i) \leftarrow Random$.
3. Loop
    (a) k++.
    (b) Perform run k of Simulation with Coupling on the time interval $[t_i, t_{i+1}[$ to build $Y_k^i(t)$ using input sequence $I(t)$.
    (c) Send to the Master: the state $Y_k^i(t_{i+1})$.
    (d) Receive from the Master: Consistent(i) and a new initial state U.
    (e) If not Consistent(i) $Y_{k+1}^i(t_i) \leftarrow U$.
4. Until Consistent(i).
5. $\forall t \in [t_i, t_{i+1}[$, $X(t) \leftarrow Y_k^i(t)$ and write $X(t)$ in shared memory.

—— Algorithm Master for Computation of an Upper Bounding sample-path ——

1. For all i Consistent(i) $\leftarrow$ False.
2. Consistent(0) $\leftarrow$ True; LastConsistent $\leftarrow 0$; $k \leftarrow 0$.
3. Loop
    (a) k++.
    (b) For all i, if not Consistent(i) Receive from LP_i the state $Y_k^i(t_{i+1})$.
    (c) $Y_1^0(t_1) \leftarrow Y_1^1(t_1)$.
    (d) $i \leftarrow$ LastConsistent.
    (e) Loop
        i) i++;
        ii) if $(Y_k^i(t_i) = Y_k^{i-1}(t_i))$ and Consistent(i-1) then Consistent(i) $\leftarrow$ True;
        iii) elsif $(Y_k^i(t_i) > Y_k^{i-1}(t_i))$ and Consistent(i-1) then Consistent(i) $\leftarrow$ True;
    (f) Until (not Consistent(i)) or (i>K);
    (g) LastConsistent $\leftarrow i - 1$.
    (h) For all i send to LP_i Consistent(i) and the state $Y_k^{i-1}(t_i)$.
4. Until LastConsistent = K.

———————————————————————————————————————

Theorem 2. *Assume that the simulation model is hv-monotone, the new version of the Master for the TPS algorithm makes the logical simulation processes build a point-wise upper bound of the sample-path faster than the original approach. Furthermore the number of runs is smaller than in the traditional approach.*

In the next section, we show we can further improve the efficiency using the envelope technique.

4 Fast Parallel Computation of Bounds with TPS Based on Coupling

We assume that the state space is endowed with a partial ordering denoted $\preceq_\alpha$. We assume that the model is hv-monotone for the point ordering on the sequences and that the output of the model is the state at time t. We use the $\preceq_\alpha$ ordering to compare states. The main constraint of the approach is the existence of two states denoted as MinState and MaxState which are smaller (resp. larger) than all other states in the state-space.

We use the following idea: if two paths beginning at MinState and MaxState, and using the same input sequence I, have coupled, then any sample-path based on sequence I will also give the same ending point for the simulation of the time-segment. We build two sample-paths in any time segment (except the first one) and these paths begin these extremal states: MinState and MaxState. A typical first run of this new version of TPS is depicted in Fig. 2. One can observe a coupling of the two sample-paths for $LP3$.

This envelope technique associated to event monotone models is the basis for the monotone version of the Coupling From The Past technique for perfect simulation (see for instance [19] for the initial idea and [3] for a new approach). It has also been proposed in [1] to obtain an approximation of the sample path when their own definition of monotony does not hold.

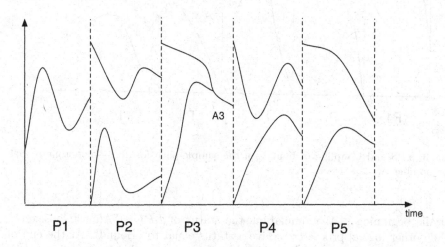

Fig. 2. TPS and Coupling of bounds of the sample-path for an hv-monotone model: first run

When the coupling occurs during the simulation at LP_i, the remaining part of the sample paths is independent of the initial state. Therefore the ending state of the segment computed at LP_i is exact and we can use it to obtain a correct sample-path of LP_{i+1} during the next run. The main advantage of this new approach is that we can obtain a consistent segment for LP_{i+1} even if LP_i is not consistent. Such a result was not true with the previous approaches. In all the algorithms proposed so far, the consistency of LP_{i+1} requires that LP_i must be consistent. To take advantage of this new property, the logical processes receive a status which can have the following values:

- "Consistent": the first state and the last state of the segment of the sample-paths are correct. By construction, the path between these two points is also correct.
- "AlmostConsistent": the first state is correct while the last state is not.
- "Coupled": the first state is unknown but as we have built upper and lower bounding paths which have coupled, the ending state is correct.
- "Bound: the first states and the last states are lower and bounds of the exact results.

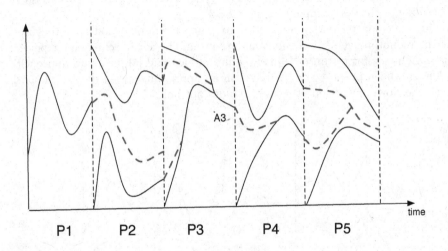

Fig. 3. TPS and Coupling of bounds of the sample-path for an hv-monotone model: run number two

At the beginning of the simulation, the status of $LP1$ is "AlmostConsistent" while other logical processes receive a status equal to "Bound". At the end of each run, the Master process modifies the status of each LP according to the results of the run and the former status of the LP and its neighbour. The Master uses the following rules to change the status and control the LP.

1. Once the status of LP_i is "Consistent", it remains "Consistent" until the end, and LP_i does not perform any new run.
2. If the former status of LP_i was "AlmostConsistent", the next simulation on LP_i builds a single path beginning with the initial state provided by LP_{i-1} and the status becomes "Consistent".

3. If the former status of LP_i was "Bound", and we observe that the two upper and lower bounding simulations have coupled during the run, the status becomes "Coupled".

4. If the status of LP_{i-1} at time t is "Consistent", and the status of LP_i is nor "Consistent", neither "AlmostConsistent", the status of LP_i is changed to "AlmostConsistent" and the final state of LP_{i-1} is used as a starting state for the next run on LP_i.

5. If the status of LP_{i-1} at time t is "Coupled", and the status of LP_i is not "Consistent", the status of LP_i is changed to "AlmostConsistent" and the final state of LP_{i-1} is used as a starting state for the next run of LP_i.

──────────── Algorithm LP_i for Coupling and Bounds ────────────

1. $k \leftarrow 0$. Read in shared memory input sequence $I(t)$ for all t in $[t_i, t_{i+1}[$.
2. Loop
    (a) k++.
    (b) Receive from the Master, Status(i) and two new initial states L (for sequence Y) and U (for sequence Z)
    (c) Perform run k of Simulation with Coupling on time interval $[t_i, t_{i+1}[$ to build $Y_k^i(t)$ using input sequence $I(t)$
    (d) If Status(i) $\neq$ "AlmostConsistent", then Perform run k of Simulation with Coupling on time interval $[t_i, t_{i+1}[$ to build $Z_k^i(t)$ using input sequence $I(t)$
    (e) Send to the Master, the states $Y_k^i(t_{i+1})$ and $Z_k^i(t_{i+1})$ if it has been computed
3. Until EndingCondition.
4. $\forall t \in [t_i, t_{i+1}[$, write $Y_k^i(t)$ and $Z_k^i(t)$ in shared memory.

──────────── Algorithm Master for Coupling and Bounds ────────────

1. Statuts(1)= "AlmostConsistent"; For all $i > 1$, Status(i)="Bound"; $k \leftarrow 0$.
2. $L_1 = a$; $U_1 = a$. For all $i > 1$, $L_i \leftarrow MinState$ and $U_i \leftarrow MaxState$;
3. Loop
    (a) k++.
    (b) For all i, if Status(i) $\neq$ "Consistent", then send to LP_i, Statuts(i) and the states L_i and U_i.
    (c) For all i, if Status(i) $\neq$ "Consistent", then receive from LP_i the states $Y_k^i(t_{i+1})$ and $Z_k^i(t_{i+1})$.
    (d) For all i such that Status(i) $\neq$ "Consistent" do
        i. If Status(i)= "AlmostConsistent" then Status(i)= "Consistent"
        ii. Else If $Y_k^i(t_{i+1}) = Z_k^i(t_{i+1})$ then Status(i)= "Coupled";
        iii. If Status(i-1)= "Consistent" then Status(i)= "AlmostConsistent".
        iv. If Status(i-1)= "Coupled" then Status(i)= "AlmostConsistent".
    (e) For all i such that Status(i) $\neq$ "Consistent" do
        i. $L_i \leftarrow Y_k^{i-1}(t_i)$
        ii. If Status(i)$\neq$ "AlmostConsistent" then $U_i \leftarrow Z_k^{i-1}(t_i)$.
4. Until EndingCondition.

Theorem 3. *This algorithm computes at each step a bound of the sample path.*

Proof: It is clear to the hv-monotone assumptions that, at the end of the first run, the two paths Y and Z provides respectively a lower bound and an upper bound of the exact sample-path. The transitions rules show that some part of the simulation are correct while the other parts give upper and bounds because they are sample paths initialized with extremal points and using the same input sequence I as all the simulations during these time segments.   □

The other advantage of this method is the convergence time. First at any time one can stop the algorithm and obtain upper and lower bounds. Second, the results improve with any new run, because parts which are "AlmostConsistent" become "Consistent", while the parts with status "Bounds" have improved the accuracy of their results. Finally, the time to obtain a correct answer decreases as soon as the first coupling occurs. Indeed, if LP_i becomes consistent at run t, LP_{i+1} becomes consistent at run $t + 1$. Therefore the estimated time decreases with a slope equal to one during this first phase. When the first coupling occur, we now have another LP which is consistent and which is not in the neighborhood of the other consistent LP. Therefore we now have two streams of consistent parts. We define the estimated time to obtain a correct sample path as the maximal number of consecutive LP which are not consistent. When coupling occurs, this number decreases very quickly (see example below) because of these number of streams used to propagate the consistency.

5   A Network of M/M/B/B Queues

It is known for a long time that many queueing networks exhibit some properties related to monotony [14]. One of the most interesting set of monotone models is described as networks of queues with index based routing (see [20] for a description and for a perfect simulation algorithm for these networks). In [20], the following property is given:

Property 1. If the indices used by index routing are non decreasing functions of the states, then the routing strategies are event monotone.

Combined with Theorem 1, this last property implies that many models are hv-monotone (see also [11]). For instance, the following routing strategies are event monotone:

- Jump the shortest queue.
- Jump the shortest response time queue.
- Route to the first available queue in an ordered list.
- Blocking between i and j: a simplest version of the previous strategy using list of size 2.
- Jump over blocking: a simplified version of the third item.

We first consider a single M/M/B/B queue to find the distribution of the coupling time. In Fig. 5, we have plotted the average time for coupling versus the

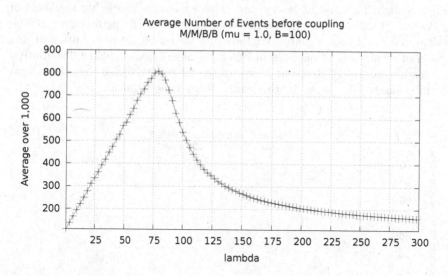

Fig. 4. Average number of events before coupling versus the arrival rate in a M/M/100/100

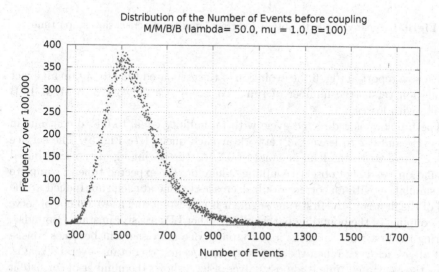

Fig. 5. Distribution of the number of events before coupling for a single M/M/100/100 when the load=0.8

arrival rate. The service rate is 1. Clearly the expected time before coupling is smaller at light load and at heavy load. The worst case is roughly at a load of 0.8. We will keep this load in the following to look at the performance of the method in a worst case scenario. We have also measured the distribution of this number of events before coupling. In Fig. 5, we have depicted such a distribution for a load equal to 0.8. Based on these numerical results we have chosen a time interval equal to 600 events for the length of the time segment.

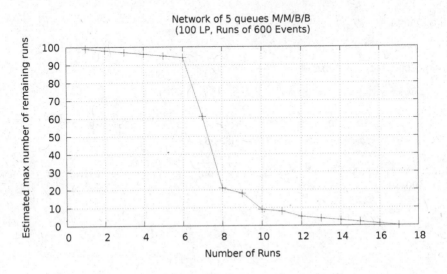

Fig. 6. Estimated Time to obtain a correct simulation versus simulation time

We now report in Fig. 6 the evolution of the estimated time to obtain an exact simulation versus the number of runs. We analyze a network of 5 M/M/B/B queues with losses.

The topology is a directed cycle with probability equal to 0.8 to continue in the cycle and 0.2 to leave the network at each queue (see Fig. 5). The service rate is equal to 1., the load is equal to 0.8. At the beginning of the distributed simulation, we do not observe coupling. Therefore the expected time to complete the simulation with an correct result decreases by one at each run. Indeed at the end of the first run, the first time segment is consistent and as we do not observe any coupling of the bounding paths, all the other LPs are still in state "Bounds". During the first runs, until the first coupling, one more segment becomes consistent after each run. When the first couplings occurs, we obtain several streams. Thus the estimated time is almost halved. Fig. 8 shows the number of consistent LP. It is also observed that as soon as the couplings occur (i.e. at runs 7 and 8), almost all the LP become consistent in a few runs. Both figures show that the coupling of the bounding paths have a large impact on the convergence speed of the algorithm.

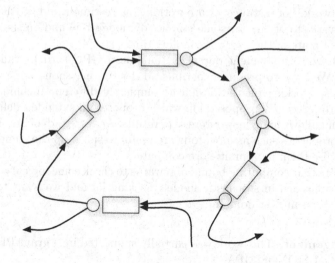

Fig. 7. The topology of the example

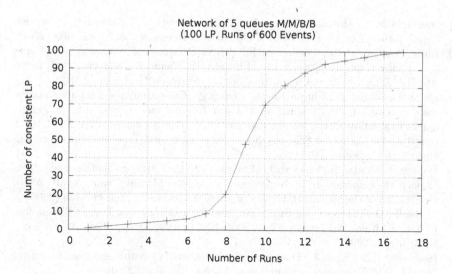

Fig. 8. Number of consistent LPs versus runs

6   Conclusion

Clearly the coupling time of the model plays an important role in the efficiency of our approach. Thus we have to further explore the theoretical and empirical issues on that domain to improve the results obtained in [4,2] for monotone queueing network. For instance we are working on Petri nets and Stochastic Automata Networks to obtain for some families of models a bound on the coupling time or an estimate of the average coupling time.

We also have to implement our algorithms on a GPU card to validate the approaches. We hope to present experimental results very soon.

We are also working on the design a completely different technique based on an algorithm recently proposed [3], which proposes an extended definition of monotony and allows many new interesting results. Again we advocate that some qualitative properties such as monotony are useful to speed up the computations or to reorganise them on a multi-core computer.

Finally note that computing bound of rewards to check some logical conditions is a typical approach in stochastic model checking [5] and we want to further test pour method in that domain..

Acknowledgement. This work was partially supported by a grant PEPS from CNRS, entitled MONOSIMPA.

References

1. Andradottir, S., Hosseini-Nasab, M.: Parallel simulation of transfer lines by time segmentation. European Journal of Operational Research 159(2), 449–469 (2004)
2. Bušić, A., Gaujal, B., Perronnin, F.: Perfect Sampling of Networks with Finite and Infinite Capacity Queues. In: Al-Begain, K., Fiems, D., Vincent, J.-M. (eds.) ASMTA 2012. LNCS, vol. 7314, pp. 136–149. Springer, Heidelberg (2012)
3. Bušić, A., Gaujal, B., Vincent, J.-M.: Perfect simulation and non-monotone markovian systems. In: Proceedings of the 3rd International Conference on Performance Evaluation Methodologies and Tools, ValueTools 2008, pp. 27:1–27:10. ICST (Institute for Computer Sciences, Social-Informatics and Telecommunications Engineering), Brussels (2008)
4. Dopper, J., Gaujal, B., Vincent, J.-M.: Bounds for the coupling time in queueing networks perfect simulation. In: Numerical Solutions for Markov Chain (NSMC 2006), Celebration of the 100th anniversary of Markov, Charleston, pp. 117–136 (2006)
5. El Rabih, D., Pekergin, N.: Statistical Model Checking Using Perfect Simulation. In: Liu, Z., Ravn, A.P. (eds.) ATVA 2009. LNCS, vol. 5799, pp. 120–134. Springer, Heidelberg (2009)
6. Fourneau, J.-M., Kadi, I.: Time parallel simulation of monotone systems. In: Poster Session, IFIP Performance Conference, Namur, Belgique (2010)
7. Fourneau, J.-M., Kadi, I., Pekergin, N.: Improving time parallel simulation for monotone systems. In: Turner, S.J., Roberts, D., Cai, W., El-Saddik, A. (eds.) 13th IEEE/ACM International Symposium on Distributed Simulation and Real Time Applications, Singapore, pp. 231–234. IEEE Computer Society (2009)
8. Fourneau, J.-M., Kadi, I., Pekergin, N., Vienne, J., Vincent, J.-M.: Perfect simulation and monotone stochastic bounds. In: Glynn, P.W. (ed.) Proceedings of the 2nd International Conference on Performance Evaluation Methodolgies and Tools, VALUETOOLS 2007, Nantes, France. Icst (2007)

9. Fourneau, J.-M., Kadi, I., Quessette, F.: Time parallel simulation and hv-monotonicity. In: Gelenbe, E., Lent, R., Sakellari, G. (eds.) Proceedings of the 26th Internation Symposium on Computer and Information Sciences. Springer Lectures Notes in Electrical Engineering, pp. 201–207 (2011)

10. Fourneau, J.-M., Pekergin, N.: An Algorithmic Approach to Stochastic Bounds. In: Calzarossa, M.C., Tucci, S. (eds.) Performance 2002. LNCS, vol. 2459, pp. 64–88. Springer, Heidelberg (2002)

11. Fourneau, J.-M., Quessette, F.: Monotone Queuing Networks and Time Parallel Simulation. In: Al-Begain, K., Balsamo, S., Fiems, D., Marin, A. (eds.) ASMTA 2011. LNCS, vol. 6751, pp. 204–218. Springer, Heidelberg (2011)

12. Fourneau, J.-M., Quessette, F.: Monotonicity and Efficient Computation of Bounds with Time Parallel Simulation. In: Thomas, N. (ed.) EPEW 2011. LNCS, vol. 6977, pp. 57–71. Springer, Heidelberg (2011)

13. Fujimoto, R.M.: Parallel and Distributed Simulation Systems. Wiley Series on Parallel and Distributed Computing (2000)

14. Glasserman, P., Yao, D.D.: Monotone Structure in Discrete-Event Systems. Series in Probability and Mathematical Statistics. Wiley Inter-Science, New York (1994)

15. Greenberg, A.G., Lubachevsky, B.D., Mitrani, I.: Algorithms for unboundedly parallel simulations. ACM Trans. Comput. Syst. 9(3), 201–221 (1991)

16. Kiesling, T.: Using approximation with time-parallel simulation. Simulation 81, 255–266 (2005)

17. Lin, Y., Lazowska, E.: A time-division algorithm for parallel simulation. ACM Transactions on Modeling and Computer Simulation 1(1), 73–83 (1991)

18. Nicol, D., Greenberg, A., Lubachevsky, B.: Massively parallel algorithms for trace-driven cache simulations. IEEE Trans. Parallel Distrib. Syst. 5(8), 849–859 (1994)

19. Propp, J., Wilson, D.: Exact sampling with coupled Markov chains and applications to statistical mechanics. Random Structures and Algorithms 9(1&2), 223–252 (1996)

20. Vincent, J.-M., Vienne, J.: Perfect simulation of index based routing queueing networks. SIGMETRICS Performance Evaluation Review 34(2), 24–25 (2006)

Compositional Approximate Markov Chain Aggregation for PEPA Models

Dimitrios Milios and Stephen Gilmore

School of Informatics, University of Edinburgh
10 Crichton Street, Edinburgh EH8 9AB, UK

Abstract. Approximate Markov chain aggregation involves the construction of a smaller Markov chain that approximates the behaviour of a given chain. We discuss two different approaches to obtain a nearly optimal partition of the state-space, based on different notions of approximate state equivalence.

Both approximate aggregation methods require an explicit representation of the transition matrix, a fact that renders them inefficient for large models. The main objective of this work is to investigate the possibility of compositionally applying such an approximate aggregation technique. We make use of the Kronecker representation of PEPA models, in order to aggregate the state-space of components rather than of the entire model.

1 Introduction

Markov chains have been used for many years for exploring the dynamic properties of systems that exhibit stochastic behaviour. They are supported by a great variety of techniques to obtain the steady-state and the transient probability distributions of such models. Many modelling formalisms generate Markov chains given some high-level description of the system. Unfortunately, even apparently simple models can generate extremely large state-spaces, a problem known as *state-space explosion*.

State-space aggregation can be an effective way to reduce the complexity of large Markov models. Aggregated models feature a reduced number of states, a fact that can accelerate transient and steady-state analysis techniques. Aggregation can be either exact or approximate. Exact aggregation of a Markov chain involves constructing a model with a smaller number of states that exhibits behaviour identical to that of the original system. If the original model is *lumpable*, then the resulting aggregated model will be a Markov chain as well. In the case of non-lumpable models, we use a reduced Markov model that approximates the behaviour of the original system. In this way, the model can be solved efficiently at the cost of loss of accuracy.

Existing approximate aggregation techniques [7][23][6] typically require the computation of several eigenvectors of the probability matrix. The great computational cost of this requirement renders these approaches not particularly popular in performance modelling. Instead, we take advantage of a compositional

M. Tribastone and S. Gilmore (Eds.): EPEW/UKPEW 2012, LNCS 7587, pp. 96–110, 2013.
© Springer-Verlag Berlin Heidelberg 2013

representation of the state-space, in order to apply approximate aggregation techniques on components rather than the entire system. The resulting reduced components are then combined to form an overall reduced state-space.

The modelling paradigm which we work with here is the PEPA language [13], and its Kronecker representation [15] in particular. A PEPA model is represented as a collection of interacting components, and each one of these has its own state-space and performs a number of actions that change its internal state. The global state of the system is expressed in terms of the local states of the components included. PEPA components can be considered as labelled continuous-time Markov chains (CTMC). We reduce the state-space of more than one component at the same time. Intuitively, the more components we approximate, the greater reduction of the global state-space we can achieve.

In order to partition the state-space of these CTMCs we apply two different approaches. The first one is a traditional approach which is related to near complete decomposability (NCD) and the spectral properties of Markov chains. The second one is a novel method that relies on the notion of quasi-lumpability. We note that in most cases we make use of the embedded discrete time Markov chain that is obtained after *uniformisation* [16].

Related work is outlined in Sect. 2. Section 3 briefly outlines the NCD-based approach. In Sect. 4 we present our approximate aggregation approach that is based on quasi-lumpability. In Sect. 5 we describe how approximate aggregation is applied in a compositional setting. Section 6 involves examples that demonstrate the performance of the two aggregation techniques. Finally, the conclusions and considerations for future work are summarized in Sect. 7.

2   Related Work

In terms of Markov chains, equivalence is formally described by the notion of *lumpability* [17]. As can be seen in [1], given a *lumpable* Markov chain we can obtain a *lumped* model which is also a Markov chain having identical transient and steady-state behaviour. State-space aggregation techniques that rely on this concept typically exploit the structure of some high-level description of the model. For example in [11], a lumpable partition is obtained by identifying isomorphic components of a PEPA model. In the general case though, a lumpable partition might not exist.

Quasi-lumpability, which was introduced in [9], captures approximate behaviour for Markov models. The term *near-lumpability* has been used to describe the same notion in [1], where the concept was generalized towards exactly and strictly lumpable Markov chains. Since we are interested in *nearly ordinarily lumpable* Markov models only, we shall use the term quasi-lumpability for the rest of the paper. Most of the research in the field so far aims at computing bounds for the state probabilities of quasi-lumpable Markov chains, assuming some partition of the state-space [9][10][8][2]. The computation of bounds of compositions of Markov chains has also been investigated in the context of Markov reward models [4] and PEPA [24]. Our goal is to develop a strategy to automatically obtain a partition of the state-space that is nearly optimal with respect to a measure related to quasi-lumpability.

Many existing approximate Markov chain aggregation techniques ([7][6]) rely on the notion of *near complete decomposability* (NCD) [3]. By definition, a completely decomposable Markov chain consists of uncoupled aggregates of states, which means that a random walk will never transition from one aggregate to another. This restriction is relaxed for nearly completely decomposable systems, where the aggregates are almost uncoupled. The relation between the spectral properties of probability matrices and NCD has been investigated in a number of works [20][22][12]. In [7], the structure of the eigenvectors has been used to partition the state-space of reversible Markov chains, in a way that minimizes the probability of transitioning between partitions. In [23], this framework has been extended to non-reversible models. In a more recent work [6], a similar approach for partitioning Markov models has been presented which is based on information theory.

However, spectral methods are not directly related to the notion of lumpability which formally captures equivalence between Markov chains. At this point, it is important to make a clear distinction between nearly completely decomposable and quasi-lumpable models. A Markov chain is nearly completely decomposable when there is a very small probability of transitioning from one part of the system to another, a fact that also implies quasi-lumpability as shown in [5]. In the general case however, a lumpable or a quasi-lumpable model does not have to be nearly completely decomposable. In this paper, we present results with respect to both quasi-lumpability and NCD approaches to approximately aggregate Markov models.

3   Aggregation Based on NCD

3.1   Spectral Segmentation of Markov Chains

Let us consider a reversible Markov chain with probability matrix P and steady-state distribution π. If $\Delta = \{A_1, \ldots, A_k\}$ is a partition of the state-space, we define the probability of the system moving from A_i to A_j in a single step:

$$Pr(A_i, A_j) = \frac{\sum_{i \in A_i, j \in A_j} \pi_i P_{ij}}{\sum_{i \in A_i} \pi_i} \tag{1}$$

Given a completely decomposable Markov model, we have $Pr(A_i, A_i) = 1$ and $Pr(A_i, A_j) = 0, \forall i \neq j$. This means that if the system is within a set of states A_i, it will never transition out of A_i. This condition is relaxed for nearly completely decomposable systems, where there is only a small probability of transitioning between parts of the system.

The eigenstructure of a probability matrix contains information about which parts of the Markov chain are almost invariant. As can be seen in [7], a probability matrix P with K invariant aggregates of states will have K eigenvalues that are equal to 1. It has been shown that states that belong to the same invariant set A_i have the same sign-structure when mapped onto the eigenvector that corresponds to eigenvalue $\lambda = 1$. Perturbation analysis that was performed in [7] shows that this property is mostly preserved for the largest K eigenvectors for a nearly completely decomposable system as well. Hence, the sign-structure of the corresponding eigenvectors has been used to identify almost invariant aggregates of states.

3.2   The Non-reversible Case

One key assumption made in the previous section is that we have a reversible Markov chain. In order to apply spectral segmentation to non-reversible Markov chains, we have to construct a reversible chain that approximates the original. Given some Markov process with probability matrix P and steady-state probability vector $\boldsymbol{\pi}$, its time reversal will have transition matrix $\bar{P}$ with elements:

$$\bar{P}_{ij} = P_{ji}\frac{\pi_j}{\pi_i} \qquad (2)$$

Of course in the reversible case, $P = \bar{P}$. In order to handle non-reversible models, we could construct a reversible one that shares some properties of the initial non-reversible Markov model and its time reversal. For instance, we consider the following process:

$$\tilde{P} = \frac{P + \bar{P}}{2} \qquad (3)$$

In the equation above, $\tilde{P}$ can be thought of as the mean process of the two. It is trivial to show that $\tilde{P}$ is a stochastic matrix with steady-state distribution $\boldsymbol{\pi}$. A similar approach appeared in [23], where a so-called *multiplicative reversibilisation* $\tilde{P} = P\bar{P}$ has been applied instead. In both cases though, there is an implicit assumption that the original non-reversible model has properties similar to those of the corresponding reversible process. This is true up to some extent, as both models have the same steady-state distribution. Thus, the eigenstructure of $\tilde{P}$ is used to obtain a partition of the state-space of P. Equation (3) implies that the closer to reversible P is, the better the approximation of its eigenproperties will be, when using $\tilde{P}$. However in cases where this is not true, this assumption could be a significant source of error. This is a consideration we try to investigate experimentally in Sect. 6.

4   Aggregation Based on Quasi-Lumpability

4.1   A Pseudo-metric Related to Quasi-Lumpability

Given a partitioning of the state-space, lumpability implies that states that belong to the same class have identical transition probabilities to each of the partitions. To describe states with approximately similar rather than identical behaviour, we have to relax this condition. Approximately similar behaviour is captured by the concept of *quasi-lumpability* [9]:

Definition 1 (Quasi-Lumpability). *A Markov chain with probability matrix P will be quasi-lumpable w.r.t. a partition $\Delta = \{A_1, \ldots, A_K\}$ with K equivalence classes, if for any two classes $A_k, A_l \in \Delta$, and for any two states $i, j \in A_k$:*

$$\left| \sum_{m \in A_l} P_{im} - \sum_{m \in A_l} P_{jm} \right| \leq \epsilon, \quad \epsilon \geq 0 \tag{4}$$

The quantity ϵ in the equation above corresponds to the maximum difference between elements that are assigned to the same class. If we consider the transition probability matrix P of a quasi-lumpable model, this can be represented as $P = P^- + P^\epsilon$, where P^- is a lumpable Markov chain and P^ϵ a matrix with no element greater than the ϵ quantity of (4). In general, most of the values of P^ϵ should be zero, while the non-zero elements should be small. As noted in [1], if ϵ is sufficiently small, the lumpable model with transition matrix P^- approximates the behaviour of the quasi-lumpable one.

Using (4), we can define a pseudo-metric that captures a kind of similarity distance between states. If we consider all the equivalence classes $A_1, \ldots, A_K$, we define the following quantity for any two states i, j that belong to the same equivalence class:

$$E_{i,j} = \sum_{l=1}^{K} \left| \sum_{m \in A_l} P_{im} - P_{jm} \right| \tag{5}$$

In the equation above, $E_{i,j}$ will be equal to zero, iff the Markov chain is lumpable with respect to the partition $\Delta = \{A_1, \ldots, A_K\}$. Since it is possible that $E_{i,j} = 0$ when $i \neq j$, $E_{i,j}$ is characterized as a pseudo-metric, rather than as a metric.

Hence, the optimal quasi-lumpable partition will be the one that minimizes the quantity $E_{i,j}$ for any two states in the same class. However, the value of $E_{i,j}$ depends not only on the transition probabilities of states i and j, but also on the way that the states are distributed across the classes. In other words, a different partitioning of the state-space will result in a completely different $E_{i,j}$ quantity for the very same i and j states. Thus, it is very difficult to design an algorithm that minimizes $E_{i,j}$ with respect to the partitioning.

Instead, we show that the pseudo-metric $E_{i,j}$ is bounded by a proper distance metric independent of the partitioning. Starting from (5), if we pull the inner sum out of the absolute value, we will have a larger value:

$$E_{i,j} \leq \sum_{l=1}^{K} \sum_{m \in A_l} |P_{im} - P_{jm}| \tag{6}$$

It is evident that the sums in the inequality above cover the entire state-space of the original Markov model. Thus, given that the initial model has N states, the right-hand side of the inequality above can be written as:

$$D_{i,j} = \sum_{n=1}^{N} |P_{in} - P_{jn}| \tag{7}$$

which is actually the *Manhattan distance* in the $\mathbb{R}^N$ space defined by the transition probabilities. To put it differently, we consider the states as N-valued vectors, where each one of the values is a transition probability to another state.

This shows that $D_{i,j} \geq E_{i,j}$. It is relatively straightforward to apply a clustering algorithm in order to identify K clusters such that the Manhattan distance $D_{i,j}$ is minimized for instances that belong to the same cluster. The minimization of $D_{i,j}$ will result in small values for $E_{i,j}$, and hence for the ϵ quantity in (4) as well.

4.2   The Clustering Algorithm

In order to obtain a partitioning of the state-space that minimizes the Manhattan distance for states in the same cluster, we have to apply a clustering algorithm. Such algorithms group the input data into *clusters* which minimize a distance metric between data in the same group. Typical clustering techniques, such as *K-means* or *Expectation-Maximization*, start from a randomly-picked initial solution and they perform a number of iterations until they converge to some optimum. Typically, multiple runs are required, as the solution obtained at each run is dependent on the initial randomly-picked solution.

In contrast, *spectral clustering* [19][21] implies that a dataset is partitioned depending on the eigenvectors of the *Laplacian* matrix, rather than on the local proximities of data-points. Concisely, the K eigenvectors that correspond to the largest K eigenvalues of the Laplacian are selected. The data is mapped to the rows of the $N \times K$ matrix formed by stacking these eigenvectors as columns. The clusters of data are well separated in this $\mathbb{R}^K$ space, meaning that it should be easy to identify a globally optimal clustering, in contrast to "conventional" clustering techniques whose solutions are only locally optimal. The algorithm of our choice is the one proposed by Ng et al in [21].

4.3   Quasi-Lumping

Assuming that we have a nearly optimal partition of the state-space, the next step is to construct a Markov chain that approximates the original model. Given some $N \times N$ lumpable matrix P with K equivalence classes $A_1, \ldots, A_K$, we define the corresponding $K \times K$ *lumped* matrix P' with entries:

$$P'_{ij} = \sum_{l \in A_j} P_{il} \tag{8}$$

where $i, j = 1, \ldots K$. We define a model to be *quasi-lumped* with respect to some matrix P, if it is lumped with respect to some matrix P^-, and $P = P^- + P^\epsilon$.

According to the definition of lumpability, the sums P'_{ij} in (8) for different states in the same class A_i will be the same. However, in the case of quasi-lumpable models they will only be approximately the same. The mean value is a reasonable approximator for populations characterized by almost the same value, so we construct the quasi-lumped matrix $\hat{P}$ with entries:

$$\hat{P}_{ij} = \frac{\sum_{k \in A_i} \sum_{l \in A_j} P_{kl}}{|A_i|} \tag{9}$$

where $|A_i|$ denotes the number of states included in class A_i. It is evident that in the lumpable case, Equation (9) degrades to (8).

5   Compositional Aggregation

So far, we have discussed two ways to approximately aggregate a Markov chain. However, neither of these is directly applicable in practice, as they both require an explicit representation of the generator matrix. Instead, we attempt to reduce only parts of the model that are going to be combined in a compositional way.

For that reason, we can use a high-level modelling formalism such as PEPA [13], that enables us to model the system as a collection of cooperating components. The idea is to utilize a compositional representation of the underlying Markov chain of a PEPA model, or more accurately, a compositional representation of the corresponding generator matrix. This is actually possible by using the Kronecker form of a PEPA model, where the "global" generator matrix is defined in terms of the "partial" generator matrices of cooperating components combined via Kronecker algebra. It should be feasible to produce reduced versions of such partial generator matrices, and then combine them to obtain an approximately aggregated state-space.

As shown in [15], the generator matrix Q that corresponds to a PEPA model can be represented as a Kronecker product of terms in the following way:

$$Q = \bigoplus_{i=1}^{N} R_i + \sum_{a \in \mathcal{A}} r_a \times \left(\bigotimes_{i=1}^{N} P_{i,a} - \bigotimes_{i=1}^{N} \bar{P}_{i,a} \right) \tag{10}$$

where

- N is the number of components in the PEPA model.
- $\mathcal{A}$ is the set of shared actions.
- R_i is the rate matrix of i-th component based on its individual actions.
- r_a is the minimum *functional rate* of the shared action a over all components. The term 'functional rate' implies that the rate of an action depends on the state of one or more components. Equivalently, there is a single rate function $r_\alpha(C)$ that describes the apparent rate of action α for each state of component C. The minimum of the functional rates over all components C_i, $i = 1 \dots N$ is defined as follows:

$$r_\alpha = \min(r_\alpha(C_1), r_\alpha(C_2), \dots r_\alpha(C_N)) \tag{11}$$

- $P_{i,a}$ is the probability matrix of the i-th component for the shared action a. $\bar{P}_{i,a}$ is a diagonal matrix that ensures that the row sums of the corresponding probability matrix are zero, i.e. it is a valid generator matrix.

A useful observation regarding (10) is that any component C_i is described by two transition rate matrices: R_i which depends on its individual actions only, and $R_i^{(coop)} = \sum_{a \in \mathcal{A}} r_a P_{i,a}$ which cannot be determined, since we do not know the apparent rates of the cooperating components. If the set of shared actions is relatively small, we can expect that R_i will be much more dense than $R_i^{(coop)}$. If this condition holds, it should be reasonable to apply an approximate aggregation algorithm to R_i, in order to obtain a nearly optimal partition of this partial state-space.

This approach could be problematic though, as eliminating a shared action in a particular component may introduce deadlocks in its behaviour. For example, consider a component C_i with rate matrices:

$$R_i = \begin{bmatrix} 0 & 0 & 0 & 0 & 2 \\ 3 & 0 & 6 & 0 & 0 \\ 0 & 3 & 0 & 0 & 4 \\ 0 & 0 & 0 & 0 & 0 \\ 0 & 0 & 0 & 5 & 0 \end{bmatrix} \quad R_i^{(coop)} = \begin{bmatrix} 0 & 0 & 3 & 0 & 0 \\ 0 & 0 & 0 & 0 & 0 \\ 0 & 0 & 0 & 1 & 0 \\ 0 & 3 & 0 & 6 & 0 \\ 0 & 0 & 2 & 0 & 0 \end{bmatrix}$$

In the example above, R_i contains a deadlock at the fourth state, meaning that there is no non-trivial steady-state distribution over R_i in isolation, hence no way to compute the reversible process needed to apply the NCD-based approach, as described in Sect. 3.2. To solve this problem, we use the $\hat{R}_i$ matrix instead, which is constructed as in the following example:

$$\hat{R}_i = \begin{bmatrix} 0 & 0 & \varepsilon & 0 & 2 \\ 3 & 0 & 6 & 0 & 0 \\ 0 & 3 & 0 & \varepsilon & 4 \\ 0 & \varepsilon & 0 & \varepsilon & 0 \\ 0 & 0 & \varepsilon & 5 & 0 \end{bmatrix}$$

where $\varepsilon > 0$ is a small rate added to some transition for each shared action. Hence, if the original PEPA model contains no deadlocks, we can be sure that $\hat{R}_i$ will have no deadlocks either. By doing so, we obtain a partition of the component's state-space by using only a part of its behaviour. The ε rates added are equally distributed and therefore imply ignorance about the shared action rates.

The partitioning obtained using $\hat{R}_i$ is applied to both R_i and $R_i^{(coop)}$. Thus, the $N_i \times N_i$ partial generator matrix $Q_i = R_i + R_i^{(coop)}$ is approximated by the $K_i \times K_i$ matrix $Q_i' = R_i' + R_i'^{(coop)}$, where K_i is the number of partitions for the component C_i. Combining the reduced partial generator matrix Q_i using the Kronecker operations defined in (10), will result in a reduced global generator as well.

The state-space of a single sequential component does not usually involve more than a few states in typical models. It would be more effective if we could approximate components with a few hundreds of states instead. For that purpose, we apply clustering to cooperations of components rather than applying it to single sequential components. The cooperation rate matrix $R^{(coop)}$ of a non-sequential C component involves only actions that are shared with components outside the cooperation. Hence, actions shared between sequential components included in the cooperation will only affect the individual rate matrix of C. In the context of this work, we apply the approximate reduction algorithms to populations of identical components.

6   A Multi-scale Example

We compare the two different approaches for approximate Markov chain aggregation. The quasi-lumpability based approach described in Sect. 4 involves applying a clustering algorithm on the row entries of the transition probability matrix of a Markov chain. The NCD based approach discussed in Sect. 3 partitions the Markov chain according to the eigenvectors that correspond to the top eigenvalues of the probability matrix. Irreversible chains are handled by constructing a reversible process according to (3). For each one of the examples that follow, we explicitly note which components have been approximated and what compression ratio has been used. Once a nearly optimal partition of the state-space is obtained using either of the two methods, a reduced Markov chain is constructed as described in Sect. 4.3.

Eventually, we compare the transient and the steady-state behaviour of the initial model with those of the approximately aggregated models. The PRISM model checker [18], its sparse engine in particular, has been used for that purpose. The Jacobi algorithm has been applied for computing the steady-state distribution, and the uniformisation method for the transient probabilities. The experiments have been performed in an Intel® Quad-Core Xeon™ @ 3.20GHz PC running Linux.

At this point, we define a simple example to demonstrate the potential of the compositional approximate aggregation. We shall consider models featuring high-population components, as even simple model descriptions can lead to very large state-spaces. In particular, multi-scale models are of interest since more efficient approaches such as fluid flow approximation [14] are not as readily applicable, because they make an assumption of continuity which is strained at low population numbers. So we consider a peer-to-peer system that involves large numbers of peers that communicate with each other with the help of an indexing server, as described in the following PEPA model:

$$PeerA \stackrel{def}{=} (localAction_A, r_{localA}).PeerA_{local}$$
$$+ (lookup_B, \top).PeerA_{lookup}$$
$$PeerA_{local} \stackrel{def}{=} (finish_A, r_{finishA}).PeerA$$
$$PeerA_{lookup} \stackrel{def}{=} (cache_A, r_{cacheA}).PeerA_{local}$$
$$+ (exchange, r_{exchangeA}).PeerA$$

$$PeerB \stackrel{def}{=} (localAction_B, r_{localB}).PeerB_{local}$$
$$+ (lookup_A, \top).PeerB_{lookup}$$
$$PeerB_{local} \stackrel{def}{=} (finish_B, r_{finishB}).PeerB$$
$$PeerB_{lookup} \stackrel{def}{=} (cache_B, r_{cacheB}).PeerB_{local}$$
$$+ (exchange, r_{exchangeB}).PeerB$$

Our system involves two classes of peers which exchange data pairwise. Both types of peers have some local functionality and a shared activity called *exchange*. Moreover, a peer will have to look up other peers in an indexing server before proceeding to any data exchange.

$$
\begin{aligned}
Index &\stackrel{def}{=} (lookup_A, r_{lookupA}).Index_{busyA} \\
&+ (lookup_B, r_{lookupB}).Index_{busyB} \\
&+ (fail, r_{fail}).Index_{broken} \\
Index_{busyA} &\stackrel{def}{=} (refresh, r_{refresh}).Index \\
&+ (fail, r_{fail}).Index_{broken} \\
Index_{busyB} &\stackrel{def}{=} (refresh, r_{refresh}).Index \\
&+ (fail, r_{fail}).Index_{broken} \\
Index_{broken} &\stackrel{def}{=} (repair, r_{repair}).Index
\end{aligned}
$$

Table 1. Rate values used in the examples

Name	Value	Name	Value	Name	Value
r_{localA}	5	r_{localB}	2	$r_{lookupA}$	10
$r_{finishA}$	4	$r_{finishB}$	3	$r_{lookupB}$	10
r_{cacheA}	1	r_{cacheB}	2	r_{fail}	0.02
$r_{exchangeA}$	1	$r_{exchangeB}$	0.5	$r_{refresh}$	10
				r_{repair}	0.5

6.1 Compositional vs Global Aggregation

In this experiment we define a system small enough to compare the compositional approximate aggregation with a globally applied approach. The first system's structure is summarized in the following system equation, with cooperation sets $\mathcal{L} = \{exchange\}$ and $\mathcal{K} = \{lookup_A, lookup_B\}$.

$$
System_{5:5:1} \stackrel{def}{=} PeerA[5] \bowtie_{\mathcal{L}} PeerB[5] \bowtie_{\mathcal{K}} Index
$$

If we apply exact aggregation as described in [11], the number of states for the $PeerA[5]$ and $PeerB[5]$ components will be 21 (these would be 243 for each with no aggregation). Therefore, we distinguish the following cases:

i. $PeerA[5]$ and $PeerB[5]$ components are further reduced independently. The compression ratio used is 0.5 for both, resulting in a reduced chain of 400 states.
ii. Approximate aggregation is applied on the entire system's generator matrix. The compression ratio used was such that it results in a reduced chain of 400 states again.

The *K-L divergence* is a very popular measure for comparing probability distributions. For two probability vectors p and q, it is defined as:

$$
KL(p\|q) = \sum_i p_i \log \frac{p_i}{q_i} \tag{12}
$$

Table 2. Execution Times for $System_{5:5:1}$

	Original	Quasi-Lumpability (Compositional)	NCD (Compositional)	Quasi-Lumpability (Global)	NCD (Global)
Approximation	-	0.15 sec	0.2 sec	205 sec	130 sec
PRISM Loading	2 sec	0.5 sec	0.5 sec	0.5 sec	0.5 sec
Transient Solution[a]	2.1 sec	0.6 sec	0.6 sec	0.6 sec	0.6 sec
Steady-State solution	0.2 sec	0.05 sec	0.05 sec	0.05 sec	0.05 sec
Total Time	4.3 sec	1.3 sec	1.35 sec	206.15 sec	131.15 sec
Number of states	1764	400	400	400	400

[a] 100 points: $0 \leq t \leq 2$

Given a partition of the state-space with K classes, we define p as a K-valued vector containing the aggregated probabilities of the original system according to the partition of the state-space used. Then, q will be a K-valued vector containing the probabilities of the corresponding reduced model, which is produced by either the quasi-lumpability or the NCD approach. We want to see which one of the approximation approaches results in the lowest K-L divergence from the original state distribution.

The quasi-lumpability and the NCD based approaches have been applied in both a compositional and a global setting. Figure 1(a) summarizes the K-L divergences at different times t, for the four approximate aggregation methods. Judging by the K-L divergences, global aggregation does not appear to be far superior to the compositional approaches. Although there is no proof that this statement generalizes to every possible model, it seems reasonable to use compositional aggregation in order to produce a reasonable approximation of the original stochastic process. This argument is supported by Table 2, which summarizes the running times for aggregating and solving the model. As expected, compositional aggregation requires a very small initial cost to reduce the model, in contrast to the global case.

A second observation with respect to Fig. 1(a) is that neither the quasi-lumpability nor the NCD based approach seems to produce significantly more accurate results. In fact, the graphs are rather contradictory, as the global setting seems to favour quasi-lumpability, while in the compositional case NCD is the method that performs better. Figure 1(b) depicts the K-L divergences for $System_{10:20:2}$ of the next section. For this larger model, the compositionally applied quasi-lumpability approach is more accurate. Therefore, it seems reasonable to conclude that approximation accuracy is dependent on the properties of the model.

6.2   Approximation of Component Behaviour

This second example provides a more detailed view of component behaviour. The following system equation is considered, with cooperation sets $\mathcal{L} = \{exchange\}$

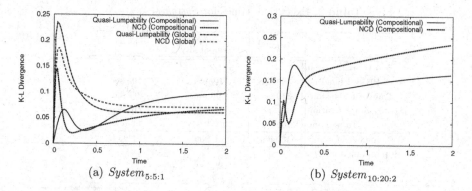

Fig. 1. Evolution of K-L divergences of various methods from the original state distribution

and $\mathcal{K} = \{lookup_A, lookup_B\}$.

$$System_{10:20:2} \overset{def}{=} PeerA[10] \underset{\mathcal{L}}{\bowtie} PeerB[20] \underset{\mathcal{K}}{\bowtie} Index[2]$$

If we apply exact aggregation as described in [11], the number of states for the $PeerA[10]$ component will be 66, while $PeerB[20]$ will have 231 states (these would be $59,049$ and $3,486,784,401$ states with no aggregation). Although neither of the components is particularly large, their combination results in a large state-space. However, it is relatively easy to further reduce $PeerA[10]$ and $PeerB[20]$ independently. The compression ratio used is 0.5 for both components.

This approximation of individual components results in significant reduction of the total state-space. As can be seen in Table 3, this reduction required only a small initial cost, while it resulted in a considerable decrease of the analysis time. A global reduction of the state-space would be practically infeasible for a models of such size. Figure 2(a) depicts the evolution of the average populations of the model components that have been reduced. Those figures seem to be reasonable approximations of the original model's average behaviour.

It would also be interesting though to look at the behaviour of the components that have not been approximated. Figure 2(b) depicts the evolution of the average $Index$ populations. Both quasi-lumpability and NCD-based approach result in approximations very close to the original solution. This provides evidence that supports the claim that the behaviour of the unreduced components will be mostly unaffected, given a good partition of the state-space. Intuitively, we can approximately aggregate components whose behaviour is of minor importance and still obtain a very good approximation for the components that have not been approximated, which might be critical. In our example, if we were interested in the indexing servers' behaviour only, the approximation error would be negligible.

Table 3. Execution Times for $System_{10:20:2}$

	Original	Quasi-Lumpability	NCD
Approximation	-	1.2 sec	1.5 sec
PRISM Loading	433 sec	105 sec	105 sec
Transient Solution[b]	310 sec	93 sec	93 sec
Steady-State solution	21 sec	6 sec	6 sec
Total Time	764 sec	205.2 sec	205.5 sec
Number of states	152460	37950	37950

[b] 100 points: $0 \leq t \leq 2$

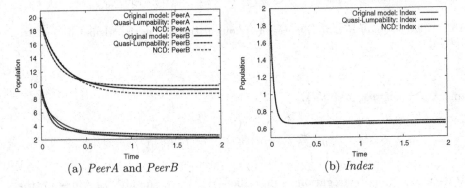

(a) *PeerA* and *PeerB*   (b) *Index*

Fig. 2. Evolution of average populations for $System_{10:20:2}$

7   Conclusions

Although approximate Markov chain aggregation is not a new concept, it has not been particularly popular in the field of Markovian modelling, since an explicit representation of the transition matrix is typically required. In this paper, we have examined two different methods to approximately aggregate a Markov chain, and we have explored the potential of applying aggregation in a compositional way.

The traditional method for selecting a nearly optimal partition of the state-space makes use of the eigenstructure of the probability matrix. We have described this family of approaches as the NCD approach, since the eigenvectors convey information about parts of the state-space that are nearly completely decomposable. We have tried to define an alternative strategy of state-space aggregation that relies on the concept of quasi-lumpability instead. More specifically, quasi-lumpability has been associated with the minimization of the $E_{i,j}$ measure between states in the same class. It has been shown that a simple clustering algorithm can be used to obtain an upper bound for this measure.

Intuitively, the quasi-lumpability approach should be superior, since a nearly completely decomposable system is essentially quasi-lumpable, but not vice-versa.

Experimental results do not support this hypothesis though. In fact, it appears that some models favour the quasi-lumpability approach, while others the NCD approach. This can be attributed to the fact that the quasi-lumpability method is suboptimal, since it minimizes only an upper bound for $E_{i,j}$. A better approximation of the total $E_{i,j}$ error will be the subject of future work.

By using the Kronecker representation of PEPA models, we were able to reduce the local state-space of the labelled CTMCs that correspond to PEPA components. This practice resulted in a great reduction of the state-space size with a small initial cost for aggregating the PEPA components, in contrast with aggregating the entire Markov chain. The multi-scale example presented demonstrates the potential of compositional approximate aggregation in two ways. Firstly, the compositional approach resulted in a reasonable approximation of the original model, especially when compared to a global approach. Secondly, the error in the approximation of the unreduced components was found to be negligible, which means that critical components can be excluded from aggregation.

A final note on the applicability of our approach is that the approximated components are required to have a set of shared actions that is relatively small when compared to their set of individual actions. That would mean that the individual rate matrix is dense enough to apply a partitioning algorithm on it. Therefore, our approach is mostly applicable to models that can be decomposed to weakly dependent components. This is apparently related to the notion of quasi-separability, which has been applied to PEPA before [25]. A characterisation of the applicability of compositional aggregation in terms of quasi-separability is an interesting direction for future work.

Acknowledgments. The authors are supported by SynthSys, a Centre for Integrative Systems Biology (CISB) funded by BBSRC and EPSRC, reference BB/D019621/1.

References

1. Buchholz, P.: Exact and ordinary lumpability in finite Markov chains. Journal of Applied Probability 31(1), 59–75 (1994)
2. Bušić, A., Fourneau, J.: Bounds based on lumpable matrices for partially ordered state space. In: ICST Workshop on Tools for Solving Markov Chains. ACM (2006)
3. Courtois, P.: Decomposability, instabilities, and saturation in multiprogramming systems. Communications of the ACM 18(7), 371–377 (1975)
4. Daly, D., Buchholz, P., Sanders, W.H.: Bound-preserving composition for Markov reward models. In: Quantitative Evaluation of Systems, pp. 243–252. IEEE Computer Society (2006)
5. Dayar, T., Stewart, W.: Quasi lumpability, lower-bounding coupling matrices, and nearly completely decomposable Markov chains. SIAM Journal on Matrix Analysis and Applications 18(2), 482–498 (1997)
6. Deng, K., Sun, Y., Mehta, P., Meyn, S.: An information-theoretic framework to aggregate a Markov chain. In: American Control Conference, pp. 731–736. IEEE Press (2009)

7. Deuflhard, P., Huisinga, W., Fischer, A., Schütte, C.: Identification of almost invariant aggregates in reversible nearly uncoupled Markov chains. Linear Algebra and its Applications 315(1-3), 39–59 (2000)
8. Fourneau, J., Lecoz, M., Quessette, F.: Algorithms for an irreducible and lumpable strong stochastic bound. Linear Algebra and its Applications 386, 167–185 (2004)
9. Franceschinis, G., Muntz, R.: Bounds for quasi-lumpable Markov chains. Performance Evaluation 20(1-3), 223–243 (1994)
10. Franceschinis, G., Muntz, R.: Computing bounds for the performance indices of quasi-lumpable stochastic well-formed nets. IEEE Transactions on Software Engineering 20(7), 516–525 (1994)
11. Gilmore, S., Hillston, J., Ribaudo, M.: An efficient algorithm for aggregating PEPA models. IEEE Transactions on Software Engineering 27(5), 449–464 (2001)
12. Hartfiel, D.: On the structure of stochastic matrices with a subdominant eigenvalue near 1. Linear Algebra and its Applications 272(1-3), 193–203 (1998)
13. Hillston, J.: A compositional approach to performance modelling. Cambridge University Press (1996)
14. Hillston, J.: Fluid flow approximation of PEPA models. In: Quantitative Evaluation of Systems, pp. 33–42. IEEE Computer Society (2005)
15. Hillston, J., Kloul, L.: An Efficient Kronecker Representation for PEPA Models. In: de Luca, L., Gilmore, S. (eds.) PAPM-PROBMIV 2001. LNCS, vol. 2165, pp. 120–135. Springer, Heidelberg (2001)
16. Jensen, A.: Markoff chains as an aid in the study of Markoff processes. Skandinavisk Aktuarietidskrift 36, 87–91 (1953)
17. Kemeny, J., Snell, J.: Finite Markov Chains. Springer (1976)
18. Kwiatkowska, M., Norman, G., Parker, D.: PRISM: probabilistic model checking for performance and reliability analysis. ACM SIGMETRICS Performance Evaluation Review 36(4), 40–45 (2009)
19. Malik, J., Shi, J.: Normalized cuts and image segmentation. IEEE Transactions on Pattern Analysis and Machine Intelligence 22(8), 888–905 (2000)
20. Meyer, C.D.: Stochastic complementation, uncoupling Markov chains, and the theory of nearly reducible systems. SIAM Review 31(2), 240–272 (1989)
21. Ng, A., Jordan, M., Weiss, Y.: On spectral clustering: Analysis and an algorithm. Advances in Neural Information Processing Systems 14(1), 849–856 (2001)
22. Pokarowski, P.: Uncoupling measures and eigenvalues of stochastic matrices. Journal of Applied Analysis 4(2), 259–267 (1998)
23. Runolfsson, T., Ma, Y.: Model reduction of nonreversible Markov chains. In: IEEE Conference on Decision and Control, pp. 3739–3744. IEEE (2008)
24. Smith, M.: Compositional abstractions for long-run properties of stochastic systems. In: Quantitative Evaluation of Systems, pp. 223–232. IEEE Computer Society (2011)
25. Thomas, N., Bradley, J.: Analysis of Non-product Form Parallel Queues Using Markovian Process Algebra. In: Kouvatsos, D.D. (ed.) Next Generation Internet. LNCS, vol. 5233, pp. 331–342. Springer, Heidelberg (2011)

A Path Connection Availability Model
for MANETs with Random Waypoint Mobility

Osama Younes and Nigel Thomas

School of Computing Science, Newcastle University, UK
{Osama.Younes,Nigel.Thomas}@ncl.ac.uk

Abstract. Understanding the factors that affect the path connection availability in multi-hop ad hoc networks can help to understand the path stability under various degrees of system dynamics. In addition, the connection availability of paths can be used as a global measure for the performance of ad hoc networks. To the best of our knowledge, there is no analytical study that provides a closed form solution for analytical analysis of connection availability of paths in multi-hop ad hoc networks with random waypoint mobility. This work proposes a closed form solution for this problem using a new stochastic reward net model. The influences of different factors, such as the number of nodes in the network, transmission range, network area size, data transmission rate, and routing protocol on the path connection availability are investigated. The proposed model is validated by extensive simulations.

1 Introduction

In MANETs, the route or path is the sequence of mobile nodes which data packets pass through in order to reach the intended destination node from a given source node. Due to the mobility of nodes, mobile ad hoc networks have inherently dynamic topologies. Therefore the routes are prone to frequent breaks (called mobility failure) which reduce the throughput of the network compared to wired or cellular networks. Consequently, the route followed by packets to reach the destination varies frequently. This is a crucial factor that affects the performance of the network.

In this work, we propose a closed form solution using a new Stochastic Reward Net (SRN) [1] model to analyse the path connection availability in multi-hop ad hoc networks where nodes move according to the random waypoint mobility model. The effects of link failure due to the mobility of nodes on the path connection availability in MANETs are analytically investigated using the proposed model. In addition, influences of different factors, such as the number of nodes in the network, transmission range, network area size, data transmission rate, and routing protocol on the path connection availability are investigated. The proposed model incorporates the characteristics of reactive routing protocols such as Dynamic Source Routing (DSR) and Ad hoc On-demand Distance Vector (AODV).

Although the random waypoint mobility model is one of the most commonly used mobility models in MANET studies, to the best of our knowledge, there is no analytical study that investigates the path connection availability in multi-hop ad hoc networks with this mobility model. This is because the spatial distribution of nodes

M. Tribastone and S. Gilmore (Eds.): EPEW/UKPEW 2012, LNCS 7587, pp. 111–126, 2013.
© Springer-Verlag Berlin Heidelberg 2013

moving with random waypoint is non-uniform which significantly complicates the analysis of the network

The rest of this paper is organized as follows. Related work is discussed in Section 2. Section 3 describes the ad hoc network model that illustrates the path failure and repair mechanisms. In Section 4, the proposed SRN model for connection availability of paths in ad hoc networks is described. Section 5 drives expressions for parameters of the SRN model. The proposed model is verified by extensive simulations in Section 6. Finally, some conclusions are drawn in Section 7.

2   Related Work

Xianren *et al* [2] proposed a model to estimate the route duration in MANETs when nodes move according to the random walk or random waypoint mobility models. This work extended [3] and [4] by relaxing their limiting conditions. The authors analysed the route duration in multi-hop paths by computing the minimum route duration of two-hop routes. The drawback of this work is that the authors assume that the probability density function (PDF) of the route duration for a two-hop route is known.

Pascoe-Chalke *et al* [5] derived statistical results of link and path availability properties. They described a probability distribution function for availability over one-hop, assuming that nodes move according to random walk mobility, which has been used to investigate multi-hop cases. However, they did not take into account the effect of node density, routing protocol, and the size and shape of the intersection regions.

Markov chain models for a two-hop MANET that incorporate three types of router failures were investigated by Dongyan *et al* [6]. The proposed models were used to study the survivability of ad hoc networks where the excess packet loss and delay due to failures are evaluated as the survivability performance metric. The network survivability was also evaluated by John *et al* [7] using a generalized Markov chain model including many types of node failure, compared to [6].

The path connection availability of a two-hop ad hoc network was presented in [8]. Analytical expressions for the leaving and returning rate in the intersection area between the source and destination were proposed. The authors tried to include the effect of routing protocol to the proposed Markov chain model, but they failed. In [9] Georgios, and Ruijie introduced a path connection availability model for wireless networks. They extended the proposed Markov model introduced in [6] by combining it to a MAC buffer survivability model which has the properties of leaky buckets.

3   Ad Hoc Network Model Description

To develop a path connection availability model, we consider a network consisting of N nodes that are distributed in a square area of dimension $L \times L$ according to a random mobility model, such as random waypoint. All nodes are independent and behave identically. Each node is equipped with omni-directional antenna and has a fixed transmission range R. The destination of any source is chosen from other nodes randomly. For the end-to-end connection, if the destination is not in the transmission range of the source, the packets are routed through N_h hops through neighbour nodes.

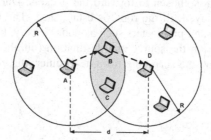

Fig. 1. Two hops communication path

Figure 1 shows two hops communication path between the source node A and destination node D, where the transmission area of each node is presented by a circle with radius R (called the transmission range). To be able to establish a connection with the node D, node A has to choose one of the nodes (B or C) located in the intersection area between the area covered by transmission range of A and D (A_{AD}) (shaded area), simply called the intersection area. As shown in Figure 1, the node A uses the node B as a router to forward its packets to node D. If there is N_i nodes in the intersection area, one of them is used as a router (called active router) and $N_i - 1$ nodes are considered as backup routers. When the active router fails, one of the backup routers is used to forward the packets.

The faults of nodes in the intersection area can be classified into two categories; node and link faults. The node fault is the failure of a node due to hardware, software, and power faults, where power fault is caused by the insufficient battery power to send the packets. The source of the link faults is the errors in the wireless channel caused by signal attenuation, signal loss, multipath fading, excessive noise and interference, and obstacle between nodes. At any instant, because of mobility, either the active or any backup router may leave the intersection area (becomes unavailable) which is considered as a link fault. In this work, we are interested in studying the effect of the node mobility on the path connection availability in MANETs. Therefore, the proposed model only considers the effect of the link faults due to mobility, but it can be easily modified to cope with other types of faults.

At any instant of time, any node can enter the intersection area A_{AD} and leave it after an average period of time of α seconds (called leaving time). We suppose that one of the nodes located outside the intersection area enters the intersection area A_{AD} every average period of time of $1/\lambda$ seconds. α and λ are the model parameters which are directly affected by many other of the network parameters such as number of nodes, size of network area, mobility pattern, speed of nodes, pause time, type of routing protocol, and transmission range.

A three hop communication path between a source node A and destination node D is shown in Figure 2. It is clear that there are two intersection areas (shaded areas) in the route between node A and D. In general, the number of intersection areas in N_h hops route is $N_h - 1$. When the active router fails due to any type of faults in any intersection area of the path, the connection between the source and destination becomes unavailable. The routing protocol then tries to re-establish the connection by starting the route recovery (maintenance) process in which one of the backup routers in the intersection area is chosen to forward the packets. During the route recovery, queued packets are delayed till the route is established. The time required for route recovery depends on many parameters such as node density, transmission range, type of fault, distance between the source and destination (number of hops), and type of routing protocol. During the searching for a new router, the connection will be completely unavailable.

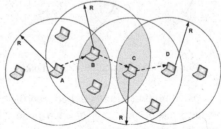

Fig. 2. Three hops communication path

For reactive routing protocols, the route recovery mechanism differs from a routing protocol to another. For On-Demand Distance Vector (AODV) protocol, there are two route recovery mechanisms; local recovery and source recovery. In local recovery mechanism, if the node that detected the link failure (called upstream node) is nearer to the destination than the source, it tries to repair the link locally itself. The upstream node sends a Route Request (RREQ) message where the Time To Live (TTL) of the message is set to (max $(N_{LH}, N_{HS}/2)$ + 2), where N_{LH} is the last known hop count to the destination, and N_{HS} is the number of hops to the source of undeliverable packet [10]. When the local repair fails (or the upstream node is nearer to the source than the destination), the upstream node starts the source repair process by sending back a Route Error (RERR) message to the source which initiates a new route discovery.

For Dynamic Source Routing (DSR) protocol, the route maintenance mechanism does not locally repair a broken link [11]. If a link failure is detected, the upstream node returns a RERR message to the source of the packet, identifying the link over which the packet could not be forward. Then, once the source node receives the RERR message, it removes the broken link from its cache and searches in it for another route to the same destination. If a cached route to the same destination exists, it sends the packet using the new route immediately. Otherwise, it may perform a new route discovery for this destination after an exponential back off delay.

4   SRN Model Description

Figure 3 shows the proposed SRN model for the connection availability of a path with N_h hops. The model consists of $(N_h - 1)$ parts with similar structure where each part models one of the intersection areas in the path. The following describes the model structure of the intersection area number k in the proposed SRN model for N_h hops.

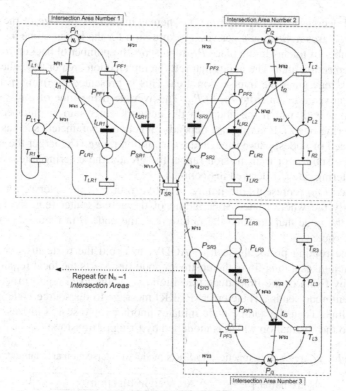

Fig. 3. SRN model for connection availability

The number of tokens in the place P_{ik} (N_i) represents the number of nodes in the intersection area which represents the number of available routers to the next hop. One of the nodes in the intersection area is used as a router (active router) in the current route between the source and destination, and the other (N_i-1) nodes work as backup routers. For random waypoint, the method introduced in [12] can be used to compute the average number of neighbour nodes which can be used to compute N_i.

At any time, there is a probability that any of the backup routers can leave the intersection area. This is modelled by the arc between the place P_{ik} and transition T_{Lk} which moves one token from the place P_{ik} to P_{Lk} after firing of transition T_{Lk}. On the other hand there is a possibility that the active router may leave the intersection area which makes the route to the destination not available. The arc between the place P_{ik} and transition T_{PFk} represents this action. The firing of transition T_{PFk} moves one token from the place P_{ik} to the place P_{Fk} which represents the failure of the path.

The average firing rate of transition T_{PFk} depends on the leaving time α (the average time that a node spends in the intersection area), whereas the average firing rate of transition T_{Lk} not only depends on α but also on the number of nodes in the intersection area. The average firing rate of T_{Lk} and T_{PFk} are $1/\alpha$ and ($\#P_{ik}/\alpha$), respectively, where $\#P_x$ is the number of tokens in the place P_x. The leaving time α depends on the size of the intersection area and the relative speed between any router in the intersection area and the source or destination node. Increasing the maximum limit of the node speed decreases the leaving time α, whereas increasing the size of the intersection area increases it. Section 4 derives an expression for the leaving time α.

The number of tokens in the place P_{Lk} represents the number of backup routers that left the intersection area. The nodes that left the intersection area or any other node in the network may enter the intersection area. This is presented by firing of transition T_{Rk} which moves a token from P_{Lk} to P_{ik}. The average firing time of transition T_{Rk} is the frequency with which the nodes in the network enter into an intersection area (called entering rate λ). Entering rate depends on network parameters such as the node density, speed of nodes, pause time, and transmission range. The larger the node density, speed of nodes, or transmission range, the greater the entering rate. An expression for entering rate λ is derived in Section 4.

The place P_{PFk} represents the failure of active router in the intersection area and consequently the whole route. After failure of the active router (e.g. the node C in Figure 2), the node that detected the failure (e.g. the node B in Figure 2), will try to recover the route.

For some routing protocols such as AODV, to avoid the route discovery by the source which takes a long time, the upstream node first starts the local repair which is presented by firing of the immediate transition t_{LRk}. If the local repair process failed, the upstream node sends a route error (RERR) message to the source node indicating the failed link. Then the source node initiates another route search process to find a new path to the destination which is modelled by firing of transition t_{SRk}.

Table 1. Arcs weight functions for SRN model of intersection area number k

Arc name	Arc weight function
W_{1k}, W_{2k}	1 IF $\#P_{SRk} > 0$ 0 ELSE
W_{3k}	$\#P_{Lk}$ IF $\#P_{SR\varepsilon} > 0$, $\varepsilon = 1, 2, \ldots,$ or $N_h - 1$ 0 ELSE
W_{4k}	1 IF $\#P_{SR\varepsilon} > 0$, $\varepsilon = 1, 2, \ldots,$ or $N_h - 1$ 0 ELSE
W_{5k}	$\#P_{Lk} + 1$ IF $\#P_{LRk} = 1$ $\#P_{Lk}$ ELSE

The firing of transition t_{LRk} puts a token in the place P_{LRk}, whose marking represents the success of the local repair process, whereas the firing of transition t_{SRk} deposits a token in the place P_{SRk} representing the failure of local repair and starting of the source repair process. Because the local repairing of the route needs at least one node to be in the intersection area, a guard function is set to disable transition t_{LRk} when $\#P_{ik} = 0$. The firing of transition T_{LRk} deposits a token in the place P_{Lk} to represent that the active router left the intersection area. As illustrated in Section 2, in some cases the local repair is not supported. So, for these cases, transition t_{LRk} and T_{LRk} should be removed from the model.

The end of source repair process is represented by the firing of transition T_{SR} which moves the token from the place P_{SRk} to P_{ik}. During the source repairing process, the source node tries to find new routers in new intersection areas. So, the failure of the nodes in the old intersection area is not a concern. Thus, we add an inhibitor arc between place P_{SRk} and transitions T_{Lk} to disable it when $\#P_{SRk} > 0$. Also, to disable transition T_{PFk} during local or source repair ($\#P_{LRk} > 0$ or $\#P_{SRk} > 0$), the inhibitor arcs from places P_{LRk} and P_{SRk} to transition T_{PFk} are added. We suppose that during search-ing for the new route, there will be N_i routers in new intersection areas. So, we added the immediate transition t_{fk} which flushes P_{Lk} and P_{LRk} and puts all tokens back in P_{ik} when $\#P_{SR\varepsilon} > 0$, where $\varepsilon = 1, 2, ...,$ or $N_h - 1$. This is controlled by the arc weight func-tions w_{3k}, w_{4k} and w_{5k}, shown in Table 1, and a guard function for transition t_{fk}. If $\#P_{SRk} = 0$, the arc weight functions w_{1k} and w_{2k} prevent depositing a token to place P_{ik} when T_{SR} fires. To disable transition T_{Lk} and enable transition T_{PFk} when all backup routers fail ($\#P_{Lk} = N_i - 1$) and only the active router is in the intersection area ($\#P_{ik} = 1$), a guard function is set to transition T_{Lk}.

For AODV, if the upstream node is far from the source node, it broadcasts RREQ with TTL set to $\left(\text{Max}\left(N_{LH}, \frac{N_{HS}}{2}\right) + 2\right)$ to repair the broken link locally. Therefore, the average firing time of transition T_{LR} is $2\,\mu\left(\text{Max}\left(N_{LH}, \frac{N_{HS}}{2}\right) + 2\right)$ where μ is the packet delay per hop. The average firing time of transition T_{SR} (τ_{sr}) is the average time needed to complete the source repair process, computed as $\tau_{sr} = \tau_L + \tau_{RERR} + \tau_{NR}$, where τ_L, τ_{RERR}, and τ_{NR} are the time required for finishing the local repair process, broadcasting RERR message, establishing a new route, respectively. Hence,

$$\tau_{sr} = 2\,\mu\left(\text{Max}\left(N_{LH}, \frac{N_{HS}}{2}\right) + 2\right) + \mu \cdot N_{HS} + 2\,\mu \cdot N_h$$
$$= 2\,\mu \cdot \left[\left(\text{Max}\left(N_{LH}, \frac{N_{HS}}{2}\right) + 2\right) + \frac{N_{HS}}{2} + N_h\right]$$

In the case of the local repair is not supported, the local repairing time is equal zero ($\tau_L = 0$) and τ_{sr} is given by $\tau_{sr} = \mu \cdot (N_{HS} + 2N_h)$

In DSR, when the source receives the RERR message and before starting a new route discovery process, it tries to use all other alternative routes in the cache to send the packet. So, to compute the average repairing time, the caching mechanism of DSR with random waypoint mobility should be modelled, which is out of the scope of this work. Therefore, it is measured by simulation.

5   Model Parameters

As illustrated above, to solve the proposed model, two important parameters should be known; the average time needed for a node to pass through the intersection area (leaving time α) and the frequency with which the nodes in the network enter into an intersection area (entering rate λ). To compute α and λ, the distance between 2-hop-apart nodes d in the path must be derived.

5.1   Distance between Nodes

To derive an expression for the distance d between 2-hop-apart nodes in the path, let's suppose that a source node A tries to send its packets to a destination node D, and the first two routers in the path are node B and C, as shown in Figure 4. The distances from D to A, B, and C are d_1, d_2, and d_3, respectively, which is called the remaining distances to the destination. The distance between any two nodes in the path (r) is called the forward distance. In [13], we introduced a technique for computing the expected values for remaining distances and forward distance.

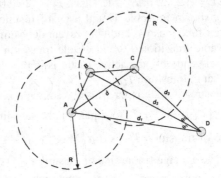

Fig. 4. Distance between nodes

From the geometry of Figure 4, the distance d between nodes A and C is

$$d^2 = d_1^2 + d_3^2 - 2d_1 d_3 Cos(\theta_1 + \theta_2) \tag{1}$$

Also, from geometry it is to be noted that

$$Cos\, \theta_1 = \frac{T_1}{2d_1 d_2} \qquad Cos\, \theta_2 = \frac{T_2}{2d_2 d_3} \tag{2}$$

where $T_1 = d_1^2 + d_2^2 - r^2$ and $T_2 = d_2^2 + d_3^2 - r^2$. It is known that

$$Cos(\theta_1 + \theta_2) = Cos\, \theta_1\, Cos\, \theta_2 - Sin\, \theta_1\, Sin\, \theta_2 \tag{3}$$

Using Equation 1, 2, and 3, we obtain the distance between nodes as:

$$d^2 = d_1^2 + d_3^2 - \frac{T_1 \cdot T_2}{2\, d_2^2} - \frac{1}{2\, d_2^2} \left(\sqrt{4d_1^2\, d_2^2 - T_1^2} \right) \cdot \left(\sqrt{4d_2^2\, d_3^2 - T_2^2} \right) \tag{4}$$

5.2   Leaving Time

The leaving time (α) is the average time needed to pass the intersection area. Consider the two hops communication path between the source node A and destination node D shown in Figure 1. The leaving time of the node B or C depends on the distance between 2-hop-apart nodes in the path (d), transmission range, and speed of nodes. In random waypoint mobility, the speed of nodes is uniformly randomly chosen from the predefined range $[V_{min}, V_{max}]$. Therefore, the average speed of nodes is given by [12]

$$V_a = \frac{V_{max} - V_{min}}{\ln\,(V_{max}) - \ln\,(V_{min})}$$

Because the intersection region is very small compared to the other network area, to simplify the analysis, it is assumed that nodes do not change their direction and speed when they cross the intersection area. The average leaving time is given by

$$\alpha = \frac{L}{E(V_r)} \tag{5}$$

where L (intersection area path length) is the average length of the path that a node passes through the intersection area and $E(V_r)$ is expected value for the relative speed between the router (i.e. node B) and the source or destination (i.e. node A or D). L depends on the distance between nodes and angle of entry to the intersection area. The average value of the intersection area path length is given by [9]

$$L = \frac{\pi R}{2} \left[1 - \frac{d\sqrt{4R^2 - d^2}}{4R^2 \; ArcCos\left(\frac{2}{d}\right)} \right] \tag{6}$$

In order to compute the average leaving time, $E(V_r)$ should be known first. According to the law of cosine, the relative velocity (V_r) between a node A and B is given by

$$V_r = \sqrt{V_A^2 + V_B^2 - 2V_A V_B \cos(\theta)} \tag{7}$$

where V_A and V_B are the velocity of the node A and B, respectively, and θ is the angle between V_A and V_B. The angle θ can vary from 0 to π. Since it is assumed that all nodes move with a velocity that is uniform distributed in the range $[V_{min}, V_{max}]$, $V_A = V_B = V_a$. Hence Equation 7 is expressed as follows

$$V_r = 2V_a \sin\left(\frac{\theta}{2}\right)$$

Therefore, the angle θ is expressed using V_r and V_a as

$$\theta = 2 \; ArcSin\left(\frac{V_r}{2V_a}\right) \tag{8}$$

Assuming that θ is uniformly distributed in the range $[0, \pi]$, the probability density function of θ can be described as follows

$$f_\theta(\theta) = \frac{1}{\pi}$$

The probability that θ is less than δ is given by

$$F_\theta(\delta) = P(\theta \le \delta) = \int_0^\delta f_\theta(\theta) \; d\theta = \frac{\delta}{\pi}$$

The cumulative distribution function (CDF) of V_r can be obtained by substituting θ from equation 8 into the last equation as follows

$$F_{Vr}(v) = P(Vr \le v) = \frac{2}{\pi} ArcSin\left(\frac{v}{2V_a}\right) \tag{9}$$

where $0 \le v \le 2V_a$. By definition the pdf of V_r ($f_{Vr}(v)$) is given by differentiation of Equation 9.

$$f_{Vr}(v) = \frac{2}{\pi\sqrt{4V_a^2 - v^2}}$$

The expected value for V_r is

$$E(V_r) = \int_0^{2V_a} v\, f_{Vr}(v)\, dv = \frac{4V_a}{\pi} \tag{10}$$

By substituting from Equation 6 and 10 into Equation 5, the expected leaving time is

$$\alpha = \frac{\pi^2 R}{8\,V_a}\left[1 - \frac{d\sqrt{4R^2 - d^2}}{4R^2\, ArcCos\left(\frac{2}{d}\right)}\right]$$

5.3   Entering Rate

At any time, any node located outside the intersection area can enter it to be used as a backup router. The frequency with which the nodes in the network enter into an intersection area is called the entering rate (λ). The entering rate depends on many parameters, such as the mobility pattern, node density, nodes speed, nodes pause time, transmission range and distance between nodes. An approximate method has been introduced in [8, 9] to compute the entering rate, but this method did not take into account the effect of mobility model or node density. This section introduces a more accurate method to compute the entering rate.

To simplify the analysis, we assume that no more than one node enters the intersection area at the same time. In addition, the path length of any node crossing the intersection area equals to the average path length computed using (6). So, we assume that only one node leaves the intersection area at a time. Therefore, the intersection area can be approximately modelled as a simple $M/M/1/K$ queue model where the intersection area and nodes present the queue and jobs. Thus, the arrival rate of jobs equals to the entering rate λ and K is the queue size which equals the number of nodes N. The queue service rate equals the rate at which the nodes leave the intersection area which depends on the number of nodes in the intersection area and α.

The steady state probabilities of the $M/M/1/K$ queue with state dependent service rates are [14]

$$P_n = \frac{P_0\, \rho^n}{n!} \tag{11}$$

$$P_0 + \sum_{n=1}^{K} P_n = 1 \tag{12}$$

where P_0 and P_n are the probability of initial state and state number n, respectively, and $\rho = \lambda \cdot \alpha$. By substituting from Equation 11 into Equation 12, we obtain

$$1 + \sum_{n=1}^{K} \frac{\rho^n}{n!} = \frac{1}{P_0} \tag{13}$$

The expected length of the queue $E(Q)$ can be evaluated as follows

$$E(Q) = \sum_{n=1}^{K} n \, P_n = \sum_{n=1}^{K} n \, \frac{P_0 \, \rho^n}{n!} = P_0 \, \rho \sum_{n=1}^{K} \frac{\rho^{n-1}}{(n-1)!} = P_0 \, \rho \sum_{n=0}^{K-1} \frac{\rho^n}{n!}$$

$$= P_0 \, \rho \left[1 + \sum_{n=1}^{K} \frac{\rho^n}{n!} - \frac{\rho^K}{K!} \right] \tag{14}$$

Substituting Equation 13 into 14 gives

$$E(Q) = \rho - P_0 \, \frac{\rho^K}{K!} \tag{15}$$

For large K, the second term in the last equation ($P_0 \frac{\rho^K}{K!}$) is very small (less than 10^{-7} in the case of $P_0 < 1$, $\rho < 10$, $K > 40$) compared to the first term (ρ), so it can be neglected. Hence Equation 14 can be evaluated to

$$E(Q) = \rho = \lambda \cdot \alpha \tag{16}$$

To compute the entering rate λ, the expected number of nodes in the intersection area (the expected queue size $E(Q)$) must be known. For random waypoint mobility, the author in [12] derived an expression for the expected number of neighbour nodes N_n (node degree) using a complex geometric probability analysis, taken into account the speed of nodes, pause time, node density, border effects and non-uniformity of nodes distribution for the mobility model. Using the average number of neighbour nodes N_n computed using the method introduced in [12], the expected number of nodes in the intersection area can be computed as follows:

$$E(Q) = \frac{A_i}{\pi \, R^2} N_n \tag{17}$$

where A_i is the size of intersection area which can be evaluated as

$$A_i = R^2 \left[2 \, ArcCos \left(\frac{d}{2R} \right) - \frac{d}{R} \sqrt{1 - \left(\frac{d}{2R} \right)^2} \right]$$

From Equation 16 and 17, the entering rate can be evaluated to

$$\lambda = \frac{N_n}{\alpha} \frac{A_i}{\pi R^2}$$

6   Validation

In this section, the proposed model is validated by comparing the analytical results obtained from solving the proposed SRN model using SPNP [15] with the simulation results obtained using the network simulator NS-2 [16].

Two performance metrics have been used to validate the proposed model; the path connection availability A_v and path failure and repair frequency f_p. The path connection availability is the probability that the route exists between a source-destination pair. It can be computed from the proposed SRN model shown in the Figure 3 using the following equation

$$A_v = Pr\left(\left(\#P_{LR1} = 0 \ \& \dots \ \& \ \#P_{LR\xi} = 0\right) \ \& \left(\#P_{SR1} = 0 \ \& \dots \ \& \ \#P_{SR\xi} = 0\right)\right)$$

where $Pr(E)$ is the probability of the event E and $\xi = N_h - 1$. The path failure and repair frequency is the frequency with which the path failure and repair occur which is computed as follows [6]

$$f_p = \frac{1}{\dfrac{1}{f_{failure}} + \dfrac{1}{f_{repair}}} = \frac{f_{failure} \cdot f_{repair}}{f_{failure} + f_{repair}}$$

$$f_{failure} = A_v \cdot Rate(T_{pfk}) \quad \text{and} \quad f_{repair} = (1 - A_v) \cdot Rate(T_{SR})$$

where $f_{failure}$, f_{repair}, and $Rate(T_x)$ are the path failure frequency, path repair frequency and firing rate of transition T_x, respectively. A series of simulation scenarios have been adopted to validate the proposed model and study the effect of network parameters such as the number of nodes, size of simulated area, transmission range, routing protocol, and data transmission rate on the path connection availability.

The settings of simulation scenarios consist of a network in a square area with the side length L varying from 800 to 1500m, number of nodes $N = 60$ or 100 (representing low and moderate node density), transmission range $R = 250$ or 200m, routing protocol is AODV or DSR, and data transmission rate (β) is 10 or 40 Kbps. All nodes move according to random waypoint mobility where the velocity of nodes is chosen uniformly from 0 to 20 m/s and the pause time is set to zero to increase the mobility of nodes. For all mobility scenarios, nodes start to move at the start of the simulation and do not stop until the end of simulation. The source-destination pairs are chosen randomly over the network where Constant Bit Rate (CBR) traffic sources are used. For all scenarios, the number of CBR sources is half of the number of nodes and the packet size is 512 byte. Identical mobility scenarios and traffic patterns are used across simulation scenarios to gather fair results. The simulation time is set to 1100s and the first 100s are discarded. All simulation results are obtained with 95% confidence interval and a maximum relative error of 2%. In Figures 5−9, solid lines refer to simulation results (labelled Sim), while dashed lines represent SRN model results (labelled Mod).

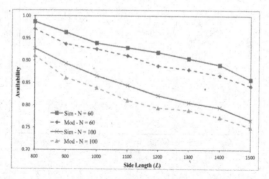

Fig. 5. Path connection availability versus the side length of the network area, where $R = 250$m, $N = 60$ or 100, and $\beta = 10$ kbps

First, the effect of increasing the size of network area and number of nodes on the path availability are investigated. The side length of the simulated area is increased from 800 to 1500m, while the number of nodes is observed for constant values (60 and 100 nodes) where $R = 250$, $\beta = 10$ Kbps, and the routing protocol is AODV. Figure 5 shows the numerical results of this scenario.

Figure 5 shows interesting results. Although increasing the number of nodes in the network increases the expected number of nodes in the intersection areas (backup routers) which increases the path availability, Figure 5 shows that the larger the number of nodes the smaller the path connection availability. This is because increasing the number of nodes has another contradictory effect on the path connection availability. Increasing the number of nodes increases the number of CBR sources and number of control/management packets which increases the interference between neighbour nodes and consequently increases the per hop delay (μ). Increasing the per hop delay increases the time needed to repair the path breaks which decreases the path availability. For this network scenario, increasing the per hop delay due to increasing the number of nodes in the network has more effects on the path availability compared to increasing the number of backup routers, as shown in Figure 5.

Also, Figure 5 shows that for a fixed number of nodes, the larger the network area size the smaller the path availability. Although increasing the network area size reduces the node density and interference between nodes which reduces the per hop delay and increases the path availability, it increases the average number of hops of the paths [13] which has much effect on reducing the path availability due to increasing of the end-to-end delay, that increases the path repairing time and probability of path break.

To analyze the impact of the data transmission rate on the path availability, we considered two data transmission rate; 10 and 40 Kbps where $N = 100$, $R = 250$m, AODV used as a routing protocol, and the side length of the network area varies from 800 to 1500m. Figure 6 shows the numerical results of this scenario. Figure 6 verifies that the data transmission rate has a significant impact on the path availability. The path availability decreases with increasing the data transmission rate because it increases contention and interference between the neighbour nodes which increases the per hop delay (μ) and the time needed for path repair.

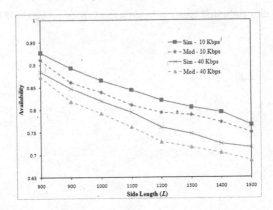

Fig. 6. Path connection availability versus the side length of the network area, where $R = 250$m, $N = 100$, and $\beta = 10$ or 40 kbps

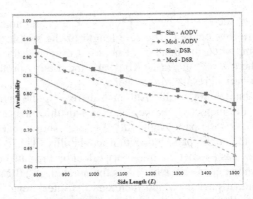

Fig. 7. Path connection availability versus the side length of the network area, where $R = 250$m, $N = 100$, $\beta = 10$ or 40 kbps and routing protocol is AODV or DSR

Figure 7 shows the effect of using DSR as a routing protocol instead of AODV where other network parameters are $N = 100$, $R = 250$, and $\beta = 10$ Kbps. It is clear that using AODV as a routing protocol provides better path availability than in the case of using DSR. This is because, for high mobility scenarios (high speed and low pause time), DSR has a larger end-to-end delay than AODV which increases the path repairing time. This can be attributed to the aggressive caching strategy used by DSR. Before starting a new route discovery, DSR tries to use all cached routes. With high mobility, the route changes fast which make all cached routes are invalid. Thus, route discovery is delayed until all cached routes fail which decreases the path availability.

The path failure frequency versus the side length of the network area is shown in Figure 8 for $N = 100$, $R = 250$, $\rho = 10$ Kbps, and AODV is the routing protocol. It is clear that the grater the network area size the greater the path failure frequency because of increasing the number of hops required to reach the destination which increases the probability of path breaks

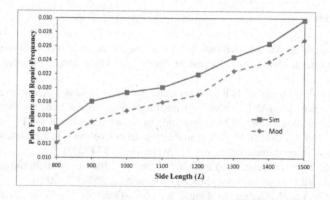

Fig. 8. Path failure frequency versus the side length of the network area, where $R = 250m$, $N = 100$, and $\beta = 10$

As shown in Figures 5–8, analytical results are close to simulation results. In order to solve the proposed model analytically, the time interval of the link failure, entering to intersection area, and path recovery are approximated to be exponentially distributed. In addition, the approximate value for the number of neighbour nodes and average number of hops computed must be rounded to the nearest integer number to be used to solve the proposed model. Therefore, simulation results have an additional overhead over analytical results For all simulation scenarios, computation time of simulation is in the order of hours, whereas the analytical results take a few seconds.

7   Conclusion

In this paper a closed form solution for analytical analysis of path connection availability in multi-hop ad hoc networks with random waypoint mobility is presented. An SRN model is proposed to study the path connection availability and failure frequency of multi-hop paths. Analytical expressions for the leaving time and the entering rate for the intersection area, which are model parameters, are derived. The proposed model is validated by extensive simulations. Compared to simulation results obtained using ns2, analytical results are accurate.

The impacts of different network parameters, such as number of nodes, data transmission rate, network size, transmission range and routing protocol, on the path connection availability are investigated. The larger the number of nodes or data transmission rate the smaller the path connection availability because of increasing the interference between neighbour nodes and consequently increases the end-to-end delay and route recovery delay. Due to increasing the number of intersection areas and number of hops in the path, increasing the network size or decreasing the transmission range increases the end-to-end delay and path break probability which decreases the path connection availability. In addition, the routing protocol has a significant effect on the path connection availability. For example, with high mobility patterns, DSR protocol decreases the path connection availability compared to AODV.

References

1. Ciardo, G., Muppala, J.K., Trivedi, K.S.: Analyzing concurrent and fault-tolerant software using stochastic reward nets. Journal of Parallel and Distributed Computing 15, 255–269 (1992)
2. Xianren, W., Sadjadpour, H.R., Garcia-Luna-Aceves, J.J.: Link Lifetime as a Function of Node Mobility in MANETs with Restricted Mobility: Modeling and Applications. In: 5th International Symposium on Modeling and Optimization in Mobile, pp. 1–10 (2007)
3. Dan, Y., Hui, L., Gruber, I.: Path availability in ad hoc network. In:10th International Conference on Telecommunications vol. 1, 381, pp. 383–387 (2003)
4. Yu-Chee, T., Yueh-Feng, L., Yu-Chia, C.: On route lifetime in multihop mobile ad hoc networks. IEEE Transactions on Mobile Computing 2, 366–376 (2003)
5. Pascoe-Chalke, M., Gomez, J., Rangel, V., Lopez-Guerrero, M.: Route duration modeling for mobile ad-hoc networks. Wireless Networks 16, 743–757
6. Dongyan, C., Sachin, G., Kishor, S.T.: Network survivability performance evaluation: a quantitative approach with applications in wireless ad-hoc networks. In: ACM International Workshop on Modeling Analysis and Simulation of Wireless and Mobile Systems. ACM, Atlanta (2002)
7. John, K., Wei, L., Demetrios, K.: A generalized model for network survivability. In: Proceedings of the Conference on Diversity in Computing, pp. 47-51. ACM, Atlanta (2003)
8. Dimitar, T., Sonja, F., Marija, E., Aksenti, G.: Ad hoc networks connection availability modeling. In: Proceedings of the 1st ACM International Workshop on Performance Evaluation of Wireless Ad Hoc, Sensor, and Ubiquitous Networks, pp. 56–60. ACM, Venezia (2004)
9. Georgios, K., Ruijie, L.: Connection availability and transient survivability analysis in wireless ad-hoc networks. In: ACM International Conference on Modeling, Analysis and Simulation of Wireless and Mobile Systems. ACM, Tenerife (2009)
10. Perkins, C., Royer, E., Das, S.: RFC 3561 Ad hoc On-Demand Distance Vector (AODV) Routing (2003)
11. Siva Ram Murthy, C., Manoj, B.S.: Ad Hoc Wireless Networks: Architectures and Protocols. Prentice Hall PTR
12. Bettstetter, C.: On the Connectivity of Ad Hoc Networks. The Computer Journal 47, 432–447 (2004)
13. Younes, O., Thomas, N.: Analysis of the Expected Number of Hops in Mobile Ad Hoc Networks with Random Waypoint Mobility. Electronic Notes in Theoretical Computer Science 275, 143–158 (2011)
14. Kleinrock, L.: Queuing Systems. Theory, vol. I. John Wiley and Sons (1975)
15. Ciardo, G., Trivedi, K.: SPNP: Stochastic Petri Net Package, http://people.ee.duke.edu/~kst/software_packages.html
16. The Network Simulator ns2, http://www.isi.edu/nsnam/ns/

Formal Performance Modelling:
From Protocols to People

Nigel Thomas, Michael Harrison, Yishi Zhao, and Xiao Chen

School of Computing Science, Newcastle University, UK
Nigel.Thomas@ncl.ac.uk

Abstract. In this paper we consider two very different case studies explored using scalable analysis techniques and stochastic process algebra. The first case study is a classical computer science problem: determining the efficiency of two non-repudiation protocols. We use PEPA to specify the model derived from the protocol specification and mean value analysis and fluid approximation to derive the desired metrics. In the second case study we model a human-centric system, concerning patient flow through a hospital clinic. The model is derived from the clinic practice and observed takt times are used to populate the model. We use PEPA and fluid approximations to derive measures. The two case studies demonstrate the power and versatility of the modelling and analysis approaches used.

1 Introduction

Stochastic process algebra, such as PEPA [1], have been used for around twenty years to formally model and analyse a wide range of computer science applications. The compositional approach to modelling has been demonstrated as being extremely efficient at specifying large models with interactions between many concurrent components. However, with that efficiency in specification has come the need for efficient and scalable analysis techniques.

Much initial work in this area was concerned with decomposing the model for solution [2], for example to derive a product form solution [3, 4]. Work on product form solutions in stochastic process algebra is still taking place, most notably using reversed processes [5, 6], but the class of model amenable to such techniques will always be limited. As a result other techniques were needed and a significant breakthrough came with the application of fluid approximations to biochemical models specified in PEPA [7]. This form of approximation uses ordinary differential equations to solve the model deterministically. Subsequent results have shown that the approximation tends to the exact solution in the limit where the number of components of each type becomes infinite [8]. This limit does not hold in the models in this paper since we have a fixed small number of service centres, however the approximation has been shown to give useful results in a number of previous studies [9–11].

In this paper we present two case studies to illustrate the applicability of the fluid approximation with PEPA. The first case study is a traditional computer

M. Tribastone and S. Gilmore (Eds.): EPEW/UKPEW 2012, LNCS 7587, pp. 127–139, 2013.
© Springer-Verlag Berlin Heidelberg 2013

science problem in analysing the performance of two security protocols. This main feature of this problem concerns the scalability of a server faced with requests from a potentially large number of pairs of client processes. The second case study is conceptually quite different, but is equally amenable to the same analysis techniques. In this case we seek to find the throughput of patients through a hospital clinic under various appointment regimes. The aim here is to minimise waiting times for patients whilst maintaining efficient working practices for consultants and other hospital staff.

The rest of the paper is organised as follows. In the next section we give a brief overview of PEPA, followed by the two case studies. In the final section we draw some conclusions and highlight some directions for future work.

2   PEPA

A formal presentation of PEPA is given in [1], in this section a brief informal summary is presented. PEPA, being a Markovian Process Algebra, only supports actions that occur with rates that are negative exponentially distributed. Specifications written in PEPA represent Markov processes and can be mapped to a continuous time Markov chain (CTMC). Systems are specified in PEPA in terms of *activities* and *components*. An activity (α, r) is described by the type of the activity, α, and the rate of the associated negative exponential distribution, r. This rate may be any positive real number, or given as unspecified using the symbol $\top$.

The syntax for describing components is given as:

$$P ::= (\alpha, r).P \mid P + Q \mid P/L \mid P \underset{L}{\bowtie} Q \mid A$$

The component $(\alpha, r).P$ performs the activity of type α at rate r and then behaves like P. The component $P + Q$ behaves either like P or like Q, the resultant behaviour being given by the first activity to complete.

The component P/L behaves exactly like P except that the activities in the set L are concealed, their type is not visible and instead appears as the unknown type τ.

Concurrent components can be synchronised, $P \underset{L}{\bowtie} Q$, such that activities in the cooperation set L involve the participation of both components. In PEPA the shared activity occurs at the slowest of the rates of the participants and if a rate is unspecified in a component, the component is passive with respect to the activities of that type. $A \overset{def}{=} P$ gives the constant A the behaviour of the component P. The shorthand $P \| Q$ is used to denote synchronisation over no actions, i.e. $P \underset{\emptyset}{\bowtie} Q$. We employ some further shorthand that has been commonly used in the study of large parallel systems. We denote $A[N]$ to mean that there are N instances of A in parallel, i.e. $A \| \ldots \| A$.

In the first case study we only consider models which are cyclic, that is, every derivative of components P and Q are reachable in the model description $P \underset{L}{\bowtie} Q$. Necessary conditions for a cyclic model may be defined on the component and model definitions without recourse to the entire state space of the model. In the second case study we employ the notion of terminating components [12]. In this case components enter a *Stop* behaviour

3   Case Study: Non-repudiation Protocols

A *Key Distribution Centre* (key exchange protocol) has been studied in our previous work, which shows the possibility of modelling by a stochastic process algebra PEPA and analysis by several alternative techniques [9–11]. In this paper, we focus on that how we can apply the modelling and analysis techniques which we developed in the *Key Distribution Centre* study, to two non-repudiation protocols. Firstly, *partial evaluation* [13] has been adopted for model simplification, then we use fluid flow approximations to solve models with large populations.

A non-repudiation service will prevent either of the principals involved from denying the contract after the agreement. The two protocols depicted here were first proposed by Zhou and Gollmann [14, 15] and use a non-repudiation server, known as a *Trusted Third Party* (TTP). We denote these two protocols by ZG1 and ZG3, respectively.

3.1   ZG1 Specification

- A: originator of the non-repudiation exchange
- B: recipient of the non-repudiation exchange
- TTP: on-line trusted third party provide network services accessible to the public
- M: message sent from A to B
- C: ciphertext for message M
- K: message key defined by A
- $NRO = sS_A(f_{NRO}, B, L, C)$: Non-repudiation of origin for M
- $NRR = sS_B(f_{NRR}, A, L, C)$: Non-repudiation of receipt of M
- $sub\_K = sS_A(f_{SUB}, B, L, K)$: proof of submission of K
- $con\_K = sS_T(f_{CON}, A, B, L, K)$: confirmation of K issued by TTP

First, A sends the ciphertext (C) and a non-repudiation origin (NRO) for message M to B, and then B replies back with a non-repudiation receipt (NRR) to A. Now B possesses the ciphertext, but cannot read it as he still hasn't got the key to decrypt M. According to the non-repudiation requirement, B is not a trusted agency to A for sending the key directly to B, they only can resort to a trusted third party (TTP). After receiving the key and proof of submission (sub_K), the TTP will generate a confirmation of K (con_K) and publish in a read only public area. Finally, B can get the key from this public area to decrypt ciphertext (C) and A fetches the confirmation of submission as non-repudiation evidence.

3.2   ZG3 Specification

- L: a unique label chosen by TTP to identify the message M
- T_s : the time that TTP received A's submission
- T_d : the time that TTP delivered and available to B
- $NRO = sS_A(f_{NRO}, TTP, B, M)$: non-repudiation of origin for M
- $NRS = sS_D(f_{NRS}, A, B, T_s, L, NRO)$: non-repudiation of submission of M
- $NRR = sS_B(f_{NRR}, TTP, A, L, NRO)$: non-repudiation of receiving a message labelled L
- $NRD = sS_D(f_{NRD}, A, B, T_d, L, NRR)$: non-repudiation of delivery of M

ZG1 describes a non-repudiation protocol with minimized involvement of a trusted third party, acting as a "low weight notary". However, timing evidence of sending and receiving is required in some applications; hence ZG3 can be adopted in this situation. A sends the plaintext (M) and a non-repudiation origin (NRO) to the trusted third part (TTP), and then fetches the time of receiving (T_s) and non-repudiation of submission (NRS) from a public area, after TTP has published this information. The TTP tells B it received M from A by sending the NRO. B generates a non-repudiation of receiving for TTP following. Finally, B and A can fetch M and the time of delivery (T_d), with other non-repudiation evidence, from the public area, after the TTP has published.

$(request)$ $1.A \rightarrow TTP$: f_{NRO}, TTP, B, M, NRO
$(response\&$
$\quad getByA1)$ $2.A \leftrightarrow TTP$: $f_{NRS}, A, B, T_s, L, NRS$
$(response)$ $3.TTP \rightarrow B$: A, L, NRO
$(sendTTP)$ $4.B \rightarrow TTP$: f_{NRR}, L, NRR
$(response\&$
$\quad getByB)$ $5.B \leftrightarrow TTP$: L, M
$(response\&$
$\quad getByA2)$ $6.A \leftrightarrow TTP$: $f_{NRD}, T_d, L, NRR, NRD$

3.3   ZG1 PEPA Model

We begin by forming components of a pair of principals A and B.

$$TTP \stackrel{def}{=} (publish, r_p).TTP$$

$$A0 \stackrel{def}{=} (sendB, r_b).A1$$
$$A1 \stackrel{def}{=} (sendA, r_a).A2$$
$$A2 \stackrel{def}{=} (sendTTP, r_t).A3$$
$$A3 \stackrel{def}{=} (publish, r_p).A4$$
$$A4 \stackrel{def}{=} (geyByA, r_{ga}).A5$$
$$A5 \stackrel{def}{=} (work, r_w).A0$$

$$B0 \stackrel{def}{=} (sendB, r_b).B1$$
$$B1 \stackrel{def}{=} (sendA, r_a).B2$$
$$B2 \stackrel{def}{=} (publish, r_p).B3$$
$$B3 \stackrel{def}{=} (getByB, r_{gb}).B4$$
$$B4 \stackrel{def}{=} (work, r_w).B0$$

$$SystemZG1 \stackrel{def}{=} TTP[K] \underset{publish}{\bowtie} (A0 \underset{\mathcal{L}}{\bowtie} B0)[N]$$

Where, $\mathcal{L} = \{sendB, sendA, work\}$.

In order to simplify the model specification and analysis, we combine A and B into a new component called AB, using a process referred to as *partial evaluation* [13]. This gives rise to the following description for the complete system when there are N pairs of principals.

$$TTP \stackrel{def}{=} (publish, r_p).TTP$$
$$AB_0 \stackrel{def}{=} (sendB, r_b).AB_1$$
$$AB_1 \stackrel{def}{=} (sendA, r_a).AB_2$$
$$AB_2 \stackrel{def}{=} (sendTTP, r_t).AB_3$$
$$AB_3 \stackrel{def}{=} (publish, r_p).AB_4$$
$$AB_4 \stackrel{def}{=} (getByA, r_{ga}).AB_5$$
$$+(getByB, r_{gb}).AB_6$$
$$AB_5 \stackrel{def}{=} (getByB, r_{gb}).AB_7$$
$$AB_6 \stackrel{def}{=} (getByA, r_{ga}).AB_7$$
$$AB_7 \stackrel{def}{=} (work, r_w).AB_0$$
$$SystemZG1 \stackrel{def}{=} TTP[K] \underset{publish}{\bowtie} AB_0[N]$$

AB_0 to AB_7 in the above ZG1 PEPA model denote the different behaviours of the AB component, and its evolution along the sequence of prescribed actions in the protocol. The choice from AB_4 to AB_5 and AB_6 means step 4 and step 5 in ZG1 can happen in any order. The *work* action is used to define that B can do something with the key and ciphertext after he has obtained these, before returning to the state AB_0 to make a new request again, which forms a working cycle to investigate the steady state.

3.4 ZG3 PEPA Model

Once again we begin by defining the behaviour of a pair of principals.

$$TTP \stackrel{def}{=} (response, r_p).TTP$$

$$A0 \stackrel{def}{=} (request, r_{t1}).A1$$
$$A1 \stackrel{def}{=} (response, r_p).A2$$
$$A2 \stackrel{def}{=} (getByA1, r_{ga1}).A3$$
$$A3 \stackrel{def}{=} (response, r_p).A4$$
$$A4 \stackrel{def}{=} (sendTTP, r_{t2}).A5$$
$$A5 \stackrel{def}{=} (response, r_p).A6$$
$$A6 \stackrel{def}{=} (getByA2, r_{ga2}).A7$$
$$A7 \stackrel{def}{=} (work, r_w).A0$$

$$B0 \stackrel{def}{=} (response, r_p).B1$$
$$B1 \stackrel{def}{=} (getByA1, r_{ga1}).B2$$
$$B2 \stackrel{def}{=} (response, r_p).B3$$
$$B3 \stackrel{def}{=} (sendTTP, r_{t2}).B4$$
$$B4 \stackrel{def}{=} (response, r_p).B5$$
$$B5 \stackrel{def}{=} (getByB, r_{gb}).B6$$
$$B6 \stackrel{def}{=} (work, r_w).B0$$

$$SystemZG3 \stackrel{def}{=} TTP[K] \underset{response}{\bowtie} (A0 \underset{\mathcal{L}}{\bowtie} B0)[N]$$

Where, $\mathcal{L} = \{getByA1, sendTTP, work\}$.

As before these are combined to form the merged component AB in the description of the complete system.

$$TTP \stackrel{def}{=} (response, r_p).TTP$$
$$AB_0 \stackrel{def}{=} (request, r_{t1}).AB_1$$
$$AB_1 \stackrel{def}{=} (response, r_p).AB_2$$
$$AB_2 \stackrel{def}{=} (getByA1, r_{ga1}).AB_3$$
$$AB_3 \stackrel{def}{=} (response, r_p).AB_4$$
$$AB_4 \stackrel{def}{=} (sendTTP, r_{t2}).AB_5$$
$$AB_5 \stackrel{def}{=} (response, r_p).AB_6$$
$$AB_6 \stackrel{def}{=} (getByB, r_{gb}).AB_7$$
$$+(getByA2, r_{ga2}).AB_8$$
$$AB_7 \stackrel{def}{=} (getByA2, r_{ga2}).AB_9$$
$$AB_8 \stackrel{def}{=} (getByB, r_{gb}).AB_9$$
$$AB_9 \stackrel{def}{=} (work, r_w).AB_0$$

$$SystemZG3 \stackrel{def}{=} TTP[K] \underset{response}{\bowtie} AB_0[N]$$

The PEPA model of ZG3 has a similar structure to that for ZG1. The main difference is the TTP component in ZG3 should respond three times for different requests in one cycle, which increases the difficulty of modelling and analysis.

3.5   ODE Analysis

ODE analysis is an approximate analysis technique based on the solution of coupled ordinary differential equations (ODEs), first applied to stochastic process algebra by Hillston [7]. In this style of model analysis, the model is expressed as a finite number of replicated components and ODEs which represent the flow between behaviours of the components. Thus, by solving the ODEs, it is possible to count the number of components behaving as a given derivative at any given time, t. In the absence of oscillations, the limit, $t \longrightarrow \infty$, then tends to a steady state value.

It is important to note that the ODE approach transforms the original stochastic discrete event system to a deterministic continuous system. In doing so, we consider fractions of any component behaving in some way at any given time, which may be difficult to interpret in a physical system. Furthermore, ODE analysis is only applicable to certain classes of model. Despite these restrictions, the technique is extremely useful when considering very large numbers of components.

In experiments we have performed with different models, we have observed that the ODEs give good predictions of the steady state behaviour only when there is at most one active minimum function [16]. This condition holds for the models considered here as there is only one type of Trusted Third Party.

The results we obtain are not exact, but converge on the true value as the number of customers increases. There is a point of maximum error, the location of which we can predict by deriving the point at which the two sides of the minimum function coincide.

The ODEs for ZG1 and ZG3 can be derived following the approach of Hillston [7].

ODEs of ZG1:

$$\frac{d}{dt}AB_0 = r_w AB_7(t) - r_b AB_0(t)$$

$$\frac{d}{dt}AB_1 = r_b AB_0(t) - r_a AB_1(t)$$

$$\frac{d}{dt}AB_2 = r_a AB_1(t) - r_t AB_2(t)$$

$$\frac{d}{dt}AB_3 = r_t AB_2(t) - r_p min(AB_3(t), TTP(t))$$

$$\frac{d}{dt}AB_4 = r_p min(AB_3(t), TTP(t))$$

$$-r_{ga}AB_4(t) - r_{gb}AB_4(t)$$

$$\frac{d}{dt}AB_5 = r_{ga}AB_4(t) - r_{gb}AB_5(t)$$

$$\frac{d}{dt}AB_6 = r_{gb}AB_4(t) - r_{ga}AB_6(t)$$

$$\frac{d}{dt}AB_7 = r_{gb}AB_5(t) + r_{ga}AB_6(t) - r_{w}AB_7(t)$$

$$\frac{d}{dt}TTP = 0$$

ODEs of ZG3:

$$\frac{d}{dt}AB_0 = r_w AB_9(t) - r_{t1}AB_0(t)$$

$$\frac{d}{dt}AB_1 = r_{t1}AB_0(t) - [r_p \frac{AB_1(t)}{AB_1(t) + AB_3t + AB_5(t)}$$
$$\times min(AB_1(t) + AB_3(t) + AB_5(t), TTP(t))]$$

$$\frac{d}{dt}AB_2 = -r_{ga1}AB_2(t) + [r_p \frac{AB_1(t)}{AB_1(t) + AB_3t + AB_5(t)}$$
$$\times min(AB_1(t) + AB_3(t) + AB_5(t), TTP(t))]$$

$$\frac{d}{dt}AB_3 = r_{ga1}AB_2(t) - [r_p \frac{AB_3(t)}{AB_1(t) + AB_3t + AB_5(t)}$$
$$\times min(AB_1(t) + AB_3(t) + AB_5(t), TTP(t))]$$

$$\frac{d}{dt}AB_4 = -r_{t2}AB_4(t) + [r_p \frac{AB_3(t)}{AB_1(t) + AB_3t + AB_5(t)}$$
$$\times min(AB_1(t) + AB_3(t) + AB_5(t), TTP(t))]$$

$$\frac{d}{dt}AB_5 = r_{t2}AB_4(t) - [r_p \frac{AB_5(t)}{AB_1(t) + AB_3t + AB_5(t)}$$
$$\times min(AB_1(t) + AB_3(t) + AB_5(t), TTP(t))]$$

$$\frac{d}{dt}AB_6 = -r_{gb}AB_6(t)$$

$$-r_{ga2}AB_6(t) + [r_p \frac{AB_5(t)}{AB_1(t) + AB_3t + AB_5(t)}$$
$$\times min(AB_1(t) + AB_3(t) + AB_5(t), TTP(t))]$$

$$\frac{d}{dt}AB_7 = r_{gb}AB_6(t) - r_{ga2}AB_7(t)$$

$$\frac{d}{dt}AB_8 = r_{ga2}AB_6(t) - r_{gb}AB_8(t)$$

$$\frac{d}{dt}AB_9 = r_{ga2}AB_7(t) + r_{gb}AB_8(t) - r_w AB_9(t)$$

$$\frac{d}{dt}TTP = 0$$

These ODEs can be solved in a number of ways. Most commonly they are simulated with a suitably small time step over a long period. This gives rise to a trace of component numbers over time. Alternatively, if we assume that a steady state exists, the ODEs can be solved analytically at the limit by taking $\frac{d}{dt}AB_i = 0$, $\forall i$, and solving the resultant set of simple simultaneous equations. Either approach gives an efficient numerical computation, even when N is extremely large.

Our analysis is interested primarily in the number of clients waiting for a *publish* (or *response* in ZG3) action from the TTP, as the clients can then fetch what they need from the public area or obtain a service results. This is represented in the model by the number of AB_3 in ZG1, AB_1, AB_3 and AB_5 in ZG3. The average queuing length $L(N)$ is the number of requests awaiting a response from the TTP. It is the number of the AB_3 (in ZG1), or AB_1, AB_3 and AB_5 (in ZG3), derivatives when $t \longrightarrow \infty$ when there are N customers in the population.

The average response time is another interesting metric for us. To obtain this we apply the arrival theorem. If an arriving request sees a free server, then the average response time will be the average service time. However, if the random observer sees all the servers busy, then the average response time will be the average service time plus the time it takes for one server to become available (including scheduling the other jobs waiting ahead of the random observer). This gives rise to the following equations.

$$W(N) = \frac{1}{r_p}\ ,\ L(N-1)+1 \leq K$$

$$W(N) = \frac{1}{r_p} + \frac{L(N-1)+1-K}{Kr_p}$$

$$= \frac{L(N-1)+1}{Kr_p}\ ,\ L(N-1)+1 > K$$

Obviously, as the TTP in ZG1 is designed as a "low weight notary", the number of waiting requests at TTP of ZG1 should always be smaller than that in ZG3 with the same parameters. However, a system engineer should clearly be very careful to choose either of these two protocols based on the trade off between performance and the need for added security functionality.

4   Case Study 2: A Rheumatology Clinic

Healthcare is subject to many performance targets and metrics used to assess the success of all clinical environments. In addition the notion of patient experience remains at the centre of all clinical operation. As such the provisioning of healthcare resources is constrained not only in providing an efficient service, but also one which meets the needs of the patients, not just clinically but also personally and socially. Important aspects in patient experience include the minimisation of waiting time and the availability of appropriate information concerning future interactions.

In this study we look at one aspect of clinical performance, namely the throughput of patients and their associate waiting times. We model a rheumatology clinic in a major NHS hospital in the UK using data captured from observations. The clinic is relatively small, consisting of a central waiting area with registration, a number of consulting rooms and treatment rooms where nurses my take blood samples or administer injections. In addition patients may be sent to a separate x-ray service outside the clinic (but still within the hospital). Patients are classified as either *new*, meaning that they have just been referred to the clinic and this is their first appointments, or *follow-up*, which denotes that the patients is attending a repeat appointment having previously attended the clinic in the past. For brevity in this presentation we will not distinguish these two classes, although in practice it adds only a little additional complexity to the specification and analysis.

A typical PEPA model of this system can be specified as follows:

$$Patient \stackrel{def}{=} (arrive, rA).Register$$

$$Register \stackrel{def}{=} (register, rR).Test$$

$$Test \stackrel{def}{=} (test, rT).Consultation$$

$$Consultation \stackrel{def}{=} (consult, rC).BloodTest$$

$$BloodTest \stackrel{def}{=} (blood, rB).Xray$$

$$XRay \stackrel{def}{=} (xray, rX).Depart$$

$$Depart \stackrel{def}{=} (depart, rD).Stop$$

$$Registration \stackrel{def}{=} (register, rR).Registration$$

$$Nurse_1 \stackrel{def}{=} (test, rT).Nurse_1$$

$$Consultant \stackrel{def}{=} (consult, rC).Consultant$$

$$Nurse_2 \stackrel{def}{=} (blood, rB).Nurse_2$$

$$XRay \stackrel{def}{=} (xray, rX).XRay$$

The complete system can be described as

$$Patient[N_p] \bowtie_{\mathcal{L}} (Registration || Nurse_1[N_1] || Consultant[N_c] ||$$
$$Nurse_2[N_2] || XRay)$$

where $\mathcal{L} = \{register, test, consult, blood, xray\}$.

The components *Registration*, *Nurse₁*, *Consultant*, *Nurse₂* and *XRay* represent the various resources in the system. Patients can only use those resources if they are available, i.e. not already in use by another patient. A key consideration therefore is in provisioning sufficient resource (denoted by N_1, N_c and N_2) such that patients do not experience excessive waiting given a particular volume, N_p. Since the *Patient* component is terminating (indicating that the patient has left the clinic), it makes no sense to derive steady state metrics. We could, if it was desired, alter the behaviour so that patients return to the *Patient* behaviour after a suitable delay following the *depart* action (as in the previous case study).

Using this model we can investigate a number of scenarios of resource availability and appointment scheduling. To do this we derive the ODEs (as in the previous case) and simulate them to derive transient metrics of interest. The particular metrics we are interested in are typically the number of patients completing their appointment within a given time, the time taken for all patients to complete, the maximum number of waiting patients at any given point and the maximum end to end response time for any patient.

As the model is specified here all the patients will begin to arrive at the same time. It turns out that this is the optimal solution for minimising the time taken for all patients to complete, hence form a process-centric view this might be thought of as a good solution. However, in this configuration some patients would be present in the clinic for the entire time, experiencing long waiting times at each stage. Other patients (those at the front of the arrival queue as dictated by the race condition on the concurrent *arrive* actions) would find each resource relatively unused as they come to it and so would experience a very fast response time.

This disparity in patient experience would clearly lead to dissatisfaction amongst those patients with very long waits. To counter this problem we have experimented with various functional rates to stagger the arrival of patients and simulate an appointment schedule. The simplest such function is to spread the arrivals over a longer period, allowing the first patients to progress through the system before other patients arrive. This has the desired effect of reducing maximum wait times, but increases the overall time to completion and reduces the average utilisation of the resources. In practice this is particularly problematic for consultants, who may then experience wait times between patients leading to an inefficient (and more costly) provision. The optimal function to reduce wait times and maintain a high utilisation of key resources is to employ a non-linear function which creates an initial load (high burst of arrivals), and then a spread of patients arriving throughout the remaining period. When the resource provision and rates in the arrival function are optimised this results in small average waits for patients at the *Consultation* phase, but otherwise a fast response through the system. The small numbers of waiting patients at the *Consultation* phase ensures that there is nearly always a patient to be seen by the consultant when they are available, so utilisation of consultants is maintained until all patients have been seen.

Using the fluid approximation we are able to introduce further functions to fluctuate the available resource (for example, to introduce scheduled breaks or unforeseen complications) or to reallocate resource between different areas. For example, with a functional rate approach to arrivals it is advantageous to process the initial burst of patients through the *test* action as quickly as possible so that the system reaches a sustainable state. This means provisioning a higher number of $Nurse_1$ components (N_1) in the initial phase, but this number can be reduced after the initial burst has gone through. At the same time during the initial phase there is less demand for later actions in the sequence, hence the number of $Nurse_2$ components can be reduced initially, but increased once patients start to complete the *consult* action. This means we can maintain a steady total of nurses $(N_1 + N_2)$ but reallocate staff between these two roles.

5 Conclusions and Future Work

The examples here show the use of PEPA and its fluid approximation in two very different scenarios. As stated in the introduction, this form of analysis was originally applied to PEPA for biochemical models, we have demonstrated here that the approach can also be applied to traditional computer science problems and to problems of a more techno-social nature involving the movement of people. The fact that the analysis can be used to derive some very useful information in both scenarios illustrates the power and flexibility of the approach.

The work described in this paper is ongoing. In the first example we aim to validate the models against real implementations of these protocols. There are clearly many more protocols of a similar nature that can also be studied using these techniques. In the case of the second example we aim to extend our work to consider other more complicated treatment pathways in different areas of healthcare. In addition we intend to develop some interface tools to enable healthcare practitioners and managers to access the analysis tools without needing to understand PEPA.

The models presented in this paper have also been solved using mean value analysis [17] which has validated the fluid approximation results. There is still some work to be done to better understand the accuracy of the fluid approximation in different scenarios. Some empirical study in this regard has been undertaken [16], but additional results on sensitivity to different distributions and functional rates (as used in the second example) remains to be undertaken.

References

1. Hillston, J.: A Compositional Approach to Performance Modelling. Cambridge University Press (1996)
2. Hillston, J.: Exploiting Structure in Solution: Decomposing Compositional Models. In: Brinksma, E., Hermanns, H., Katoen, J.-P. (eds.) EEF School 2000 and FMPA 2000. LNCS, vol. 2090, pp. 278–314. Springer, Heidelberg (2001)
3. Hillston, J., Thomas, N.: Product form solution for a class of PEPA models. Performance Evaluation 35(3-4), 171–192 (1999)

4. Hillston, J., Thomas, N.: A syntactic analysis of reversible PEPA processes. In: Proceedings of the 6th International Workshop on Process Algebra and Performance Modelling, Nice (1998)
5. Harrison, P.G.: Turning back time in Markovian process algebra. Theoretical Computer Science 290, 1947–1986 (2003)
6. Harrison, P.G., Thomas, N.: Product-Form Solution in PEPA via the Reversed Process. In: Kouvatsos, D.D. (ed.) Next Generation Internet. LNCS, vol. 5233, pp. 343–356. Springer, Heidelberg (2011)
7. Hillston, J.: Fluid flow approximation of PEPA models. In: Proceedings of QEST 2005, pp. 33–43. IEEE Computer Society (2005)
8. Hayden, R., Bradley, J.: A fluid analysis framework for a Markovian process algebra. Theoretical Computer Science 411(22-24), 2260–2297 (2010)
9. Zhao, Y., Thomas, N.: Approximate Solution of a PEPA Model of a Key Distribution Centre. In: Kounev, S., Gorton, I., Sachs, K. (eds.) SIPEW 2008. LNCS, vol. 5119, pp. 44–57. Springer, Heidelberg (2008)
10. Thomas, N., Zhao, Y.: Fluid flow analysis of a model of a secure key distribution centre. In: Proceedings of the 24th UK Performance Engineering Workshop. Imperial College, London (2008)
11. Zhao, Y., Thomas, N.: Efficient solution of a PEPA model of a key distribution centre. Performance Evaluation 67(8), 740–756 (2010)
12. Thomas, N., Bradley, J.: Terminating processes in PEPA. In: Proceeding of the 17th UK Performance Engineering Workshop, University of Leeds (2001)
13. Clark, A., Duguid, A., Gilmore, S., Tribastone, M.: Partial Evaluation of PEPA Models for Fluid-Flow Analysis. In: Thomas, N., Juiz, C. (eds.) EPEW 2008. LNCS, vol. 5261, pp. 2–16. Springer, Heidelberg (2008)
14. Zhou, J., Gollmann, D.: A Fair Non-repudiation Protocol. In: Proceedings of IEEE Symposium on Security and Privacy (SP 1996). IEEE Computer Society (1996)
15. Zhou, J., Gollmann, D.: Observation on Non-repudiation. In: Kim, K.-C., Matsumoto, T. (eds.) ASIACRYPT 1996. LNCS, vol. 1163, pp. 133–144. Springer, Heidelberg (1996)
16. Thomas, N.: Using ODEs from PEPA models to derive asymptotic solutions for a class of closed queueing networks. In: 8th Worshop on Process Algebra and Stochastically Timed Activities, University of Edinburgh (2009)
17. Thomas, N., Zhao, Y.: Mean value analysis for a class of PEPA models. The Computer Journal 54(5), 643–652 (2011)

SRN Models for Analysis
of Multihop Wireless Ad Hoc Networks

Osama Younes and Nigel Thomas

School of Computing Science, Newcastle University, UK
{Osama.Younes,Nigel.Thomas}@ncl.ac.uk

Abstract. Mobile Ad hoc Networks (MANETs) are becoming very attractive
and useful in many kinds of communication and networking applications. Due
to the advantage of quick construction and numerical analysis of analytical modelling techniques, such as Stochastic Petri nets, Queueing Networks and Process
Algebra, have been broadly used for performance analysis of computer networks. In addition, analytical modelling techniques generally provide the best
insight into the effects of various parameters and their interactions. To the best
of our knowledge, there is no analytical study that investigates the effect of
various factors of multihop ad hoc networks, such as communication range,
density of nodes, random access behavior, mobility patterns, speed of nodes,
traffic patterns, and traffic load, on the performance indices such as packet
delay and network capacity. The main objective of this work is designing an
analytical framework that can be used to study the effect of all these factors on
the performance of MANETs, where nodes move according to random waypoint mobility model. We employ a verbose modelling approach which includes
organizing a framework into several models to break up the complexity of
modelling the complete network, and make it easier to analysis each model of
the framework as required. The proposed framework can be used to evaluate
any of transport, network, or data link layer protocols. The proposed models are
validated using extensive simulations.

1   Introduction

Traditional wireless communication networks, namely cellular and satellite networks,
require a fixed infrastructure over which communication takes place. Accordingly,
considerable effort and resources are required for such networks to be set up, before
they can actually be used. In cases where setting up an infrastructure is a difficult or
even impossible task, such as in emergency/rescue operations, military applications or
disaster relief, other alternatives need to be devised. Mobile Ad hoc Networks
(MANETs) are stand alone wireless networks that lack the service of a backbone
infrastructure [1]. They consist of a collection of mobile nodes, where the nodes act as
both sources and routers for other mobile nodes in the network. A node can send a
message to another one beyond its transmission range by using other nodes as relay
points and thus a node can function as a router. This mode of communication is
known as wireless multihop.

M. Tribastone and S. Gilmore (Eds.): EPEW/UKPEW 2012, LNCS 7587, pp. 140–155, 2013.
© Springer-Verlag Berlin Heidelberg 2013

Mobile Ad hoc Networks share many of the properties of wired and infrastructure wireless networks but also has certain unique features which come from the characteristics of the wireless channel. Nodes in MANETs are free to move randomly; thus, the network topology changes rapidly at unpredictable times. Therefore, the nodes need to collect connectivity information from other nodes periodically. Mobility is a crucial factor affecting the design of MANET's protocols, including Medium Access Control (MAC), Transmission Control Protocol (TCP), and routing protocols.

High performance is a very important goal in designing communication systems. Therefore, performance evaluation is needed to compare various architectures for their performance, study the effect of varying certain parameters of the system and study the interaction between various parameters that characterize the system. It is to be noted that most of research that studies the performance of MANET were evaluated using Discrete Event Simulation (DES) utilizing a broad range of simulators, such as NS2 [2], OPNET [3], and GloMoSim [4]. The principal drawback of DES is the time taken to run such models for large, realistic systems, particularly when results with high accuracy (i.e., narrow confidence intervals) are desired. In order to get a reliable value, one has to run simulation tens of iterations with different seed values of a random generator. In other words, it tends to be expensive. A large amount of computation time may be needed in order to obtain statistically significant result. In highly variable scenarios, with number of nodes ranging from tens to thousands, node mobility varying from zero to tens of m/s, the simulation time of most current systems will increase dramatically to an unacceptable level.

Due to the advantage of quick construction and numerical analysis of analytical modelling techniques, such as Petri nets and process algebra, have been used for performance analysis of networks. In addition, analytical modelling is a less costly and more efficient method. It generally provides the best insight into the effects of various parameters and their interactions [5]. Hence analytical modelling is the method of choice for a fast and cost effective evaluation of a network protocol.

Ad hoc networks are too complex to allow analytical study for explicit performance expressions. Consequently, the number of analytical studies of MANET is small [6-10]. In addition, most of these studies have many drawbacks, which can be summarized as follows:

1. Most of analytical research in MANET suppose that the nodes are stationary or the network is connected all the times to simplify the analytical analysis.
2. Most of analytical research in MANET study the behaviour of one protocol in a specific layer, not the whole network. For example in [11-16] they only proposed models for MAC protocols in Data Link Layer.
3. To reduce the state space of the analytical models of MANET, most of research are macroscopic (dynamics of actions are aggregated, motivated by limit theorems) and not scalable.
4. Some of research is restricted to analysis of single hop ad hoc networks.
5. To simplify the analysis, most of research study MANETs in the case of saturated traffic load (i.e. all the time every node has a packet to send).

To the best of our knowledge, there is no analytical study that investigates the effect of various factors of ad hoc networks, such as communication range, density of nodes, random access behavior, mobility patterns, speed of nodes, traffic patterns, and traffic load, on the performance indices such as packet delay and network capacity. This work introduces an analytical framework that can be used to study the effect of all these factors on the performance of MANETs. The proposed framework is organized into several models to break up the complexity of modelling the complete network, and make it easier to later analysis of each model of the framework as required. The proposed framework can be used to evaluate any of transport, network, or data link layer protocols. In addition this framework can be used to study the effect of the interaction between different protocols in different layers on the performance of MANETs.

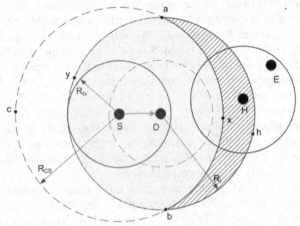

Fig. 1. One hop communication

2   Network Model and Assumptions

To develop a Stochastic Reward Net (SRN) models for MANET, we consider a network consisting of N nodes that are distributed in a square area of dimension LxL according to a mobility model, such as random waypoint. All nodes are independent and behave identically. Each node is equipped with omni-directional antenna and has a fixed transmission range R_{tx}. Each node in the network is a source of traffic, where it generates packets with rate λ. The destination of any source is chosen from other nodes randomly. For the end-to-end connection, if the destination is not in the transmission range of the source, the packets are routed through N_h hops through neighbour nodes. The neighbour nodes (intermediate nodes) are used as connection relays to forward packets to destinations. Therefore, the mobile nodes work as both sources and routers for other mobile nodes in the network. We suppose that each node forward the same average number of packet per unit time (λ_r) to other neighbour nodes. The traffic load in the network is represented by λ and λ_r. The number of routed packets per unit time (λ_r) is one of the network layer model parameters. An expression for λ_r is derived in Section 4.

In wireless networks, all nodes with multi-directional antennas have three radio ranges related to the wireless radio: transmission range (R_{tx}), carrier-sensing range (R_{cs}) and interference range (R_i). To illustrate these ranges, Figure 1 shows one hop communication between the source node S and destination node D, where the circles with radii R_{tx}, R_{cs} and R_i present the transmission range of the node S, carrier sensing range of the node S and interference range of the node D, respectively.

Carrier sense range is a physical parameter for a wireless radio. It depends on the sensitivity of the antenna. Any transmissions from other nodes in the carrier sense range of a node S will trigger carrier sense detection, and S detects the channel as busy. If the channel is detected to be busy, node S will wait for the channel to become idle for at least the duration of distributed inter-frame space (DIFS) before it starts trying to transmit a packet. The area covered by the carrier sense range of a node is called carrier sense area for the node. The nodes located in the carrier sensing area are called carrier sensing nodes (N_{cs}).

All nodes located within the area covered by the transmission range of a node S, called neighbour nodes, can receive a packet from S or send a packet to S successfully, if there is no interference from other radios. The area covered by the transmission range of a node is called capture area for the node. If a node S transmits to a node D, as shown in Figure 1, any transmission from any node located within the interference range of D interferes with the signal sent by S.

Transmission and carrier sense range are determined by the transmission and reception power threshold and path loss of signal power. To simplify analysis, we assume that both carrier sense and transmission ranges are fixed and identical in all the nodes. The interference range of any node varies depending on the distance between S and the destination and the sending and receiving signal power.

The hidden area (the dashed area shown in Figure 1) is the area covered by the interference range of the destination node D and not covered by the carrier-sensing range of the source node S. The nodes located in the hidden area are called the hidden nodes. For example, as shown in Figure 1, the node H is in the interference range of D and out of the carrier sensing range of S. Therefore, the node H is hidden from S. The node S will not be able to hear transmission by the hidden node H. Consequently, if it transmits packets to the node D at the same time, there will be packet collisions at D. The hidden nodes problem is a well-known problem in multihop ad hoc networks.

The nodes located in the intersection of the carrier sensing range of the source and the interference range of the destination are called interfering nodes. For example, for the source and destination nodes S and D shown in Figure 1, the interfering nodes are located in the shaded area. Any transmission from these nodes is sensed by S and interferes with the transmission from S. For random waypoint mobility model, we introduced a mathematical analysis in [17] and [18] to compute the average number of carrier sensing nodes (N_{cs}), interfering nodes (N_i) and hidden nodes (N_H).

3   Proposed Framework

MANETs are a multi-layer problem. The physical layer must adapt to rapid changes in link characteristics. The multiple access control layer should allow fair access, minimize collisions, and transport data reliably over the shared wireless links in the

presence of hidden or exposed terminals and rapid changes. The network layer protocols should determine and distribute information used to calculate paths in an efficient
way. The transport layer should be able to handle frequent packets loss and delay that
are very different than wired networks. In addition, the topology of MANET is highly
dynamic because of frequent nodes mobility. Thus, there are many interacting parameters, mechanisms, and phenomena in the area of mobile ad hoc networking.
Therefore, Ad hoc networks are too complex to allow analytical study for explicit
performance expressions.

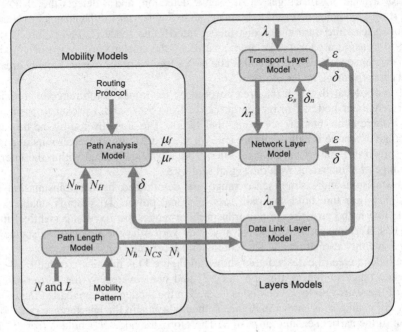

Fig. 2. Proposed framework for modelling MANET

To overcome all drawbacks of other research explained in Section 1, we propose an
analytical framework that can be used to evaluate MANETs or a specific protocol in
any layer. To present an approach for the modelling and analysis of large-scale ad hoc
network systems, there are two requirements in advance. First, the model should be
detailed enough to describe some important network characteristics that have a significant impact on performance. Second, it should be simple enough to be scalable
and analyzable. It is clear that these two requirements are contradictory. Therefore, to
solve this problem, we will model the MANET by a framework that consists of four
models, as shown in Figure 2, instead of building one analytical model for the whole
network. These four models and the interactions between them will be similar to the
four main layers and their interactions in TCP/IP model.

Figure 2 illustrates the analytical framework for modelling mobile ad hoc networks. It consists of five models which are divided into two groups; Mobility Models
and Layers Models, as shown in Figure 2. The five models interact with each other by

exporting and importing some parameters from other models, as shown in Figure 2. The mobility models are used to make analysis of the path between any source and destination. It consists of two models, Path Length Model and Path Analysis Model. According to the number of nodes (N), mobility pattern (random way point, random walk point, free way, etc.), and the size of the network area (L^2), the Path Length Model is used to compute the expected number of hops between any source-destination pair (N_h). According to the routing protocol (AODV, DSR, SSA, LMR, etc.) and N_h, the Path Analysis Model is used to study connection availability of the path and calculates the average rate of failure (μ_f) and repair (μ_r) of any path between any source and destination. The Path Length Model is a mathematical model, whereas the Path Analysis Model is Stochastic Reward Net model, which have been introduced in [17] and [18], respectively.

The Layers models consist of three models; Data Link Layer Model, Network Layer Model, and Transport Layer Model. Data link layer protocols (MAC protocols) are modelled by the Data Link Layer Model. This model uses the throughput of the Network Layer Model (λ_n) to compute the packet loss probability (ε) and the average delay of packets (δ) in data link layer. In [19], we introduced the Data Link Model. The actions in the network layer are modelled by the Network Layer Model. It uses μ_r, μ_f, λ_T (the throughput of Transport Layer Model) and ε to calculate the average number of packets per unit time that is sent to Data Link Layer model (λ_n), Packet loss probability when the node buffer is full (ε_B), and the average delay of packets in the Network Layer Model (δ_n). The network layer SRN model is introduced in Section 5. The Transport Layer Model (TLM) represents the analytical model for any of the transport layer protocols such as TCP or UDP. The inputs of the TLM are λ, ε_B, δ_n, and ε, and the output is λ_T. To simplify the analytical analysis, only UDP protocol is adopted as a transport layer protocol. Because of its simplicity, modelling of UDP protocol is included in network layer model introduced in Section 5.

The proposed models are solved iteratively using fixed point iteration technique to compute the required performance indices, such as the average delay and throughput per hop. This is explained in Section 4. Also, Section 4 shows how to use the performance indices per hop to compute the performance indices per path.

4   Traffic Load and Packet Forward Rate

The traffic load in the multihop ad hoc networks depends on the packets generation rate (λ) and packets forward rate (λ_r) per node. Packets generation rate is a network parameter, whereas the packets forward rate depends on λ and other network parameters such as network size, number of nodes, and mobility model. This section derives an expression for λ_r.

Figure 3 shows N_h hops communication path between the source node S and destination node D, where λ_t is the average number of packets that is successfully sent by any node per unit time, and λ_1, λ_2, ..., λ_{Nh} are the average number of packets sent by the source S and received by the nodes R_1, R_2, ... , D, respectively. Throughput ratio (α) is the ratio between the average number of received and successfully transmitted packets per node per unit time. Because all nodes are similar and behave identically, we suppose that throughput ratio for all nodes are equal. The throughput ratio can be computes as follows:

$$\alpha = \frac{(\lambda_t - \lambda_1) + \lambda_1}{\lambda_r + \lambda} = \frac{\lambda_t}{\lambda_r + \lambda} = \frac{\lambda_1}{\lambda} = \frac{\lambda_t - \lambda_1}{\lambda_r}$$

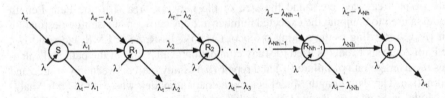

Fig. 3. A network communication path

Therefore, the average number of packet that the node R_1 received from the source S per unit time is $\lambda_1 = \alpha\,\lambda$. For the node R_1, the throughput ration is computed as follows:

$$\alpha = \frac{(\lambda_t - \lambda_2) + \lambda_2}{(\lambda_r - \lambda_1) + \lambda_1 + \lambda} = \frac{\lambda_t}{\lambda_r + \lambda} = \frac{\lambda_t - \lambda_2}{(\lambda_r - \lambda_1) + \lambda} = \frac{\lambda_2}{\lambda_1}$$

So, the average number of packet that are sent by S and received by R_2 is

$$\lambda_2 = \alpha\,\lambda_1 = \alpha^2\,\lambda$$

In the same way, we can deduce that the average number of packet that a node R_k received from the source S per unit time is

$$\lambda_k = \alpha^k\,\lambda \tag{1}$$

Consequently, the average number of packets received by the destination D per unit time, which represents the throughput per path, is

$$Throughput = \lambda_{N_h} = \alpha^{N_h}\,\lambda \tag{2}$$

The number of packets sent by a source S and forwarded (routed) by the intermediate nodes (routers) between the source S and destination D in the path can be computed as follows:

$$\lambda_x = \lambda_1 + \lambda_2 + \dots + \lambda_{N_h - 1}$$

From equation 1 and 2, λ_x can be computed as

$$\lambda_x = (\alpha + \alpha^2 + \cdots + \alpha^{N_h - 1}) \cdot \lambda \tag{3}$$

If the number of sources in the network is N_s, the average number of routed packets per unit time (λ_r) is

$$\lambda_r = N_s \cdot \lambda_x = N \cdot \lambda_r \tag{4}$$

From equation 3 and 4, the average number of routed packets per node is

$$\lambda_r = (\alpha + \alpha^2 + \cdots + \alpha^{N_h - 1}) \cdot \frac{N_s}{N} \cdot \lambda \tag{5}$$

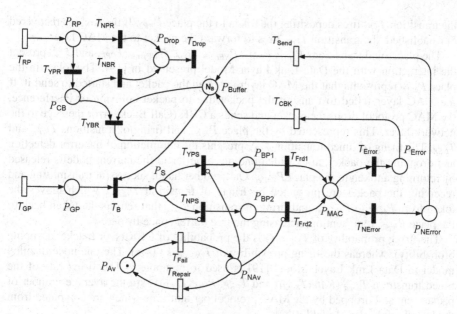

Fig. 4. Network layer model

5   Network Layer Model

The main goal of network layer protocols (Routing Protocols) is the correct and efficient route establishment and maintenance between a pair of nodes in order that the messages are sent or forwarded reliably and in a timely manner. In addition, because the nodes work as a router, the routing protocols maintain information about the routes in the network to be used to forward any received packets. The design of MANET routing protocols is a challenge because they operate in resource-constrained devices and networks with highly dynamic topologies.

The proposed network layer model is shown in Figure 4. It is a Stochastic Reward Net (SRN) model for network layer events in MANETs. Transition T_{GP} represents the generation of packets in the transport layer. When transition T_{GP} fires, a token is deposited in the place P_{GP}. The mean firing time of T_{GP} is the mean time of generation of UDP packets in transport layer. The place P_{Buffer} contains tokens corresponding to the free buffer spaces in the current node. The initial number of tokens in P_{Buffer} (N_B) is the total number of free buffer spaces in the node. The firing of immediate transition T_B reserves a buffer space for outgoing packets by removing a token from P_{Buffer} and depositing a token into the place P_s which represents receiving of packets by the network layer.

When a token arrives in the place P_s, there are two possibilities at this point. The first, the path to the destination is available, so the transition T_{YPS} fires moving the token from the place P_s to the place P_{BP1}. The firing of transition T_{Frd1} moves the token from P_{BP1} to P_{MAC} which represents forwarding the packet from the network layer to the MAC layer. The second, the path to the destination is not available, therefore the transition T_{NPS} fires depositing the token to the place P_{BP2}. If the route is recovered or established, the transition T_{Frd2} fires to forward the packet to the MAC layer.

The places and transitions P_{MAC}, P_{Error}, P_{NError}, T_{Error}, T_{NError}, T_{CBK}, and T_{send} present the interaction with the Data Link Layer Model presented in [19]. The token in the place P_{MAC} represents that the MAC layer received the packet and started to send it. If the MAC layer failed to transmit the packet due to packet collision or interference, the MAC protocol drops the packet and sends a CBK (Call Back) error message to the network layer. This represented by the place P_{Error} and firing of transitions T_{Error} and T_{CBK}. The firing of timed transition T_{CBK} presents the completion of the error detection and dropping the packet, after which one place buffer in the current node is released by returning a token to the place P_{Buffer}. On the other hand, successful transmitting and receiving the packet are presented by fringe of transition T_{NError}, which moves the token from P_{MAC} to P_{NError}, and firing of transition T_{Send} that returns the token back to the place P_{Buffer} representing increasing the free buffer space by one.

The firing probability of T_{Error} (ε) is the probability of CBK error (packet dropping probability), whereas the firing probability of T_{NError} is $(1-\varepsilon)$. The one node detailed model in Data Link Layer Model [19] is used to compute ε. The firing rate of the timed transition T_{Send} $(Rate(T_{Send}))$ and T_{CBK} $(Rate(T_{CBK}))$ are the average number of packet sent and dropped by the MAC protocol per unit time which are computed from the Data Link Layer Model [19].

In MANETs, each node has a routing table that indicates for each destination which is the next hop and number of hops to the destination. The main function of the routing protocols is building and updating the routing table. The routing protocols work in the network layer. For any packet entering the network layer, the routing protocol checks all available paths to the destination and chooses the best one. Because of mobility of nodes, there are frequent failures for paths between sources and destinations. The average time of failure of any path between any source and destination depends on the density distribution of nodes and the type of mobility pattern. For any path failure, the routing protocol tries to recover the path to the destination. The average time of the path recovery depends on the type of routing protocols, density of nodes, and mobility pattern.

The places P_{Av} and P_{NAv}, and transitions T_{Fail} and T_{Repair} model the effect of path failure and repairing process. The token in P_{Av} means that the path between the source and destination is available. Whereas, the token in P_{NAv} means that the path between the source and destination is not available. The timed transitions T_{Fail} and T_{Repair} present the completion of failure and repair of the path between the source and destination, respectively. The rate of firing of transitions T_{Fail} (μ_f) and T_{Repair} (μ_r) are the average rate of failure and repair of any path, respectively, which are computed using the Path Analysis Model that we proposed in [18]. The inhibiter arcs from places P_{AV} and P_{NAv} to transitions T_{Frd2}, T_{NPS} and T_{YPS} ensure that if there is no path to the destination in the routing table, the packet (token) will not be forwarded from the routing layer (P_s) to the data link layer (P_{MAC}).

Any node in MANET may work as a source, destination or router. The neighbours of any node may send packets to it to forward them to another node (works as a router) or absorb them (works as destination). The firing of timed transition T_{RP} and depositing a token in the place P_{RP} present the completion of receiving a packet from a neighbour node. The firing rate of T_{RP} depends on the average number of received packet to forward per unit time (λ_r). Section 4 derived an expression for λ_r. If the path that is required by the received packet is not available, the node drops the packet immediately. This is modelled by the place P_{Drop} and transitions T_{NPR} and T_{Drop}. Otherwise, the node tries to save the packet in the buffer which is presented by transition T_{YPR} and place P_{CB}.

Firing of transition T_{NBR} means that the buffer is full ($\#P_{Buffer} = 0$) and the node is unable to forward the packet which is dropped. If the buffer can accommodate a packet ($\#P_{Buffer} > 0$), the packet enters a queue and waits in order to be processed by MAC protocol. This is presented by firing transition T_{YBR} that moves a token from P_{CB} to P_{MAC}. Transitions T_{GP} and T_{RP} are assigned with guard functions that preventing firing of these transitions when the buffer is full ($\#P_{Buffer} = 0$). If ψ is the average probability that any path in the network is available, the firing probabilities of the transition T_{YPR} and T_{YPS} are ψ, whereas the firing probabilities of transitions T_{NPR} and T_{NPS} are $(1-\psi)$. The probability of the path availability is computed using the Path Analysis Model that we proposed in [18].

As explained in Section 3, the proposed frame work consists of three main SRN models; Data Link (MAC) Layer Model, Path Analysis Model, Network Layer Model. To compute the required performance indices, such as delay and throughput, the three models are solved iteratively using the fixed point iteration technique. The following procedure and Figure 2 summarize the iterative process to solve the proposed models to compute the delay per hop and throughput ratio which is used to compute the end-to-end delay and throughput per path:

Step 1: Using the Path Length Model, the parameters N_H, N_{cs}, N_h, and N_i, are computed.

Step 2: Solve the Data Link Layer Model using the procedure introduced in [19] to compute ε and δ considering that $\lambda_n = \lambda$.

Step 3: Solve the Path Analysis Model to compute μ_f and μ_r.

Step 4: Considering that $\alpha = 0.5$, as an initial value, the Network Layer Model is solved to compute the new value for α and λ_n. Also, any of the performance metric τ^n, such as throughput per hop, is computed, where n is the number of iteration.

Step 5: If $n = 1$ (initial iteration), increase n by one and go to Step 2.

Step 6: Compute the error of the performance metric using the following equation

$$\text{err}(\tau) = |\tau^n - \tau^{n-1}| / \tau^n$$

Step 7: If the err(τ) is less than a specified threshold, stop the iteration process, otherwise increase n by one and go to Step 2.

The number of iterations depends on the error threshold. In all validation scenarios introduced in the validation section, the error threshold is set to 0.05. In all cases the convergence of the performance metric is achieved in only a few iterations.

6   Validation and Results

In this section, the proposed model is validated by making extensive comparisons of its results with the results of many simulation experiments. The simulation results are obtained by using ns-2 simulator [2], whereas the analytical results derived from the proposed models are obtained using SPNP tool [20].

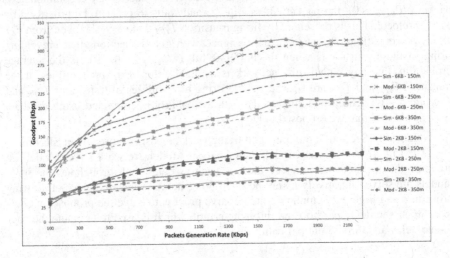

Fig. 5. Goodput versus packets generation rate for the BA method, in the case of packet size = 2kB or 6kB, R_{cs} = 150m, 250m or 350m, L = 600m, and R_{tx} = 150m

Two fundamental performance metrics are used to evaluate the proposed SRN models; goodput and end-to-end delay. The goodput is the number of data bits, not including protocol overhead and retransmitted bits, received correctly at a destination per unit time. Thus, goodput represents the application level throughput. End-to-end delay of data packets is the average time that a packet takes from the beginning of transiting the packet at a source node until the packet delivery to a destination. This includes delay time caused by buffering of data packets during route discovery, queuing at the interface queue for transmission at MAC layer, retransmission delays at MAC layer, and propagation and transfer delay times. In simulation, the throughput is computed by dividing the total number of received packets at all receivers by the simulation time, whereas end-to-end delay is obtained by summing up individual packet delays at all receivers and dividing the sum by the total number of received packets. The average goodput per source-destination pair and packet end-to-end delay for all simulation scenarios of the network are obtained by averaging over goodput of all source-destination pairs and end-to-end delay of all packets received by any destination, respectively.

For all simulation scenarios, all nodes move according to random waypoint mobility where the velocity of nodes is chosen uniformly from 0 to 20 m/s and the pause time is set to zero. For all mobility scenarios, nodes start to move at the start of the simulation and do not stop until the end of simulation. The source-destination pairs are chosen randomly over the network where Constant Bit Rate (CBR) traffic sources are used. The number of CBR sources is equal to the number of nodes where the destinations are randomly chosen. Identical mobility scenarios and traffic patterns are used across simulation scenarios to gather fair results. The simulation time is set to 1100s. The first 100s are discarded to be sure that the network has reached the steady state. All simulation results are obtained with 95% confidence interval. In Figures 10–20, solid lines refer to simulation results (labeled Sim), while dashed lines represent results of SRN models (labeled Mod).

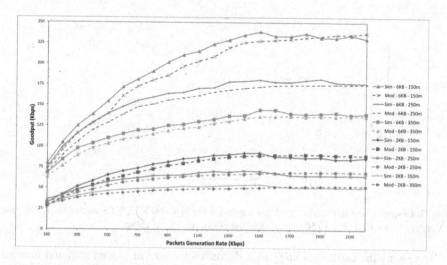

Fig. 6. Goodput versus packets generation rate for the RTS/CTS method, in the case of packet size = 2kB or 6kB, R_{cs} = 150m, 250m or 350m, L = 600m, and R_{tx} = 150m

To validate the proposed models, many network simulation scenarios are conducted. The settings of simulation scenarios consist of a network in a square area with side length L, where the number of nodes varies from 60 to 240, packets generation rate varies from 100 to 2200 kb/s, transmission range R_{tx} = 150 or 250m.

The first scenario is based on varying the packet generation rate in each source node from 100 to 2200 kb/s where the number of nodes N = 60, the size of network area is 600X600m, and transmission range is 150m. To investigate the effect of increasing the carrier sensing range and packet size on the performance of the network, R_{cs} is set to 150, 250, or 350m and the packet size is set to 2 or 6 kB. For this scenario, Figure 5 and 6 show the average goodput per source-destination pair verses increasing value for the packet generation rate for Basic Access (BA) and RTS/CTS (Request to Send/Clear to send) method [19], respectively.

As clear in Figure 5 and 6, in the case of light load conditions (small packet generation rate) the greater the packet generation rate the greater the goodput. However, in heavy load conditions, increasing the packet generation rate does not much affect on the goodput. This is because, in heavy load conditions when every node has a packet to send all the time, the contention to access the channel increases which increases the packets collision probability, interference between nodes, and buffer overflow. Thus, the number of packets losses increases that make any more increase in the packet generation rate has not a significant effect on goodput. Also, Figure 5 and 6 show the effect of increasing the carrier sensing range and packet size on the average goodput per source-destination pair under various channel traffic loads.

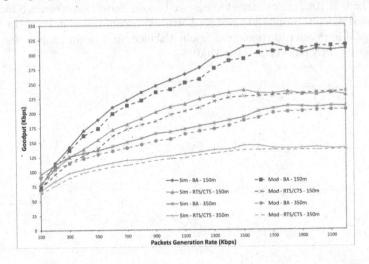

Fig. 7. Goodput versus packets generation rate for the BA and RTS/CTS methods, in the case of packet size = 6kB, R_{cs} = 150m or 350m, L = 600m, and R_{tx} = 150m

Increasing the carrier sensing range decreases the size of hidden area and number of hidden nodes N_H which consequently decreases the packet collision probability. However, the greater the carrier sensing range the greater the size of interference area and number of interfering nodes N_i which increase the packet collision probability and decreases the channel availability. Therefore, from Figure 5 and 6, it can be observed that a larger carrier sensing range results in a smaller goodput for both BA and RTS/CTS schemes.

Although increasing the packet size increases the packet collision probability due to hidden nodes and exponential backoff time per packet, it reduces the number of data packets sent per unit time that reduces the contention between nodes, and the packet collision probability due to interfering nodes. In addition, although the number of received packets per unit time in the case of lager packet size is smaller than that in the case of small packet size; the number of received bits per unit time is larger. Thus, as clear from Figure 5 and 6, the larger packet size improves the performance of the network for different carrier sensing ranges in both BA and RTS/CTS schemes.

As shown in Figure 5 and 6, with very light traffic load, increasing the packet size or carrier sensing range has not much significant effect on the performance of the network because the network load is very low, so most packet arrivals can be serviced successfully . In addition, with the same traffic load, with large packet size, it is to be noted that decreasing the carrier sensing range has more effect on the network goodput compared to small packet size. This is because, the smaller packet size increases interference and contention between nodes that make the goodput saturate fast with increasing the traffic load.

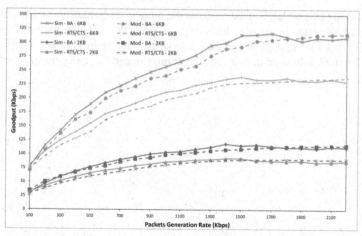

Fig. 8. Goodput versus packets generation rate for the BA and RTS/CTS methods, in the case of packet size = 2kB or 6kB, $R_{cs} = 150m$, $L = 600m$, and $R_{tx} = 150m$

In Figure 7 and 8, the comparison of the BA and RTS/CTS methods are made against the packet size and carrier sensing range. Figure 7 and 8 show the goodput versus the packet generation rate for BA and RTS/CTS method where in Figure 7 the packet size is 2 or 6 kB and $R_{cs} = 150m$, and in Figure 8 the packet size is 6 kB and $R_{cs} = 150$ or 350m. The figures reveal that in multi-hop ad hoc networks, in contrary to single hop ad hoc networks, BA method outperforms RTS/CTS method especially in heavy load and large packet size conditions. In the case of packet size is 6kB, increasing the carrier sensing range from 150m to 350m decreases the saturated goodput with 32.1% and 40.2% for BA and RTS/CTS methods, respectively and saturated goodpute for BA method is 32.4% higher than that for RTS/CTS method. This is because of the exposed terminal and blocking area problems for RTS/CTS.

To investigate the influence of the number of nodes on the end-to-end delay, Figure 9 shows the end-to-end delay versus increasing values of the number of nodes in the network (from 80 to 240 nodes) for BA method, where packet size = 2 kB, $R_{cs} = 250$ or 450m, L=1200, packets generation rate = 1000 kB/s, and Rtx = 250m. In Figure 9, it can be seen that for small number of nodes (less than180) the greater the number of nodes the greater the end-to-end delay because increasing number of nodes increases the collision probability and contention between nodes which increase the random exponential backoff time that increases the end-to-end delay. However, for large number of nodes, the end-to-end delay slightly increases with the increasing of the number of nodes because the system starts to saturate and becomes unable to serve any more packets.

As shown in Figures 5–9, the analytical results agree closely with simulation results. The difference between analytical and simulation results is due to the following approximations: (1) the time intervals of many events in the Data Link Layer Model, Network Layer Model, and Mobility Models, have been approximated to be exponentially distributed to be able to solve the proposed models analytically, (2) the approximate value for the number of neighbour nodes computed using the method introduced in [18], which is used to drive the number of hidden and interfering nodes, must be rounded to the nearest integer to be used to solve the models, and (3) the number of hops computed using the method introduced in [17] is usually overestimates the actual value and also it must be approximated to an integer number.

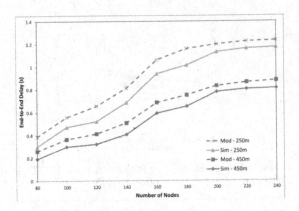

Fig. 9. End-to-end delay versus number of nodes for the BA method, in the case of packet size = 2kB, R_{cs} = 250m or 450, L = 1200m, and R_{tx} = 250

7   Conclusion

This work introduces an analytical framework for modelling MANETs that can be used to study the effect of various factors, such as communication range, density of nodes, random access behaviour, mobility patterns, and traffic load, on the performance indices such as packet end-to-end delay and network throughput, for performance analysis of MANETs. The proposed framework consists of five models; Path Analysis Model, Path Length Model, Data Link Layer Model, Network Layer Model, Transport Layer Model. To compute the required performance indices, such as delay and throughput, the three models are solved iteratively using the fixed point iteration technique. The proposed models are validated using extensive simulations.

References

1. Sarkar, S.K., Basavaraju, T.G., Puttamadappa, C.: Ad Hoc Mobile Wireless Networks: Principles, Protocols and Applications. Auerbach Publications (2004)
2. The Network Simulator ns2, http://www.isi.edu/nsnam/ns/
3. OPNET Modeler. Opnet Technologies, http://www.opnet.com
4. Zeng, X., Bagrodia, R., Gerla, M.: GloMoSim: a library for parallel simulation of large-scale wireless networks. In: Proceedings of the Twelfth Workshop on Parallel and Distributed Simulation, PADS 1998, pp. 154–161 (1998)
5. Jain, R.: The Art of Computer Systems Performance Analysis: Techniques for Experimental Design, Measurement, Simulation, and Modelling. John Wiley & Sons, New York (1991)

6. Zhang, C., Zhou, M.: A stochastic Petri net-approach to modeling and analysis of ad hoc network. In: Proceedings of the International Conference on Information Technology: Research and Education, ITRE 2003, pp. 152–156 (2003)

7. Lin, C., Chang-jun, J., Yu, F., Fei, L.: Performance evaluation of ad hoc networks based on SPN. In: Proceedings of the 2005 International Conference on Wireless Communications, Networking and Mobile Computing, vol. 2, pp. 816–819 (2005)

8. Gollakota, S., Ramana, B.V., Murthy, C.S.R.: Modeling TCP over Ad hoc Wireless Networks using Multi-dimensional Markov Chains. In: 3rd International Conference on Broadband Communications, Networks and Systems, BROADNETS 2006, pp. 1–10 (2006)

9. Nabhendra, B., Alhussein, A.: Queuing network models for delay analysis of multihop wireless ad hoc networks. In: Proceedings of the 2006 International Conference on Wireless Communications and Mobile Computing. ACM, Vancouver (2006)

10. Ghadimi, E., Khonsari, A., Diyanat, A., Farmani, M., Yazdani, N.: An analytical model of delay in multi-hop wireless ad hoc networks. Wirel. Netw. 17, 1679–1697

11. Jianhua, H., Dritan, K., Alistair, M., Yiming, W., Angel, D., Joe, M., Zhong, F.: Performance investigation of IEEE 802.11 MAC in multihop wireless networks. In: Proceedings of the 8th ACM International Symposium on Modeling, Analysis and Simulation of Wireless and Mobile Systems. ACM, Montreal (2005)

12. van den Berg, H., Mandjes, M., Roijers, F.: Performance Modeling of a Bottleneck Node in an IEEE 802.11 Ad-Hoc Network. In: Kunz, T., Ravi, S.S. (eds.) ADHOC-NOW 2006. LNCS, vol. 4104, pp. 321–336. Springer, Heidelberg (2006)

13. Wang, B., Song, F., Zhang, S., Zhang, H.: Throughput modeling analysis of IEEE 802.11 DCF mechanism in multi-hop non-saturated wireless ad-hoc networks. In: International Conference on Communications, Circuits and Systems, ICCCAS 2008, pp. 383–387 (2008)

14. Fangqin, L., Chuang, L., Hao, W., Peter, U.: Throughput Analysis of Wireless Multi-hop Chain Networks. In: Eighth IEEE/ACIS International Conference on Computer and Information Science, ICIS 2009, pp. 834–839 (2009)

15. Yu, C., Yang, Y., Darwazeh, I.: A Cross-Layer Analytical Model of End-to-End Delay Performance for Wireless Multi-Hop Environments. In: Global Telecommunications Conference (GLOBECOM 2010), pp. 1–6. IEEE (2010)

16. Sweedy, A.M., Semeia, A.I., Sayed, S.Y., Konber, A.H.: The effect of frame length, fragmentation and RTS/CTS mechanism on IEEE 802.11 MAC performance. In: 10th International Conference on Intelligent Systems Design and Applications (ISDA), pp. 1338–1344 (2010)

17. Younes, O., Thomas, N.: Analysis of the Expected Number of Hops in Mobile Ad Hoc Networks with Random Waypoint Mobility. Electronic Notes in Theoretical Computer Science 275, 143–158

18. Yones, O., Thomas, N.: A Path Connection Availability Model for MANETs with Random Waypoint Mobility. In: Tribastone, M., Gilmore, S. (eds.) EPEW/UKPEW 2012. LNCS, vol. 7587, pp. 111–126. Springer, Heidelberg (2013)

19. Younes, O., Thomas, N.: An SRN Model of the IEEE 802. 11 DCF MAC Protocol in Multi-Hop Ad Hoc Networks with Hidden Nodes. The Computer Journal 54, 875–893 (2011)

20. Ciardo, G., Muppala, J., Trivedi, K.: SPNP: stochastic Petri net package. In: Proceedings of the Third International Workshop on Petri Nets and Performance Models, PNPM 1989, pp. 142–151 (1989)

Don't Just Go with the Flow:
Cautionary Tales of Fluid Flow Approximation

Alireza Pourranjbar[1], Jane Hillston[1], and Luca Bortolussi[2,3]

[1] LFCS, School of Informatics, University of Edinburgh, UK
[2] DMG, University of Trieste, Italy
[3] CNR/ISTI, Pisa, Italy

Abstract. Fluid flow approximation allows efficient analysis of large
scale PEPA models. Given a model, this method outputs how the mean,
variance, and any other moment of the model's stochastic behaviour
evolves as a function of time. We investigate whether the method's results, i.e. moments of the behaviour, are *sufficient* to capture system's
actual dynamics.

We ran a series of experiments on a client-server model. For some
parametrizations of the model, the model's behaviour can accurately be
characterized by the fluid flow approximations of its moments. However,
the experiments show that for some other parametrizations, these moments are not sufficient to capture the model's behaviour, highlighting
a pitfall of relying only on the results of fluid flow analysis. The results
suggest that the sufficiency of the fluid flow method for the analysis of
a model depends on the model's concrete parametrization. They also
make it clear that the existing criteria for deciding on the sufficiency of
the fluid flow method are not robust.

1 Introduction

One of the features of Performance Evaluation Process Algebra, or PEPA, is that
the concise set of formal primitives it provides is rich enough to be used to model
a wide range of systems [1,2,3,4]. In general, analysis of a PEPA model involves
deriving the model's underlying Continuous Time Markov Chain (CTMC) and
applying Markovian analysis. When PEPA is used to model a large scale system,
i.e. a system with large populations of entities, the size of the underlying CTMC
becomes so large that Markovian analysis becomes expensive, time consuming
or even, due to the memory constraints, practically infeasible; a famous problem
referred to in the literature as the problem of *state space explosion*.

For the analysis of large scale PEPA models, methods have been developed
which provide us with *approximate* results. One such method is Monte Carlo
stochastic simulation. Here, given a large scale PEPA model, the modeller runs
a number of simulations over the underlying CTMC, sampling the state of the
system at the time t of interest. The obtained set of samples are then used
to characterize the system performance metric's approximate distribution. The
approximate distribution, found by applying the Monte Carlo method, tends to

M. Tribastone and S. Gilmore (Eds.): EPEW/UKPEW 2012, LNCS 7587, pp. 156–171, 2013.

the exact one as the number of simulation runs tends to infinity. Depending on the size of the system, running the stochastic simulations can be computationally expensive. An alternative approach for the analysis of large scale models is fluid flow approximation [5]. Using this method, one derives from a PEPA model, a set of ordinary differential equations (ODEs) whose solutions approximate the moments of the underlying CTMC to a given order. When the fluid flow method is used to analyse a model, the modeller characterizes the system's stochastic behaviour by the moments of its associated CTMC.

Compared with Monte Carlo simulation, the fluid flow method is orders of magnitude more efficient. However, it only captures the first few moments of the underlying CTMC and, under some conditions, it can suffer from a significant amount of error. These two observations raise the question of *sufficiency* of the fluid flow method: having a large scale PEPA model, is it *sufficient* to use *only* the fluid flow method for its analysis and are the results of this method enough to characterize the system's dynamics?

Our focus is on these two questions: we present the results of our experiments, in which we investigated if the fluid flow method is a sufficient tool for the analysis of variants of a simple client-server system. These experiments showed that, whilst for some models the results of fluid flow method can be used to accurately characterize the system's behaviour, for other models the results contain a large amount of error or are even misleading about the system's real executions.

The issue of sufficiency and related questions have previously been considered in the literature. In [6] Hayden and Bradley show that the state space of each PEPA model can be partitioned into regions. The suitability of the fluid flow method depends on the region that the system's execution resides in; the accuracy of the results of the fluid flow method decreases as the dynamics of the system gets closer to the *unsafe* regions. In [7], Stefanek et al. suggest that for periods of time when the system is performing in unsafe regions, one needs to run a large number of stochastic simulations, use such trajectories to calculate the moments (mean, variance, etc.) of the system's behaviour, and use them in place of the result of the fluid flow method. Our experiment results show the same phenomenon with respect to the quality of the fluid flow approximation as well as the importance of calculating accurate moments. Nevertheless, they also show that some systems have a particular type of dynamics which cannot be captured only by looking at the moments of its behaviour.

The work presented in [8] provides the basis of this paper. In [8], Bortolussi et al. suggest that one requirement for applying the fluid flow method when analysing a model, is for the all of the model's transitions to have *continuous* effect on model's dynamics. It is argued in [8] that this requirement might not be fully respected by all models. Such non-conforming models suggested in [8] are: models where a small population of components are interacting with a large population or models in which there is an interplay of slow and fast transitions. For these models, the authors suggest that the appropriate analysis of the model is performing *hybrid stochastic simulation*. In this analysis method, the *continuous* and *discrete* transitions, both necessary for capturing the model's dynamics, are taken into account. In [8] Bortolussi et al. looked at the necessary conditions for sufficiency of the fluid flow method and provided some heuristics or criteria for checking, by looking at a model, if the fluid flow approximation is sufficient for its analysis. Our experiments showed that, given a PEPA model, more robust criteria than the ones presented in [8] are needed for one to decide on sufficiency of the fluid flow method.

Structure of this paper: Section 2 describes the model which we considered in our experiments. Section 3 shows the results of analysis of our model, where different methods have been applied. Section 4 describes the results of our experiment with respect to the sufficiency of the fluid flow method. In Section 5 we present our concluding remarks about sufficiency results and elaborate on future work.

2   The Model

To illustrate our argument throughout the paper we use variants of a simple client-server system. The following is the PEPA model of this system, where n_c is the number of client and n_s is the number of servers:

$$C_{thinking} \overset{def}{=} (think, r_t).C_{requesting}$$
$$C_{requesting} \overset{def}{=} (req, r_c).C_{thinking}$$
$$S_{idle} \overset{def}{=} (req, r_s).S_{logging}$$
$$S_{logging} \overset{def}{=} (log, r_l).S_{idle}$$
$$CS \overset{def}{=} S_{idle}[n_s] \underset{\{req\}}{\bowtie} C_{thinking}[n_c]$$

Model 1. PEPA model of a simple client-server system

A server's initial state is S_{idle} when it is waiting for a client to synchronize with it on the action req[1]. A client's initial state is $Client_{thinking}$. Each client, initially, performs an action *think* and when her thinking is finished, she undertakes the shared action *req* synchronizing with an idle server. When *req* is done, the client goes to her initial state and the server goes to the state $Server_{logging}$. Here the server undertakes the action *log* and then becomes *idle* again. In PEPA each action has a *rate* which is the parameter of an *exponentially distributed random variable* that governs the *delay* associated with performing that action. For instance, the rate of the action *think* is r_t.

In this paper we assume that the objective of the analysis of this model is to find the *distribution* of the number of clients who are in the state $Client_{requesting}$ at the equilibrium. These are the clients being queued, waiting to get the service. We also want to know how the length of this queue changes as we reconfigure

---

[1] *req* stands for "request".

the system: adding servers, considering more complicated behaviour for servers, changing the service rate of the existing servers, or when the population of clients increases.

Preliminaries

We use the notion of *numerical vectors* to build the underlying state space of our client-server system [5]. Each state of this system is represented as a vector, consisting of four *state variables*: $\langle S_i, S_l, C_t, C_r \rangle$, where in the current state, S_i represents the number of *idle* servers, S_l is the number of *logging* servers, C_t is the number of *thinking* clients and finally C_r is the number of clients who are requesting. At any given time, $\langle S_i, S_l, C_t, C_r \rangle \in \mathbb{Z}^{+^4}$.

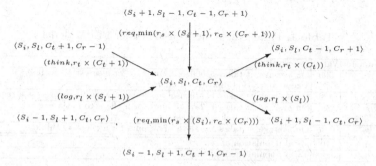

Fig. 1. Transitions into and out of a typical state $\langle S_i, S_l, C_t, C_r \rangle$

Figure 1 shows a typical state of this system and how the system might transition into or out of it. Each transition's rate is a function of the rate of the transition's action and the population count which enables that transition. For instance, in state $\langle S_i, S_l, C_t, C_r \rangle$ the rate of the action *log* is $r_l \times S_l$. According to [9] when two components synchronize on an action, the rate of the shared action is defined to be the minimum of the rates at which the synchronizing components can perform that action. This notion can be lifted to *populations* of components [10]. When components of two populations synchronize on an action, the rate at which the action takes place is the minimum of the rates which each of those populations *offer* for the shared action. In Fig. 1, when the system is in state $\langle S_i, S_l, C_t, C_r \rangle$, the server population can perform action *req* with rate $S_i \times r_s$ and client population with the rate $C_r \times r_c$. Consequently, for state $\langle S_i, S_l, C_t, C_r \rangle$, the action *req* happens with the rate $\min(S_i \times r_s, C_r \times r_c)$.

Given concrete values for parameters of the client-server system (activity rates and the initial populations), one can use the pattern shown in Fig. 1 to build the complete state space $\mathbb{D}$ ($\mathbb{D} \subseteq \mathbb{Z}^{+^4}$) underlying the model. This state space can be treated as a Continuous Time Markov Chain on the space $\mathbb{D}$ and be used as the basis of performance evaluation [5]. An important aspect of a dependable client-server system is to have short queues for the clients and serving them in a timely manner. Hence, in the analysis of this model, we want to find the behaviour of state variable C_r.

3   Analysis of the Model

Typically, a client-server system involves a large population of clients communicating with a relatively smaller population of servers. Let us make a concrete client-server model based on Model 1 with the parameter values shown in Table 1. Our concrete model describes a system with 10000 clients and 10 fast servers. The rates are chosen in a way to make the length of the client waiting queue be sensitive to the number of servers available in the system and enable us to study an interesting behaviour exhibited by an extension of this model which will be shown later in Sec. 4.2.

Table 1. Parameter values considered for PEPA Model 1

Parameter	Value	Description
r_s	500	On average, it takes 1/500th of an hour for a server to initiate a communication link with a client.
r_l	120	On average, it takes 1/120th of an hour for a server to process a request.
r_c	2	On average, it takes 1/2 of an hour for a client to initiate a communication link with a server.
r_t	0.06	On average, it takes 1/0.06th of a hours for a client to think.
n_s	10	Total population of servers.
n_c	10000	Total population of clients.

In order to find C_r's equilibrium distribution one can construct the model's underlying CTMC, use Markovian analysis to solve it and find C_r's *exact* distribution. However, when the client population is large, even in the range of a few thousands, the size of the CTMC becomes so large that solving it incurs a large computational cost. Therefore, a more feasible way to find C_r's behaviour is to use alternative approaches, such as the Monte Carlo method or the fluid flow method [5], to find more efficiently *approximations* to the *exact* solutions.

The Monte Carlo method was first applied to find C_r's distribution at the equilibrium. We performed 20000 simulations over the model's underlying CTMC, collected C_r's value at $t = 15000$ (hours) and built a histogram, shown in Fig. 2.1. One can use this histogram to derive information such as C_r's mean ($\mathbb{E}_{M.C.}[C_r]$) and standard deviation ($\sigma_{M.C.}[C_r]$)[2]. Running 20000 simulations guarantees that the mean *self distance* [11] of resulting histogram is bounded by $\log 2\sqrt{\pi/20000}$; an indication that the histogram is reasonably stable.

Another way to find C_r's behaviour, is to use the fluid flow method. For a PEPA model, this method constructs a set of ordinary differential equations (ODEs) which approximates how the *mean*, *variance* (and higher order moments) of state variables evolve over the course of time [6,10]. Tools such as

---

[2] The subscript M.C. expresses that the measure is a result of applying the Monte Carlo method.

the PEPA Eclipse Plugin [12] and the Grouped PEPA Analyser [13] can be used
to automatically derive a PEPA model's underlying ODEs. Here in this paper, we
will use Chapman-Kolmogorov forward equations, related to the model's underlying CTMC, to derive its corresponding ODEs [6] to shows how exactly ODEs
are constructed and what they describe about our model's CTMC. Assuming

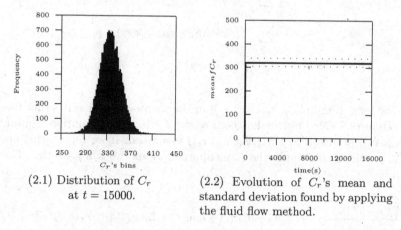

(2.1) Distribution of C_r
at $t = 15000$.

(2.2) Evolution of C_r's mean and
standard deviation found by applying
the fluid flow method.

Fig. 2. C_r's behavior, found by applying the Monte Carlo method and fluid flow
method

that the model's underlying CTMC is completely defined by the pattern shown
in Fig. 1, one can write the Chapman-Kolmogorov forward equations which
express, as a function of time, how the probability of being in any given state
$\mathbf{v} = \langle S_i, S_l, C_i, C_t \rangle \in \mathbb{D} \subset \mathbb{Z}^{+^4}$ evolves. Let $p_{\langle S_i, S_l, C_t, C_r \rangle}(t)$ be the probability of
being in state $\langle S_i, S_l, C_i, C_t \rangle$ at time t. Then we have:

$$
\frac{d\, p_{\langle S_i, S_l, C_t, C_r \rangle}(t)}{d\, t} = \tag{1}
$$
$$
\begin{aligned}
&+ (C_t + 1) \times r_t \times p_{\langle S_i, S_l, C_t+1, C_r-1 \rangle}(t) \\
&+ (S_l + 1) \times r_l \times p_{\langle S_i-1, S_l+1, C_t, C_r \rangle}(t) \\
&+ \min(\ (S_i + 1) \times r_s\ , (C_r + 1) \times r_c\ ) \times p_{\langle S_i+1, S_l-1, C_t-1, C_r+1 \rangle}(t) \\
&- \min(\ S_i \times r_s\ , C_r \times r_c\ ) \times p_{\langle S_i, S_l, C_t, C_r \rangle}(t) \\
&- S_l \times r_l \times p_{\langle S_i, S_l, C_t, C_r \rangle}(t) \\
&- C_t \times r_t \times p_{\langle S_i, S_l, C_t, C_r \rangle}(t).
\end{aligned}
$$

This ODE system has one equation for each state $\mathbf{v} \in \mathbb{D}$. Having a large number
of states means one cannot form and solve equations for all states of the model's
CTMC. However, we reconfigure the equations and for each state variable,

find one equation describing how the mean of that state variable evolves. For state variable C_r:

$$\frac{d\,\mathbb{E}[C_r](t)}{d\,t} = \sum_{\langle S_i,S_l,C_t,C_l\rangle \in \mathbb{D}} \frac{C_r \times p_{\langle S_i,S_l,C_t,C_r\rangle}(t)}{d\,t} \qquad (2)$$

$$= + \sum_{\langle S_i,S_l,C_t,C_l\rangle \in \mathbb{D}} C_t \times r_t \times p_{\langle S_i,S_l,C_t,C_r\rangle}(t)$$

$$- \sum_{\langle S_i,S_l,C_t,C_l\rangle \in \mathbb{D}} \min(S_i \times r_s, C_r \times r_c) \times p_{\langle S_i,S_l,C_t,C_r\rangle}(t)$$

$$= + r_t \times \mathbb{E}[C_t](t) - \mathbb{E}[\min(S_i \times r_s, C_r \times r_c)](t).$$

Note the term $\mathbb{E}[\min(S_i \times r_s, C_r \times r_c)]$ in the above equations. In order to *close* the system of ODEs and make them solvable, the approximation $\mathbb{E}[\min(S_i \times r_s, C_r \times r_c)] \approx \min(\mathbb{E}[S_i \times r_s], \mathbb{E}[C_r \times r_c])$ is applied. If we repeat this process for C_t, S_i and S_l and apply the same approximation, we will have the following equations[3].

$$\frac{d\,\mathbb{E}_{F.F.}[C_t](t)}{dt} = -r_t \times \mathbb{E}_{F.F.}[C_t](t) + \min(r_c \times \mathbb{E}_{F.F.}[C_r](t), r_s \times \mathbb{E}_{F.F.}[S_i](t)) \quad (3)$$

$$\frac{d\,\mathbb{E}_{F.F.}[C_r](t)}{dt} = -\min(r_c \times \mathbb{E}_{F.F.}[C_r](t), r_s \times \mathbb{E}_{F.F.}[S_i](t)) + r_t \times \mathbb{E}_{F.F.}[C_t](t)$$

$$\frac{d\,\mathbb{E}_{F.F.}[S_i](t)}{dt} = -\min(r_c \times \mathbb{E}_{F.F.}[C_r](t), r_s \times \mathbb{E}_{F.F.}[S_i](t)) + r_l \times \mathbb{E}_{F.F.}[S_l](t)$$

$$\frac{d\,\mathbb{E}_{F.F.}[S_l](t)}{dt} = +\min(r_c \times \mathbb{E}_{F.F.}[C_r](t), r_s \times \mathbb{E}_{F.F.}[S_i](t)) - r_l \times \mathbb{E}_{F.F.}[S_l](t)$$

Due to the approximation step, the solutions $\mathbb{E}_{F.F.}[C_t]$, $\mathbb{E}_{F.F.}[C_r]$, $\mathbb{E}_{F.F.}[S_i]$ and $\mathbb{E}_{F.F.}[S_l]$ are approximations to $\mathbb{E}[C_t]$, $\mathbb{E}[C_r]$, $\mathbb{E}[S_i]$ and $\mathbb{E}[S_l]$ which, could have been derived by solving the model's underlying CTMC. Here, in order to save space, we did not include the ODEs related to variance of the state variables. Figure 2.2 shows $\mathbb{E}_{F.F.}[C_r]$ found by the fluid flow analysis of our model. The dotted lines above and below $\mathbb{E}_{F.F.}[C_r]$'s trajectory show $\mathbb{E}_{F.F.}[C_r] + \sqrt{Var_{F.F.}[C_r]}$ and $\mathbb{E}[C_r] - \sqrt{Var_{F.F.}[C_r]}$ respectively. Note that the system reaches its equilibrium within seven seconds. This means that $t = 15000$ (hours), which was the sampling time when running the Monte Carlo method, is a time when the system has reached its equilibrium.

4   Sufficiency of Fluid Flow Analysis

When analysing a large scale PEPA model, the decision has to be made about an appropriate analysis method. The fluid flow approximation is an efficient way

---

[3] The subscript F.F. expresses that the measure is the result of applying the fluid flow approximation.

to analyse the model. However, its results might be insufficient to capture the actual dynamics of the system. Moreover, the approximation:

$$\mathbb{E}[\min(g(x), h(x))] \approx \min(\mathbb{E}[g(x)], \mathbb{E}[h(x)])]$$

introduces a certain amount of error in the fluid flow approximation's results, which is difficult to control. These issues raise the question of *sufficiency* of the fluid flow method as an analysis tool when analysing a PEPA model. In the following, we provide evidence that whilst the fluid flow approximation is a sufficient method for analysis of some models, applying this method might not be appropriate (and may even be misleading) for others.

4.1   The Client-Server System

Let us consider again Model 1. Considering the equation set (3), we know that in the equilibrium:

$$\frac{d\ C_t(t)}{dt} = \frac{d\ C_r(t)}{dt} = \frac{d\ S_i(t)}{dt} = \frac{d\ S_l(t)}{dt} = 0 \qquad (4)$$

In the equilibrium, depending on the rates and populations of the clients and servers, one of the following cases can happen:

- A: No contention case: $\min(r_s \times S_i, r_c \times C_r) = r_c \times C_r$. In this case, there is enough service capacity to satisfy the requirements of the clients. Simplifying the equations we have:

$$C_r = \frac{r_t}{r_t + r_c} n_c, \quad C_t = \frac{r_c}{r_c + r_t} n_c, \quad S_i = n_s - \frac{r_c}{r_l} \frac{r_t}{r_t + r_c} n_c, \quad S_l = \frac{r_c}{r_l} \frac{r_t}{r_t + r_c} n_c. \quad (5)$$

- B: Contention case: $\min(r_s \times S_i, r_c \times C_r) = r_s \times S_i$. In this case, clients become blocked, because there is not enough service capacity to satisfy their needs. In this case:

$$C_r = n_c - \frac{r_s}{r_t} \frac{r_l}{r_s + r_l} n_s, \quad C_t = \frac{r_s}{r_t} \frac{r_l}{r_s + r_l} n_s, \quad S_i = \frac{r_l}{r_s + r_l} n_s, \quad S_l = \frac{r_s}{r_s + r_l} n_s. \quad (6)$$

For the parameter values of Table 1, the system settles in case A.

We wished to check whether it is sufficient to use *only* the fluid flow method when analysing this model and how the sufficiency depends on the concrete population levels of clients and servers. For this purpose, initially, we ran experiments where we considered various populations for the servers (n_s varies from three to 18) and for each population level, the analysis results derived by the fluid flow method were compared against those derived from the Monte Carlo method. The client population was kept constant ($n_c = 10000$). Table 2 summarises the results of these experiments. In Table 2, $\mathbb{E}_{M.C.}[C_r]$ and $\sigma_{M.C.}[C_r]$ are respectively, the mean value of C_r and C_r's standard deviation found by the Monte Carlo method. Similarly $\mathbb{E}_{F.F.}[C_r]$ and $\sigma_{F.F.}[C_r]$ are C_r's mean and the associated standard deviation found by the fluid flow method. As the results of the Monte Carlo method are closer to C_r's exact behaviour, we consider such results as the basis of checking the validity of the results of the fluid flow method. Hence, the error associated with $\mathbb{E}_{F.F.}[C_r]$ (similarly for other measures) is defined as:

$$Err(\mathbb{E}_{M.C.}[C_r], \mathbb{E}_{F.F.}[C_r]) = \left| \frac{\mathbb{E}_{M.C.}[C_r] - \mathbb{E}_{F.F.}[C_r]}{\mathbb{E}_{M.C.}[C_r]} \right| \times 100.$$

Table 2. Comparing results of the fluid flow method and Monte Carlo simulation

	n_s	3	4	5	6	7	8	9	10	12	14	16	18
$\mathbb{E}[C_r]$	F.F.A.	5645	4193	2741	1290.3	322	322	322	322	322	322	322	322
	M.C.	5644	4192	2740	1290	490	384	349	335	325	323	322.6	322.3
	Err.(%)	0.01	0.01	0.03	0.04	34	16	7.7	3.8	0.9	0.3	0.18	0.12
$\sigma[C_r]$	F.F.A.	60.62	70	78.26	85.73	17.66	17.66	17.66	17.66	17.66	17.66	17.66	17.66
	M.C.	60.45	69.45	78.79	86.5	36.90	23.49	19.84	18.72	17.99	17.72	17.76	17.74
	Err.(%)	0.26	0.25	0.67	0.9	52.3	25.20	11.44	5.6	1.8	0.3	0.5	0.4

Considering $Err(\mathbb{E}_{M.C.}[C_r], \mathbb{E}_{F.F.}[C_r])$ in Table 2, we observed that whilst in some configurations of the client-server system, $\mathbb{E}_{F.F.}[C_r]$ reasonably approximates $\mathbb{E}_{M.C.}[C_r]$ ($n_s \leq 6$ or $n_s \geq 9$, $Err(\mathbb{E}_{M.C.}[C_r], \mathbb{E}_{F.F.}[C_r]) < 5\%$), in other configurations, the error is relatively high ($n_s = 7$ or $n_s = 8$). Based on the notion of *switching points* defined in [6], one explanation for this phenomenon is that when the system's dynamics keeps *switching* between case A and case B, then the quality of the approximation $\mathbb{E}[\min(r_s \times Si, r_c \times n_c)] = \min(\mathbb{E}[r_s \times S_i], \mathbb{E}[r_c \times C_r])$ is poorer and the mean behaviour shown by the fluid flow method has more error than the case when the system's dynamics settles down in one mode. Looking at the results of the Monte Carlo method, the relatively large value of the *coefficient of variation* ($\frac{\sigma_{M.C.}[C_r]}{\mathbb{E}_{M.C.}[C_r]}$) associated with $\mathbb{E}_{M.C.}[C_r]$ when $n_s = 7$ or $n_s = 8$, shows that C_r's distribution is relatively wide and hence the system's dynamics is likely to switch *more often* between the case of having a small number of clients requesting (A) and the case of having a large number of them (B).

Figure 3.1 summarises another aspect of the fluid flow approximation for this experiment. It shows that for this particular example, if $n_s > 6.6 + \epsilon$ the system converges to the behaviour associated with case A, i.e. $C_r = 322$ and when $n_s < 6.6 + \epsilon$ the system's dynamics converges to case B. The values of Table 2 suggest that the maximum error associated with $\mathbb{E}_{F.F.}[C_r]$ happens when n_s is chosen to be in the interval (6,8).

We extended the previous experiments to also consider different populations of clients. Here, n_c takes values in $[1000, 100000]$, n_s in $[1, 50]$ and the rate values were again chosen based on Table 1. For each pair of (n_s, n_c) we plot $\mathbb{E}_{F.F.}[C_r]$. Figure 3.2 shows the result. As we can see, for each n_c, there is a n_s which defines the border between cases A and B for that n_c. For instance, when $n_c = 30000$, if $n_s > 21$ then in the equilibrium, $\min(r_s \times S_i, r_c \times C_r) = r_c \times C_r$ (the system resides in case A) and if $n_s < 21$ then in the equilibrium, the system resides in case B. The same phenomenon happens when $n_s = 70000$ and

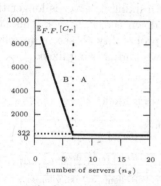
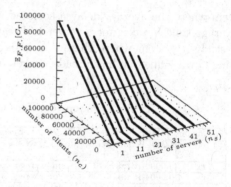

(3.1) $\mathbb{E}_{F.F.}[C_r]$ at the equilibrium. (3.2) $\mathbb{E}_{F.F.}[C_r]$ at the equilibrium. Both n_s and
Here n_s varies and $n_c = 10000$. n_c vary.

Fig. 3. $\mathbb{E}_{F.F.}[C_r]$ at the equilibrium for various populations considered for clients and servers

$n_s = 40$. The results in Table 2 and the fact that the mode change occurs in the given configurations of this particular model, suggests that the accuracy of C_r's moments, found by the fluid flow method, increases, i.e. the error associated with the moments decreases, if the system's populations are changed in a way that reduces the probability that the system settles near the switching points. The experiments showed that in cases where the error associated with $\mathbb{E}_{F.F.}[C_f]$, $\sigma_{F.F}[C_r]$ (or higher moments) is small, the fluid flow method can be considered as an efficient way to characterize C_r's behaviour. In such cases, the modeller can efficiently find accurate moments such as mean, variance, skewness and kurtosis and then construct an *approximate histogram*, similar to the one that can be derived by the application of the Monte Carlo method. The knowledge that C_r's exact distribution is uni-modal (see the histogram of Fig. 2.1) makes it easier to construct C_r's approximate histogram from the moments. Here, the fluid flow approach is sufficient to form a reasonable characterization of C_r's behaviour.

4.2   An Extension of Client-Server System

In this subsection we consider Model 2 which is an extension of Model 1. The structure of the Model 2 is the same as Model 1 except that in Model 2 each server might occasionally *break down* and stop serving the clients:

$$S_{idle} \stackrel{def}{=} (req, r_s).S_{logging} + (brk, r_b).S_{broken}$$
$$S_{logging} \stackrel{def}{=} (log, r_l).S_{idle}$$
$$S_{broken} \stackrel{def}{=} (fix, r_f).S_{idle}$$

Table 3 shows the chosen values for the new rates r_s, r_b and r_f. The rest of the parameters in Model 2 are as in Table 1. For illustration purposes, we consider a system where the average delay associated with fixing a server is longer than the average time it takes for a server to break down (i.e. $r_f < r_b$). This helps us to study a system where there is a higher probability to see more servers breaking down while one has already broken down and is being fixed.

Table 3. Parameter values used for Model 2

Parameter	Value	Description
r_s	200	Compared to Model 1, we have made the servers slower in this model.
r_b	0.0006	It takes 70 days, on average, for a server to break down.
r_f	0.0004	It takes 100 days, on average, for a server to get fixed.
r_t	0.05	Compared to Model 1, we have made a clients' thinking longer.

The results of the analysis of Model 2, through the Monte Carlo technique as well as the fluid flow method is depicted in Fig. 4. Figure 4.1 shows that this model, with the current parameter values, exhibits a *multi-modal* behaviour. The first *mode* corresponds to the situation where there is no broken server ($S_b = 0$). The experiment showed that in 7100 trajectories out of 20000 simulation trajectories, at $t = 15000$, the system was observed to be in this mode. When a server breaks down, the system changes its *mode*. Due to the decrease in S_i, the overall service rate offered by the servers decreases and C_r's values cluster around a higher level in the new mode.

Figures 4.2, 4.3, 4.4 and 4.5. show that until $t \approx 4000$, $\mathbb{E}[C_r]$ remains constant, $\mathbb{E}[S_i]$ is *decreasing* and $\mathbb{E}[S_b]$ is increasing. This shows a phase of execution where in spite of the fact that $\mathbb{E}[S_i]$, experienced by the clients, is decreasing, still, the overall service rate offered by the servers ($r_s \times S_i$) is large enough to keep $\mathbb{E}[C_r]$ at the same level. Interestingly, at $t \approx 4000$, $\mathbb{E}[S_b]$ becomes large enough, i.e. $\mathbb{E}[S_i]$ becomes small enough, so that $\mathbb{E}[C_r]$ starts to increase. This is the second phase of the system's execution. During this period of time, $\mathbb{E}[S_i]$ keeps decreasing and $\mathbb{E}[C_r]$ increasing. Eventually, at $t = 10000$ the system reaches its equilibrium.

In order to check the sufficiency of the fluid flow analysis for analysing this model we ran a similar experiment to the one described in Section 4.1. The population of clients was kept constant at $n_c = 10000$ and different populations of servers in the range $[3, 32]$ were considered. Table 4 summarizes the results. Checking the sufficiency property for this model was more interesting as it is capable of showing a multi-modal behaviour.

Table 4. Comparison between results of the fluid flow method and the Monte Carlo method. $n_c = 10000$ and n_s varies.

	n_s	3	4	5	6	7	8	9	10	12	14	16	18	24	32
$\mathbb{E}[C_r]$	F.F.A.	7119	6159	5199	4239	3279	2319	1359	399	243	243	243	243	243	243
	M. C.	7156	6177	5236	4295	3387	2599	1975	1460	843	533	378	309	251	244
	Err.(%)	0.6	0.2	0.7	1.3	3.18	10.77	31.1	72.6	71.1	54.4	35.7	21	3	0.1
$\sigma[C_r]$	F.F.A.	1240	1432	1601	1753	1894	2025	2148	959	15.42	15.42	15.42	15.42	15.42	15.42
	M.C.	1245	1420	1609	1758	1808	1792	1656	1456	1048	713	470	314	76	17.80
	Err.(%)	0.42	0.79	0.52	0.25	4.7	13	29	34.1	98	97	96	95	79	13

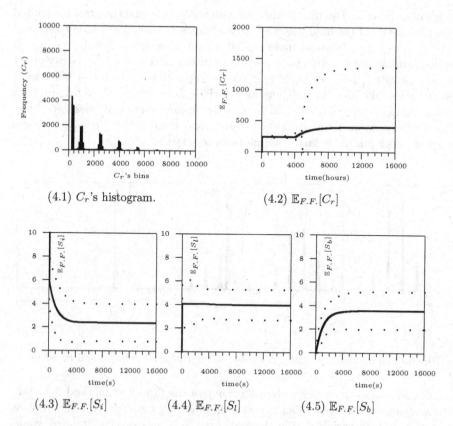

Fig. 4. State variables' behaviour in Model 2 when $n_c = 10000$ and $n_s = 10$

Considering the error $Err(\mathbb{E}_{M.C.}[C_r], \mathbb{E}_{F.F.}[C_r])$, one can see the same trend as in the results of Model 1: as we gradually increase the number of servers, the error between the results of the fluid flow analysis and the Monte Carlo method with respect to $\mathbb{E}[C_r]$ first rises and then decreases. In order to explain this trend, we use Fig. 5, which shows the results of Monte Carlo simulations for each case.

We observed that again the quality of the approximation $\mathbb{E}[\min(r_s \times S_i, r_c \times C_r)] \approx \min(r_s \times \mathbb{E}[S_i], r_c \times \mathbb{E}[C_r])$ plays an important role in the accuracy of the results of the fluid flow method. In a model where n_s is relatively small (e.g. $n_s = 4$), despite the fact that system's dynamics has *different modes*, still, in *any* of those modes, the above approximation is exact:

$$\mathbb{E}[\min(r_s \times S_i, r_c \times C_r)] \approx \min(r_s \times \mathbb{E}[S_i], r_c \times \mathbb{E}[C_r]) = r_s \times S_i.$$

As n_s increases, we see models whose dynamics contain mode(s) where $\min(r_s \times \mathbb{E}[S_i], r_c \times \mathbb{E}[C_r]) = r_s \times S_i$ and mode(s) where $\min(r_s \times \mathbb{E}[S_i], r_c \times \mathbb{E}[C_r]) = r_c \times C_r$. For example, when $n_s = 6$ or $n_s = 10$, the system keeps switching between *a series of modes* where there are not enough servers to keep C_r small and *the mode* where there are enough servers to satisfy client requests. In models with such a behaviour, the quality of approximation is poorer and the error associated with the results of the fluid flow method increases. For relatively larger values of n_s (e.g. $n_s > 12$), it becomes more probable that when a server fails, the overall service rate offered by other active servers remain large enough to satisfy client requesting rate. This means, in spite of having different modes of behaviour, less switches take place in the dynamics of the system with respect to minimum approximation (see Fig. 5.4) and hence, the approximation is more accurate. Consequently, as we see in Table 4, the error associated with $\mathbb{E}_{F.F.}[C_r]$ decreases as we consider relatively larger populations of servers.

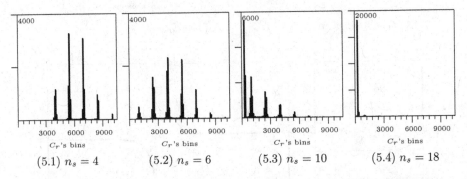

C_r's bins	C_r's bins	C_r's bins	C_r's bins
(5.1) $n_s = 4$	(5.2) $n_s = 6$	(5.3) $n_s = 10$	(5.4) $n_s = 18$

Fig. 5. The histogram of $\mathbb{E}[C_r]$ for some of the cases, $n_c = 10000$ and n_s varies

Another aspect of checking the sufficiency of the fluid flow method is to take into account the fact that this method is finding *only moments* (mean, variance, etc.) of the state variables. We checked, for the client-server system of Model 2, if these moments alone are providing enough information about the system's actual execution.

Figure 6.1 describes the solution of the ODEs for C_r, when $n_s = 18, n_c = 10000$. Figure 6.2 shows one trajectory of C_r considering the same populations. In this particular trajectory, in a large portion of the time, C_r's value fluctuates in close proximity of $\mathbb{E}_{F.F.}[C_r]$. In this part of the simulation $\mathbb{E}_{F.F.}[C_r]$ and $\sigma_{F.F}[C_r]$ can accurately represent C_r's evolution. Figure 6.2 also shows that there can also be some *spikes* which occur due to a combination of contention and one (or more) servers being broken. In this period of time, $\mathbb{E}_{F.F.}[C_r]$ and $\sigma_{F.F}[C_r]$ cannot represent C_r's behaviour. One might logically argue that these spikes have happened only in this particular trajectory and can be ignored. However, Fig. 5.4 indicates that in 800 out of 20000 simulation runs, we observe $C_r > \mathbb{E}_{F.F.}[C_r] + 20 \times \sigma_{F.F}[F]$. Therefore, having occasional long queues of the clients, requesting the service, is one of the intrinsic characteristics of the system with the assumed populations. We conclude that characterising the dynamics of the system by only the results of the fluid flow method, i.e. $\mathbb{E}[C_r]$ and $\sigma_{F.F}[C_r]$, does not account for such occasional spikes. These spikes can be especially important from the performance modelling point of view, for instance when the designers of a client-server system are going through the capacity planning phase.

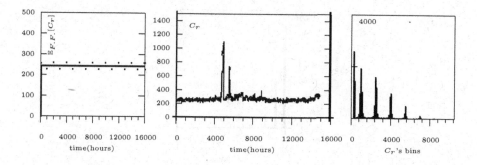

(6.1) $\mathbb{E}_{F.F.}[C_r]$ $n_s = 18$ (6.2) A trajectory of C_r, $n_s = 18$ (6.3) C_r's distribution, and $n_c = 10000$.   and $n_c = 10000$ $n_s = 9$ and $n_c = 10000$.

Fig. 6. Comparing an actual trajectory of C_r with $\mathbb{E}_{F.F.}[C_r]$

The client-server systems where C_r has a multi-modal distribution, show another sufficiency issue with respect to the fluid flow method. In such cases, C_r's mean and standard deviation are too *crude* to reflect C_r's actual behaviour. For instance, consider the model where $n_c = 10000, n_s = 9$. Figure 6.3 shows C_r's distribution. Table 4 shows that for this case $\mathbb{E}_{F.F.}[C_r] = 1359$ and $\sigma_{F.F}[C_r] = 2148$. By looking at the histogram, we observed that only in 5500 out of 20000 simulations,

$$\mathbb{E}_{F.F.}[C_r] - 0.25 \times \sigma_{F.F}[C_r] < C_r < \mathbb{E}_{F.F.}[C_r] + 0.25 \times \sigma_{F.F}[C_r].$$

In other words, in contrast with what one might expect from a *mean* measure, $\mathbb{E}_{F.F.}[C_r]$ is showing a value that the system's dynamics is more likely to be away from.

Figure 6 shows that in the analysis of a model, any given approach which only outputs the moments of beaviour, might not be sufficient to analyse that model. For instance, running stochastic simulations and *only* extracting the average, which is a common analysis method, might keep hidden some of the important aspects of the system's execution.

As we have seen, some ranges of values for n_s and n_c give rise to instantiations of Model 2 for which the results of fluid flow analysis alone, are too *abstract* to characterize the system's dynamics. However, experiments showed that for the same model but with different parameters, the multi-modality disappears, and for these instantiations of Model 2, $\mathbb{E}_{F.F.}[C_r]$ and $\sigma_{F.F}[C_r]$ can *accurately* exhibit the system's executions. For instance, if we consider larger populations for the servers ($n_s > 32$), even when one or more servers are broken, the remaining service capacity is large enough to prevent a sudden increase in C_r. Or as another example, consider $n_s = 14, n_c = 10000$ (the condition as seen in Fig. 5.1, but decrease the thinking rate from $r_t = 0.05$ to $r_t = 0.01$ and make clients communication with servers faster: increase $r_c = 2$ up to $r_c = 200$. Effectively, each client now spends more time thnking independently and once she enters the request queue, because she communicates with a servers more efficiently, she

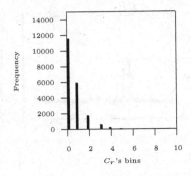

Fig. 7. C_r's histogram when $r_t = 0.01, r_c = 200$

leaves the queue more quickly. This stops high contention in the system (see Fig. 7) and consequently server's breakdowns will not have any effect on C_r.

5   Conclusion and Future Work

Our experiments led us to the following conclusions:

1. In performance evaluation studies, there are models which exhibit multi-modal behaviour. For such systems, using analysis approaches which only capture the behaviour's moments might not be sufficient to reveal the actual dynamics of the system. This insufficiency is not exclusively related to the fluid flow method. Even with stochastic simulations, it might not be sufficient to look only at the *average* of the simulation trajectories — *averaging* might hide some aspects of the system's performance.

2. It was shown in [6] that the accuracy of the fluid flow method depends on the quality of the approximation:

$$\mathbb{E}[\min(g(x), h(x)) \approx \min(\mathbb{E}[g(x)], \mathbb{E}[h(x)])].$$

The results of the fluid flow approximation are more accurate when it is less probable for the system to be in regions of the state space where the quality of this approximation is poor. In the context of our experiments we showed that this accuracy criterion can also be applied for multi-modal systems: if the dynamics of the system does not enter the unsafe regions, even though the system observes different modes, the moments of the behaviour can still be accurately calculated by applying the fluid flow method.

3. For a PEPA model which is capable of exhibiting multi-modal behaviour, the sufficiency of the fluid flow method depends on the concrete values one considers for the model's parameters. Moreover, the multi-modal behaviour is very sensitive to parameter values and model structure.

4. In a PEPA model, having a small population of components interacting with a larger one, or having a combination of slow and fast transitions, does not necessarily imply the insufficiency of the fluid flow method for the analysis of that model. However, for models in these classes [8], the modeller must run a rigorous validation of the results of the fluid flow method.

5.1   Future Work

Our experiments showed some models for which the fluid flow method was concluded to be *insufficient*. However, such conclusions could only be made after running numerous computationally expensive stochastic simulations. Our future work will focus on finding algorithms or analytical results which, for a given PEPA model, can decide whether the fluid flow method is a sufficient analysis tool. Specifically we aim to build a method which can statically analyse a completely parametrized PEPA model and reveal if the model has the potential to show multi-modal behaviour. This involves improvements on the sufficiency criteria offered in [8].

References

1. Bradley, J.T., Gilmore, S., Hillston, J.: Analysing distributed internet worm attacks using continuous state-space approximation of process algebra models. J. Comput. Syst. Sci. 74(6), 1013–1032 (2008)
2. Harrison, M.D., Massink, M., Latella, D.: Engineering crowd interaction within smart environments. In: Proc. of the 1st ACM SIGCHI Symposium on Engineering Interactive Computing Systems, EICS 2009, pp. 117–122. ACM, USA (2009)
3. Wang, H., Laurenson, D., Hillston, J.: PEPA analysis of MAP effects in hierarchical mobile IPv6. In: Proc. 15th Int. Symposium on Modeling, Analysis, and Simulation of Computer and Telecommunication Systems, MASCOTS 2007, pp. 337–342. IEEE Computer Society (2007)
4. Ding, J., Hillston, J., Laurenson, D.: Performance modelling of content adaptation for a personal distributed environment. Wirel. Pers. Commun. 48(1), 93–112 (2009)
5. Hillston, J.: Fluid flow approximation of PEPA models. In: 2nd Int. Conf. on the Quantitative Evaluation of Systems, pp. 33–42 (September 2005)
6. Hayden, R., Bradley, J.T.: A fluid analysis framework for a Markovian process algebra. Theoretical Computer Science 411(22-24), 2260–2297 (2010)
7. Stefanek, A., Hayden, R., Bradley, J.T.: Hybrid analysis of large scale PEPA models. In: 9th Workshop on Process Algebra and Stochastically Timed Activities (PASTA 2010) (September 2010)
8. Bortolussi, L., Galpin, V., Hillston, J., Tribastone, M.: Hybrid semantics for PEPA. In: 7th Int. Conf. on the Quantitative Evaluation of Systems (QEST), pp. 181–190 (September 2010)
9. Hillston, J.: A compositional approach to performance modelling. Cambridge University Press (1996)
10. Tribastone, M., Gilmore, S., Hillston, J.: Scalable differential analysis of process algebra models. IEEE Trans. on Software Engineering 38(1), 205–219 (2012)
11. Cao, Y., Petzold, L.: Accuracy limitations and the measurement of errors in the stochastic simulation of chemically reacting systems. Journal of Computational Physics 212(1), 6–24 (2006)
12. Tribastone, M., Duguid, A., Gilmore, S.: The PEPA eclipse plugin. SIGMETRICS Perform. Eval. Rev. 36(4), 28–33 (2009)
13. Stefanek, A., Hayden, R., Bradley, J.T.: GPA - a tool for fluid scalability analysis of massively parallel systems. In: Proc. 8th Int. Conf. on Quantitative Evaluation of SysTems, QEST 2011, pp. 147–148. IEEE Computer Society (2011)

PCTMC Models
of Wireless Sensor Network Protocols

Marcel C. Guenther and Jeremy T. Bradley

Imperial College London, 180 Queen's Gate,
London SW7 2AZ, United Kingdom
{mcg05,jb}@doc.ic.ac.uk

Abstract. Wireless Sensor Networks (WSNs) consist of a large number of spatially distributed embedded devices (nodes), which communicate with one another via radio. Over the last decade improvements in hardware and a steady decrease in cost have encouraged the application of WSNs in areas such as industrial control, security and environmental monitoring. However, despite increasing popularity, the design of end-to-end software for WSNs is still an expert task since the choice of middleware protocols heavily influences the performance of resource-constrained WSNs. As a consequence, WSN designers resort to discrete event simulation prior to deploying networks. While such simulations are reasonably accurate, they tend to be computationally expensive to run, especially for large networks. This particularly limits the number of distinct protocol configurations that engineers can test in advance of construction and hence their final setup may be suboptimal. To mitigate this effect we discuss how highly efficient mean-field techniques can be brought to bear on models of wireless sensor networks. In particular, we consider the practical modelling issues involved in constructing appropriately realistic Population CTMC (PCTMC) models of WSN protocols.

Keywords: Mean-field Analysis, PCTMC Modelling, WSN Modelling.

1   Introduction

Recent hardware improvements and decreasing deployment costs have increased the popularity of Wireless Sensor Network (WSN) in various application areas. Examples include security and surveillance [1], forest fire detection [2], structural monitoring and controlling [3,4] as well as wildlife habitat monitoring [5] and healthcare [6] to name but a few. The emphasis of WSNs is to sample different kinds of environment data and forward the information to data sinks for further processing and analysis. While the general architecture of such networks is simple, the challenge lies in guaranteeing a number of Quality of Service (QoS) constraints for different application scenarios. Most commonly, sensor network applications require a specific balance between energy-efficiency, link reliability, security, bandwidth, and latency.

To ensure, prior to installing a WSN, that the software meets QoS demands, many WSN designers simulate their applications using discrete event simulation

M. Tribastone and S. Gilmore (Eds.): EPEW/UKPEW 2012, LNCS 7587, pp. 172–187, 2013.

(DES) frameworks such as Castalia [7], ns 2/3 [8] and TOSSIM [9]. These low-level network simulators have fairly sophisticated models for channel noise and interference and generally provide a realistic simulation environment for WSN applications [10]. However, discrete event simulation becomes computationally expensive as we increase the number of nodes in the network [11]. Therefore predicting the behaviour of a large network for a particular configuration cannot be done in real-time and optimising protocols by means of parameter sweeping can become computationally infeasible even if it is done offline. Mean-field analysis methods [12] for Population Continuous Time Markov Chains (PCTMCs) may help to overcome this problem. Originally, PCTMC models were used to approximate molecule levels in chemical reaction systems [13,14]. Recently, this paradigm has gained popularity in the performance analysis community as an efficient means to study large scale client-server systems [15,16]. The use of PCTMC models for WSNs has been rare in the literature, despite encouraging results presented in [17,18]. One of the main reasons for this is that PCTMCs only allow negatively exponentially distributed state sojourn times,[1] which may at first seem unsuitable for WSN modelling since these networks feature many deterministic, clock driven state changes. In this paper we will illustrate that this does not necessarily disqualify PCTMCs as a useful modelling paradigm for WSNs. In particular when analysed using the fast mean-field analysis method, PCTMC models can be seen a heuristic tool that enables a designer to discount certain configurations without the need for expensive simulations.

Our paper is organised as follows. In Section 2 we present an overview over WSN hardware, middleware and other protocol related issues. Moreover, we formally introduce PCTMC models and mean-field analysis. Subsequently Section 3 looks at how WSNs can be represented as PCTMCs and further points out open modelling challenges. Section 4 compares an example PCTMC model of the dataflow behaviour in a fail-safe WSN to the behaviour observed in an analogous low-level Castalia simulation of the same network. In Section 5 we present our conclusions and propose further research opportunities.

2   Background

The most compelling reason for studying fast performance analysis techniques is that they allow designers to conduct real-time behavioural prediction and efficient offline parameter sweeping for large networks. While protocol parameterisation has often been ignored in former studies [19], recent WSN protocol research highlights the performance benefit of optimising protocols for a given environment. In [20] the authors use a low-level network simulation to optimise the IEEE 802.15.4 MAC protocol, to show that it can deliver good performance when tuned correctly. Due to the simulation complexity, however, the authors only investigate a limited number of parameter setups. Clearly, a faster analysis method would help to reject inefficient protocol setups without the need for

---

[1] In practice any short-tailed distribution can be approximated via combinations of exponential distributions or phase-type distributions.

simulation. In [21] a promising centralised real-time protocol optimisation framework is presented, which uses deterministic formulas to infer the current network behaviour. Subsequently multi-objective programming is applied to find a better global parameter configuration for the network. Despite showing significant performance improvements in empirical tests, the framework currently cannot guarantee network improvements as protocol parameter changes alter the network state. Therefore the optimisation has to be run frequently to continually improve the network based on the latest performance measurements. Here, a fast prediction method could potentially reduce the optimisation frequency. In the following we briefly introduce the WSN hardware and software landscape. Subsequently, we formally present the PCTMC formalism and the mean-field method, which has the potential to provide a computationally efficient way of analysing large WSN models.

2.1   The WSN Protocol Stack

Nodes, also referred to as Motes, are small, embedded, battery powered radio devices with significant processing, bandwidth, radio and energy constraints [22]. The radio range heavily depends on the environment in which the network is deployed [23]. As for bandwidth, nodes such as the MicaZ can transmit up to 250 Kbps [22], although in many applications the actual throughput is much lower because of channel contention and other communication overheads. Similarly, as many types of nodes are battery powered, energy has to be used efficiently. In the literature the energy aspect has received the largest attention among all of these hardware related constraints. For deployments in which node batteries are hard to replace, application and middleware need to be tuned to increase network lifetime, i.e. the time until the WSN stops functioning due to energy depletion in one or more nodes. Since idle listening is the largest source of energy waste [24], the main method for reducing nodes' energy consumption is to introduce duty-cycling. When duty-cycling, nodes turn off their radio units whenever possible. If, over a time period T, a node has its radio turned on $x\%$ of the time, we say that the node has a duty-cycle of $x\%$. The lower x, the longer the network lifetime will be. Yet, while duty-cycling increases battery lifetime, it has a great impact on bandwidth, latency and reliability. To overcome the resulting QoS related challenges, a vast number of protocols have been suggested over the last decade [25], each of which aims to optimally balance different QoS aspects.

   Figure 1 gives a high-level overview over the basic software architecture of wireless sensor applications. A more detailed representation can be found in [26]. The **Application layer** contains the logic required for data acquisition and processing. A simple application might measure quantities such as temperature, humidity or luminosity in regular intervals and forward the data to a sink node. Other applications might also process measured data, serve data requests or send messages in response to external events. Furthermore applications also need to decide which nodes to forward their data to. This can either be specific nodes or a high-level destinations such as data sinks. The **Network layer** [25] is responsible for ensuring that data from the application layer is routed towards

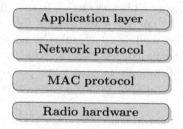

Fig. 1. A simple wireless sensor network protocol stack

its destination. A common communication pattern is convergecast, where all nodes in the network sample information and forward the data to dedicated sink nodes via multi-hop routes. In multi-hop networks, routing protocols need to relay incoming packets from other nodes in addition to handling packets coming from their own application layer. Network protocols are either centralised or a decentralised. A centralised routing protocol elects one or several nodes which control the routing behaviour of the network, whereas decentralised protocols let nodes autonomously decide where to forward messages to. Protocols in the latter category are sometimes referred to as swarm intelligence or bio-inspired protocols [27]. **MAC layer** protocols on the other hand determine how neighbouring sensor nodes communicate with each other. There are three classes of MAC protocols, contention based protocols, schedule based protocols and hybrid approaches. In contention based protocols such as CSMA, nodes can send messages at any time provided the channel is clear, whereas in schedule based protocols like TDMA each node is allocated a time window during which it can transmit messages [28]. Additionally MAC protocols are in charge of managing the node's duty-cycle behaviour to ensure nodes are only awake when necessary. Finally the **Radio layer** controls nodes' radio hardware and can be used to configure signal modulation, frequency or transmission power.

Even though the vast protocol landscape provides solutions for nearly any kind of WSN application, building software for WSNs still requires experienced designers, who choose appropriate protocol setups that match QoS demands. To simplify the WSN application development process, researchers have come up with a variety of universal middleware frameworks [29,30,31,32] some of which are already capable of dynamically adapting their setup for performance gain [33]. Despite being suitable for particular application types, there is no guarantee that they will perform optimally in all scenarios. To balance the demand for application optimised WSN middleware and ease of application development, other researchers have proposed auto-generating bespoke middleware based on the application profile [34].

2.2 PCTMCs

Population models assume that a large number of identical individuals belonging to a particular population interact with individuals from other populations and thereby alter population levels. This abstraction from individuals to populations vastly reduces the complexity and the state-space of the underlying model. Common examples of population models are chemical reaction models [14,35] where populations represent molecule concentrations, ecology models [36] describing the behaviour of groups of animals or plants and software performance models [37,38] capturing the interactions between components in massively parallel systems.

Population continuous time Markov chains (PCTMCs) have a finite set of populations D, $n = |D|$ and a set E of transition classes. States are represented as an integer vector $\boldsymbol{p} = (p_1, \ldots, p_n) \in \mathbb{Z}^n$, with the ith component being the current population level of species $S_i \in D$. A transition class $(r_e, \boldsymbol{c}_e) \in E$ for an event e describes a transition with negatively exponentially distributed firing delay that occurs at rate $r_e : \mathbb{Z}^n \to \mathbb{R}$ and changes the population vector $\boldsymbol{p}$ into $\boldsymbol{p} + \boldsymbol{c}_e$. The analogue to PCTMCs in the systems biology literature are Chemical Reaction Systems, were $\boldsymbol{p}$ describes a molecule count vector and transition classes represent chemical reactions between the molecules with r_e being the reaction rate function and $\boldsymbol{c}_e$ the stoichiometric vector for a specific reaction. For notational convenience we write an event/reaction e as

$$\underbrace{S_* + \cdots + S_*}_{\text{in}} \to \underbrace{S_* + \cdots + S_*}_{\text{out}} \qquad \text{at } r_e(\boldsymbol{p}) \qquad (1)$$

where $S_* \in D$ represent different species that are affected by the event. The corresponding change vector $\boldsymbol{c}_e = (s_1^{\text{out}} - s_1^{\text{in}}, \ldots, s_n^{\text{out}} - s_n^{\text{in}}) \in \mathbb{Z}^n$ where s_i^{in} represents the number of occurrences of a species $S_i \in D$ on the left hand side of the event and s_i^{out} the number occurrences on the right hand side. The event rate is

$$\begin{cases} r_e(\boldsymbol{p}) & \text{if } p_i \geq s_i^{\text{in}} \text{ for all } i = 1, \ldots, n \\ 0 & \text{otherwise} \end{cases}$$

An important aspect of PCTMC models is that approximations to the evolution of population moments of the underlying stochastic process can be represented by a system of ODEs [16]

$$\frac{\mathrm{d}}{\mathrm{d}t}\mathbb{E}[T(\boldsymbol{p}(t))] = \sum_{e \in E} \mathbb{E}[(T(\boldsymbol{p}(t) + \boldsymbol{c}_e) - T(\boldsymbol{p}(t)))\, r_e(\boldsymbol{p}(t))] \qquad (2)$$

To obtain the ODE describing the evolution of the mean of a population p_i for instance, all we need to do is to substitute $T(\boldsymbol{P}) = P_i$ in the above equations, where P_i is the random variable representing the population count of species S_i. In the literature the resulting ODEs are often referred to as mean-field approximations [12,38]. Similarly ODEs for higher joint moments can be obtained by choosing adequate $T(\boldsymbol{P})$, e.g. $T(\boldsymbol{P}) = (P_i - \mu_i)^2$ for the variance of P_i. Alternatively stochastic simulation [35] can be used to evaluate PCTMCs. Like discrete event simulation for low-level protocol models, this latter simulation technique captures the stochastic behaviour of the PCTMC exactly, but it also does not scale for models with large populations.

When modelling spatially distributed networks such as WSNs, it is often easier to use a subclass of PCTMCs, so-called spatial PCTMCs (SPCTMCs). SPCTMCs have a discrete, finite number of locations each with a finite population of different agent states. By agent state population we mean the number of agents that are in a specific state of the underlying discrete state automata representing the agent, i.e. each agent description generates a number of species in the resulting PCTMC. When evaluating an SPCTMC we keep track of the evolutions of all agent state populations in all locations. The reason we distinguish between SPCTMCs and PCTMCs is that the population replication and the spatial notion of neighbourhoods can be exploited in order to simplify the higher-order moment ODE analysis [39]. A common way to design SPCTMC models is to use stochastic Petri nets or stochastic process algebras. The idea behind such high-level languages is to first describe local agent states, which can then be put together in a composite model. The composite model describes the topology, initial agent state populations in different locations and the interactions between neighbouring agent populations. For simplicity we refer to a species S at location l as $S@l$ [14,40]. Moreover, $S@l_*$ is used as a shorthand when defining events that occur in all locations in the same way.

3   PCTMC Models of WSNs

When simulating WSN protocol stacks in network simulators like Castalia, TOS-SIM or ns 2/3, each protocol is commonly represented as an individual module. While this works well in low-level modelling, we found that for PCTMC modelling it is easier to create models of cross-layer protocols which express the behaviour of the entire application. In the following we outline which features can be expressed in PCTMC models of WSNs and how this can be achieved.

3.1   WSN Message Exchange and Buffers

In a PCTMC model of a WSN we assume that there are a discrete number of locations, each of which hosts one WSN node. Moreover, we assert that the radio range is fixed, so that every node has a set of neighbours that it can send messages to. Take for instance Figure 2, a simple topology with 15 nodes where each node has at most 4 neighbours. Even though this is an extremely regular topology, it is not hard to see that we can also express more sophisticated topologies with asymmetric links or varying neighbourhood densities in a similar way. Another important feature of a WSN node is its buffer. Generally a node's message buffer is small, allowing it to temporarily cache packets before forwarding them to other nodes in the network. Packet transmission is atomic in the sense that packets are either received entirely or not at all. Packet loss occurs due to channel interference, modulation errors and congestion control mechanisms. The biggest challenge in representing a buffer as a population of a PCTMC is

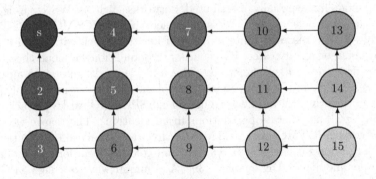

Fig. 2. Node 's' is the sink to which all other nodes route their messages. Any two nodes that are connected by arrows can communicate. In more realistic topologies some links may only be unidirectional since radio links can be asymmetric.

to ensure that nodes send messages at a constant bandwidth until the buffer is empty. In the following we will explain how this can be done for synchronised unicast communication. Synchronised broadcast communication can be modelled similarly. Assuming interference free communication without packet loss, we obtain the following evolutions for a node at location l_1 that is sending unicast messages to nodes l_2 and l_3

$$
\begin{aligned}
\emptyset &\to Buf@l_1 && \text{at } sampleRate \\
Buf@l_1 &\to Buf@l_2 && \text{at } bw^* TX@l_1{}^* RX@l_2{}^* \mathbb{P}_{12} \\
Buf@l_1 &\to Buf@l_3 && \text{at } bw^* TX@l_1{}^* RX@l_3{}^* \mathbb{P}_{13}
\end{aligned} \tag{3}
$$

where $Buf@l_*$ is the buffer population at each location with $Buf@l_* = 0$ initially. The rate constants $sampleRate$ and bw are the average number of sensor readings and the average number of packets that can be sent per time unit, 8/respectively. Moreover, we assume that a single node is either in state RX or TX. Naturally communication can only happen if the sender is in TX and the receiver is in RX mode. The $\mathbb{P}_{ab}$ terms express the proportion of messages that node l_a sends to a node located at l_b such that $\sum_i \mathbb{P}_{ai} = 1$. To incorporate message loss we can add evolutions such as

$$
Buf@l_1 \to \emptyset \qquad\qquad \text{at } msgLossRate
$$

When analysing the evolutions shown in Eqn. (3) using mean-field techniques, the continuous buffer representation causes problems as it introduces indicator function terms to the ODEs. To overcome this problem we decided to use a discrete buffer representation instead. Assuming a single node has buffer states $\{Buf_0, \ldots, Buf_m\}$, where Buf_i represents the state in which the buffer contains

i messages. The corresponding unicast communication reactions for lossless message transmission from l_1 to l_2 and l_3 are

$$Buf_i@l_1 \rightarrow Buf_{i+1}@l_1 \qquad\qquad\qquad \text{at } sampleRate$$

$$Buf_j@l_1 + Buf_i@l_2 \rightarrow Buf_{j-1}@l_1 + Buf_{i+1}@l_2 \quad \text{at } bw^* TX@l_1{}^* RX@l_2{}^*$$
$$\mathbb{P}_{12}{}^* Buf_i@l_1{}^* Buf_j@l_2$$

$$Buf_j@l_1 + Buf_i@l_3 \rightarrow Buf_{j-1}@l_1 + Buf_{i+1}@l_3 \quad \text{at } bw^* TX@l_1{}^* RX@l_3{}^*$$
$$\mathbb{P}_{13}{}^* Buf_i@l_1{}^* Buf_j@l_3$$

where initially $Buf_0@l_* = 1$, $0 \leq i < m$ and $0 < j \leq m$ and $(1 - Buf_0@l)$ is 1 whenever l has a non-empty buffer. In this case the transmission rate is always bw or 0 and the ODEs representing the evolution of the mean of populations $Buf_*@l_1$ and $Buf_*@l_2$ can be integrated everywhere. To simplify this model, in Section 4 we assert that nodes can always receive messages and attempt to send messages whenever their buffer is non-empty, i.e. we can ignore all $RX@l_*$ and $TX@l_*$ terms the above evolutions. In the mean-field ODEs the gradient for the expected buffer level $\mathbb{E}[Buf_i@l(t)]$ then becomes the sum of

$$\mathbb{E}[Buf_i@l(t)]^* bw^* \left(\sum_k \mathbb{P}_{kl}{}^*(1 - \mathbb{E}[Buf_0@k(t)]) \right) \qquad (4)$$

and

$$-\mathbb{E}[Buf_i@l(t)]^* bw^* \left(\sum_k \mathbb{P}_{lk}{}^*(1 - \mathbb{E}[Buf_m@k(t)]) \right) \qquad (5)$$

which represent the terms for the incoming and the outgoing messages respectively. To approximate the average buffer size for any location l at time t we then simply evaluate

$$\sum_{i=1}^m i^* \mathbb{E}[Buf_i@l(t)] \qquad (6)$$

There are two drawbacks to the discrete buffer approach. Firstly, representing buffer levels as a discrete number of m populations creates m extra mean-field ODEs for every location. Secondly, when analysing the resulting mean-field ODEs, we have to bear in mind that the use of small populations ($\sum Buf_i@l = 1$) can lead to significant errors in the mean-field estimate of the real population means. Despite the latter shortcoming our example in Section 4 shows that this PCTMC buffer representation works qualitatively well, when comparing the mean-field solution to the results of a realistic low-level discrete event simulation of a WSN.

3.2   Network Protocol

Having discussed how to represent basic WSN message exchange in PCTMC models, we now discuss how network protocols can be modelled. As mentioned in Section 2.1, there exist centralised and decentralised routing approaches. In our opinion the best way to create a PCTMC model of a centralised WSN routing protocol is to write an algorithm, which, given the network topology and the behaviour of the centralised routing protocol, generates the reactions outlined in Eqn. (3), with $\mathbb{P}_{ij}$ chosen to reflect the network topology. The network shown in Figure 3, for example, could have been generated according to a centralised routing algorithm executed at node 's'. Even though static routing models can be

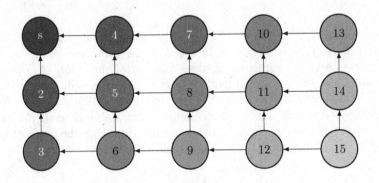

Fig. 3. Node 's' is the sink to which all other nodes route their messages

analysed efficiently using mean-field methods, we are generally more interested in dynamic routing behaviour, for instance when studying fail-safe protocols [41]. We will now show how decentralised dynamic routing can be represented in a PCTMC model. Decentralised schemes require nodes to make decisions as to where they send messages to. To make informed decisions, nodes need to collect meta-information about their immediate neighbours, e.g. their buffer occupancy, link reliability, distance to the sink or battery status. This information can subsequently be used to compute $\mathbb{P}_{ij}$. In [18] the authors abstract such neighbourhood information as pheromone levels. From zoology, pheromone is a hormone used by foraging insects to mark routes between their nest and food sources. The higher the pheromone level along a certain path, the more insects will travel along that route. In models where peripheral nodes need to relay messages towards a sink node, e.g. Figure 3, we assume all nodes disseminate pheromone and that they infer routing decisions based on the resulting pheromone gradient. While Bruneo *et al.* [18] use discrete pheromone levels, represented in a manner similar to our buffer representation, we suggest a continuous pheromone level representation. A typical pheromone model for a convergecast network will assert that sink nodes are the pheromone sources, whereas all other nodes spread the pheromone emitted by the sinks. This way a pheromone gradient, represented by the shading in Figure 3, between sink and peripheral nodes emerges. As long as the pheromone level of nodes decreases with increasing hop distance from surrounding sink(s), we can easily use the resulting gradient to make local routing decisions that guarantee message delivery to the nearest sink(s). The reactions for the pheromone spread look as follows

$$\emptyset \to Ph@l_* \qquad \text{at } pheroInc@l_*$$
$$Ph@l_* \to \emptyset \qquad \text{at } pheroDec@l_*$$

where $pheroInc@l_*$ is the sum of the difference between a node's pheromone level and that of its neighbours, e.g. at location 3

$$pheroInc@l_3 = \max(0, Ph@l_2 - Ph@l_3) + \max(0, Ph@l_6 - Ph@l_3) \qquad (7)$$

and for sinks we assume that $pheroInc$ is some constant. Moreover, let

$$pheroDec@l_* = \min(0.1, Ph@l_* - 2) \qquad (8)$$

The min term ensures that the pheromone level will not fall below 0. Although the pheromone gradient presented here only encodes a node's distance from the sink, it is possible to incorporate other neighbourhood information such as buffer levels or battery status in the pheromone concentration in case further QoS constraints have to be met by the protocol. Having shown how to express continuous pheromone levels in a PCTMC model, we can further utilise these levels to make dynamic routing decisions. A straightforward way of doing this is illustrated by the following reactions for the node at location 3 in Figure 3.

$$Buf_i@l_1 \to Buf_{i+1}@l_1 \qquad \text{at } sampleRate$$
$$Buf_j@l_3 + Buf_i@l_2 \to Buf_{j-1}@l_3 + Buf_{i+1}@l_2 \quad \text{at } RouteUp@l_3 * Buf_j@l_3 *$$
$$bw^* Buf_i@l_2$$
$$Buf_j@l_3 + Buf_i@l_6 \to Buf_{j-1}@l_3 + Buf_{i+1}@l_6 \quad \text{at } RouteRight@l_3 * Buf_j@l_3 *$$
$$bw^* Buf_i@l_6$$
$$Buf_j@l_2 + Buf_i@l_3 \to Buf_{j-1}@l_2 + Buf_{i+1}@l_3 \quad \text{at } RouteDown@l_2 * Buf_j@l_2 *$$
$$bw^* Buf_i@l_3$$
$$Buf_j@l_6 + Buf_i@l_3 \to Buf_{j-1}@l_6 + Buf_{i+1}@l_3 \quad \text{at } RouteLeft@l_6 * Buf_j@l_6 *$$
$$bw^* Buf_i@l_3$$
$$(9)$$

In contrast to the static centralised approached, where we assumed fixed routing probabilities for all neighbours, we now have $RouteUp@l_*$, $RouteDown@l_*$, $RouteLeft@l_*$ and $RouteRight@l_*$ instead of $\mathbb{P}_{ij}$. We can express $RouteLeft@l_6$ as

$$RouteLeft@l_6 = \frac{max(0, Ph@l_3 - Ph@l_6)}{pheroInc@l_6} \qquad (10)$$

i.e. the pheromone excess of node 3 over 6 divided by the sum of the excesses of all neighbours of node 6. Clearly, if location 3 has a lower pheromone level than location 6, node 6 will not route messages via node 3. If node 3 has a higher pheromone level, a proportion of messages from node 6 is relayed to the sink via location 3. Sink nodes have to be handled separately as they would have 0 denominators. However, fractions of populations are undesirable in moment approximating ODEs as they cause significant loss of accuracy for small denominators, which can cause errors when approximating higher-order moments. A suitable alternative that works better for mean-field analysis can be obtained by treating the routing probabilities as populations

$$RouteUp@l_6 \rightarrow RouteLeft@l_6 \quad at \; max(0, Ph@l_3 - Ph@l_6) * RouteUp@l_6$$
$$RouteDown@l_6 \rightarrow RouteLeft@l_6 \quad at \; max(0, Ph@l_3 - Ph@l_6) * RouteDown@l_6$$
$$RouteRight@l_6 \rightarrow RouteLeft@l_6 \quad at \; max(0, Ph@l_3 - Ph@l_6) * RouteRight@l_6$$

Reactions for $RouteUp@l_*$, $RouteDown@l_*$ and $RouteRight@l_*$ follow a similar pattern. If we ensure that $RouteUp@l_* + RouteDown@l_* + RouteLeft@l_* + RouteRight@l_* = 1$ then this will yield routing populations that have similar steady state behaviour as Eqn. (10).

3.3 MAC Protocol

While we argue that it is possible to model and evaluate non-trivial routing protocols using PCTMCs and mean-field analysis, it is much harder to represent sophisticated MAC protocols using the PCTMC formalism. In [17] Gribaudo *et al.* show that PCTMCs can represent duty-cycled MAC protocols with sender initiated transfers, i.e. protocols where nodes that want to propagate a message stay awake until the receiving node wakes up. Protocols like S-MAC, however, which require nodes to wake up in regular, synchronised intervals are hard to represent using PCTMCs. This is because feasible phase-type approximations cannot accurately represent deterministic or even near deterministic delays. Whether a MAC protocol can be represented by a PCTMC thus depends on how deterministic the cycles are.

3.4 Physical Layer

One of the most challenging aspects of WSN modelling is to capture the behaviour of the wireless medium [42]. The two most important factors are the natural variation in signal strength and packet collisions. Despite the use of log-normal shadowing for path loss and sophisticated collision models that simulate capture effects,[2] even simulators such as Castalia do not manage to replicate the exact behaviour of empirical networks [42]. In this light it is unrealistic to expect PCTMC models to capture the characteristics of the wireless medium with high quantitative accuracy. Nevertheless, it is worth aiming at obtaining

---

[2] When considering capture effects, collisions only occur if interfering signals are sufficiently strong.

qualitative agreement, especially when using PCTMC models for protocol optimisation. Thus far, however, attempts to recreate the effects of radio interference in our PCTMC models have only been moderately successful and are subject to further research.

3.5   Other Limitations and Opportunities

Many publications on WSN protocols deal with the prediction and optimisation of energy consumption in WSNs. As we mentioned earlier, common energy saving features such as duty-cycling are generally hard to express in PCTMC models. Similarly, the evolution of battery levels is difficult to represent in models since batteries discharge in a highly non-linear fashion [43,44]. Regardless of these restrictions, PCTMC models can be used to analyse the dataflow of messages under static and dynamic routing conditions (cf. Section 4). Insights into the dataflow of a WSN application can be used to estimate the energy consumption. Generally, a more evenly distributed message load in the network will equate to better energy durability in individual nodes.

A final aspect of WSNs is node mobility. While it is straightforward to model node failure in particular locations, thus far we have not found a strategy for representing mobile nodes in PCTMC models. Nevertheless it might be possible to port some of the concepts developed for gossip models [45] and epidemics [46], to represent roving nodes.

4   Worked Example

In Section 3 we described how a PCTMC can be used to model unicast communication in a WSN with decentralised dynamic routing. We now illustrate that the mean-field analysis for our PCTMC abstraction of such a WSN can indeed produce a good qualitative representation of the dataflow behaviour in a WSN, even in presence of light interference. The comparison shown in Table 1 was taken from [47]. It compares our mean-field results for the pheromone model discussed in Section 3 to the average obtained from 200 Castalia simulations of the same WSN. Note that Castalia is a low-level network simulator, which simulates the exchange of every message separately. Since Castalia simulations use a sophisticated collision model, we also added a simple collision model to our PCTMC model. The modified PCTMC model makes receivers discard messages when two or more neighbours send messages simultaneously. The heat map in Table 1 shows the normalised buffer sizes in a network with 100 nodes, where every node produces 1 message per second and can relay up to 20 messages per second. To normalise these mean buffer levels at steady state, we set the non-sink node with the highest buffer to 100%. The resulting spatial heat maps represent relative buffer levels. To create a strong contrast, all nodes with a relative buffer size between $x\%$ to $(x - 5)\%$ are coloured black at $x\%$ opacity, and sink nodes are coloured at 100% opacity. Sinks are marked 's' and broken nodes are left white and are marked 'x'.

Table 1. Data flow in a network with 100 nodes several sinks and broken nodes in presence of interference [47]. Hotspot regions have darker shades, sink locations are marked 's', broken nodes are marked 'x'.

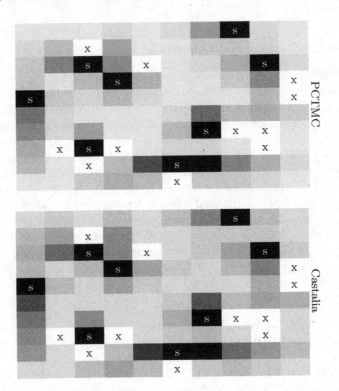

5   Conclusions and Future Work

We have illustrated how PCTMC models can be used to represent various aspects of WSN protocol stacks. Even though it is undoubtedly true that realistic low-level simulations will remain predominant in the WSN community, our aim is to establish mean-field analysis techniques as a rapid heuristic that can be used to focus computationally expensive low-level simulations. Analysing the routing behaviour and the dataflow of nodes running decentralised routing protocols is one such example, but we aim to provide more case studies in the future. Current limitations for our PCTMC models are the lack of techniques to express interference, synchronous duty-cycle behaviour and mobility. Clearly these features deserve further attention, as they are key concepts whose implementation would make PCTMC modelling more appealing to the WSN community. In case PCTMC models are not capable of capturing all of these aspects, mean-field evaluation techniques for Generalised Semi-Markov Processes (GSMPs) [16] are worth investigating too. Aside from mean-field approaches we also intend to consider hybrid modelling paradigms such as HYPE [48]. Moreover, in the future we plan to perform formal benchmarks in order to compare the speed and accuracy of realistic low-level network simulations of WSN protocols with analysis techniques for abstract WSN performance models.

References

1. Viani, F., Oliveri, G., Donelli, M., Lizzi, L., Rocca, P., Massa, A.: WSN-based Solutions for Security and Surveillance. Computer, 1762–1765 (September 2010)
2. Al-Fares, M.S., Sun, Z.: Self-Organizing Routing Protocol to achieve QoS in Wireless Sensor Network for Forest Fire Monitoring. Systems Research, 211–216 (2009)
3. Xu, N., Rangwala, S., Chintalapudi, K.K., Ganesan, D., Broad, A., Govindan, R., Estrin, D.: A wireless sensor network For structural monitoring. In: Proceedings of the 2nd International Conference on Embedded Networked Sensor Systems SenSys 2004, vol. 20(7), pp. 13–24 (2004)
4. Akhondi, M.R., Talevski, A., Carlsen, S., Petersen, S.: Applications of Wireless Sensor Networks in the Oil, Gas and Resources Industries. In: 2010 24th IEEE International Conference on Advanced Information Networking and Applications, pp. 941–948 (2010)
5. Bagree, R., Jain, V.R., Kumar, A., Ranjan, P.: TigerCENSE: Wireless Image Sensor Network to Monitor Tiger Movement. In: Marron, P.J., Voigt, T., Corke, P., Mottola, L. (eds.) REALWSN 2010. LNCS, vol. 6511, pp. 13–24. Springer, Heidelberg (2010)
6. Micallef, J., Grech, I., Brincat, A., Traver, V., Monto, E.: Body area network for wireless patient monitoring. IET Communications 2(2), 215–222 (2008)
7. Boulis, A.: Castalia: revealing pitfalls in designing distributed algorithms in WSN. In: Jha, S. (ed.) Proceedings of the 5th International Conference on Embedded Networked Sensor Systems, pp. 407–408. ACM (2007)
8. Ns, The Network Simulator - ns-2 (2002)
9. Levis, P., Lee, N.: TOSSIM: A Simulator for TinyOS Networks, UC Berkeley, pp. 1–17 (September 2003)
10. Bergamini, L., Crociani, C., Vitaletti, A., Nati, M.: Validation of WSN simulators through a comparison with a real testbed. In: Proceedings of the 7th ACM Workshop on Performance Evaluation of Wireless Ad Hoc Sensor and Ubiquitous Networks, pp. 103–104. ACM (2010)
11. Egea-Lopez, E., Vales-Alonso, J., Martinez-Sala, A., Pavon-Mario, P., Garcia-Haro, J.: Simulation Scalability Issues in Wireless Sensor Networks. IEEE Communications Magazine 44(7), 64–73 (2006)
12. Opper, M., Saad, D.: Advanced Mean Field Methods: Theory and Practice. MIT Press (2001)
13. Van Kampen, N.G.: Stochastic Processes in Physics and Chemistry. North-Holland personal library, vol. 11. North-Holland (1992)
14. Ciocchetta, F., Hillston, J.: Bio-PEPA: A framework for the modelling and analysis of biological systems. Theoretical Computer Science 410(33-34), 3065–3084 (2009)
15. Hillston, J.: Fluid flow approximation of PEPA models. In: Second International Conference on the Quantitative Evaluation of Systems, QEST 2005, pp. 33–42 (2005)
16. Hayden, R.A.: Mean-field approximations for performance models with generally-timed transitions. Accepted for publication in ACM SIGMETRICS Performance Evaluation Review (2011)

17. Gribaudo, M., Cerotti, D., Bobbio, A.: Analysis of On-off policies in Sensor Networks Using Interacting Markovian Agents. In: 6th IEEE International Conference on Pervasive Computing and Communications, PerCom 2008, pp. 300–305 (2008)
18. Bruneo, D., Scarpa, M., Bobbio, A., Cerotti, D., Gribaudo, M.: Markovian agent modeling swarm intelligence algorithms in wireless sensor networks. Performance Evaluation 69(3-4), 135–149 (2012)
19. Förster, A., Murphy, A.L.: A Critical Survey and Guide to Evaluating WSN Routing Protocols. In: The First International Workshop on Networks of Cooperating Objects (CONET), Stockholm (2010)
20. Anastasi, G., Conti, M., Francesco, M.D.: A Comprehensive Analysis of the MAC Unreliability Problem in IEEE 802. 15. 4 Wireless Sensor Networks. IEEE Transactions on Industrial Informatics 7(1), 52–65 (2011)
21. Zimmerling, M., Ferrari, F., Mottola, L., Voigt, T., Thiele, L.: pTunes: Runtime Parameter Adaptation for Low-power MAC Protocols. In: Proceedings of the 11th International Conference on Information Processing in Sensor Networks - IPSN 2012, p. 173. ACM Press, New York (2012)
22. Crossbow: Crossbow datasheet on MicaZ (2006)
23. Sohrabi, K., Manriquez, B., Pottie, G.J.: Near ground wideband channel measurement in 800-1000 MHz. In: 1999 IEEE 49th Vehicular Technology Conference Cat No99CH36363, vol. 1(3), pp. 571–574 (1999)
24. Van Dam, T., Langendoen, K.: An adaptive energy-efficient MAC protocol for wireless sensor networks. In: Akyildiz, I.F., Estrin, D., Culler, D.E., Srivastava, M.B. (eds.) Proceedings of the First International Conference on Embedded Networked Sensor Systems, SenSys 2003, vol. 03, p. 171. ACM Press (2003)
25. Yick, J., Mukherjee, B., Ghosal, D.: Wireless sensor network survey. Computer Networks 52(12), 2292–2330 (2008)
26. Yadav, P.: Cross-Layer Protocols to Support Periodic Data Collection and Event Driven Wireless Sensor Network Applications. Phd thesis, Imperial College (2011)
27. Paone, M., Paladina, L., Bruneo, D., Puliafito, A.: A Swarm-based Routing Protocol for Wireless Sensor Networks. In: Sixth IEEE International Symposium on Network Computing and Applications, NCA 2007, vol. 3(Nca), pp. 265–268 (2007)
28. Bachir, A., Dohler, M., Watteyne, T., Leung, K.K.: MAC Essentials for Wireless Sensor Networks. IEEE Communications Surveys Tutorials 12(2), 222–248 (2010)
29. Römer, K., Kasten, O., Mattern, F.: Middleware challenges for wireless sensor networks. ACM SIGMOBILE Mobile Computing and Communications Review 6(4), 59–61 (2002)
30. Chatzigiannakis, I., Mylonas, G., Nikoletseas, S.: 50 ways to build your application: A survey of middleware and systems for Wireless Sensor Networks. In: 2007 IEEE Conference on Emerging Technologies Factory Automation, EFTA 2007, pp. 466–473 (2007)
31. Tong, S.: An Evaluation Framework for middleware approaches on Wireless Sensor Networks. Tech. Rep., Helsinki University of Technology, Helsinki (2007)
32. Wang, M.-M., Cao, J.-N., Li, J., Dasi, S.K.: Middleware for Wireless Sensor Networks: A Survey. Journal of Computer Science and Technology 23(3), 305–326 (2008)
33. Liu, T., Martonosi, M.: Impala: a middleware system for managing autonomic, parallel sensor systems. In: System, PPoPP 2003, vol. 38, pp. 107–118. ACM (2003)
34. Buckl, C., Sommer, S., Scholz, A., Knoll, A., Kemper, A.: Generating a Tailored Middleware for Wireless Sensor Network Applications. In: IEEE International Conference on Sensor Networks Ubiquitous and Trustworthy Computing, SUTC 2008, pp. 162–169 (2008)

35. Gillespie, D.T.: Exact stochastic simulation of coupled chemical reactions. Journal of Physical Chemistry 81(25), 2340–2361 (1977)
36. Wangersky, P.J.: Lotka-Volterra population models. Annual Review of Ecology and Systematics 9(1), 189–218 (1978)
37. Stefanek, A., Hayden, R.A., Bradley, J.T.: Fluid computation of the performance-energy trade-off in large scale Markov models. Accepted for Publication in ACM SIGMETRICS Performance Evaluation Review (2011)
38. Benaim, M., Le Boudec, J.: A class of mean field interaction models for computer and communication systems. Performance Evaluation 65(11-12), 823–838 (2008)
39. Stefanek, A., Guenther, M.C., Bradley, J.T.: Normal and inhomogeneous moment closures for stochastic process algebras. In: 10th Workshop on Process Algebra and Stochastically Timed Activities (PASTA 2011), Ragusa (2011)
40. Galpin, V.: Towards a spatial stochastic process algebra. In: Proceedings of the 7th Workshop on Process Algebra and Stochastically Timed Activities, PASTA, Edinburgh (2008)
41. Liu, A.-F., Ma, M., Chen, Z.-G., Gui, W.-H.: Energy-Hole Avoidance Routing Algorithm for WSN. In: Fourth International Conference on Natural Computation, ICNC 2008, vol. 1, pp. 76–80 (2008)
42. Halkes, G.P., Langendoen, K.G.: Experimental Evaluation of Simulation Abstractions for Wireless Sensor Network MAC Protocols. EURASIP Journal on Wireless Communications and Networking 2010, 1–10 (2010)
43. Perla, E., Catháin, A.O., Carbajo, R.S., Huggard, M., Mc Goldrick, C.: Power-TOSSIM z: Realistic Energy Modelling for Wireless Sensor Network Environments. In: Proceedings of the 3rd ACM Workshop on Performance Monitoring and Measurement of Heterogeneous Wireless and Wired Networks, pp. 35–42. ACM (2008)
44. Jongerden, M.R., Haverkort, B.R.: Which battery model to use? IET Software 3(6), 445 (2009)
45. Chaintreau, A., Le Boudec, J.Y., Ristanovic, N.: The age of gossip: spatial mean field regime. Evolution, 109–120 (2009)
46. Caravagna, G., Hillston, J.: Modeling biological systems with delays in Bio-PEPA. In: Electronic Proceedings in Theoretical Computer Science, MeCBIC, vol. 40, pp. 85–101 (2010)
47. Guenther, M.C., Bradley, J.T.: Mean-field analysis of data flows in Wireless Sensor Networks. Submitted to VALUETOOLS (2012),
http://www.doc.ic.ac.uk/~mcg05/wsnrouting
48. Galpin, V., Bortolussi, L., Hillston, J.: HYPE: A Process Algebra for Compositional Flows and Emergent Behaviour. In: Bravetti, M., Zavattaro, G. (eds.) CONCUR 2009. LNCS, vol. 5710, pp. 305–320. Springer, Heidelberg (2009)

A Novel Approach to Energy Efficient Content Distribution with BitTorrent

Matthew Forshaw and Nigel Thomas

School of Computing Science
Newcastle University, Newcastle upon Tyne, UK
{m.j.forshaw,nigel.thomas}@ncl.ac.uk

Abstract. The energy efficiency aspects of IT infrastructure and communications systems are facing increased scrutiny, and a broad range of compelling financial, social, political and legislative factors is emerging. In this paper, energy efficiency considerations are addressed in the context of BitTorrent. We provide mechanisms to facilitate energy efficiency and energy proportionality, and propose an energy-efficient content distribution system employing these mechanisms to minimise energy consumption and reduce cost.

Keywords: Energy efficiency, Peer to Peer (P2P), Content distribution, BitTorrent.

1 Introduction

Energy costs now dominate IT infrastructure total cost of ownership (TCO), with data centre operators predicted to spend more on energy than hardware infrastructure in the next five years. With western european data centre power consumption estimated at 56 TWh/year in 2007 and projected to double by 2020 [4], the need to improve energy efficiency of IT operations is imperative. The issue is compounded by social and political factors and strict environmental legislation governing organisations.

BitTorrent [7] is a peer-to-peer (P2P) file sharing protocol, accounting for approximately 17.9% [15] of overall Internet bandwidth use. Contrary to traditional client-server approaches, BitTorrent relies less on the distributor's centralised infrastructure and bandwidth, offering a scalable content distribution solution with reduced provider-side power consumption and cost. This scalability makes BitTorrent particularly resilient to *flash crowds* [10], vast numbers of users accessing content simultaneously, a behaviour often observed for new and popular content.

In this paper we introduce provider-side mechanisms to promote energy-efficient and energy-proportional operation of a BitTorrent based content distribution system. Our approach is complementary to the proxy scheme proposed in [1], and alleviates the need for centralised peer control as imposed in [2] and [5]. In this research we consider situations where such centralised control cannot be guaranteed, and present mechanisms which do not require alterations to client logic.

M. Tribastone and S. Gilmore (Eds.): EPEW/UKPEW 2012, LNCS 7587, pp. 188–196, 2013.

These relaxed conditions make our approach more broadly applicable as well as simplifying deployment.

2   Related Work

Early research considering BitTorrent energy efficiency focused primarily on file sharing using devices with limited battery and computational power [11].

Anastasi et al. [1] propose a scheme allowing multiple peers within a typical LAN environment to delegate the task of downloading to a designated proxy server which takes part in the BitTorrent protocol on their behalf. Meanwhile these peers "behind" the proxy can be switched off without interrupting the download. Upon completion of the download, the requested files are transferred back to the peers.

Blackburn and Christensen [5] introduce a wake-up semantic to the BitTorrent protocol, allowing peers to sleep while remaining active in the system. Centralised control is assumed whereby these peers may be sent a packet and woken up remotely.

Andrew et al [2] propose a system to balance the power consumption of servers and peers involved in a peer-to-peer download. This approach assumes centralised control over all peers, enabling these peers to be powered on and off to maximise the download rate of a subset of awake peers.

3   BitTorrent

When a downloader (*peer*) initiates a download via BitTorrent, they first obtain a *torrent file*, a file containing metadata for the requested content. This metadata includes an endpoint to a BitTorrent tracker node. The *tracker* is essential to the operation of any BitTorrent system. The tracker maintains records of all peers uploading or downloading particular content (known collectively as the *swarm*), and coordinates content distribution and enables peer discovery. This component must remain online at all times in order for newly arriving peers to be able to connect.

Once the peer has established a connection with the tracker, the tracker responds with a peer list containing the details of a random subset of the other peers transferring the requested content. The peer may then connect to, and obtain content from, these peers. Additionally, the peer may elect to obtain up-to-date peer lists from the tracker periodically according to an *announce interval* specified by the tracker.

Files in BitTorrent are split into multiple *pieces*, allowing peers to share pieces of the file they hold while obtaining the pieces they require. BitTorrent peers' ability to download and upload simultaneously benefits performance and makes BitTorrent significantly more scalable than client-server file distribution approaches.

BitTorrent peers may belong to one of two states; *leeching* or *seeding*. Peers actively downloading in the system but who do not currently hold a full copy of the file are referred to as *leechers*. Once a peer has obtained all the pieces of their download, they may either depart from the system or remain active as a *seed.* Seeds remain active participants in the system, altruistically sharing upload bandwidth to distribute content to other peers.

4   System Models and Objectives

In our model we represent peer power consumption as manufacturer specified *nameplate* power consumption figures. Selecting readily available power consumption values provides sufficient accuracy for our system to make valuable energy savings while minimising the overhead associated with collecting the information. We also maintain details of the download and upload capacity of individual peers. These may be figures obtained out of band or taken from real-time observations of the running system.

We model a *seed pool* as a group of servers under centralised control, heterogeneous in terms of power consumption and upload capacity. The upload capacity of these servers is assumed to be considerably greater than that of typical peers. Membership is assumed to be dynamic, with servers arriving to and departing from the pool periodically. Where members of the seed pool may be considered internal architecture across one or more data centre facilities, we may assume physical access for detailed in-situ power profiling. Multiple linear regression models calibrated for each resource will provide accurate estimates based on real-time resource utilisation measurements, including CPU, RAM and disk activity. Software agents instrumenting each machine communicate this utilisation data to the tracker.

Our model considers tracker and seed instances to belong to one of two distinct states; *sleep* or *active*. An active resource is fully powered up and is able to execute operations and serve requests from the system. A resource may be placed in a sleep state, where the machine is no longer able to serve requests but consumes significantly less power. While asleep, system state is stored in memory allowing the machine to transition into an active state quickly. We model the time taken to transition between these two states, during which the resources consume power but are unable to contribute to the system.

Content distribution networks are typically large shared infrastructures, distributed across multiple data centre facilities nationally or globally. Hence, it is imperative that our system model adequately represents the differences between data centre facilities and global variation in the cost and cleanliness of their power sources. Facility modeling includes the Power Usage Effectiveness (PUE) rating, a metric representing the proportion of facility overheads (for example, power, cooling and lighting infrastructure) in terms of the power consumption of the IT equipment. We account for variations in the price and ecological impact of energy supply in our model, representing these in pence and kg CO_2 per kWh respectively.

We consider modeling of network devices outside the data centre facility as beyond of the scope for this research. Peer-to-peer approaches have greater total bandwidth requirements than client-server approaches due to peers communicating with one another. The impact of this communication overhead on power consumption is difficult to assess. Despite significant recent improvements in energy-efficiency of hardware [16], typical network hardware is found to be energy-disproportional [13]. This power characteristic results in a narrow dynamic power range, limiting the potential impact of variable traffic workload on power consumption. Furthermore, these network devices must remain online at all times and are outside of the administrative control of content providers. Existing research has compared client-server and peer-to-peer approaches, finding peer-to-peer to demonstrate greater network-related power consumption but lower overall power consumption in a communication-intensive scenario such as file distribution [14].

It is unrealistic for an organisation to minimise its power consumption without first considering the trade-offs between energy efficiency, cost and reliability. In an inter-organisational scenario such as software patch distribution in an office environment or large-scale deployment across a cluster, stakeholders of the system will most likely be concerned with minimising the aggregate energy consumption and cost of a system. Conversely, in situations where peers are external to the organisation (e.g. video on demand or public content distribution), stakeholders are likely to prioritise provider-side energy efficiency and cost over those of the peers. Our approach must remain flexible in order to satisfy the various optimisation goals of the stakeholder.

5   Approach

5.1   Energy Proportional Tracker Migration

Energy Proportional Tracker Migration leverages heterogeneous hardware to promote energy proportionality of the tracker component. During periods of low utilisation the tracker will reside on a computationally constrained but energy-efficient machine, autonomically migrating to a more performant (but more costly in terms of power) server during periods of increased load. This will minimise the load-independent component of our system's overall power consumption and achieve near energy proportional operation.

Existing research has demonstrated the ability to compose a number of non energy-proportional servers, combining power saving mechanisms to deliver an energy-proportional aggregate system [17] [12]. We acknowledge the heterogeneous nature of typical real-world data centres (often caused by machine failures, and upgrades, etc) [9] and contribute mechanisms which specifically leverage hardware heterogeneity to achieve aggregate energy proportionality.

5.2   Elastic Capacity Provisioning

In Elastic Capacity Provisioning, we propose a variation of typical BitTorrent use, whereby a content distributor operates a pool of specialised seeds. It is the role of these seeds to share content to other peers, ensuring satisfactory levels of performance, energy consumption and cost. This pool is said to be elastic because instances are provisioned dynamically in response to real-time service demand. We consider the heterogeneous nature of this pool of specialised seeds when periodically recalculating and provisioning the minimum active set of seed resources to achieve desired performance, cost and energy optimisations.

Traditionally, BitTorrent seeds abide by strategy where seeder upload capacity is allocated proportionally to those peers with higher download rates, optimistic that those peers may themselves become seeds more quickly and serve other peers. We propose a hybrid scheme whereby upload bandwidth is allocated on a combination of observed download rates and peer energy inefficiency. Peers who are particularly energy-inefficient relative to the rest of the swarm will be provided with a larger proportion of the seeder's upload capacity. Enabling these peers to complete their download and leave the system more quickly reduces their power consumption. In situations where upload capacity is limited among members of the swarm, and such actions threaten the overall health of the swarm, the traditional strategy is observed to prevent starvation.

5.3   Peer Connectivity Shaping

Peer Connectivity Shaping augments the peer lists returned by the tracker, giving some peers preferential treatment by providing them with the details of a larger peer set, or of peers with greater available upload bandwidth. This promotes greater connectivity between the peer and the swarm, lowering the peer's download time and consequently reduces its energy consumption.

Once a peer list has been received, a client typically selects a random subset of peers with which to connect to in the first instance. Peers are unaware of the upload capacity of the peers when they select which peers to connect to, so it is important when a peer requests its initial peer list that the list comprises a smaller proportion of peers with slow upload rates. Subsequent peer lists may include a wider range of peer upload capabilities, as BitTorrent's "tit-for-tat" mechanism will favour peers with higher upload rates and ensure the peer receives fair download rates. In the case of a particularly energy-inefficient peer, it may be more beneficial to provide small peer lists to increase download performance at the expense of increasing the peer's connectivity with the swarm.

The interval between a peer's requests to the tracker may also be optimised to improve performance and lower energy consumption and cost. In highly dynamic systems where peers and seeds are arriving and departing frequently, it may be preferable to lower the interval between peer requests in order for them to remain responsive to the changing state of the system. Increased requests to the tracker will place the tracker under greater load so there is a subtle trade-off between increasing performance for peers without incurring greater power consumption.

The impact of these approaches should be both equitable and proportional, such that energy-efficient peers are not penalised excessively in terms of download performance, and be beneficial to the swarm as a whole. Decisions made by the system are informed by comprehensive measures of system performance collected by the tracker, and are subject to the optimisation goals of the policy currently being enforced by the service provider, and the current state of the system.

6   Experimentation

To evaluate the efficacy of our approach we have developed a simulation environment based on TorrentSim [3]. Our simulation environment extends the underlying simulation framework to allow dynamic provisioning of nodes during execution, adds power consumption modelling support, and augmented BitTorrent tracker and seed components implementing our proposed energy efficiency approaches. A monitoring component periodically collects real-time power consumption and performance metrics for offline analysis. Simulation studies are carried out for scenarios with varying levels of swarm heterogeneity and bandwidth availability. We also compare our approach with traditional client-server and naive BitTorrent approaches.

A lightweight implementation of our energy-efficient BitTorrent system is written in Python, with system models and operational data stored in a MySQL database. The implementation will be tested locally using a virtualised testing environment [8], providing greater control over the conditions under which the implementation is evaluated. Large scale testing is to be carried out on Planet-Lab [6].

7   Preliminary Findings

In the initial evaluation of the Energy Proportional Tracker Migration approach we consider two normalised tracker workload traces shown in Figures 1 and 2. Workload traces WL_1 and WL_2 represent tracker requests during the arrival and service of 100 and 200 peers respectively. In each case three seeds are active in the system, and all peers depart from the system upon completing their download.

Workload WL_1 is characterised by larger peer inter-arrival times and greater availability, resulting in smaller mean peer service time. Conversely, in WL_2 peer inter-arrival times are much smaller and peer download rates are constrained by limited availability and greater competition for available upload capacity. The request rate at a given period is largely dependant on the number of peers and seeds active in the system. Observed increases in request rate over time indicate the arrival of new peers, while decreases signify peers' completion and subsequent departure from the system.

The efficacy of our provisioning approach is evaluated for two groups of servers. The first group is homogeneous in terms of both performance and power consumption, while the second comprises servers from two heterogeneous classes of server. In Figure 3 we present relative energy savings for our approach when compared to a group of servers right-sized to satisfy the peak request rate observed over the duration of the traces. In each case we find increasing the number of servers is beneficial in reducing energy consumption, allowing for finer grained provisioning of resources to satisfy the offered workload.

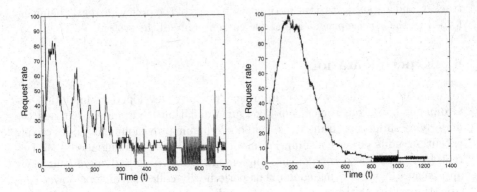

Fig. 1. Tracker workload trace WL_1 **Fig. 2.** Tracker workload trace WL_2

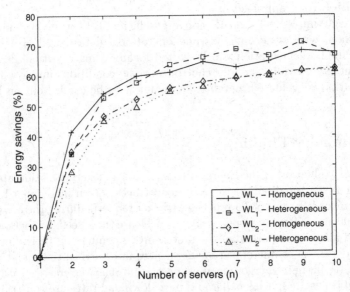

Fig. 3. Comparison of energy savings for two workload traces with homogeneous and heterogeneous groups of servers of size n

Our initial results demonstrate the potential for considerable energy savings and reduction in the load-independent portion of aggregate power consumption with negligible SLA violations. Further detailed analysis is ongoing and will form the basis of future publications.

8   Conclusions and Further Work

The potential trust and security implications of the system proposed in this paper are of great interest. We acknowledge complexities in guaranteeing the veracity of a peer's self-reported power consumption profile in inter-organisational settings, and design the system ensuring that any free riding permitted by our mechanisms is not detrimental to the overall performance or energy efficiency of the system.

A common challenge in peer-to-peer systems is accountability [18]. The usage data collected by our energy-efficient tracker not only informs the behaviour of our system, but also allows fine-grained attribution of utility, energy-efficiency and cost. The application of this accountability information in a class of energy-aware incentive mechanisms for BitTorrent will be addressed in our ongoing research.

Peer Exchange (PEX) [19] is an extension to the BitTorrent protocol enabling decentralised peer discovery in BitTorrent swarms. In PEX, peers periodically communicate directly among themselves, sharing details of the peers with whom they are connected. PEX has been shown to be beneficial to performance. However, as peers are not equipped with global knowledge of the system this approach cannot easily be made energy-aware. We will look to investigate approaches to an energy-aware PEX-like system without impacting upon overall performance.

This paper considers the use of BitTorrent as a content distribution mechanism in a single management domain. An interesting area of future research is to extend our approach to facilitate energy-efficient use of BitTorrent in a federated network of interconnected content distribution networks. Such a federated approach would allow organisations to share resources, further reducing the need to over-provision to meet peak demand. Service Level Agreements (SLAs) between these organisations may be enforced on a combination of utility, cost and energy efficiency. Audit and accountability information may be used to facilitate billing for service between organisations. Of particular interest is the ability to reconcile the conflicting optimisation goals of multiple service providers on shared infrastructure, and energy-aware incentive mechanisms in a federated context.

References

1. Anastasi, G., Giannetti, I., Passarella, A.: A BitTorrent proxy for green internet file sharing: Design and experimental evaluation. Comput. Commun. 33, 794–802 (2010)
2. Andrew, L.L.H., Sucevic, A., Nguyen, T.T.T.: Balancing peer and server energy consumption in large peer-to-peer file distribution systems. In: Proc. IEEE Green-Com (2011)
3. Barcellos, M., Mansilha, R., Brasileiro, F.: Torrentlab: investigating BitTorrent through simulation and live experiments. In: IEEE Symposium on Computers and Communications, ISCC 2008, pp. 507–512 (July 2008)
4. Bertoldi, P., Atanasiu, B.: Electricity consumption and efficiency trends in european union. Renewable Energy Status Rep. (2009)
5. Blackburn, J., Christensen, K.: A simulation study of a new green BitTorrent. In: IEEE International Conference on Communications Workshops, ICC Workshops 2009, pp. 1–6 (2009)
6. Chun, B., Culler, D., Roscoe, T., Bavier, A., Peterson, L., Wawrzoniak, M., Bowman, M.: Planetlab: an overlay testbed for broad-coverage services. SIGCOMM Comput. Commun. Rev. 33, 3–12 (2003)

7. Cohen, B.: Incentives build robustness in BitTorrent (2003)
8. Deaconescu, R., Milescu, G., Aurelian, B., Rughiniş, R., Ţăpuş, N.: A virtualized infrastructure for automated BitTorrent performance testing and evaluation. Internation Journal on Advances in Systems and Measurements 2(2&3), 236–247 (2009)
9. Heath, T., Diniz, B., Carrera, E.V., Meira Jr., W., Bianchini, R.: Energy conservation in heterogeneous server clusters. In: Proceedings of the Tenth ACM SIGPLAN Symposium on Principles and Practice of Parallel Programming, PPoPP 2005, pp. 186–195. ACM, New York (2005)
10. Izal, M., Uroy-Keller, G., Biersack, E., Felber, P.A., Hamra, A.A., Garces-Erice, L.: Dissecting BitTorrent: Five months in torrent's lifetime, pp. 1–11 (2004)
11. Kelenyi, I., Ludanyi, A., Nurminen, J.: Energy-efficient BitTorrent downloads to mobile phones through memory-limited proxies. In: 2011 IEEE Consumer Communications and Networking Conference (CCNC), pp. 715–719 (2011)
12. Krioukov, A., Mohan, P., Alspaugh, S., Keys, L., Culler, D., Katz, R.H.: Napsac: design and implementation of a power-proportional web cluster. In: Proceedings of the First ACM SIGCOMM Workshop on Green Networking, Green Networking 2010, pp. 15–22. ACM, New York (2010)
13. Mahadevan, P., Sharma, P., Banerjee, S., Ranganathan, P.: A Power Benchmarking Framework for Network Devices. In: Fratta, L., Schulzrinne, H., Takahashi, Y., Spaniol, O. (eds.) NETWORKING 2009. LNCS, vol. 5550, pp. 795–808. Springer, Heidelberg (2009)
14. Nedevschi, S., Ratnasamy, S., Padhye, J.: Hot data centers vs. cool peers. In: Proceedings of the 2008 Conference on Power Aware Computing and Systems, HotPower 2008, p. 8. USENIX Association, Berkeley (2008)
15. Price, D.: An estimate of infringing use of the internet. Tech. rep. Envisional Ltd. (2011)
16. Ryckbosch, F., Polfliet, S., Eeckhout, L.: Trends in server energy proportionality. Computer 44(9), 69–72 (2011)
17. Tolia, N., Wang, Z., Marwah, M., Bash, C., Ranganathan, P., Zhu, X.: Delivering energy proportionality with non energy-proportional systems: optimizing the ensemble. In: Proceedings of the 2008 Conference on Power Aware Computing and Systems, HotPower 2008, p. 2. USENIX Association, Berkeley (2008)
18. Turcan, E., Graham, R.L.: Getting the most from accountability in P2P. In: 1st International Conference on Peer-to-Peer Computing (P2P 2001), pp. 95–96 (2001)
19. Wu, D., Dhungel, P., Hei, X., Zhang, C., Ross, K.: Understanding peer exchange in BitTorrent systems. In: 2010 IEEE Tenth International Conference on Peer-to-Peer Computing (P2P), pp. 1–8 (2010)

Performance Modelling
of Magnetohydrodynamics Codes

R.F. Bird, S.A. Wright, D.A. Beckingsale, and S.A. Jarvis

Performance Computing and Visualisation
Department of Computer Science
University of Warwick, UK
bob@dcs.warwick.ac.uk

Abstract. Performance modelling is an important tool utilised by the High Performance Computing industry to accurately predict the run-time of science applications on a variety of different architectures. Performance models aid in procurement decisions and help to highlight areas for possible code optimisations. This paper presents a performance model for a magnetohydrodynamics physics application, Lare. We demonstrate that this model is capable of accurately predicting the run-time of Lare across multiple platforms with an accuracy of 90% (for both strong and weak scaled problems). We then utilise this model to evaluate the performance of future optimisations. The model is generated using SST/macro, the machine level component of the Structural Simulation Toolkit (SST) from Sandia National Laboratories, and is validated on both a commodity cluster located at the University of Warwick and a large scale capability resource located at Lawrence Livermore National Laboratory.

1 Introduction

Increasing compute performance and maximising supercomputer utilisation has long been a major goal within the High Performance Computing (HPC) industry. Users of these supercomputers are building increasingly more complex and computationally intensive applications, furthering research in a wide variety of science and engineering areas.

In order to meet the demands of the industry, HPC centres are starting to move away from traditional architectures and towards new technologies. One such technology is that of many-core, utilising large numbers of processor units, possibly as part of a heterogeneous architecture. The highly parallel SIMD nature of many-core units, such as GPUs and Intel MIC, allows faster processing of large amounts of data, and can offer performance gains for scientific applications [1,2,3].

With this increase in technical complexity, it is important to ensure these resources are used effectively. By being able to accurately predict the run-time of a code for a given architecture, we are not only able to make more efficient use of the hardware, but we can also rapidly compare code performance on a variety of different architectures. Furthermore, we are also able to extrapolate results past existing core counts, making predictions of code performance at scale.

M. Tribastone and S. Gilmore (Eds.): EPEW/UKPEW 2012, LNCS 7587, pp. 197–209, 2013.
© Springer-Verlag Berlin Heidelberg 2013

In order to predict run-time performance, we need to capture the run-time behaviour of the application and the performance characteristics of the target system. We can then infer information from this data. This process is known as performance modelling. In this paper we describe the development of a performance model for the 2-dimensional variant of *Lare*, a representative plasma physics application. Lare is a Lagrangian remap code, used for solving magneto-hydrodynamics (MHD) equations [4], and is being developed at the University of Warwick.

Specifically we make the following contributions:

- We develop a performance model for Lare. This is the first known predictive performance model for Lare and allows for the prediction of run-time on a variety of current and future architectures based on a minimal number of input parameters. It has been developed such that any future changes or optimisations in the code base can be readily incorporated into the model;

- We validate this performance model on two HPC systems: a commodity cluster located at the University of Warwick and a 260 TFLOP/s capability resource located at Lawrence Livermore National Laboratory (LLNL). We demonstrate an accuracy of greater than 90% for both weak and strong scaled problems;

- Finally, we use our model to provide an evaluation of possible optimisations to Lare. Specifically we perform an investigation into the potential improvements that can be gained from a move towards an Arbitrary Lagrangian-Eulerian (ALE) code in which a more expensive remap step can be applied less frequently.

The remainder of the paper is organised as follows: Section 2 provides a summary of related work; Section 3 provides a background to performance modelling and the operation of Lare; Section 4 discusses the approach taken in developing the performance model; Section 5 provides a validation of the accuracy of the model; Section 6 uses the model to detail potential gains from future optimisations. Finally Section 7 concludes this paper.

2 Related Work

Performance models are a vital tool used by the HPC industry in order to predict the run-times of an application. These predictions can then be used to aid procurement decisions, identify optimisation opportunities, or to predict the behaviour of an application running on a hypothetical future architecture at scale [5].

Hammond et al. [6] show how performance modelling can be used to provide a comparison between two different systems, and use this comparison to aid procurement decisions. They show that the ability to make predictions at scale can be more valuable than the information obtained from small scale benchmarks. In [7], Herdman et al. use a performance model of an industry strength hydrodynamics benchmark to provide guidance for the procurement of future systems. The authors use their performance model to generate a range of predicted values for comparison, spanning multiple architectures and compiler configurations.

In addition to allowing us to assess current architectures, performance modelling also plays a vital role in enabling us to look at the performance of applications on future architectures at scale. Pennycook et al. [8] show how performance modelling can be used to provide an insight into how applications will perform on a variety on architectures, highlighting the potential benefits of using many-core architectures. Finally, in [9] it is shown that performance modelling can be applied to emerging distributed memory heterogeneous systems to provide an analysis of the performance characteristics and to accurately predict run-times for an application [10].

In [11] a model of parallel computation, LogGP, based on the LogP [12] model, is introduced. It extends the predictive performance of LogP by including the ability to accurately predict communication performance for small messages. This in turn forms the basis on which plug-and-play models can be built, as shown in [13]. The authors show that a model can be built that is able to accurately predict the run-time of an application on a variety of architectures, whilst taking a minimal set of input parameters. This approach has successfully been used by others, including Davis et al. [14] and Sundaram-Stukel et al. [15], and is the basis of the approach taken in this paper.

The previous methods of developing an analytical performance model have been purely mathematically based, but as levels of concurrency and message passing continue to climb this is becoming increasingly difficult to do accurately. By instead simulating the topologies of machines, and message passing behaviour of applications, we can hope to gain increased accuracy. This simulation of hardware can be done using an abstraction of the machine, using both virtual processors and interconnect. By providing values for the specifications of the processors and the interconnect, we can then reproduce the communications performed by the application. By having this closeness between software and hardware it allows for greater performance optimisation of both, as seen in the co-design approach that is being used to move us towards exascale [16,17,18].

One such tool that facilitates this machine level simulation is SST/macro, one component of Structural Simulation Toolkit [17] from Sandia National Laboratories. SST/macro allows for simulation style models to represent both the control flow of an application, and the message passing behaviour. In doing this it can fully consider such factors as contention and network topology, areas which had previously introduced inaccuracy into analytical models. In order to make use of these advantages, SST/macro has been used to construct the model used in this paper.

3   Background

3.1   Lare

To solve MHD equations, Lare uses an approach based on control volume averaging using a staggered grid. This approach is extended to include complex
components such as magnetic fields and shock forces. Lare is run on a fixed size
grid for a set number of iterations, an outline of which is shown in Figure 1. The
grid used in Lare is 2-dimensional with its width (N_x) and height (N_y) set at
run time. This grid is then decomposed in two dimensions ($P_x \times P_y$) such that
each processor receives $nx \times ny$ cells, where $nx = N_x/P_x$ and $ny = N_y/P_y$.

```
1 DO
2       ...
3       CALL lagrangian_step
4       CALL eulerian_remap(i)
5       ...
6 END DO
```

Fig. 1. The main compute loop of Lare, operated over for a fixed number of iterations

The main area of computation in Lare is represented by two key steps, each
executed once per iteration: the *Lagrangian step*; and the *Lagrangian remap*. The
Lagrangian step contains the majority of the computationally intensive physics,
representing a significant proportion of the run-time. During this step the grid on
which the calculations are performed gets distorted. The gridding scheme used
in Lare cannot tolerate large distortions of the computational domain without
frequent remapping operations. And thus, some work must be done to correct the
grid before computation can continue. The *Lagrangian remap* reforms the grid
to its proper coordinates, and involves a significant amount of computation and
a series of near-neighbour exchanges are required, which ensures neighbouring
cells hold the appropriate values.

3.2   Performance Modelling

The general run-time of a parallel application can be described by Equation 1,
which states that the total run-time is the combined total of the compute and
communication times.

$$T_{total} = T_{compute} + T_{comms} \tag{1}$$

When developing a performance model it is usual to start with the simplistic
case of a serial run, as it contains no communications. In doing this you are able
to simplify Equation 1, to that shown in Equation 2.

$$T_{total} = T_{compute} \qquad (2)$$

This compute term can then be broken down further, to describe the run-time at a function level. This is shown in Equation 3, where w_g is refered to as the 'grind time', and both nx and ny represent the decomposed grid size in the relevant direction.

$$T_{compute} = \sum w_g \times (nx \times ny) \qquad (3)$$

The term grind time is used to describe the per-cell cost of a function. To obtain these values the code can be instrumented with timers. This can either be done using a profiler such as *gprof* or *scalasca*, alternatively the instrumentation can be done manually. Once these grind times have been found they can be put back into Equation 3 to calculate the total compute time.

4   Developing a Performance Model

In order to fully understand the run-time characteristics of Lare, the code was profiled for both serial and parallel runs. This quantifies the time spent in each subroutine, allowing us to focus our efforts when building our simulation.

In order to construct a model using SST/macro, a skeleton of the code has to be constructed that includes the main areas of compute and communication. As the generation of a comprehensive skeleton application can be a non-trivial process, a small tool was written to facilitate this. The tool performs static analysis on the Fortran source code, and transforms this information into a SST/macro skeleton model. The tool parses the Fortran source code line by line, splitting the line into tokens based on whitespace. These tokens are then matched against an in-built list of keywords, identifying key areas such as subroutine declarations and invocations. Once a keyword is matched, the line is processed. Subroutine declarations are parsed and replicated in the skeleton code. These subroutines are then populated by any function calls made within them. One of the key benefits of the tool is that it identifies MPI communications and is able to flag these to the user and input them into the skeleton. The tool is able to auto-complete much of the information about the MPI call, leaving only the size of the communication buffer to be provided by the user.

In addition to the skeleton, SST/macro requires machine specific details to be specified, such as: topology, network bandwidth and on-node and off-node latencies. These values are obtained using a series of micro-benchmarks.

In order to accurately populate the skeleton application, the main contributors of run-time need to be identified. By profiling Lare and combining this with our existing understanding, it is clear that the two most significant contributors are the Lagrangian step and the Lagrangian remap as previously discussed.

By combining these two steps, we can develop an equation that accurately and concisely summarises the total run-time of Lare as shown in Equation 4.

$$T_{total} = \sum_{i=0}^{iterations} (t_{lagrangian\_step} + t_{remap}) \tag{4}$$

In order to make use of this equation, an incremental approach to building a model was taken, starting with the construction of a serial model.

4.1 Serial Model

For a serial run of Lare, there is no inter-process communication – the run-time is singularly representative of the compute, allowing us to apply Equation 2.

This equation can be decomposed further. The term $T_{compute}$ can further be broken up into its subcomponents, as shown in Equation 3. A table of the relevant grind times for Lare can be found in Table 1.

Table 1. A table depicting the grind times used in modeling Lare, along with their relative location in the source code

File Name	Subroutine	w_g Term
diagnostics.f90	energy_account	$w_{energy\_account}$
lagran.f90	lagrangian_step	$w_{lagrangian\_step}$
lagran.f90	predictor_corrector_step	$w_{predictor\_corrector}$
xremap.f90	remap_x	w_{remap_x}
yremap.f90	remap_y	w_{remap_y}
zremap.f90	remap_z	w_{remap_z}
remap.f90	eulerian_remap	$w_{remap\_remainder}$
diagnostics.f90	set_dt	w_{set_dt}

We are able to derive values of the relevant w_g times by running a version of Lare instrumented with timers. Using these values we are able to develop a model that can predict serial run-time to an exceptionally high level of accuracy, using Equation 4.

4.2 Parallel Model

Once a serial model was developed, a parallel model could then be considered in the form shown in Equation 1.

The communication in Lare is dominated by two MPI functions, send-receives and all reduces. The send-receive functions are used to swap neighbour cells, whilst the all reduces collate data. By summing the times taken by these operations, we can represent the communications time as:

$$T_{comms} = \sum t_{Sendrecv} + \sum t_{Allreduce} \tag{5}$$

During the point-to-point communications, the amount of data sent is dependent on the grid size set at compile time. The grid undergoes a coarse decomposition in two dimensions, and is distributed among the processors. This method of decomposition is performed with the aim of minimising the surface-area-to-volume ratio, which in turn increases the ratio of computation to communication. This decomposition strategy is replicated in the model, with SST/macro simulating an exact copy of the communications. Once all the required terms have been identified, they can be incorporated into the model. In order for SST/macro to accurately simulate communications, it requires values for the latency and bandwidth of the target system. These values can be found experimentally with a set of micro-benchmarks that are distributed with SST/macro.

Figure 2 shows elements of both the model and original Lare source code for two methods, dm_x_bcs and remap_x. It compares the original source to the equivalent representation in the model. In (a) we see the dm_x_bcs subroutine that features an *MPI_Sendrecv*. In (b) we can see this has been translated to the equivalent SST/macro MPI call, to be dealt with by the simulated network. Similarly (c) shows an area of compute performed by the original source, this is then replaced by a w_g based calculation in (d).

5 Validation

In order to validate our model, we compare application run times with simulation times for a variety of grid sizes and processor counts on 2 different machines.

5.1 Machines

The two machines used in the validation of the model were the resident supercomputer at the University of Warwick, Minerva, and a large scale capability resource, Sierra, located at LLNL. The specification of the two machines used in this study are summarised in Table 2.

Table 2. Details of the experimental machines used

	Sierra	Minerva
Processor	Intel Xeon 5660	Intel Xeon 5650
Processor Speed	2.8 GHz	2.66 GHz
Cores/Node	12	12
Nodes	1849	258
Memory/Node	24 GB	24 GB
Interconnect	QLogic TrueScale 4X	QDR InfiniBand
Compilers	Intel 12.0	Intel 12.0
MPI	MVAPICH2 1.7	OpenMPI 1.4.3

(a) Original Fortran dm_x_bcs Subroutine

```
1  SUBROUTINE dm_x_bcs
2     ...
3     CALL MPLSENDRECV(dm(nx-1, 0:ny+1), ny+2, mpireal, &
4            proc_x_max, tag, dm(-1, 0:ny+1), ny+2, mpireal, &
5            proc_x_min, tag, comm, status, errcode)
6     ...
7  END SUBROUTINE dm_x_bcs
```

(b) Model dm_x_bcs Subroutine

```
1  void dm_x_bcs(int rank) {
2     ...
3     mpi->sendrecv(ny + 2, sstmac::sw::mpitype::mpi_real, \
4     proc_x_max, tag, ny + 2, sstmac::sw::mpitype::mpi_real, \
5     proc_x_min, tag, world(), stat);
6     ...
7  }
```

(c) Original Fortran remap_x Subroutine

```
1  SUBROUTINE remap_x ! remap onto original Eulerian grid
2     ...
3     DO iy = -1, ny+2
4        iym = iy - 1
5        DO ix = -1, nx+2
6           ixm = ix - 1
7           ...
8        END DO
9
10    END DO
11    ...
12 END SUBROUTINE remap_x
```

(d) Model remap_x Subroutine

```
1  void remap_x(int rank) {
2     ...
3     sstmac::timestamp t(remap_x_w * nx * ny);
4     compute(t);
5     ...
6  }
```

Fig. 2. Code snippet comparing original source code with its representation in the model, including a w_g based compute call and a SST/macro MPI call

5.2 Weak Scaled Problem

For a weak scaled problem, the grid size is increased with the processor count with the aim of keeping the compute per processor fixed. This is the approach taken for solving increasingly difficult problems in a fixed amount of time. As the processor count increases, more communication between grid cells is required, leading to a general increase in communication time. As the compute per processor remains the same throughout, we expect that our w_g will not change, allowing us to be confident of the predictions for compute time. Table 3 presents a comparison of the experimental run-times against predicated run-times for a weak scaled problem with 3,000,000 cells per core, running for 100 iterations.

Table 3. A table comparing the run-times to simulation times of Lare for Minerva and Sierra

(a) Minerva

Nodes	Grid Size	Time (s)	Prediction (s)	Error (%)
1	6000	543.10	527.03	-3.05
4	12000	554.90	528.57	-4.98
9	18000	560.63	541.55	-3.52
16	24000	569.41	549.06	-3.71
21	30000	570.08	551.14	-3.44
36	36000	578.24	558.15	-3.60

(b) Sierra

Nodes	Grid Size	Time (s)	Prediction (s)	Error (%)
1	6000	480.70	465.46	-3.29
4	12000	485.26	466.17	-4.10
9	18000	493.59	466.83	-5.73
16	24000	498.32	476.30	-4.62
21	30000	499.07	478.43	-4.31
36	36000	499.01	480.49	-3.85
49	42000	499.47	481.98	-3.63
64	48000	499.15	483.68	-3.20
81	54000	499.31	487.22	-2.48
100	60000	499.58	488.59	-2.25
121	66000	500.00	490.12	-2.02
144	72000	500.57	491.54	-1.84
169	78000	500.29	492.91	-1.50
196	84000	500.27	495.44	-0.98
225	90000	500.85	496.88	-0.80
256	96000	500.29	499.44	-0.17

From the table we can see that the model was able to accurately predict the run-time to an accuracy of greater than 90%. The predicated runtime being consistently slightly lower than the experimental time can be attributed to a small percentage of the run time behaviour not being incorporated in the prediction, such as the set up costs, which are not captured by the model.

5.3   Strong Scaled Problem

Strong scaling describes the process of solving a fixed problem size with an increasing number of processors. As the processor count increases the aim is to decrease the run-time. A comparison between experimental run-time and predicted run-time is shown in Table 4 for a 16,800 × 16,800 strong scaled problem, running for 100 iterations. This problem size was chosen to give a sufficiently long run time, but still fit in the available memory.

Table 4. A table comparing the run-times to simulation times of Lare for Minerva and Sierra fora strong scaled problem

(a) Minerva

Nodes	Time (s)	Prediction (s)	Error (%)
8	518.01	532.85	2.78
12	348.16	364.61	4.51
16	262.74	277.77	5.41
24	172.01	189.51	9.24
32	128.67	133.48	3.61

(b) Sierra

Nodes	Time (s)	Prediction (s)	Error (%)
16	251.06	236.00	-6.38
32	119.60	121.78	1.79
64	61.02	64.16	4.90
128	33.38	35.55	6.12

The performance model was able predict the run-time to an accuracy of greater than 90% for a range of core counts.

6   Evaluation of Future Optimisations

An Arbitrary Lagrangian Eulerian (ALE) generalisation of Lare is under development. This would mean the requirement to remap each iteration will no longer hold, and instead a move to ALE would allow the remap step to only be done once the grid becomes sufficiently deformed. By performing an investigation into the expected performance of an hypothetical ALE variant of Lare we can gain valuable insight into the potential performance gains.

By moving to an ALE code, we can vary the frequency of the remap, a metric will be developed to formally determine the value of this frequency (F_r), but initial indications show that remapping will be required, on average, once every tenth iteration ($F_r = 0.1$) over the course of the simulation. By varying the frequency of the remap, the code will be affected in two main ways. Firstly, it will significantly reduce the general cost per iteration in terms of compute, as the remap step will no longer be present. Secondly, reducing the frequency of the remap step reduces the frequency of inter-process communication. In changing the code in this way, the total cost is no longer as described in Equation 4, but instead includes a term to denote the new remap, as in Equation 6.

$$T_{total} = T_{lagrangian\_step} + T_{remap\_new} \tag{6}$$

This equation can then be reduced further, as shown in Equation 7.

$$T_{total} = \sum_{i=0}^{iterations} (t_{lagrangian\_step}) + \sum_{j=0}^{iterations/F_r} t_{remap\_new} \tag{7}$$

In order to express the new total cost, relative to the old, we can extend Equation 4 to include terms for the relative costs. This is shown in Equation 8.

$$T_{total\_new} = (T_{lagrangian\_step} \times C_{lagrangian\_step}) +$$
$$(T_{lagrangian\_remap} \times C_{remap\_new} \times F_r) \tag{8}$$

If we assume no change to the cost of the Lagrangian step ($C_{lagrangian\_step} = 1$), we can perform an investigation into how the frequency of remap and the cost of remap affect the overall performance. Table 5 shows the percentage decrease in run-time obtained for different values of F_r and C_{remap_new} for a 8,192 square problem on 36 processors performing 100 iterations, in which the remap step contributes just under 65% of the run-time.

Table 5. A table showing the percent decrease in run-time for different values of F_r and C_{remap_new} for a 8,192 square problem on 36 processors performing 100 iterations

C_{remap_new}	F_r					
	1	0.5	0.2	0.25	0.1	0.001
1	0.00	32.15	48.22	51.44	57.87	64.24
2	-64.30	0.00	32.15	38.58	51.44	64.17
4	-192.90	-64.30	0.00	12.86	38.58	64.04
5	-257.20	-96.45	-16.07	0.00	32.15	63.98
10	-578.69	-257.20	-96.45	-64.30	0.00	63.66

From Table 5 we can clearly see that reducing the remap frequency offers large performance gains as the remap frequency decreases for reasonable values of C_{remap_new}. Optimistic projections for this optimised code hope that it will have a similar cost for the lagrangian step ($C_{lagrangian\_step} = 1$), a remap cost that is around twice as large ($C_{remap\_new} = 2$) and allow the remap to be performed on average every ten steps ($F_r = 0.1$). From Table 5 we can see this may offer a speed-up greater than 50%.

7 Conclusion

In this paper we have presented a predictive performance model for Lare, a MHD code developed by, and maintained at, the University of Warwick. This model allows us to predict the run-time of Lare accurately on a variety of platforms. We have validated the accuracy of the model to 90% on two clusters, a commodity cluster located at the University of Warwick and a 360 TFLOP/s capability resource located at LLNL.

The model was shown to perform well for both weak and strong scaling over a wide range of core counts. We have also used our model to provide a forward look at possible optimisations in the Lare code base, with an evaluation of the gains that may be expected. We also plan to extend the model to the 3-dimensional version of Lare and develop predictive performance models for similar physics codes with the aim of drawing comparisons between these and Lare.

Acknowledgements. We would like to thank Todd Gamblin and Scott Futral for their invaluable help in utilising Sierra and the other Open Compute Facility resources at Lawrence Livermore National Laboratory. This work is supported by the EPSRC grant: A Radiation-Hydrodynamic ALE Code for Laser Fusion Energy (EP/I029117/1).

References

1. Pang, B., Li Pen, U., Perrone, M.: Magnetohydrodynamics on Heterogeneous architectures: a performance comparison. CoRR abs/1004.1680 (2010)
2. Ryoo, S., Rodrigues, C.I., Baghsorkhi, S.S., Stone, S.S., Kirk, D.B., Hwu, W.-M.W.: Optimization principles and application performance evaluation of a multithreaded GPU using CUDA. In: Proceedings of the 13th ACM SIGPLAN Symposium on Principles and Practice of Parallel Programming, PPoPP 2008, pp. 73–82. ACM, New York (2008)
3. Griebel, M., Zaspel, P.: A multi-GPU accelerated solver for the three-dimensional two-phase incompressible Navier-Stokes equations. Computer Science - Research and Development 25, 65–73 (2010), doi:10.1007/s00450-010-0111-7
4. Arber, T., Longbottom, A., Gerrard, C., Milne, A.: A Staggered Grid, Lagrangian-Eulerian Remap Code for 3-D MHD Simulations. Journal of Computational Physics 171 (2001)
5. Kerbyson, D., Hoisie, A., Wasserman, H.: Modelling the performance of large-scale systems.. IEE Proceedings – Software 150, 214 (2003)
6. Hammond, S.D., Mudalige, G.R., Smith, J.A., Davis, J.A., Jarvis, S.A., Holt, J., Miller, I., Herdman, J.A., Vadgama, A.: To upgrade or not to upgrade? Catamount vs. Cray Linux Environment. In: 2010 IEEE International Symposium on Parallel Distributed Processing, Workshops and Phd Forum (IPDPSW), pp. 1–8 (2010)
7. Herdman, J.A., Gaudin, W.P., Turland, D., Hammond, S.D.: Benchmarking and Modelling of POWER-7, Westmere, BG/P, and GPUs: An Industry Case Study. ACM SIGMETRICS Performance Evaluation Review 38 (2011)
8. Pennycook, S.J., Hammond, S.D., Mudalige, G.R., Wright, S.A., Jarvis, S.A.: On the Acceleration of Wavefront Applications using Distributed Many-Core Architectures. The Computer Journal 55, 138–153 (2011)
9. Mudalige, G.R., Giles, M.B., Bertolli, C., Kelly, P.H.: Predictive modeling and analysis of OP2 on distributed memory GPU clusters. In: Proceedings of the Second International Workshop on Performance Modeling, Benchmarking and Simulation of High Performance Computing Systems, PMBS 2011, pp. 3–4. ACM, New York (2011)

10. Giles, M.B., Mudalige, G.R., Sharif, Z., Markall, G., Kelly, P.H.: Performance analysis of the OP2 framework on many-core architectures. SIGMETRICS Perform. Eval. Rev. 38, 9–15 (2011)
11. Alexandrov, A., Ionescu, M.F., Schauser, K.E., Scheiman, C.: LogGP: incorporating long messages into the LogP model - One step closer towards a realistic model for parallel computation. In: Proceedings of the Seventh Annual ACM Symposium on Parallel Algorithms and Architectures, SPAA 1995, pp. 95–105. ACM, New York (1995)
12. Culler, D., Karp, R., Patterson, D., Sahay, A., Schauser, K.E., Santos, E., Subramonian, R., von Eicken, T.: LogP: towards a realistic model of parallel computation. In: Proceedings of the Fourth ACM SIGPLAN Symposium on Principles and Practice of Parallel Programming, PPOPP 1993, pp. 1–12. ACM, New York (1993)
13. Mudalige, G.R., Vernon, M.K., Jarvis, S.A.: A Plug-and-Play Model for Evaluating Wavefront Computations on Parallel Architectures. In: 22nd IEEE International Parallel and Distributed Processing Symposium, IPDPS 2008 (2008)
14. Davis, J.A., Mudalige, G.R., Hammond, S.D., Herdman, J., Miller, I., Jarvis, S.A.: Predictive Analysis of a Hydrodynamics Application on Large-Scale CMP Clusters. In: International Supercomputing Conference (ISC 2011). Computer Science (R & D), vol. 26, pp. 175–185. Springer, Heidelberg (2011)
15. Sundaram-Stukel, D., Vernon, M.K.: Predictive analysis of a wavefront application using LogGP. SIGPLAN Not. 34, 141–150 (1999)
16. Hammond, S.D., Mudalige, G.R., Smith, J.A., Jarvis, S.A., Herdman, J.A., Vadgama, A.: WARPP: A Toolkit for Simulating High Performance Parallel Scientific Codes. In: 2nd International Conference on Simulation Tools and Techniques, SIMUTools 2009 (2009)
17. Janssen, C.L., Adalsteinsson, H., Kenny, J.P.: Using simulation to design extremescale applications and architectures: programming model exploration. SIGMETRICS Perform. Eval. Rev. 38, 4–8 (2011)
18. Rodrigues, A.F., Hemmert, K.S., Barrett, B.W., Kersey, C., Oldfield, R., Weston, M., Risen, R., Cook, J., Rosenfeld, P., CooperBalls, E., Jacob, B.: The structural simulation toolkit. SIGMETRICS Perform. Eval. Rev. 38, 37–42 (2011)

Optimisation of Patch Distribution Strategies for AMR Applications

D.A. Beckingsale, O.F.J. Perks, W.P. Gaudin, J.A. Herdman, and S.A. Jarvis

Performance Computing and Visualisation,
Department of Computer Science, University of Warwick, UK
dab@dcs.warwick.ac.uk

Abstract. As core counts increase in the world's most powerful super-computers, applications are becoming limited not only by computational power, but also by data availability. In the race to exascale, efficient and effective communication policies are key to achieving optimal application performance. Applications using adaptive mesh refinement (AMR) trade off communication for computational load balancing, to enable the focused computation of specific areas of interest. This class of application is particularly susceptible to the communication performance of the underlying architectures, and are inherently difficult to scale efficiently. In this paper we present a study of the effect of patch distribution strategies on the scalability of an AMR code. We demonstrate the significance of patch placement on communication overheads, and by balancing the computation and communication costs of patches, we develop a scheme to optimise performance of a specific, industry-strength, benchmark application.

1 Introduction

In the race to exascale, floating point operations are becoming cheaper and the real challenge is providing data to utilise the available computational power. Communications are therefore becoming more important in scientific computing and efficiently transferring data will be key to scaling the existing generation of petascale applications.

Adaptive mesh refinement (AMR) is a technique used to increase the resolution of computation in areas of interest—such as shock fronts and material interfaces—avoiding the necessity of a uniform fine-grained mesh [1,2]. The technique uses multiple levels of refinement, where areas of interest are identified and the accuracy of computation is increased, by subdivision of the problem domain. This decomposition and refinement creates a natural computational load imbalance as work will be clustered around the areas of interest. The technique uses a distribution strategy to share the increased workload between under-utilised compute resources. The basic unit of distribution is a *patch*, a rectangular sub-grid of cells which result from mesh refinement. The decrease in computation time offered by AMR comes at the cost of increased communication overheads, caused by additional boundary communications, and data transfer between refinement levels. The management of patches and associated AMR metadata

M. Tribastone and S. Gilmore (Eds.): EPEW/UKPEW 2012, LNCS 7587, pp. 210–223, 2013.
© Springer-Verlag Berlin Heidelberg 2013

creates an additional computational overhead, however, it is not the primary focus of this paper.

In this paper we present a cost-benefit analysis of patch distribution strategies and identify optimisation opportunities. We present our study in the context of Shamrock, a 2-dimensional, Lagrangian hydrodynamics code utilising AMR, developed at the UK Atomic Weapons Establishment (AWE). Shamrock is an industry-strength benchmark supporting a range of architectures. It is a key tool in evaluating future high-performance computing technologies at AWE, and provides a robust software framework for our investigation [3].

Specifically, we study how allowing workload imbalance can, under certain conditions, reduce the communication overheads and thus, by identifying situations where patch distribution has a negative effect on overall runtime, improve the scalability of the code. Initially, we demonstrate the application of AMR on a symmetric, and therefore, naturally load balanced problem. In this case, any distribution of patches will increase communication time and harm overall performance. We extend this simple example to motivate the use of patch distribution on inherently more representative asymmetric problems, where load balance is not guaranteed. For these asymmetric problems we demonstrate the available trade-off between communication and computation costs, and highlight the potential advantages of an optimal distribution strategy.

The specific contributions of this work are as follows:

- A cost-benefit analysis of AMR patch distribution on symmetric and asymmetric input decks is documented.
- We implement an AMR-level distribution threshold to mitigate cost between fully enabled and fully disabled patch distribution strategies.
- We demonstrate the potential of an intelligent, environment-driven, patch distribution strategy, through hand tuning, motivating the case for a runtime-based heuristic distribution strategy.

The remainder of this paper is structured as follows: in Section 2, we present an overview of related work. Section 3 presents a more detailed discussion of the key aspects of AMR. In Section 4 we analyse the load imbalance caused by two different problem input decks. In Section 5 we analyse the scalability of two patch distribution schemes, and Section 6 presents an analysis of the application of a distribution threshold-based on the AMR level. Section 7 then demonstrates how, with prior knowledge of expected communication and computation costs, we can improve the runtime and scalability of the application. Finally, in Section 8 we conclude the paper and discuss future work.

2 Related Work

The structured AMR techniques developed by Berger and Oliger [1] have been successfully applied to a number of problem domains including cosmology [4,5], astrophysics [6], and shock hydrodynamics [7,8]. The power of AMR in increasing solution accuracy without the requirement of a uniform fine-grained mesh has motivated investigation into ensuring the scalability of these techniques.

Codes utilising AMR typically contain a number of distinct steps that can have an impact on scalability: adding refined patches to flagged areas of interest, balancing the load of patches across processors, and communication and synchronisation between patches during calculations.

Adding refined patches, or re-gridding, is a computationally intensive process involving identifying areas of interest, flagging the cells in these areas, and creating a set of refined patches to cover all the flagged cells. Luitjens and Berzins present a study of three common re-gridding techniques, remarking on the communication and computation complexity of the three algorithms, and demonstrating scalable results from the Berger-Rigoustous algorithm [9,10].

Optimal distribution of refined patches is key to achieving efficient execution and acceptable runtimes. Lan *et al.* present reductions in runtime of up to 47% when using a grid-splitting technique to move work from overloaded processors to underloaded ones [11]. Using system measurements provides an effective way to ensure work is evenly balanced [12], and the optimisations presented in Section 7 make use of a set of simple measures of system performance to develop an efficient patch distribution scheme. Our work differs from previous research by building on work in performance modelling [13,14], using measured parameters to estimate the optimal distribution of patches.

Identifying the factors limiting the scalability of AMR is an ongoing problem, however, the key features identified by Colella *et al.* provide a platform for investigation: minimising communications, efficiently computing patch metadata, and optimising communication between coarse and fine patch boundaries [15]. Van Straalen *et al.* extend these features, concluding that the traditional concerns over load imbalance and communication volume were not as critical to application performance as identifying and isolating subtle use of non-scalable algorithms in the grid management infrastructure of the AMR framework [16].

3   Adaptive Mesh Refinement

Adaptive mesh refinement is the process of increasing the resolution of computation at specific areas of interest, allowing increased accuracy where it is most needed. Figure 1(a) illustrates how AMR would be applied to a simple area of interest. An area of interest is a portion of the problem where there is a high degree of entropy, such as at material interfaces or at shock fronts.

The AMR capability of Shamrock is provided by custom AMR library, rather than third-party AMR package such as SAMRAI [17] or Chombo [18]. Areas of interest are identified and the cells containing them are flagged. These flagged cells are then grouped into rectangular patches, which may contain some unflagged cells. Computation is carried out over all patches, and hence, all levels. Solutions are transferred between the patches on different levels, with coarse solutions being mapped up to higher levels, and the more accurate solutions being projected back down. A typical arrangement of patches is illustrated in Figure 1(b).

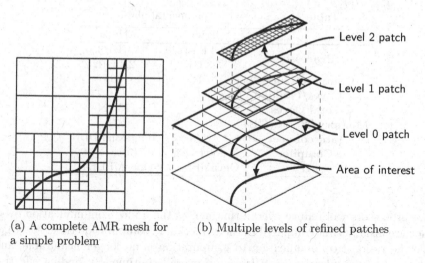

(a) A complete AMR mesh for   (b) Multiple levels of refined patches
a simple problem

Fig. 1. AMR mesh and corresponding application of patches

The complexity of AMR, and the associated metadata required, present some problems for a parallel implementation: (i) newly created patches need to be assigned to a processor, (ii) boundaries must be communicated between patches, sometimes across AMR levels, and (iii) solutions must be mapped and projected between patches.

Once areas of the problem have been refined, work required in that area, and hence CPU time spent computing that area, will increase. In order to combat this it is common to distribute the extra work to processors with a smaller workload. Refinement may happen in only one small area of the problem, and if the newly created patches are not distributed in an effective way then the resulting load imbalance is likely to negatively affect the amount of time spent in computation. However, distributing the patches will increase the cost of both the boundary communications and the transfer of solutions between patches.

Boundary communications occur at patch interfaces and involve the swapping of variables in ghost cells between adjacent patches. However, boundary communications may also have to cross refinement levels, since a patch may be adjacent to another patch on a different level. Boundary communications across refinement levels involve some additional computational overhead as solution values must be interpolated onto the grid due to the differing resolution. Solution transfer occurs where patches on different refinement levels overlap, and involves the transfer of the necessary variables, between levels, for each overlapping cell. The data needs to be transferred every timestep, so high transfer costs affect the scalability of the code.

The competing factors of communication and computation need to be effectively managed in order to minimise runtime. At small scale the addition of

Table 1. Summary of experimental platforms

	Tricca	Hera
Processor	Intel E3-1240 3.3 GHz	AMD 8356 2.3 GHz
Compute Nodes	1	864
Cores/Node	4	16
Total Cores	4	13,824
Memory/Node (GB)	12	32
Interconnect	N/A	Infiniband DDR
Compiler	Intel 11.1	Intel 12.1
MPI	OpenMPI 1.4.3	OpenMPI 1.4.3

more processors will reduce overall runtime, as the added communication overheads are insignificant compared to the reduction in computation time. At larger scale the ratio of communication to computation is no longer favourable, and the added communication cost drives up overall runtime. By finding effective ways to balance the computation-communication trade off, we can increase the performance and scalability of the code.

4   Symmetric and Asymmetric AMR

As discussed in Section 3, a key component of AMR is patch distribution. This enables local fine grained analysis in areas of interest, whilst maintaining an even workload for all processors.

With the existing patch distribution strategy, patches are always distributed, regardless of locality, with a probability based on an estimation of current computational workload. The implication of this strategy is that previously neighbouring patches, in both the horizontal and vertical domain, can be physically distributed across the whole machine, increasing communication times. The nature of Shamrock means that the majority of communication is the exchange of boundary cells and transfer of solutions, and although some global communication is required, physical proximity is crucial for keeping communication costs at a minimum, and in turn improving scalability.

Throughout this paper we make use of results obtained from two different computing platforms, illustrated in Table 1. The first is a quad-core workstation, used to demonstrate behaviour at small scale, the second is a large 127 TFLOP/s supercomputer, located at the Lawrence Livermore National Laboratories (LLNL) Open Compute Facility, used to demonstrate the scalability of our techniques.

4.1   Symmetric AMR

We demonstrate a symmetric decomposition using a square multi-material problem, executed on four processors. Although the resulting mesh is not symmetrical, the processors receive the same number of refined cells, giving an approximately equal and naturally balanced decomposition. With the original distribution policy, patches will be distributed to different processors, reducing the physical proximity of neighbouring patches. Whilst the goal is to reduce load imbalance, this distribution strategy actually introduces a small imbalance due to the order of patch distribution. The added communication cost of this distribution also has a significant impact on runtime. We also note that despite the obvious symmetry of the problem mesh, the refinement may be asymmetrical due to the nature of the underlying algorithm. Whilst this may not be a representative AMR computation, it demonstrates a situation where patch distribution will perform poorly. From this example we can then infer potential performance gains from alternative patch distribution strategies in more representative problems.

(a) A simple three material problem.

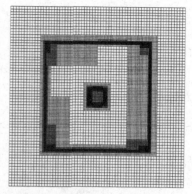

(b) The initial mesh, including refined areas.

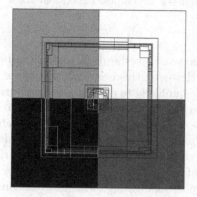

(c) Patch assignment without distribution.

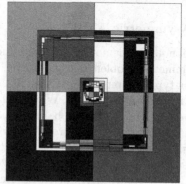

(d) Patch assignment with distribution.

Fig. 2. A symmetric multi-material problem, with the corresponding AMR mesh and patch assignments

Figure 2(a) presents the problem, with its area of interest, coupled with the resulting mesh, Figure 2(b), from an AMR level of four. We illustrate the patch distribution when decomposed over four processors firstly from a no distribution policy, Figure 2(c), and secondly a round-robin distribution, Figure 2(d).

The amount of time spent in computation time and communication time is presented in Figure 3. Both decompositions are load balanced, with each processor spending an average of 268.98s in the computation portion of the application. However, the distribution of the patches in Figure 2(d) has destroyed the spatial locality of the patches and increased the communication times to an average of 60.67s. By keeping patches local the communication time is reduced to an average of 19.96s, which provides a speedup of 1.14×. These differences are caused wholly by on-node patch distribution, where communication times are significantly lower than off-node.

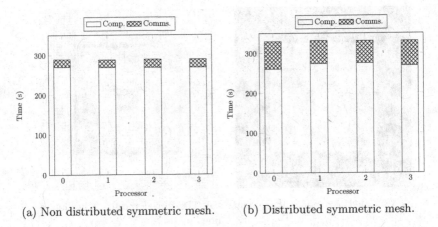

(a) Non distributed symmetric mesh.   (b) Distributed symmetric mesh.

Fig. 3. Runtime breakdown for a symmetric decomposition on four cores

4.2   Asymmetric AMR

In Section 4.1 we demonstrated the unnecessary overheads of patch distribution on a symmetric problem decomposition. However, this is an unrealistic representation of typical input data, as such data is unlikely to decompose symmetrically across a range of processors. Whilst a lack of symmetry in decomposition does not inherently imply load imbalance, we can no longer guarantee it. Patch distribution strategies may improve performance by reducing this load imbalance.

In this section we illustrate the benefit of patch distribution on asymmetric decompositions. Using an single quadrant of Figure 2(a), presented in Figure 4(a), we obtain a naturally asymmetric decomposition, through which we can compare the two distribution strategies by analysing the impact of the load imbalance. Without distribution, all of the patches obtained through mesh refinement will be assigned to the same local processor, illustrated in Figure 4(c), rather than being shared between all processors.

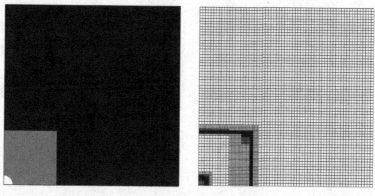

(a) A simple, asymmetric, three material problem.

(b) The initial mesh, including refined areas.

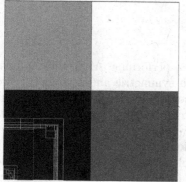

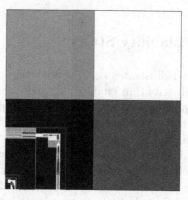

(c) Patch assignment without distribution.

(d) Patch assignment with distribution.

Fig. 4. An asymmetric multi-material problem, with the corresponding AMR mesh and patch distributions

In Figure 5 we present the breakdown of computation and communication time for each processor, illustrating the available performance gains afforded through patch distribution. The disparity between computational workload is illustrated in the communication times of the remaining processors as they wait for the overloaded processor. For patch distribution we see a reduction in the worst case communication times, from 120s down to 24s, and a levelling of computation times, resulting in a reduction in runtime.

This extreme case illustrates the runtime increases created when the load imbalance is maximal, thus highlighting the benefit of patch distribution to load balance in AMR applications. The cost of this technique is the 25% of time spent in the communication phase, which has wide implications in the scalability of the code.

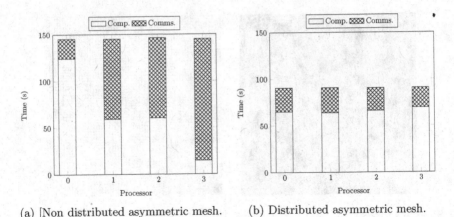

(a) [Non distributed asymmetric mesh.   (b) Distributed asymmetric mesh.

Fig. 5. Runtime breakdown for an asymmetric decomposition on four cores

5   Scalability Study

Section 4 illustrates the disparity between performing AMR with and without patch distribution enabled, through both symmetric and asymmetric problem decompositions. Both of the examples presented were designed to illustrate the performance of the techniques in ideal circumstances. However, in more realistic scenarios a middle ground between the two examples is likely to be observed.

To illustrate this more realistic scenario we perform a scalability study of the two techniques applied to the same problem decomposition. For this study we use the problem from Figure 2(a), which is initially symmetrically decomposed, and strong scale it, by increasing the processor count but keeping the global problem size constant. For our study we selected a problem comprised of 1 million cells, computed on a selection of processor counts ranging from 4 to 1024, in powers of 2. Evaluating the proportion of runtime spent in computation and communication allows us to comment on the scalability of each distribution strategy.

Figure 6 presents the breakdown of computation and communication times for runs of the symmetric problem at 9 different processor counts on Hera. The reduction in communication time with patch distribution disabled is shown to vastly increase the scalability of the code. Initially, the problem is symmetrically decomposed over 4 processors, hence the lower runtime when patches are not distributed. As core counts increase, the computation and communication times become more diverse between the two distribution strategies. Whilst the lowest overall runtime time is found on 32 processors with patch distribution enabled, as the number of processors increases communication becomes the dominant factor – accounting for 71.4% of the total runtime on 1024 processors. When patch distribution is disabled, we no longer see such a marked increase in communication times and total runtime, although average computation time remains higher due to the load imbalance. It is this trade off, spending more time computing

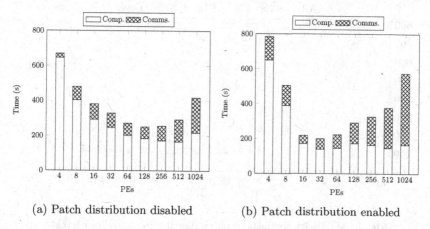

(a) Patch distribution disabled   (b) Patch distribution enabled

Fig. 6. Scalability study of strong scaled AMR problem evaluating patch distribution

locally in order to communicate less, that provides the improved run times at scale.

In the following sections we try to address the balance between computation time and communication time, finding a threshold to achieve both a reduction in runtime and an increase in scalability.

6   Level-Based Distribution Threshold

In Section 5 we demonstrated the influence of problem symmetry in the performance of patch distribution techniques. In the following section we illustrate how applying a distribution level threshold can form a 'middle ground' between these two techniques. To control communication overheads we apply a threshold on patch refinement levels for distribution. With a threshold level of 2, only patches at the second level of refinement and higher will be considered for distribution. With a higher distribution threshold, we will increase the load imbalance, but minimise the communication time, and vice versa.

Using the asymmetric problem presented in Figure 4(a) we demonstrate the effect of a patch distribution threshold as the problem is strong scaled.

Figure 7 shows how the different threshold levels span the runtimes of fully enabling or disabling patch distribution. What is also clear, and intuitive, is that all threshold-based results are bounded. Therefore the motivation for a threshold-based patch distribution strategy lies in risk mitigation. Without ahead-of-time runtime prediction, through modelling or execution, the best strategy is unknown, thus a threshold strategy reduces risk of poor performance and scalability.

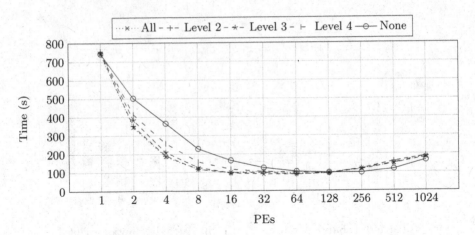

Fig. 7. Scalability analysis of patch distribution threshold levels

7   Optimising Patch Distribution

In previous sections we have demonstrated the importance of using patch distribution techniques to balance computational work across processors against the communication costs incurred by data transfers. However, these schemes were developed using simple, intuitive heuristics, without consideration for the more complex relationship between computation time and communication time.

To make more optimal decisions about the distribution of patches during program execution we utilise a model based on three measured parameters: computation time per cell (W_g), network latency (l), and network bandwidth (G). We use these parameters to estimate the time required to compute and communicate a patch q on a processor p using the following formula:

$$t_{q,p} = W_g\left(cells_p\right) \times \left(l_p\left(q\right) + \frac{q}{G_p\left(q\right)}\right) \tag{1}$$

where l_p and G_p are the latency and bandwidth obtained when sending the patch to processor p. These network parameter values will change based on the type of communication (on or off-node) being performed.

Rather than evaluating only computational workload, we take communication overheads into account to select the most appropriate processor for the current patch, considering: (i) increased communication time incurred by the patch, and (ii) how this overhead compares with the estimated computational saving. Our new patch distribution scheme utilises this information by maintaining a list of the total estimated work on each processor, and selecting a processor for a given patch that will increase the current maximum runtime the least. Equation 2 describes this scheme mathematically:

$$p_q = \min_{p \in processors}\left(t_p + t_{q,p}\right) \tag{2}$$

where p_q is the processor selected for patch q, and t_p is the total estimated work time currently assigned to processor p.

Using W_g values measured from a single processor run on the target system, and latency and bandwidth values estimated using the SKaMPI benchmark [19], Figure 8 demonstrates the obtained performance increases of our model-based patch distribution strategy.

The performance of our optimised strategy is generally equivalent to the best performance of out the two previous strategies, but out performs it in certain configurations, on 16 and 32 cores by 18.1% and 29.1% respectively. The lack of performance increase in other configurations is attributed to lack of sufficient computation and the increased overheads of maintaining this new mapping. More efficient metadata management would decrease the overhead of patch selection and improve performance of the optimised strategy.

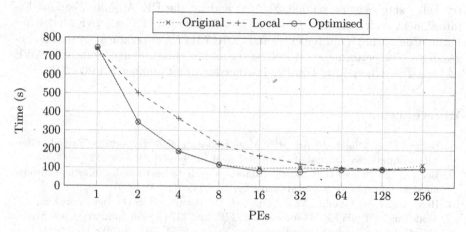

Fig. 8. Runtime comparison of patch distribution strategies.

8   Conclusions and Future Work

As the size of high-performance computers increases, applications will be constrained not by computational power, but by data availability. AMR presents a technique to increase the efficiency of computation by focusing work on areas of interest. This, however, will create an imbalance of work, as refined patches will typically occur in highly localised areas of the problem. Load balancing can be used to reduce load imbalance at the expense of increased communication costs. We have demonstrated the benefits and limitations of patch distribution strategies on both symmetric and asymmetric problem decompositions. Additionally we have shown how a threshold-based distribution strategy can mitigate risk between the two extremes. By utilising an optimised patch-distribution strategy that considers the runtime impact of patch distribution, we can make informed decisions about more optimal patch locations, with up to 29% improvements over the current strategies. In future research we plan on employing a more sophisticated performance model of the Shamrock code to enhance performance predictions to improve patch distribution decisions. Combined with a more efficient metadata management strategy, runtime improvements offered by the optimised distribution strategy are expected to be even more significant. We will combine this investigation with work to port Shamrock to an external AMR framework, to benefit from a wide variety of research into scalable AMR techniques.

Acknowledgements. We wish to give special thanks to Todd Gamblin and Scott Futral for providing continued assistance in accessing the Open Compute Facility resources at Lawrence Livermore National Laboratory, specifically the Hera machine on which the majority of experiments in this paper have been performed.

This work is supported in part by The Royal Society through their Industry Fellowship Scheme (IF090020/AM) and by the UK Atomic Weapons Establishment under grants CDK0660 (The Production of Predictive Models for Future Computing Requirements) and CDK0724 (AWE Technical Outreach Programme). The performance modelling research is also supported jointly by AWE and the TSB Knowledge Transfer Partnership grant number KTP006740.

References

1. Berger, M.J., Oliger, J.: Adaptive Mesh Refinement for Hyperbolic Partial Differential Equations. Journal of Computational Physics 53(3), 484–512 (1984)
2. Berger, M.J., Colella, P.: Local Adaptive Mesh Refinement for Shock Hydrodynamics. Journal of Computational Physics 82(1), 64–84 (1989)
3. Herdman, J.A., Gaudin, W.P., Turland, D., Hammond, S.D.: Benchmarking and Modelling of POWER7, Westmere, BG/P, and GPUs: An Industry Case Study. SIGMETRICS Performance Evaluation Review 38(4), 16–22 (2011)
4. Bryan, G.: Fluids in the Universe: Adaptive Mesh Refinement in Cosmology. Computing in Science & Engineering 1(2), 46–53 (1999)
5. Wu, J., Gonzalez, R., Lan, Z., Gnedin, N., Kravtsov, A., Rudd, D., Yu, Y.: Performance Emulation of Cell-Based AMR Cosmology Simulations. In: Proceedings of the 13th IEEE International Conference on Cluster Computing, pp. 8–16 (September 2011)
6. Fryxell, B., Olson, K., Ricker, P., Timmes, F., Zingale, M., Lamb, D., MacNeice, P., Rosner, R., Truran, J., Tufo, H.: FLASH: An adaptive mesh hydrodynamics code for modeling astrophysical thermonuclear flashes. The Astrophysical Journal Supplement Series 131, 273–334 (2000)
7. Baeza, A., Mulet, P.: Adaptive mesh refinement techniques for high-order shock capturing schemes for multi-dimensional hydrodynamic simulations. International Journal for Numerical Methods in Fluids 52(4), 455–471 (2006)
8. Quirk, J.: A parallel adaptive grid algorithm for computational shock hydrodynamics. Applied Numerical Mathematics 20(4), 427–453 (1996)
9. Luitjens, J., Berzins, M.: Scalable parallel regridding algorithms for block-structured adaptive mesh refinement. Concurrency and Computation: Practice & Experience 23(13), 1522–1537 (2011)

10. Berger, M.J., Rigoutsos, I.: An Algorithm for Point Clustering and Grid Generation. IEEE Transactions on Systems Man and Cybernetics 21(5), 1278–1286 (1991)
11. Lan, Z., Taylor, V., Bryan, G.: Dynamic Load Balancing for Structured Adaptive Mesh Refinement Applications. In: Proceedings of the 30th International Conference on Parallel Processing, pp. 571–579 (September 2001)
12. Sinha, S., Parashar, M.: Adaptive Runtime Partitioning of AMR Applications on Heterogeneous Clusters. In: Proceedings of the 3rd IEEE International Conference on Cluster Computing, vol. 22, pp. 435–442 (2001)
13. Davis, J.A., Mudalige, G.R., Hammond, S.D., Herdman, J.A., Miller, I., Jarvis, S.A.: Predictive Analysis of a Hydrodynamics Application on Large-Scale CMP Clusters. Computer Science - Research and Development 26(3-4), 175–185 (2011)
14. Mudalige, G.R., Vernon, M.K., Jarvis, S.A.: A Plug-and-Play Model for Evaluating Wavefront Computations on Parallel Architectures. In: Proceedings of the 22nd IEEE International Parallel and Distributed Processing Symposium, pp. 1–14 (April 2008)
15. Colella, P., Bell, J., Keen, N., Ligocki, T., Lijewski, M., Straalen, B.: Performance and Scaling of Locally-Structured Grid Methods for Partial Differential Equations. Journal of Physics: Conference Series 78(13), 012013 (July 2007)
16. Van Straalen, B., Shalf, J., Ligocki, T., Keen, N., Yang, W.-S.: Scalability Challenges for Massively Parallel AMR Applications. In: Proceedings of the 23rd IEEE International Parallel and Distributed Processing Symposium, pp. 1–12 (May 2009)
17. Wissink, A.M., Hornung, R.D., Kohn, S.R., Smith, S.S., Elliott, N.: Large Scale Parallel Structured AMR Calculations Using the SAMRAI Framework. In: Proceedings of the 14th ACM/IEEE Conference on Supercomputing, pp. 6–19 (November 2001)
18. Colella, P., Graves, D., Ligocki, T., Martin, D.: Chombo Software Package for AMR Applications Design Document. Technical report, Lawrence Berkeley National Laboratory (April 2009)
19. Reussner, R., Sanders, P., Prechelt, L., Müller, M.S.: SKaMPI: A Detailed, Accurate MPI Benchmark. In: Alexandrov, V.N., Dongarra, J. (eds.) PVM/MPI 1998. LNCS, vol. 1497, pp. 52–59. Springer, Heidelberg (1998)

Energy Consumption in the Office

Anton Stefanek, Uli Harder, and Jeremy T. Bradley

Department of Computing, Imperial College London
Huxley Building, 180 Queen's Gate, London, SW7 2RH
{as1005,uh,jb}@doc.ic.ac.uk

Abstract. In this paper we present measurements of energy usage of standard office computing equipment. Using a data trace lasting for all of March 2012 we analyse the energy use of office equipment such as desktop computers, a printer and a fridge. The interest in a more detailed knowledge of the energy usage patterns of these appliances is driven by the desire to manage, and if possible reduce, the energy consumption of computing equipment in a university department. The reason behind this can be financial to reduce electricity costs and/or environmental to reduce the carbon foot print of an office environment. We analyse the data and show simple autoregressive time series models to predict the energy usage of appliances. We also show that it's feasible to accurately approximate the power consumption of a desktop computer using the CPU utilisation information. We describe a future set-up where we plan to monitor the energy usage of a student lab.

Keywords: Energy consumption, Measurement, Forecasting.

1 Introduction

In this paper we present data collected with several energy monitors in an office environment. The data comprises a number of different desktop computers, a fridge, a printer, a mobile phone / laptop charger and a digital radio. In addition we also monitor the office temperature. The data we present here can be downloaded from [3].

The motivation behind this measurement exercise is to understand what the environmental impact of computing is. In order to make computing greener we first need to know how much energy is used by computers. This measurement exercise is a warm-up for a larger experiment, where we aim to monitor the energy usage of an entire computer lab used by undergraduate students. Given that conservative estimates of peak usage indicate that departments and companies pay thousands of GBP for the electricity usage of their computing equipment, being able to quantify how money could be saved is very useful in the current economic climate. In the long-term we would also like to be able to investigate how different scheduling policies for CPU scavenging applications like Condor [7] could be improved to use less energy.

M. Tribastone and S. Gilmore (Eds.): EPEW/UKPEW 2012, LNCS 7587, pp. 224–236, 2013.
© Springer-Verlag Berlin Heidelberg 2013

In the following sections we first describe the experimental setup. We perform a survey of the data and show a few insightful visualisations. In the next section we describe simple statistical models forecasting future demand. Finally we discuss the implications of our observations and sketch a future larger measurement exercise.

2   Experimental Setup

For this experiment we used ten *SmartPlug* meters from *AlertMe*[1]. Each Smart-Plug was placed between the device and the mains network and measured the actual power consumption with an accuracy of around $1W$. The plugs reported power measurements via the Zigbee wireless protocol to a *SmartHub* controller, approximately every 10 seconds. The hub is a low power ARM based computer running a version of the Linux operating system. It is connected to the Internet and reports the measurements from the plugs to the AlertMe website. In addition, we used a *SmartDisplay* device to report the current temperature of the office to the hub.

The data from AlertMe can either be viewed on a dashboard with limited capabilities or obtained via an API. However, the API does not allow detailed history requests. Therefore, we ran a simple script that retrieved the current measurements from the AlertMe API at regular intervals of 12 seconds (a rate just below the limits imposed by AlertMe) and uploaded all the data to *Cosm* [2] website, which provides an online storage of time series data.

On each monitored desktop computer we ran a simple script that measured the CPU utilisation and deposited the data onto Cosm every 12 seconds.

For convenience, we wrote a simple HTML dashboard that displays an overview of all the current and historical measurements via calls to Cosm. We retrieved detailed historical data from Cosm via the Cosm API and used various data visualisation and statistical analysis tools to gain insights from the experiment. Figure 1 shows an overview of the whole setup.

2.1   Monitored Devices

We monitored the following appliances:

- Four desktop computers. Computer 1 is an HP model with 3GHz Intel Core 2 Duo E8400 processor. Computer 2 is a Dell model with 2.8GHz Intel Core 2 Duo E7400 processor. Computer 3 has a quad core 3.4 GHz Intel Core i5-670 processor. Computer 4 has a single core 3.6 GHz Intel Pentium 4 processor. All the computers are running a custom version of the Ubuntu Linux operating system and are used for common office tasks such as web browsing, programming and scientific computing.
- Monitors. We monitored two screens (21 inch NEC LCD monitor and 20 inch Dell LCD monitor) attached to Computer 1 and one 22 inch Sun monitor attached to Computer 2.

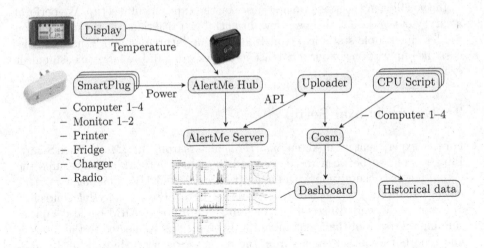

Fig. 1. Overview of the experimental setup. Images of the SmartPlug, Display and Hub taken from `www.alertme.com`

- A large shared HP printer. The printer is part of a college-wide printing system. Users can submit jobs to a central queue and then start printing after physically logging into the printer.
- A fridge.
- A mains socket used for occasional charging of a mobile phone and a laptop.
- A digital radio.

3   Survey of the Data

We ran the experiment described above throughout March 2012. Overall, there were only a few hours when we lost data due to a crashed uploader script and outages of the AlertMe and Cosm servers. In total, we collected around $200k$ power measurement data points for each device and $230k$ CPU measurement data points for each CPU core of each computer.

Due to various delays in the system, the resulting time series data points do not come from regular time intervals. We performed a simple re-sampling of the data, producing a regular time series where each data point corresponds to a time-average of all the original points in its interval. Figure 2 shows the measured data for the four computers, Figure 3 for the other devices, when re-sampled into 20 minute intervals.

Figure 3 also shows the corresponding room temperature and number of active jobs submitted to the Condor system obtained via the `condor_stats` command. Condor monitors the activity of a large number of computers. If the computers are idle for a period of time, Condor schedules any pending jobs for processing on the available computer. In our experiments, Computers 1 and 3 are assigned

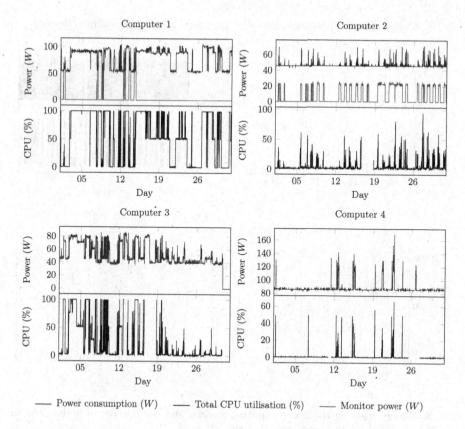

Fig. 2. Energy use and CPU utilisation of the monitored computers. The shown dates correspond to Mondays.

to a Condor pool. This is manifested in some of the high CPU utilisation during periods of time when the monitors are switched off.

The plots show quite clearly that the usage patterns are very different for all four computers. It is clear that the power consumption is highly correlated with the total CPU utilisation. We will look at this relationship in Section 3.3. Moreover, similar load patterns for Computer 1 and Computer 3 suggest that there is a correlation between the number of active Condor jobs and the CPU utilisation of the computers. We will look at this relationship in Section 3.4. Table 1 summarises the total energy consumption of all the devices.

3.1   Day of Week Averages

We average the above data for each week day. Figure 4 shows the averaged data for the 4 computers. We can clearly distinguish the weekend and standard working hours. Figure 5 shows the averaged data for the non-computer devices and for the number of condor jobs and the temperature.

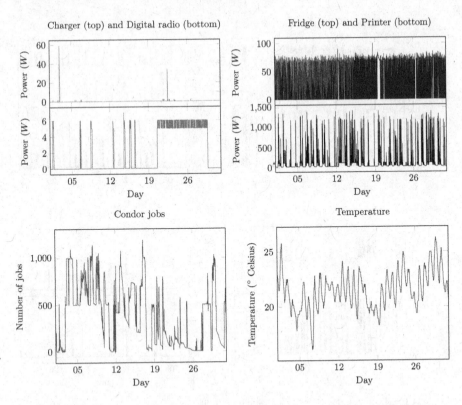

Fig. 3. Energy used by the non-computing devices and the number of active jobs in the Condor pool and the temperature in the office

Table 1. Total energy consumption of all the devices in March 2012

Device	Total (kWh)
Computer 1	59.2
Computer 2	34.6
Computer 3	37.4
Computer 4	64.5
Monitor 1	2.9
Monitor 2	5.5

	Total (kWh)
Charger	0.16
Radio	1.3
Fridge	19.9
Printer	108.4

3.2   Duration Histograms

We look at the proportion of time the devices stay at particular power levels. For each time series, we divide the range of its values into 25 intervals. We keep track of the duration of how long the value stays within a single interval. At each time of a change to a different interval, we record the total duration and the power level interval. We then plot a histogram of the total time the device stayed within an interval. Figure 6 shows these histograms for the 4 computers.

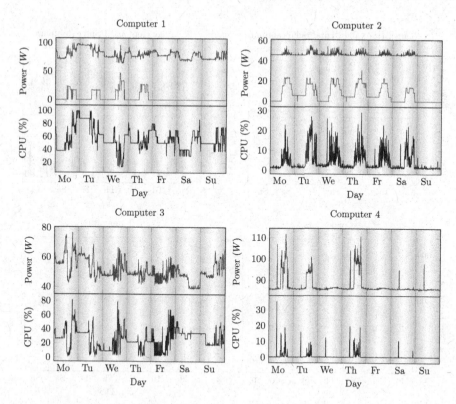

Fig. 4. Week day average of the CPU utilisation and power consumption of the 4 computers

For example, the upper left figure shows the histogram for the power consumption of Computer 1. It can be seen that there are roughly 3 distinct power levels at which the computer stays most of the time. The lowest power level of around 56 W, corresponding to the machine being idle, is mostly maintained for periods of time around 1000 seconds long. The plot on the right hand side shows the CPU utilisation histogram for the same machine. Here, the 3 different levels are even more clear and show that most of the long running tasks are at the highest utilisation. The tall peak showing this is not present in the power histogram, because the power values had show larger fluctiations and do not stay within the same tight interval for a long time. This is probably a manifestation of the fact that the power consumption also depends on various other factors, such as the usage of the disk drive, graphics card or the room temperature.

Figure 8 in the following section shows the histograms for the Computers 1 and 3 where the values are summed over the range of possible durations.

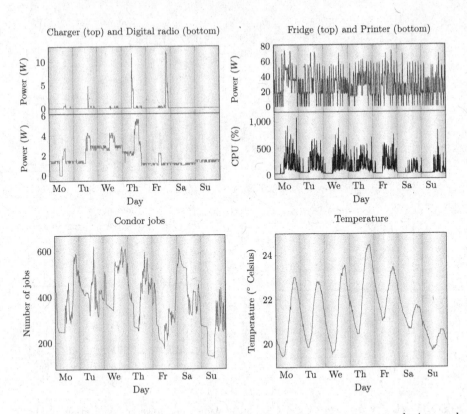

Fig. 5. Week day average of the power consumption of the non-computer devices and the week day average of the number of active Condor jobs and the temperature

Figure 7 shows the histogram for the Fridge and the Printer. The histogram for the Fridge clearly shows the two different states of the fridge. In case of the Printer, it can be seen that it is mostly idle, except for very short spikes of very high power consumption corresponding to the print jobs.

3.3   Power vs. CPU Relationship

In this section, we look at the relationship between the power consumption and CPU utilisation for the monitored computers. We will try to come up with a simple model that will estimate the power from just the CPU utilisation information.

Figure 8 shows the distribution of the power consumption and CPU utilisation for Computers 1 and 3, which are part of a Condor pool and therefore showed a larger variety of utilisation and power levels during the experiment. There are clearly several distinct power and CPU levels at which the computers stay for most of the time. For example, the utilisation of the Computer 1 is around 0%, 50% or 100% most of the time and similarly 0%, 25%, 50%, 7% and 100% for Computer 3. This corresponds to the number of CPU cores of the computers.

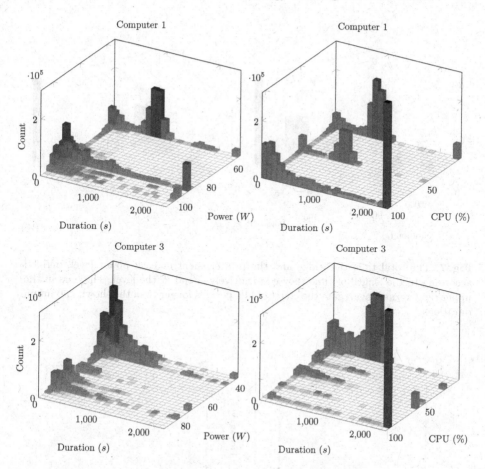

Fig. 6. Plot of the total time the computers stay at different power/CPU utilisation levels. For each power/utilisation interval, the plots show all possible durations in seconds for which the device stayed within the interval. For each level/duration pair, the total time in such state is plot. The time spent in states where the duration is larger than shown is included in the total value for the largest duration.

Usually, each Condor job fully utilises one core so this is expected. Figure 9 further shows the histogram of the relative changes of the power consumption and CPU utilisation for Computers 1 and 3. As expected, the values for the computer with more cores change in smaller relative steps.

Figure 10 plots the power consumption against CPU utilisation. The left hand side plot shows that the power consumption can be approximated by a quadratic function of the CPU utilisation. This confirms expectations from literature. It is suggested that adding a higher order term to a linear function can often accurately capture the relationship between the power consumption and CPU speed [6].

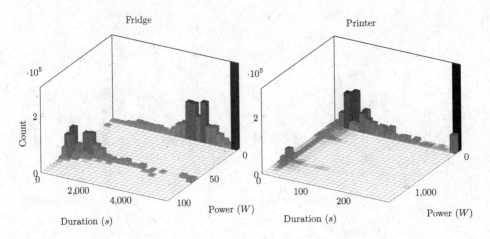

Fig. 7. The total time the fridge and the printer spent at each power level, divided according to the length of time they consecutively spend at the level. The bars in the upper right corners aggregate the count of idle periods longer than the shown maximum durations.

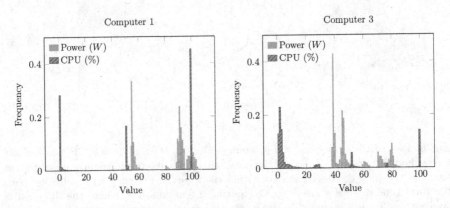

Fig. 8. Histogram of the power consumption and CPU utilisation levels for Computer 1 and 3

The solid lines in Figure 10 are the fitted quadratic polynomials for Computer 1 and 3. Their parameters are

$$\text{Power}_1(x) = 54.7W + x \cdot 0.94W/\%CPU - x^2 \cdot 5.3 \cdot 10^{-3}W/\%CPU^2$$
$$\text{Power}_3(x) = 40.0W + x \cdot 0.83W/\%CPU - x^2 \cdot 4.4 \cdot 10^{-3}W/\%CPU^2$$

respectively, where x is the CPU utilisation.

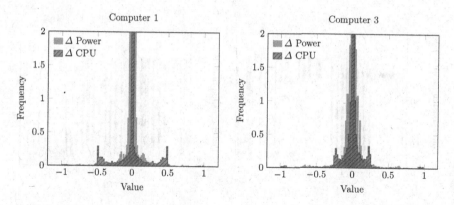

Fig. 9. Histogram of the normalised changes in power consumption and CPU utilisation

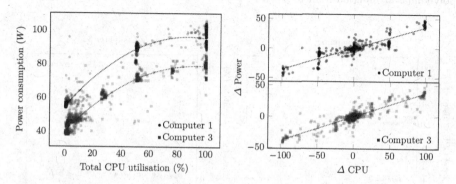

Fig. 10. Plots of power consumption (change in) against CPU utilisation (change in, respectively). The left hand side plot suggests that the power consumption can be characterised as a quadratic function in the CPU utilisation.

Figure 11 shows the power consumption of Computers 1 and 3 obtained from CPU utilisation and the above best fit functions. The sum of the absolute error at each time point for both computers is around 10% of the total power consumption.

3.4   CPU vs. Condor Relationship

Much of the load on Computers 1 and 3 is caused by jobs executed by the Condor system. Figure 12 looks at the relationship between the CPU utilisation and the number of active jobs submitted to Condor. Apart from some load for Computer 1 when there are a few Condor jobs, it looks like the load increases almost as a step function as soon as the number of jobs is over a certain threshold (around 500 jobs).

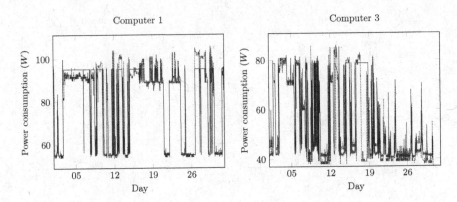

Fig. 11. Power consumption as obtained from the CPU utilisation and the quadratic polynomial fit function from Figure 10

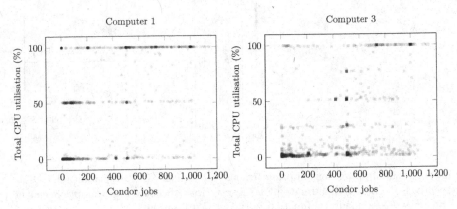

Fig. 12. Plots of CPU utilisation against the number of active Condor jobs

4   Forecast Model of Energy Consumption

Predicting the CPU utilisation and power consumption for an immediate future time interval can be useful in many applications. For example, if a scheme is employed that puts inactive computers to sleep, a forecast model could detect possible candidates by looking for computers with 0% CPU utilisation. We demonstrate that such a prediction could be feasible. Figure 13 shows the results from a simple auto-regression forecast model, similar to a model previously used for predicting arrivals in a health-care system [5]. We take the data from the first 10 days as an initial training set. At each hour after the 10-th day, we forecast the value for the next hour and plot the corresponding 95% confidence interval. We form a new training set, replacing the data for the first hour with the real data for the predicted hour. We continue until the end of the data set.

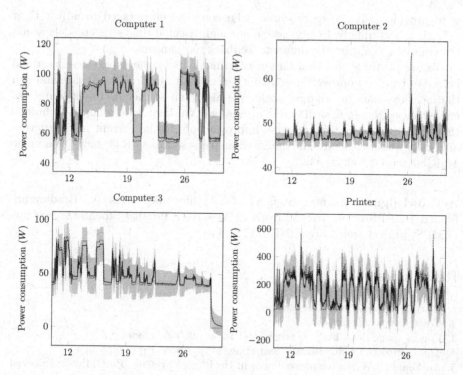

Fig. 13. Autoregression model for Computers 1-3 and the Printer. At each hour shown, the data from the last ten days was used to predict the consumption for the next hour. The shaded area shows the 95% confidence interval of the prediction. The dotted lines are the actual values.

The predictions look fairly accurate. However, they do not immediately react to sudden changes in the time series value. This can be crucial in many applications such as the sleep algorithm mentioned above. Therefore we plan to explore alternative, more accurate models.

5 Conclusion

In this paper we have shown how the energy usage of standard office equipment can be measured using common power monitors. We presented some insightful visualisations of the data and observed a simple quadratic relationship between the power consumption and CPU utilisation. This relationship could be used to reduce the number of needed power monitors. After a suitable calibration, the power consumption could be estimated from the easily accessible CPU utilisation information.

We demonstrated that is possible to use the measured data to predict future use. This can lead to many potential applications. For example, the Condor scheduling algorithms could use the predictions to choose computers suitable for running submitted jobs and ones suitable for hibernation. Another possibility is to provide guidance to the users who could be encouraged to adjust their behaviour accordingly. In any case, more sophisticated time series models would be required to capture the different feedback mechanisms.

We are planning to run a larger experiment using the experience described here. We plan to improve the reliability of the data recording software and run the measurements on a larger scale. We also plan to include other sources of energy measurements, such as clamp meters. We hope to develop a technique that will help to discover possible improvements to the current infrastructure and energy management. The data and analysis scripts in R [4] have been made available on our website [3].

Acknowledgment. Anton Stefanek, Uli Harder and Jeremy T. Bradley are funded by EPSRC on the Analysis of Massively Parallel Stochastic Systems (AMPS) project (reference EP/G011737/1).

References

1. AlertMe, http://www.alertme.com/
2. Cosm, https://cosm.com/
3. Energy usage data, http://aesop.doc.ic.ac.uk/tools/energy/
4. The R Project for Statistical Computing, http://www.r-project.org
5. Au-Yeung, S.W.M.: Response Times in Healthcare Systems. Ph.D. thesis, Imperial College London (2008),
   http://pubs.doc.ic.ac.uk/response-times-in-healthcare/
6. Rivoire, S., Ranganathan, P., Kozyrakis, C.: A comparison of high-level full-system power models. In: Proceedings of the 2008 Conference on Power Aware Computing and Systems, HotPower 2008, p. 3 (2008)
7. Thain, D., Tannenbaum, T., Livny, M.: Distributed computing in practice: the Condor experience. Concurrency - Practice and Experience 17(2-4), 323–356 (2005)

On the (Page) Ranking of Professional Tennis Players

Nicholas Dingle[1], William Knottenbelt[2], and Demetris Spanias[2]

[1] School of Mathematics, University of Manchester,
Oxford Road, M13 9PL, United Kingdom
nicholas.dingle@manchester.ac.uk
[2] Department of Computing, Imperial College London,
South Kensington Campus, SW7 2AZ, United Kingdom
{wjk,ds406}@doc.ic.ac.uk

Abstract. We explore the relationship between official rankings of professional tennis players and rankings computed using a variant of the PageRank algorithm as proposed by Radicchi in 2011. We show Radicchi's equations follow a natural interpretation of the PageRank algorithm and present up-to-date comparisons of official rankings with PageRank-based rankings for both the Association of Tennis Professionals (ATP) and Women's Tennis Association (WTA) tours. For top-ranked players these two rankings are broadly in line; however, there is wide variation in the tail which leads us to question the degree to which the official ranking mechanism reflects true player ability. For a 390-day sample of recent tennis matches, PageRank-based rankings are found to be better predictors of match outcome than the official rankings.

1 Introduction

The rankings of the world's top tennis players are the subject of much global popular interest. Indeed, a number one ranking can bring with it a great deal of prestige and celebrity, as evidenced by Association of Tennis Professionals (ATP) player Novak Djokovic's recent appearance in Time magazine's 2012 list of the Top 100 most influential people in the world[1]. Rankings can also cause a great deal of controversy, as evidenced by the recent debate over Women's Tennis Association (WTA) player Caroline Wozniacki's ranking. Wozniacki held the number one position in the WTA rankings for 67 weeks leading up to 23 January 2012, despite her failure to win a Grand Slam tournament. This led former Wimbledon champion Martina Navratilova to observe in early 2012: "If we still had the same ranking system we were using six years ago... Kvitova would have ended up number one... [Wozniacki]'s number one because that's how they set up the computer ranking... *It weighs too much on quantity and not enough on quality*... Caroline doesn't need to explain why she was number one, it's the WTA that needs to explain that."[2]

---

[1] See http://www.time.com/time/specials/packages/article/
0,28804,2111975_2111976_2111961,00.html
[2] See http://www.reuters.com/article/2012/01/23/
us-tennis-open-navratilova-idUSTRE80M0JY20120123

M. Tribastone and S. Gilmore (Eds.): EPEW/UKPEW 2012, LNCS 7587, pp. 237–247, 2013.
© Springer-Verlag Berlin Heidelberg 2013

To some, the notion of an overall ranking might seem simplistic in a sport like tennis which features an unknown degree of transitivity (one of the primary requirements for any total ordering) and a plethora of variables that might potentially affect the outcome of any individual match – e.g. player handedness, player height, playing surface, match location, weather conditions, and even recent changes in marital status [6]. To others, the concept of a ranking system for elite sportspersons invokes moral revulsion and a questioning of the values they might be understood to promote [9]. Despite these issues, there is no denying the public's fascination with rankings, as well as the public's strong desire that any ranking system should be "fair" in some sense.

Naturally, not all interest in rankings can be ascribed to purely altruistic motives. Researchers and speculators have been keen to assess the predictive power of rankings. For example, Clarke and Dyte proposed an approach based on logistic regression to use ATP rating points to predict the outcome of tournaments [4]. Corral proposed a probit model to assess the degree to which differences in official rankings are good predictors of the outcome of Grand Slam matches [5].

Some authors have made the case that the official tennis ranking system does not actually rank players according to their relative abilities but rather simply measures their cumulative progress through various tournament rounds. This is because, under both the official ATP and WTA ranking systems (both of which will be described more fully later), points are awarded according to the highest round reached in each tournament, irrespective of the quality of opposition defeated or the margins of victory. By way of example, winning an ATP Tour 500 tournament like Memphis will yield more ranking points than making the quarter finals of a Grand Slam[3]. Nevertheless, there is a limit on the total number of tournaments that can count towards the rankings for any given player, together with the requirement to include the Grand Slams and certain more prestigious mandatory tournaments. This means that players (especially those in the top 20) cannot gain a high ranking by accumulating a large number of victories in minor tournaments alone.

Clarke [3] proposed an alternative ranking system whereby players are assigned a numerical rating which is adjusted using exponential smoothing according to the difference between the match result one would expect given the difference in ratings between the players participating and the actual match result. This difference might be measured in terms of "sparks" – or Set-Point mARKS – which are earned for winning games and points. More recently, Radicchi [8] proposed a method similar to Google PageRank [2] to rank players according to the opponents they have defeated over a period of time. The particular context was an investigation into the greatest male tennis player of all time[4].

In the present paper we compare and contrast the PageRank-style tennis rankings proposed by Radicchi with the rankings systems used in the sport today. We show an up-to-date (April 2012) comparison of official and PageRank-based

---

[3] Source: http://grandslamgal.com/atp-mens-tennis-rankings-explained/

[4] Surprisingly this turned out to be not Roger Federer or Rafael Nadal but Jimmy Connors.

rankings for both the ATP and WTA tours. We also investigate the predictive power of the official and PageRank-based ranking systems in forecasting the outcomes of matches.

The remainder of this paper is organised as follows. Section 2 describes the current ATP and WTA rankings systems. Section 3 describes the PageRank algorithm and how it can be applied to the ranking of tennis players. Section 4 presents results while Section 5 concludes.

2 Current Ranking Systems

2.1 ATP

The current ranking system used in professional men's tennis is the South African Airways ATP Rankings, developed by the ATP in 2009 with the intention of providing an "objective merit-based method ... for determining qualification for entry and seeding in all tournaments..." [1]

Table 1. ATP ranking points structure for larger tournaments (excludes Challengers and Futures tournaments, the Olympics and Tour Finals)

	W	F	SF	QF	R16	R32	R64	R128	Qual.[5]
Grand Slams	2000	1200	720	360	180	90	45	10	25
Masters 1000	1000	600	360	180	90	45	10(25)	(10)	25
ATP Tour 500	500	300	180	90	45	20	-	-	20
ATP Tour 250	250	150	90	45	20	(10)	-	-	12

A player's ATP Ranking is computed over the immediate past 52 weeks, and is based on the total points a player accrues in the following 19 tournaments (18 if he did not qualify for the ATP World Tour Finals):

- The four so-called Grand Slam tournaments (Australian Open, French Open, Wimbledon US Open)
- The eight mandatory ATP World Tour Masters 1000 tournaments,
- The previous Barclays ATP World Tour Finals count until the Monday following the final regular-season ATP event of the following year.
- The best four results from all ATP World Tour 500 tournaments played in the calendar year
- The best two results from all ATP World Tour 250, ATP Challenger Tour, and Futures Series tournaments count.

In those years when the Olympics are held, results from the Olympics also count towards a player's world ranking.

As shown in Table 1, points are awarded according to the round (beginning with Qualifying, and ending with the Final) in which a player is eliminated – or if they win the tournament.

---

[5] Points awarded for qualifying subject to adjustment depending on draw size.

2.2 WTA

Similarly to ATP rankings, a player's WTA ranking is computed over the immediate past 52 weeks, and is based on the total points a player accrues at a maximum of 16 tournaments. As shown in Table 2, points are awarded according to the round in which a player is eliminated or for winning the tournament. The tournaments that count towards the ranking are those that yield the highest ranking points. These must include:

- The four Grand Slam tournaments (Australian Open, French Open, Wimbledon US Open)
- Premier Mandatory tournaments (Indian Wells, Miami, Madrid, Beijing)
- The WTA Championships (Istanbul)

For top 20 players, their best two results at Premier 5 tournaments (Doha, Rome, Cincinatti, Montreal, Toronto and Tokyo) also count[6]. As for the ATP tour, in those years when the Olympics are held, results from the Olympics also count towards a player's world ranking.

Table 2. WTA ranking points structure for larger tournaments (excludes ITF Circuit tournaments, the Olympics and Tour Finals)

	W	F	SF	QF	R16	R32	R64	R128	Qual.[5]
Grand Slams	2000	1400	900	500	280	160	100	5	60
Premier Mandatory	1000	700	450	250	140	80	50(5)	(5)	30
Premier 5	800	550	350	200	110	60(1)	(1)	-	30
Premier	470	320	200	120	60	40(1)	(1)	-	20
International	280	200	130	70	30	15(1)	(1)	-	16

3 PageRank Applied to Tennis Players

The original formulation of PageRank [2] uses a random surfer model to measure the relative importance of web-pages. The central idea is that pages which are linked to by a large number of other pages are regarded as being more important than those with fewer incoming links; a surfer clicking through links on web-pages at random is therefore more likely to land on the more important web-pages.

For a web-graph with N pages, PageRank constructs an $N \times N$ matrix R that encodes a surfer's behaviour in terms of the matrices W, D and E.

The first behaviour modelled is where a surfer randomly clicks on links on a given page to move to another page. The corresponding matrix W has elements w_{ij} given by:

$$ w_{ij} = \begin{cases} \frac{1}{deg(i)} & \text{if there is a link from page } i \text{ to page } j \\ 0 & \text{otherwise} \end{cases} $$

where $deg(i)$ denotes the total number of links out of page i.

---

[6] Source: http://www.wtatennis.com/SEWTATour-Archive/Ranking_Stats/howitworks.pdf

The second behaviour is that when a surfer encounters a page that has no outgoing links, they randomly jump to any other page in the web-graph. This is described by the matrix $D = du^T$, where d and u are column vectors:

$$d_i = \begin{cases} 1 \text{ if } deg(i) = 0 \\ 0 \text{ otherwise} \end{cases}$$

$$u_i = 1/N \ \ \forall i, 1 \leq i \leq N$$

We note that other probability distributions for u are possible; here we consider only a uniformly distributed choice. The two behaviours are then combined into a single-step transition matrix $W' = W + D$.

The third and final behaviour to be modelled is that of a surfer deciding to ignore the links on the current page and to surf instead to some other random page. This is captured in a dense matrix E with elements $e_{ij} = u_j \ \forall i, j$.

The surfer's overall behaviour is determined by the whether or not they choose to follow the link structure of the web-graph or to jump about at random. The balance between the two is controlled by the parameter α ($0 \leq \alpha \leq 1$). The overall one-step PageRank DTMC transition matrix R is therefore defined as:

$$R = (1 - \alpha)W' + \alpha E \tag{1}$$

which is a dense matrix due to the presence of E. The PageRank of the web-graph is calculated by solving the DTMC steady-state problem:

$$x = xR \tag{2}$$

To avoid calculations with a dense matrix we rewrite Eq. 2 using Eq. 1, the definition of the matrix E and the fact that $\sum_i x_i = 1 \ \forall i$, so that the calculation only involves sparse matrices [7]:

$$x = (1 - \alpha)xW' + \alpha u$$

This can easily be manipulated into the form $Ax = b$:

$$(I - (1 - \alpha)W')^T x^T = \alpha u^T$$

and then solved for x using a method such as Conjugate Gradient Squared.

The idea of applying a PageRank-like algorithm to tennis players was first proposed by Radicchi [8]. Radicchi's formulation of the problem is equivalent to the matrix-based description of PageRank given above. When using PageRank to model tennis, the pages in the web-graph become the records of the players in their head-to-head encounters, and instead of N pages we have N players. The major difference from standard PageRank is that PageRank disregards multiple outgoing links from a single source page to a given target page, while we count the number of times a single player loses to each of their opponents.

Each player (node) in the network is assigned a "prestige score" which is passed on to other players through weighted edges. The prestige scores, P_i in a network of N nodes, can be found by solving the system of equations:

$$P_i = (1 - \alpha) \sum_j P_j \frac{w_{ji}}{s_j^{out}} + \frac{\alpha}{N} + \frac{(1-\alpha)}{N} \sum_j P_j \delta(s_j^{out}) \qquad (3)$$

for $i = 1, ..., N$ with the constraint $\sum_i (P_i) = 1$. In this equation, w_{ji} is the outgoing weight from player j to player i and by that we mean the number of defeats player j has suffered against player i, s_j^{out} is the total out-strength of player j (i.e. $s_j^{out} = \sum_i w_{ji}$), α is a damping parameter where $0 \leq \alpha \leq 1$ and N is the total number of players in the network. The δ function takes a value of 1 for an input of 0 and a value of 0 otherwise.

Radicchi's model defines the (i,j)th entry of W, denoted w_{ij}, as the number of matches player i has lost to player j normalised over the total number of matches player i has lost. Just as web-pages linked to by a large number of other pages will achieve a high PageRank score, so too will players who defeat a large number of other players.

The definitions of D, E and α are unchanged but we interpret them differently. We need D in the cases where a player has no defeats recorded against them – in reality this is unlikely to occur, but it may be the case in our data-sets given that we only have access to results from a limited time period. In this case, we assume the player is equally likely to lose to all other players given the absence of any information to the contrary.

Just as a surfer may disregard the links on a current page and surf to a random page, we believe that it is possible for any player to lose to any other (due to a variety of unpredictable external factors) and this is how we interpret E. The scalar parameter α lets us decide how likely we think it is that this will happen. In the experiments that follow we set α to 0.00001.

4   Results

4.1   The January 2012 WTA Rankings

We return briefly to the January 2012 debate over the WTA rankings mentioned in the introduction. Table 3 presents a comparison of the official WTA rankings and PageRank-based WTA rankings as at 12 January 2012. While both rankings feature the same set of players in the top 10 (all of whom of are undoubtedly among the sport's elite female players), the PageRank-based rankings do appear to support the contention that Petra Kvitova may have been a more appropriate number 1 in early 2012.

Table 3. Official and PageRank-based WTA Rankings on 12 January 2012

	Official WTA Rankings		PageRank-based WTA Rankings	
1	Caroline Wozniacki	(DEN)	Petra Kvitova	(CZE)
2	Petra Kvitova	(CZE)	Vera Zvonareva	(RUS)
3	Victoria Azarenka	(BLR)	Caroline Wozniacki	(DEN)
4	Maria Sharapova	(RUS)	Victoria Azarenka	(BLR)
5	Samantha Stosur	(AUS)	Samantha Stosur	(AUS)
6	Na Li	(CHN)	Marion Bartoli	(FRA)
7	Vera Zvonareva	(RUS)	Na Li	(CHN)
8	Agnieszka Radwanska	(POL)	Agnieszka Radwanska	(POL)
9	Marion Bartoli	(FRA)	Maria Sharapova	(RUS)
10	Andrea Petkovic	(GER)	Andrea Petkovic	(GER)

4.2   Official and PageRank-Based Rankings of Contemporary Players

Fig. 1 compares the ranks generated by the PageRank approach described in Section 3 with the current ATP ranks for the top 120 male players. Players located on the dashed line have the same PageRank as ATP rank; those players above the line have a higher PageRank than ATP rank while the opposite holds for those below it. We observe that the top 8 players have the same ranks under both systems, but that there is an increasing disparity between the two ranking systems for lower ranked players.

Fig. 2 compares the ranks predicted by the PageRank approach described in Section 3 with the current WTA ranks for the top 120 female players. Again, we observe that agreement between the two ranking systems is best for higher ranked players, although even within the higher ranked players there are some surprising differences. This might be because of the gentler (relative to the ATP rankings) gradient between the score achieved by a tournament winner compared to players reaching later tournament rounds.

The seeding system used in tournaments may explain why there is less agreement between the PageRank and official ranks for the weaker players. Lower ranked players are more likely to be matched with higher ranked players in the initial rounds, and this makes it harder for the weaker players to proceed. This has two possible effects on rankings. First, weaker players have less opportunity to proceed to the later rounds of tournaments where the ranking points received per victory are significantly higher. In contrast, under PageRank players are compensated with an appropriate amount of PageRank when they defeat an opponent of a given level of ability irrespective of the round. Second, lower ranked players tend to play fewer tournament games than high ranked ones and this limits the amount of data on which to base rankings under any system.

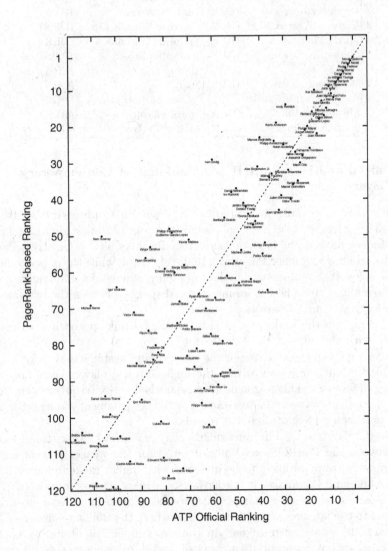

Fig. 1. PageRank-based Ranking vs. Official Ranking for ATP players (April 2012)

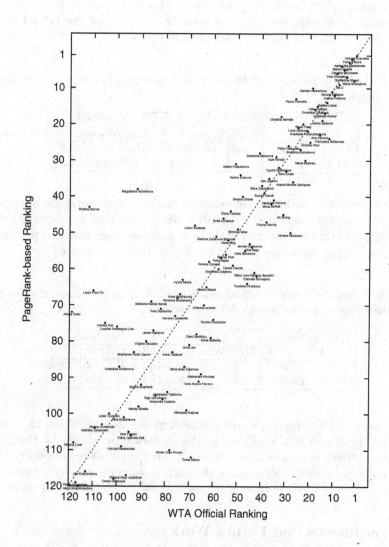

Fig. 2. PageRank-based Ranking vs. Official Ranking for WTA players (April 2012)

4.3   Predictive Power

We are interested in comparing the predictive power of ranking systems. The simplest approach to forecasting the winner of a tennis match is to select the player with the lowest rank. We now investigate how good the official system and the PageRank approach are when used in this way.

Table 4. Predictive power of official and PageRank tennis rankings over 390 days of recent matches

Tour	# Matches	Official			PageRank		
		Right	Wrong	%	Right	Wrong	%
ATP	12 022	7 987	4 035	66.4%	8 055	3 967	67.0%
WTA	12 775	8 406	4 369	65.8%	8 470	4 305	66.3%

Table 4 compares the success of using the two approaches over 390 days worth of historical matches played in 2011/2012. We observe that approximately 66% of the time selecting the lower ranked player is correct, and that this percentage is about the same regardless of how the player's rank is computed.

Table 5. Predictive power of official and PageRank tennis rankings in those cases where the different systems predict different outcomes

Tour	# Matches	Official			PageRank		
		Right	Wrong	%	Right	Wrong	%
ATP	1 738	835	903	48.0%	903	835	52.0%
WTA	1 876	906	970	48.3%	970	906	51.7%

There are times, however, where the prediction based on official rank differs from that produced by PageRank. In this situation, as shown by the results in Table 5, there is an advantage to using the PageRank results over the official rankings because they predict the correct outcome correctly more often (approximately 52% of the time as opposed to 48% with the official ranks).

5   Conclusions and Future Work

We have taken Radicchi's PageRank-inspired tennis ranking system and applied it to calculate rankings for players currently playing on the ATP and WTA tours. We observed that the two systems tend to rank the top players consistently but that there is considerable disagreement for lower-ranked players. We believe this can be attributed to the seeding system used in tournaments. We have also investigated the use of the two ranking approaches to predict the outcome of tennis matches and have observed that, when the predictions so generated differ, the PageRank approach appears to be (on average) a slightly better predictor.

In future we could conduct a wider experiment similar to [5], which investigated whether differences in rankings were good predictors of the outcome of Grand Slam tennis matches, but using PageRank-based ranking rather than official rankings. This will build on the prediction work reported in this paper. It may be interesting to experiment with PageRank-based systems that take into account the margin of victory of matches and to see if this approach yields greater predictive power. We could also investigate the predictive power of a more fine-grained PageRank-based approach that is constructed from set-level results, rather than the match-level results presented in this paper.

We would like to investigate the parameter α in more detail, both to assess the sensitivity of our results to particular values and to estimate accurate values from available statistics. We will also evaluate to what extent the length of the match (3 sets or 5 sets) has on the chances of an upset, and whether this could account for the fact that our PageRank-derived rankings more closely match the official rankings for male players than for female players.

Acknowledgements. The authors would like to thank the anonymous referee for their insightful comments and suggestions.

References

1. ATP Tour, Inc: The 2009 ATP Official Rulebook (2011), http://www.ATPWorldTour.com
2. Brin, S., Page, L.: The anatomy of a large-scale hypertextual web search engine. Computer Networks and ISDN Systems 30(1-7), 107–117 (1998), http://www.sciencedirect.com/science/article/pii/S016975529800110X, Proceedings of the Seventh International World Wide Web Conference
3. Clarke, S.R.: An adjustive rating system for tennis and squash players. In: de Mestre, N. (ed.) 2nd Conference on Mathematics and Computers in Sport, pp. 43–50 (1994)
4. Clarke, S.R., Dyte, D.: Using official ratings to simulate major tennis tournaments. International Transactions in Operational Research 7(6), 585 (2000)
5. del Corral, J., Prieto-Rodriguez, J.: Are differences in ranks good predictors for Grand Slam tennis matches? International Journal of Forecasting 26(3), 551–563 (2010)
6. Farrelly, D., Nettle, D.: Marriage affects competitive performance in male tennis players. Journal of Evolutionary Psychology 5, 141–148 (2007)
7. Langville, A., Meyer, C.: Deeper inside PageRank. Internet Mathematics 1(3), 335–380 (2004)
8. Radicchi, F.: Who is the best player ever? A complex network analysis of the history of professional tennis. PLoS ONE 6(2), e17249 (2011)
9. Tännsjö, T.: Is it fascitoid to admire sports heroes? In: Tännsjö, T., Tamburrini, C. (eds.) Values in Sport: Elitism, Nationalism, Gender Equality and the Scientific Manufacturing of Winners, ch. 1, pp. 9–23 (2000)

Towards a Volunteer Cloud Architecture

Abdulelah Alwabel, Robert Walters, and Gary Wills

Electronics and Computer Science School,
University of Southampton
{aala10,rjw1,gbw}@ecs.soton.ac.uk

Abstract. Volunteer cloud computing is a new type of clouds aiming at moving volunteer computing towards the cloud. The new cloud type is motivated by the fact that building a cloud out of non-dedicated resources can be useful for scientific projects which cannot afford the cost of consumption of cloud services provided by cloud service providers such as Amazon. However, Volunteer Clouds are in its infancy level with some challenges and issues that ought to be tackled. This paper presents a new architecture which can facilitate volunteer clouds being a viable cloud solution.

1 Introduction

Volunteer cloud computing (VCC) mixes the concepts of cloud computing (Armbrust et al., 2010) and volunteer computing (Anderson & Fedak, 2006) by offering all or some of cloud services without charging. VCC has some advantages compared to commercial clouds. The First advantage is the cost effectiveness of volunteer clouds since all resources are offered voluntarily which can be very useful for projects that cannot afford commercial clouds' services (Chandra & Weissman, 2009). Secondly, it reduces energy consumption and gas emissions because it utilises computing resources that would otherwise remain idle. Arpaci et al., (1995) show that the average percentage of local resources being idle within an organisation is about 80%. In contrast, commercial clouds set up a huge number of dedicated resources in their data centres, thus, they have a negative impact on the environment since their data centres consume massive amounts of electricity (Gupta & Awasthi, 2009). Finally, comm. ercial clouds are inefficient in terms of data mobility and pay little attention to the location of clients (Weissman et al., 2011). This paper presents and discusses a new architecture which can facilitate volunteer clouds being a viable cloud solution

2 The Architecture

The abstract level of the architecture, Figure 1, divides VCC into three layers: (i) a service layer; (ii) a middleware layer; and (iii) a physical layer. The service layer is concerned with delivering services in a way similar to commercial clouds.

M. Tribastone and S. Gilmore (Eds.): EPEW/UKPEW 2012, LNCS 7587, pp. 248–251, 2013.
© Springer-Verlag Berlin Heidelberg 2013

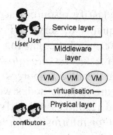

Fig. 1. VCC Architecture

2.1 Service Layer

The service layer provides services via an interface to customers based on SOA approach. The business model in VCC is similar to that of commercial clouds. VCC's contributors volunteer their resources to form a VCC for a certain time, and they may be services consumers at the same time if they wish.

2.2 Middleware Layer

The aim of the layer is to provide resources to the service layer as they would be provided by a commercial cloud. The layer, shown in Figure 2, consists of *task management* and *QoS management*. *Task management* works with tasks received from the service layer. It involves *task scheduler, load balancing* and *self-automation*. The task *scheduler* organises tasks coming from the service layer by passing them to suitable resources which are offered in the physical layer. *The load balancing* ensures that the load is distributed appropriately, thus minimizing the required time to process a task. *Self-automation* helps to provide the rapid elasticity in VCCs. It allows users to scale services up or down according to their needs. *QoS management* ensures that a minimum quality level is maintained. The *performance monitor* in *QoS management* ensures that the performance of each task is maintained at an acceptable level which is reported in the *SLA reporting* component. Node volatility is quite high in VCCs, so the *performance monitor* must cooperate with the *resource management* to find reliable nodes among available resources that suite each task. The *fault recovery* component can be vital with regards to improving the performance of the overall VCCs.

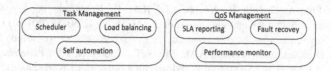

Fig. 2. Middleware Layer

2.3 Physical Layer

Resource manager, Figure 3, is responsible for resource aggregation, resource allocation and resource monitoring. It aggregates volunteer nodes denoted by the public.

An aggregation mechanism can classify resources according to a number of criteria with the aim of optimising the quality of service. For example, the history of each volunteer node can be useful in terms of recognising which node should be selected by the resource allocator for each task. The *allocator* receives tasks from tasks management and allocates them to the required resources. The *allocator* can decrease the interruption of services by assigning tasks to nodes with higher reliability. The *monitor* component observes allocated resources regularly in case any of them becomes unavailable. In this case, the *monitor* informs the *fault recovery* in the middleware in order to recover the task from a replicated node.

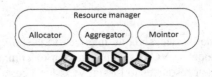

Fig. 3. Physical Layer

3   Conclusion

In conclusion, this paper presented an architecture for volunteer clouds which can be used to enhance volunteer clouds. The architecture has three layers: service layer which is an interface between customers and a volunteer cloud; middleware which is responsible of processing tasks while preserving QoS as requested by customers; and physical layer which contains raw resources (typically PCs, laptops ...etc) managed by *resource manager*. Our future work will be about improving the quality level of services provided by VCCs. This involves designing performance metrics tool and employing fault recovery techniques to improve the overall reliability of VCCs.

References

Anderson, D.P., Fedak, G.: The Computational and Storage Potential of Volunteer Computing. In: Sixth IEEE International Symposium on Cluster Computing and the Grid (CCGRID 2006), vol. 101, pp. 73–80. IEEE (2006), doi: 10.1109/CCGRID.2006.101

Armbrust, M., Fox, A., Griffith, R., Joseph, A.D., Katz, R., Konwinski, A., Lee, G., et al.: A view of cloud computing. Communications of the ACM, 53(4), 50–58 (2010), http://portal.acm.org/citation.cfm?id=1721672 (retrieved)

Arpaci, R.H., Dusseau, A.C., Vahdat, A.M., Liu, L.T., Anderson, T.E., Patterson, D.A.: The Interaction of Parallel and Sequential Workloads on a Network of Workstations. In: Science, vol. 23. ACM (1995), http://portal.acm.org/citation.cfm?id=223618 (retrieved)

Chandra, A., Weissman, J.: Nebulas: Using distributed voluntary resources to build clouds. In: Proceedings of the 2009 Conference on Hot Topics in Cloud Computing, p. 2. USENIX Association (2009), http://citeseerx.ist.psu. edu/viewdoc/summary?doi= 10.1.1.148.7267 (retrieved)

Gupta, A., Awasthi, L.K.: Peer enterprises: A viable alternative to Cloud computing? In: 2009 IEEE International Conference on Internet Multimedia Services Architecture and Applications (IMSAA), vol. 2, pp. 1–6. IEEE (2009), http://ieeexplore.ieee.org/xpls/abs_all.jsp?arnumber=5439456 (retrieved)

Weissman, J.B., Sundarrajan, P., Gupta, A., Ryden, M., Nair, R., Chandra, A.: Early experience with the distributed nebula cloud. In: Proceedings of the Fourth International Workshop on Data-intensive Distributed Computing, pp. 17–26. ACM, http://portal.acm.org/citation.cfm?id=1996019 (retrieved)

Author Index